MY
COUNTRY,
MY RIGHT
TO SERVE

MY COUNTRY, MY RIGHT TO SERVE

Experiences of Gay Men and Women in the Military, World War II to the Present

Mary Ann Humphrey

HarperPerennial

A Division of HarperCollins*Publishers*

*This book is dedicated to
my life partner, Debra Sue Keever,
and to my son,
Parke Edward-Ashton Humphrey I.*

Photograph of Robert "Jess" Jessop © 1988 by Maile Klein.

Designed by Barbara DuPree Knowles

LIBRARY OF CONGRESS CATALOGING-IN-PUBLICATION DATA
Humphrey, Mary Ann.
    My country, my right to serve: experiences of gay
men and women in the military, World War II to the
present / Mary Ann Humphrey.—
    1st ed.
        p.   cm.
    Includes bibliographical references.
    ISBN 0-06-092126-9
    1. United States—Armed Forces—Gays.   I. Title.
UB418.G38H86   1990
355'.008'664—dc20   89-46538

---

93 94 CG/HC 10 9 8 7 6 5 4 3 2

CONTENTS

⭐ PART THREE *Post-Vietnam Years and the Present*   173

FOREWORD

One day last year, an active-duty soldier came into my office to discuss antigay harassment and discrimination in our nation's armed forces. When it was her turn to speak, she stood and, with a respectful military bearing, quietly detailed the soul-wrenching ordeal to which she was even then being subjected.

Here she was, literally the perfect soldier, her record replete with commendations, top-notch evaluations, and glowing testimony from her superiors. She had not had one bad evaluation or comment in over five years of rapid advancement in the service. By all that is right and just, she should have been able to look forward with anticipation and pride to fulfilling her life's ambition, a military career.

There was just one problem. She was, some said, a lesbian. As a result, this brave woman's life was now filled not with promotions but with rumors. Government investigators were harassing her both on and off duty and interrogating her friends and acquaintances for information or even innuendo about her private life. She was being vilified in front of family and friends. Her career, into which she had poured the energies and disciplines of a lifetime, was being destroyed. And for what? To satisfy a Defense Department policy of discrimination against homosexuals—a policy that is irrational, ineffective, and incalculably harmful both to our nation's armed forces and to the significant component of those forces that is, notwithstanding the policy, lesbian or gay.

The case of the woman soldier who came to my office is not unique; she is one of thousands, male and female, officers and enlisted personnel, who are victimized every year. In case after case, the story is the same. Accomplishments, loyalty, dedication, intelligence, discipline, energy—all mean nothing. What counts is sexual orientation. What counts is six simple words of Defense Department policy: "Homosexuality is incompatible with military service."

The Pentagon can provide no basis for its policy—no facts, no figures, no logic, no bottom line. Thus, when the Pentagon's own researchers examined the issue in 1989, they found—unequivocally—that homosexuals *are* suitable for military service and recommended that the Defense Department take steps to end its ban on gays (see Appendix B).

Their report—bought and paid for by you, the taxpayer—was immediately suppressed by the Department of Defense. I and some of my colleagues in the House of Representatives had to press the Pentagon for over *nine months* to obtain it. To this day, the Pentagon has not officially released the report, and my office routinely receives requests for copies from military officers who cannot get it any other way. [Document PERS–TR–89–002 is available from your state congressman.]

These attempts by the Pentagon to bury information that contradicts its antigay policy should come as no surprise. In 1957, the Navy commissioned the so-called Crittenden report, which reached the same basic conclusions as the latest study. It took twenty years and, ultimately, a court order to pry that report from Pentagon vaults.

Perhaps the Defense Department should consider why, every time it studies the issue seriously, it gets an answer it considers wrong. Perhaps it should think about the information and the findings contained in these reports instead of trying to conceal them. Perhaps it should summon the courage to ask some basic questions about the harm being done to its own people by the current policy. Perhaps, in short, it should enter the twentieth century before the start of the twenty-first.

Instead, the Pentagon persists in its prejudices, arguing on the basis not of fact but of myth. Department officials maintain that homosexuals present a serious security risk and thus cannot serve in a military environment. Gays, they say, are easily blackmailed by enemy agents who learn of their sexual orientation and threaten to expose it. The only problem with this old argument is that it is not true. Pentagon officials cannot point to one case in military history in which such blackmail occurred and security was breached—not one.

Of course, this hypothetical security risk could be forever eliminated if the military were to lift its ban on homosexuals—thereby immunizing its gays against blackmail. I once pointed this out to a high-ranking Defense Department official, who had earlier conceded that in all likelihood at least 10 percent of U.S. service members were gay. Why then, I wondered, would the Pentagon persist in actually *creating* a potential security risk for such a substantial portion of its own force? He had no answer.

Security issues aside, the Pentagon argues that it cannot permit gays to serve because the military's straight majority would not tolerate such integration. A straight soldier, the Pentagon claims, would never take an order from a "dyke" or a "fag"—despite the fact that thousands already do, wittingly or unwittingly, every day. Thus, the Pentagon's policy is to accede to a prejudice, right or wrong, simply because it perceives that prejudice to be held by a majority of those serving in our armed forces.

To me, this is a cockeyed notion of leadership, especially for those whose very purpose is to defend the principles of equality and freedom upon which our nation is based. Unfortunately, it is an attitude with some precedent within the Defense Department.

In 1948, the Pentagon objected strenuously to President Truman's executive order to desegregate the military, maintaining that white men would never take orders from black men and that to force them to do so would disrupt "good order, discipline, and morale." Undoubtedly, some in the military were unhappy when desegregation proceeded. But can anyone argue that it was not necessary, or right, or ultimately successful? Today, after forty years, each and every U.S. soldier, sailor, aviator, and marine—from privates to generals—takes orders from a chairman of the Joint Chiefs of Staff who happens to be black.

I submit that discrimination on the basis of sexual orientation is as wrong and harmful as discrimination on the basis of race. The difference is that, with homosexuals, the discrimination often occurs *after* one has joined the military. Gays cannot, after all, be detected simply by the color of their skin. And as you will learn from the stories in Dr. Humphrey's timely book, they often are forced to pay a terrible price in order to serve their country. Some are hunted down and hounded out, but the vast majority quietly and effectively do their jobs, all the while living with the fear of being discovered.

Gay men and lesbians—like those given a voice in *My Country, My Right to Serve*—have served and continue to serve their country well and with honor. Surely many have died in that service; died for a country they loved, fighting for a military whose respect they had earned, but which denied them not only that respect but simple dignity as well.

Mary Ann Humphrey's book is a welcome and long overdue look into the lives of these courageous men and women. She has completed exhaustive research in support of this effort, and has gathered together compelling insights on the many gays and lesbians who have and are still serving in our armed forces.

I believe that these stories will inspire, shock, anger, and sadden all who read them, whether the reader is committed to change, or fearful of it. They contain dramatic lessons about the price of prejudice borne by those who possess it and by those who have been victims of it. They raise some larger questions not only about the policies of one institution but about the wisdom and the values of a society that has allowed that institution to be so wrong for so long at so great a cost. But above all, the stories are about people—people who want only to do their jobs and serve their country and live their lives and win a little respect. This book, like the country they wish to serve, is dedicated to a proposition no more or less profound than that they should have the right to do just that.

—Gerry E. Studds (D-Mass.)

United States House of Representatives

December 1989

Gerry E. Studds (D-Mass.), the first openly gay member of Congress, is currently serving his ninth term in the U.S. House of Representatives. He is a senior member of the House Foreign Affairs Committee and the House Merchant Marine and Fisheries Committee, where he serves as chairman of the Subcommittee on Fisheries and Wildlife Conservation and the Environment.

PREFACE

Many people ask how one goes about writing a book. Where do you get the idea? What is the impetus, the catalyst?

For me, inspiration began in January 1986, when I was the Equal Opportunity–Affirmative Action Officer (an ironic title if ever there was one) in the 364th Civil Affairs Brigade of the U.S. Army Reserve. I held the rank of captain-promotable, which means I had passed all boards and was merely waiting for my promotion date. With nearly seven years in, I was planning on at least thirteen more until retirement.

One sunny Sunday afternoon (drills always seemed to fall on weekends when the sun shone brightly), I was called in to headquarters by the soon-to-be commander of the unit, a full colonel who was a circuit court judge pro tem and a lawyer from St. Helens, Oregon. The two other men present were both majors. One was a chief prosecutor for a city near Portland; the other was a lawyer from Eugene. No one else was in the room—just we four "weekend warriors," as reservists were called.

The colonel looked at me and said, "You have been accused of being a practicing homosexual."

I wanted to say, "Hell, I don't need any practice. I've been doing this for years, and I'm quite good at it, thank you." But I bit back the urge, knowing there is a regulation prohibiting homosexuals, bisexuals, or anyone who's had any incidents involving either of those sexual orientations from all branches of the military. Such individuals are disallowed. They are against regulation.

"A former colleague of yours has accused you," the colonel went on to say, and he proceeded to question me. I thought about asking for legal representation, but thought it would help if I just answered his questions. Besides, I had to know who could have been angry or vengeful enough to make this accusation. I was not offered any representation, nor was I given my rights which was a process similar to that used in civilian law situations. But since this was just a friendly conversation, I was told, we didn't need such things.

After an hour of degrading and humiliating questions—the colonel had turned the interrogation over to the chief prosecutor by this time—I was finally told who had made the accusation. I was not surprised to learn who it was and explained why I felt this person had come forward. But it didn't seem to make any difference, and the seedy form of questioning continued.

The man who had accused me was a former colleague of mine on the P.E. teaching staff of Portland Community College. In the spring of 1985, I had been given a RIF (reduction in force) notice by the associate dean at my home-base campus. I felt I should never have been riffed and gathered evidence to support my view. The fact that I held a doctorate in education should have been enough to maintain my position. I also had more seniority, more overall campus teaching experience, and more program experience than several other faculty members who were not riffed. When I presented my case to the president of the college, the administration corrected their mistake. Unfortunately, their solution was to rif the next person in line, a friend of mine who was *also* a weekend warrior, a lieutenant colonel in the Marine Corps Reserves.

In addition to working together, this man and I had been friends for nearly twelve years. He shared some of my interests; he once helped me move. He knew of my sexual orientation, as did most of the other faculty members, even though I didn't shout it out loud. This man blamed me *personally* for the administration's decision to rif him. He went after me with a vengeance, telling other colleagues on the faculty that I would be in trouble if I got my job back, because he would then "get" me in the Army Reserve. At school, we are protected against any discrimination for being gay. Not so in the military.

During my service to the Army and this country, I'd never had any problems. I never made sexual innuendos to anyone in any of my units. What I did in my private life was and always has been just that—private. But this man, this friend, knew about the regulation and did indeed know how to "get" me. He went to my military unit and supplied them with a list of names so they could conduct an investigation. I feel he went—not as a citizen but as another lieutenant colonel—to the lieutenant colonel and the colonels in my unit and said, "Gee, you really need to know about this person. I *just* found out, and golly, gee, shucks, you must get rid of her. We all know the regulation against queers in the military, so you guys should probably do your work and take care of this. The security of this country is at stake if she remains—it's my duty to let you know." (Later I discovered he was so obsessed with the situation that he returned several times to *make sure* the unit was doing its job.) They were forced to act.

Clearly, this was a case of revenge. My accuser had never before been concerned about my sexual orientation. If he had been, surely he would have come forward with the information years ago.

After my own interrogation, the major/prosecuting attorney was given the task of calling all the people on the list the man had submitted. None of these people were under military jurisdiction. Technically, they did not have to cooperate, but the major led them to believe they had to answer his questions. As I later learned, he was not interested in anything positive they had to say about me. Many plainly stated that they knew nothing about my personal life and let it go at that. He even interrogated my lover over the phone, but she was noncommittal. When he asked her about my sexual orientation, she replied that I was asexual. ("Asexual?" I said later that evening. "Don't you realize a *worm* is asexual?")

Although I tried to keep my sense of humor, it was very embarrassing and emotionally draining to know that my fellow workers and friends were being asked such personal questions about me. I hired a lawyer, who tried to put together stopgaps, but we knew that sooner or later the case would go to an administrative board (where evidence is heard on cases of this nature—where discharge types and procedures are determined) and I would be forced to resign or take legal action against the well-known military monster.

Because of military bungling, it took approximately two years. In May 1987, I was finally notified that an administrative board date had been set. At that point, I decided I would resign. It took another six months for the Army to complete the paperwork. Technically, I drilled in my capacity from January 1986, when I was accused, until December 1987, when I was removed and given an honorable discharge. At that point, I had officially completed nine years.

I don't wish to downplay the stress and trauma this incident created in my life. My relationship with my partner, Debra, was then fairly new. My son, Parke, was being continually upset. Why were they kicking Mommy out of the Army when she liked it so much? (At a very young age he had been told of my gayness, and he saw it as merely another way of living.) I tried to explain it to him, but he still couldn't understand. "Gee," he said, "if you don't do anything wrong, why should you be kicked out anyway?" I had no answer for him.

What I did have was a massive amount of unresolved anger toward the colleague who had made the accusation. I lost my trust in any individual with his kind of self-righteousness. In fact, I was beginning to distrust mankind in general.

I sought psychiatric help to resolve these negative feelings. It was Dr. Kenneth Paltrow who first suggested that something positive might come out of the entire experience. At the time, I was livid that he could even think such a thing, but then he said, "Perhaps you could be a pioneer, a spokesperson. You could even write a book."

That was all I needed to turn my negative energy into a positive force. I realized that many individuals had similar, if not more traumatic, experiences and undoubtedly had stories to tell. I could write a book that would give the military gay a platform to tell his or her story. Such a book could also contribute to our society's education regarding homosexuality.

Our society's problems with sexual orientation result from its acceptance or rejection of that orientation. However, many European countries have little or no problem with homosexual orientation. The United States has been slower to learn. Through education we can attain understanding and acceptance of those who are a little different from "normal."

People cannot go on believing that because someone is homosexual, something has gone "wrong" with him. That is not true, as much validated research shows. For example, in his years of work at Johns Hopkins Medical Center, Dr. John Money has encouraged research that has demonstrated that fetal exposure to certain hormones causes animals to become either homosexual or heterosexual in early developmental stages. There is evidence that this same research applied to the development of sexuality would also be true of human fetuses. In other words, it is not a change in one's life that causes a person to become homosexual or heterosexual. This research supports the conclusion that we are born with our sexual orientation, just as we are born with brown, blue, or green eyes.

Being gay is not something that happens to you all of a sudden. I believe and feel in my heart that I was always gay. I did not *act* upon those feelings until I was in my early twenties, but that doesn't mean I wasn't gay from birth.

When I excitedly told my parents about my plans for this book, the idea was not greeted with enthusiasm. Therefore, I made a conscious decision that day never to share another thing about the book with my family. Despite this lack of familial support, I went ahead eagerly with my research. I found that there had been thousands of people removed from the military for being against regulation, and just as many more removed for "other reasons." But the underlying reason was homosexuality.

And so I started my task, recording the personal histories of those individuals willing to tell their stories. I found them by placing notices in straight and gay newspapers around the country and by contacting various gay organizations. The word spread quickly. I was asked to be a guest on the Sally Jessy Raphael show, which proved to be a turning point for the book: Craig Nelson, my editor at Harper Collins, spotted a notice I'd placed in the *New York Native*, which mentioned the upcoming program date.

I had expected to encounter some marvelous things, some unusual things, and, certainly, many ironies while writing this book. But the feelings I experienced during the interviews were something I hadn't bargained on.

There was the man living with his lover of thirty-plus years out in the country near San Diego who, on the day I came to interview him, flew the traditional "gay" flag in addition to the Stars and Stripes that already waved from his tall flagpole. "I feel this is a very important project," he told me, "and I wanted you to know I support it totally." I was touched by his gesture.

And I felt the pain when a fifty-six-year-old man in the Chicago area began to cry softly as he talked about his lover who had been murdered years before. "I bet those straight people out there just can't understand that I could love another man for over thirty-two years and still carry the torch," he said.

I held one woman in my arms as she cried over the loss of her infant. "Why did the military care so little for me that they'd let my baby die when it was just twelve days old?" she asked me. "Was it because they knew I'm a lesbian and so they felt my life and the life of my child had no value?"

And there was Robert "Jess" Jessop, the former medic who was hospitalized for complications from AIDS at the time of our interview. He told me how he had tried to take his own life after he'd been interrogated by the military because he was gay: he'd tried to destroy what he called "his own gay spirit." Recalling the brutality of Vietnam, he was so overcome by grief that he broke down several times. He described those terrifying moments of going into a firefight, finding one of his own people torn apart by a grenade, then killing a man by firing a .45 point-blank at his face, even though he'd sworn never to draw a weapon on another human being. I tried to calm Jess as he talked about those things that happen in war, those things that happen when you feel you're not a good person and so you throw everything aside and try to take your own life to keep anyone else from learning your secret. We held each other tight as he haltingly told his story. His tears burned my cheek and rolled onto my shoulder.

No, I was not prepared for the feelings these interviews often evoked. The emotions I felt during the entire project were unbelievably strong. I did not realize I would get so involved in this issue; I am not an activist. (In fact, I was *accused* of being an activist by one journalist, when I asked him to assist in running a notice for interviews.)

I remember Perry Watkins telling me he was not an activist. If the Army had quietly let him retire, he would have done so. But because they did not recognize the contract they had with him, after all those years of telling him he could reenlist even though they knew he was gay, he said, "No. You didn't treat me fairly. You've made me mad. Therefore, I will take you to court."

The stories that resulted from these interviews need to be told. They are of paramount importance, not only for our gay military history but for society at large.

I use the term *gay history* because, to me, we are all gay whether we are male or female. Therefore, I see our contribution to military history as a gay contribution to military history. I do not use the terms *lesbian* and *gay*. We are already fragmented and splintered in our own directions. I see no reason to further that schism. However, each individual used whatever term he or she was comfortable with in telling his or her story, and I have edited only when it was necessary for the sake of clarity.

For the reader who is not gay, the important thing to understand as you read this book is that gays participate in all walks of life. We are a viable, contributing force in the human race, a force that has given much to the arts, the sciences, writing, music, psychiatry, teaching—we are everywhere. You may know gay individuals at your place of work, at school, or in your family. You should make the effort to see that our lives are as important as yours. We need your understanding, your willingness to see us as equals, your caring, and your concern. Without these the harassment, misunderstanding, and ignorance about what a gay person really is or isn't will continue.

I've heard many times, "Well, gays never have lasting relationships." If you could put yourself in our place and realize the pressure society puts on gay people to hide, to keep "it" undercover and never talk about their lovers, never shout from the rooftops about that love, perhaps you would understand some of the difficulties we face.

How would you feel if someone said to you, "Okay, why don't *you* be gay for a day?" As gays, we have the same feelings when someone says to us, "Why don't *you* be straight for a day?" We can't do it; it can't be changed. People don't "turn gay." If society would accept this fact, much of the stress, turmoil, and emotional duress surrounding us could be alleviated.

Many people in these stories have family situations similar to mine, but that doesn't mean all gay individuals come from families who reject them once their gayness is acknowledged. The contrary is often true. Many parents are very open and loving and continue to be as supportive as ever upon learning their child is gay.

During the final phase of assembling this manuscript, I obtained research material prepared by the Defense Personnel Security Research and Education Center in Monterey, California. The Defense Department assigned the center the task of proving that homosexuals were a security risk in the military. The resulting document, PERS-TR–89–002, Nonconforming Sexual Orientations and Military Suitability (found in Appendix B of this book), supports none of the reasons for removing gays from the military. Indeed, it says homosexuals should not be removed simply because they are gay. A companion document, PERS-TR–89–004, Pre-Service Adjustment of Homosexual and Heterosexual Military Accessions—Implications for Security Clearance Suitability, further supports the gay military person and his or her stability.

The oral histories in this book provide more personal evidence that gays are good workers in the military. We do a good job, we are not security risks, and there is no reason to kick us out. The act of committing treason is caused by a character flaw, not sexual orientation. The security risk myth has been promoted by the same mentality that says all gay men are child molesters.

The military is a meaningful occupation for many individuals, as it was for me. I went into the Army Reserve in 1979 to complete a personal obligation I'd undertaken in 1962 yet never completed with the Marine Corps. (I'd entered the Corps for a short time when I was younger and decided it just wasn't for me.) But I also wanted to enter the Reserves to give myself an ideal way to have a "second retirement" (college retirement being the first) and to give my strengths, training, and education to my country in the meantime. It was my constitutional right.

When I went for my physical and written tests for my direct commission (my education warranted a direct to captain), I knew that the regulation against homosexuality could keep me out of the military. I was concerned as to how that stumbling block would be handled. *No paperwork was given directly to me.* However, I do remember very clearly how the military doctor stated the question about homosexuality. "Do you have any problems with homosexuality, alcohol, or drugs?" he asked. "No," I answered, "I have no problem." I remember leaving the physical, coming home to my partner, and saying, "I made it through. I didn't have to lie." And as far as I was concerned, I did not lie. I have no problem with any of the things that doctor mentioned. The military might have a problem with them, but I don't. I had a right to be there, and I felt what I was doing was not against regulations.

To have had to resign after nine good years, halfway to my retirement, left me hurt and angry. But this book helped dissolve that anger and soothed the hurt. It was a catharsis of sorts. (I was also able to forgive the man from my college, but I would never forget what he did to me.) I have now realized that this book will do much more for the military gay than I could ever have done by serving the remainder of my time. That makes me feel good.

This contribution to our gay history and, more specifically, to our gay military history was an idea thrust upon me almost by accident. But I am glad I accepted the challenge. And I offer this collection of personal experiences in the hope that one day we can all say, "Gay people are just like everyone else. I don't understand why it's against regulation."

—Mary Ann Humphrey, Ed.D.
August 1990

AUTHOR'S NOTE: *Beginning in early 1990, a surprising and overwhelming ground swell of protest has come forward from colleges and universities across the country regarding the military's banning of and discrimination against gays. The ban they are protesting affects the Reserve Officer Training Corps programs (ROTC) located on all campuses. Letters have come from all the higher-education representation groups and from Congress, urging a change in the policy. This unexpected explosion of protest, given further exposure by the media, is gaining incredible support, and may well be the stone for David's slingshot that will finally bring down the military giant's policy.*

ACKNOWLEDGMENTS

One of the beginning stages of any written work involves the assembly of the proposal. So I thank Cliff Martin for taking the time to read my proposal and telling me it had great potential as a contribution to the military gay history. Likewise, my editor, Craig Nelson, and his assistant editor, Jennifer Hull, also receive my praise for their professional guidance and editorial work.

I want to thank my friends and associates at the Rock Creek Campus of Portland Community College and, in particular, the "coffee klatch" for letting me know you care: Joan Barker, Charleen Carter, JoAnn Prall, Connie Vinciguerra, and Bill Hilderbrand (our token male). You supported me, wanted to know how things were going, held my hand, and, heck, I could always get a good hug out of Charleen! Dean Kruse, truly an officer and a gentleman, you gave assistance that was most appreciated and was a lifesaver. My boss at Rock Creek, Steve Rathman, has been supportive from the day I began working for him. He initially made the statement "Please don't think I judge you the way others have judged you before. Let me have a chance to know you, and I will make up my own mind." Thank you for giving me that chance to be who I really am, a professional who happens to be gay. To you, Sandy Ryan, my professional editor, confessor, fount of wisdom, mystical rose, and lady bountiful; and to shy, quiet Rick Kruger, her other half of Creative Characters—you were tops. And Carolyn Hulbert, special flowers and accolades to you. You've always been that cherished lady in my life who taught me how to feel with my heart, with my emotions. That ability was indispensable during the tough times in completing this project. Your words, "I know if anybody can do it, you can," came true. And to Norman Laurilla, my agent, for plugging away, trying to do what was best for me; we did it.

Thanks to Chuck Schoen, for his assistance in California; to Copy

Berg, for his great artwork and cartoons; and especially to Tom Butenhoff, Miriam Ben-Shalom, Kathy Gilberd, Jeff Boler, Jay Hathaway, Johnnie Phelps, Leonard Dean, Jim Woodward, Ellen Nesbitt, and Ken Devon, for their hospitality along the way. Technical assistance was provided by many professionals. Among them, Judy Binder, my chief transcriber, was a great help because she understood where I was coming from and saw quite clearly where all this would go. Thanks also to Frances Reed and Joan Nolan, my typists, and particularly to Al Mayer, my computer whiz, helper-outer. (If not for you, Al, everything would still be jumbled on my disks!)

I would like to thank Gary Pohrman for his many years of support, no matter where his assignments took him; Roger Meyer for his counsel and assistance, Karen Keeney for answering my many legal questions; and Susan Hauser for her initial editorial help and, of course, for introducing me to Jerry Packard and Merl Grossmeyer, who have become my/our two best friends. Jerry, thanks for all your assistance, advice, information, and clarification on military questions involving Germany, and all your well-tested information on publishing and writing. And to you, Merl, my solid rock, that voice of experience, thanks for being there.

Heartfelt appreciation is given to Congressman Gerry Studds for his foreword for *My Country, My Right to Serve* and to his aide, Kate Dyer, who did a fine job tying up all the loose ends. I would also like to thank all those gay servicemen and women from the past and present, because without them the book would never have been possible. I know many still can't stand up and say, "I'm gay and I'm proud to be a marine," or "I'm gay and I'm proud to be a sailor," but perhaps that day will come. Their contribution to this country, to help us stay strong and safe, is truly appreciated.

A special thanks to Vi and Kay Laudon for making me feel like a part of their family and inviting my family—Parke and Debra—to be a part of theirs, too. And as I speak of family, Debra Sue, you have probably been the most important person in this entire project. Without your love, support, and understanding through all the rough times, I wouldn't have been able to finish it. Without you stepping in, taking on those extra tasks, being there when I was gathering all my research material, and talking to me late into the night by telephone when I was away on my many excursions around the country doing interviews—without all your help, it couldn't have been done. It was your gift of unselfish love that made it possible. And to you, Parke Edward-Ashton, my son—our son—who initially couldn't understand why they were "kicking Mommy out of the Army" but who now understands even more clearly that we weren't the ones who lost, they were—thanks to you, my dear son, for all your love, hugs, and sweet kisses. You were able to learn and grow from this experience, and if I can leave anything for you, it's my words on these pages. I feel confident that someday you will be able to carry on the ideals of equality, because as a child of gay parents, you understand there's nothing wrong with love, caring, and individuality.

INTRODUCTION

Since the beginning of recorded trials, homosexuals have been judged and punished. The homosexual or, to use a common definition, "one who has committed sodomy," has been fined, banished, beheaded, hanged, drowned, burned, and dismembered. Such punishments have been recorded as early as 1444.

Clearly, the person who commits acts that are considered "unnatural" has never been held in any great esteem. Although the punishments have been tempered to some degree, a similar attitude toward homosexuals persists in society today and has been carried into the military. Gay men and women who choose the military as a profession are often caught in a web of homosexual purges, indirect investigations, and discrimination. In most cases, they are removed from service with less than honorable discharges. Many are court-martialed.

In most professions, being gay is not grounds for dismissal. In the military, however, the mere suggestion of homosexuality is a career death sentence. The military has a practiced way of eliminating "moral threats" to its community; each branch has a specific regulation that addresses the issue of homosexuality. All are basically the same. Most are described in the Personnel Regulations, specifically, U.S. Army Regulations AR 135–175 and AR 135–178 (see Appendix A), which outline purpose, definition, and policy for discharge due to homosexuality.

In the military environment the gay individual must hide the sexual side of his or her personality. He or she may become nearly "asexual," or may be forced to fabricate a lover of the opposite sex. Military personnel are quick to point a finger at the male who is very effeminate or the female who is very masculine acting, whether or not that person is gay. The straight individual who associates with a suspected homosexual is also at risk.

The resulting emotional and mental stress is enormous. Many acquiesce to the pressure and do not hide their orientation, therefore risking dismissal by letting their sexual preference be known to others. Others may hide their sexuality until they complete their enlistment, then live in fear that the military may still come for them. (Another regulation on the books allows the military to bring people back in *after* retirement, if evidence is presented about their orientation, then discharge them so their benefits can be taken away. However, in the present climate, the military would be hard-pressed to carry out such a process.)

Despite the military's current attitude toward homosexuals, the gay presence in the military environment is not a recent one and was once considered acceptable. Historical evidence suggests that Alexander the Great, Julius Caesar, Frederick the Great, and Napoleon were either homosexual or bisexual. Classical military forces often had paired homosexual lovers within their ranks. Homosexuality was an accepted lifestyle for those choosing the military in ancient Sparta and during certain periods in Japan. But this was not a lasting military direction.

Abuse and expulsion of homosexuals in the United States military environment were recorded during the beginning of the Republic. General George Washington issued orders as early as 1778 to remove defendants court-martialed for sodomy. The accused were subjected to a gauntlet of fifers and drummers marking their ouster and disgrace as they were literally "drummed from the corps." These methods have changed only slightly with the passage of time.

As the military evolved, so did its treatment of suspected homosexuals. There were periods when the homosexual was removed by the "sickie theory," as if the individual had a mental disease, and by the "criminal theory," as if he had committed a crime. In the late forties and early fifties, a concerted effort was mounted to expel only "true homosexuals," a term hard to define when early research showed that by age twenty, nearly 40 percent of American men had experienced at least one orgasm with another man.

The military has been much like a fickle lover, embracing gays and other minorities as welcome cannon fodder when there is a need for maximum manpower. During limited action or peacetime, however, that same erratic lover becomes more selective, and the purges begin again with increased fervor. Lives and military careers have been disrupted and destroyed, when gays are no longer useful.

Individuals have been put in chains, disgraced, and sentenced to prison for their "gay crimes." They have been given general, undesirable, other than honorable, or dishonorable discharges. They received "blue discharges" (because they were printed on blue paper) during World War II. Section Eights, the military's psychiatric classification, were given out particularly during World Wars I and II. As late as 1988, three women in the Marine Corps were each ordered to serve a one-year prison term for being gay. (In one of the latter cases, the prosecuting attorney had asked for forty-plus years!)

The military fears that if the homosexual is allowed in its ranks, there will be such rampant sexual activity among the men and women (men with men, women with women) that it will lead to promiscuous behavior. And they frequently refer to "situational" homosexuality in their arguments.

Situational homosexuality, when individuals engage in same-sex acts without necessarily identifying with being homosexual, has occurred in instances where there is confined space or lack of choices, and when sex is used as a means of power and control rather than for actual sexual pleasure. It has occurred in prisons and in war situations. In general, it occurs anyplace where there is not easy access to the opposite sex. The individual who has participated in a homosexual act may contend, "I was drunk. I didn't know what was going on," or "I must have lost my head for a moment." Situational homosexuality seems to occur more readily in conditions where the individual is under great stress, particularly in the military under the strain of war or even in prison camps. In these circumstances, the activity may be more of a stress reliever than a source of pleasure.

Situational homosexuality is a valid expression of sexuality, but it does not necessarily mean the person is not a heterosexual. And it does not necessarily recur once the individual is no longer under the same set of circumstances.

The military uses the above examples of situational homosexuality and other charges that have not been validated and cannot be proved, such as security risk and moral degradation, as the basis for the regulation. Yet the document recently completed by the Defense Personnel Security Research and Education Center in Monterey, California, PERS–TR–89–002, Nonconforming Sexual Orientations and Military Suitability (see Appendix B), states:

Homosexuals are like heterosexuals in being selective in choice of partners, in observing rules of privacy, in considering appropriateness of time and place, in connecting sexuality with the tender sentiments, and so on. To be sure, some homosexuals are like some heterosexuals in not observing privacy and priority rules. In fact, the manifold criteria that govern sexual interests are identical for homosexuals and heterosexuals, save for only one criterion, the gender of the sexual partner. Therefore, those who resist changing the traditional policies support their positions with statements of the negative aspects of discipline, morale, and other abstract values of military life. Buried deep in the supporting conceptual structure is the fearful imagery of homosexuals polluting the social environment with unrestrained and wanton expressions of deviant sexuality. It is as if a person with nonconforming sexual orientation will always indiscriminately and aggressively seek sexual outlets.

In 1987, there were approximately 597,000 Army service members discharged for all reasons. Of those, homosexual discharges totaled 242 male enlisted and 6 officers; and 107 female enlisted and no officers. The other services had gay discharges proportional to their total numbers. The Navy was an exception with fewer members discharged overall but a greater number of gay discharges than the Army. In the Navy, 550 male enlisted and 7 officers, and 104 female enlisted and 2 officers were discharged for being gay. The Marine Corps discharged 67 gay male enlisted and 2 officers, and 31 gay female enlisted and no officers.

For years there has been great controversy over the fact that women are subjected to witch hunts more often than men. Overall, women comprise about one tenth of total military personnel, yet the percentages for females discharged are three or four times greater than those for males (PERS–TR–89–002). Of the Army's total discharges, 5 percent were enlisted gay men compared to 17 percent enlisted gay women. The Navy had 13 percent of enlisted men discharged for homosexuality and 27 percent of enlisted women. The Marine Corps discharged 4 percent of enlisted men for being gay and 33 percent of enlisted women. (Keep in mind that the Marine Corps is the smallest of the four military forces!) The Air Force discharged 4.3 percent of enlisted men for homosexuality and 10 percent of enlisted women.

According to regulations a discharge shall be characterized as honorable or under honorable conditions where the sole purpose of separation is homosexuality, unless aggravated acts are included in the findings. A separation under other than honorable conditions may be issued if there is a finding that the service member attempted, solicited, or permitted a homosexual act by using force, coercion, or intimidation with a person under sixteen years of age, with a subordinate in circumstances that violate the customary military superior-subordinate relationship, openly, in public view, for compensation, aboard a military vessel or aircraft, or in other locations subject to military control (PERS–TR–89–002).

Currently, if a person is discovered to be homosexual and admits

it, he or she is given an administrative discharge, which usually involves a board proceeding with presented "evidence"; an honorable is
usually given. But it will state on the discharge form, DD 214 (a form
future employers will be able to see), "admitted homosexuality."
Therefore, even though the discharge is honorable, the reason for discharge is still going to have an impact on the individual's life after
the military, particularly if he or she seeks employment in a homophobic atmosphere.

Blacks and other minorities have been discriminated against in the
military for decades, and a parallel may be drawn between these
groups and gays. In both world wars there were separate units for
blacks and other minority groups. When the armed forces were ordered to integrate all the units in 1948, as Gerry Studds pointed out,
they argued that integration would destroy morale, affect the completion of the mission, and so on. Those same arguments were raised
regarding allowing women into the ranks. At the time the military was
opened to women in the early 1940s there were fears that they would
destroy the morale, activate the sexual proclivities of men, and destroy the decorum of the previously all-male, segregated environment.

The evidence shows that the military is slow to follow the path of
social change. It has dragged its feet on many issues, trying to keep
its community a totally separated environment, apart from the rest of
society. Women, blacks, and other minorities still have a problem ris-
ing through the ranks in the military. Women are not promoted as
readily as men, and they are more suspect. If a woman is not married,
there is suspicion that she may be gay, or she may be considered a
"whore" or "slut"—terms commonly used by military males in the
sixties and seventies and even in the eighties. Any military male who
forms a very close relationship with another male can be suspect as
well.

The Navy demonstrated this mentality when it investigated the 1989
explosion of the USS *Iowa*. The Navy blamed the incident on a sailor,
Clayton Hartwig, and accused him without evidence of being a homosexual. Because he had left an insurance policy to a close friend,
the Navy concluded that Hartwig was distraught over a "cooled relationship" with a former lover and took his own life along with forty-
seven others. A full congressional investigation was ordered and found
no evidence to support the Navy's charge.

With such archaic thinking at the highest level of the military, it is
gratifying to note that for the first time a female is in charge of the
4,000-plus cadets at West Point. In 1989, Kristin Baker was chosen
"captain of the corps," a truly prestigious position. And in August of

the same year, President Reagan nominated and promoted the first black four-star general, Colin Powell, to chairman of the Joint Chiefs of Staff. These two instances prove that while the military is hard to change, the change just may be coming. General Powell just may be the one to spearhead a change in this policy against gays.

A premonition of that change came in the early 1970s, when two gay individuals stood up against the military for the first time. Sergeant Leonard Matlovich, U.S. Air Force, and Ensign Vernon "Copy" Berg III, U.S. Navy, took their cases to the highest courts. As they tell in the following pages, both lost their right to remain in the military and failed to get their positions back, but they were given out-of-court settlements. Matlovich, a highly decorated sergeant with nearly twelve years of service, had the following epitaph written on his tombstone: "When I Was in the Military, They Gave Me a Medal for Killing Two Men and a Discharge for Loving One."

The stories contained in this book are the experiences of the gay man or woman who either has served honorably and not been discovered, or has been ousted from the military. In each of the three parts, the reader will be able to see through the individual's own words what it has been and is like to be gay and be a member of the military. Of the 130 people interviewed, 42 were chosen for the final work, 28 men and 14 women. There are 19 from the Army, 12 from the Navy, 9 from the Air Force, 1 from the Marine Corps, and 1 from the National Guard. Most ranks are represented in the four services. The general officer corps (generals and admirals) are not represented—the fear of discovery is too great for any of those ranking officers to come forward. (This is not to say there are not gays at that level. Statistics and the stories in this book prove that gay general officers do exist.) Some subjects are still on active duty, and a pseudonym was necessary to protect them from discovery.

These oral histories emphasize the stress and struggle of the military gay. They are the stories of individuals who are serving their country, as is their constitutional right, yet who are theoretically not allowed in the military because of an unfair regulation. They are not allowed to prove themselves because they are always in disguise, always leading a double life. If the regulation were not in place, these individuals could undoubtedly contribute even more to their particular military occupation.

While this book was being written, Lieutenant Colonel Oliver North of the U.S. Marine Corps stood trial and was convicted of, among other things, shredding government documents and obstructing Congress. Many of the people interviewed commented on how this trial illustrated the incongruity of the military's way of thinking. Colonel North's conviction was *reason enough* to remove him from service under less than honorable conditions. Many felt that he should be honored rather than tried. Yet on November 2, 1989, the U.S. Senate unanimously voted to restore North's $23,000 pension. Senator Jesse Helms was quoted as saying, "Ollie North has been punished enough."

Individuals in this book have been given prison sentences, undesirably or dishonorably removed from the military, deprived of all benefits, harassed, degraded, and abused and have had their futures totally destroyed when their only "crime" was that they were gay.

As you read their stories, you will notice the survivor instinct inherent in many of the interviewees. These men and women may have been pummeled and verbally abused—in many cases, they were physically abused as well. While the military tried to break their spirits and destroy their dignity, they survived and often went on to become even better citizens because of their innate ability to come back and say, "You can't do this to me. You cannot destroy my inner self."

Many of the individuals interviewed stated that their particular military occupation was in an area where people did tolerate them. In other words, their colleagues looked the other way. They probably knew that the individual was gay but decided it wasn't important. Whether they accepted his or her homosexuality is not the issue. If the majority of the personnel who work with gays in the military can choose to ignore one's sexual orientation or, better yet, adopt a live-and-let-live attitude, there is absolutely no reason why the entire regulation should not be removed.

It is not the intent of this introduction to answer all the reader's questions about homosexuality but merely to give basic information about the subject and to show how it applies to the military gay. For further information an expanded bibliography, a service organization list, and other appropriate resources can be found in the back of the book.

I hope this book will help initiate a movement in this country similar to those that have occurred in Canada, Denmark, the Netherlands, Sweden, and Israel where gays are now allowed to serve. If the regulation in the U.S. armed forces were also removed, we could get on with living and with serving our country as we have a right to do—a right we should all be able to exercise.

THE U.S. MILITARY

Rankings Effective 1945–47, Officers and Enlisted

Army/Air Force*	Navy/Coast Guard	Marine Corps
General of the Army	Admiral of the Fleet	General
General	Admiral	Lieutenant General
Lieutenant General	Vice Admiral	Major General
Major General	Rear Admiral	Brigadier General
Brigadier General	Commodore	Colonel
Colonel	Captain	Lieutenant Colonel
Lieutenant Colonel	Commander	Major
Major	Lieutenant Commander	Captain
Captain	Lieutenant	First Lieutenant
First Lieutenant	Lieutenant Junior Grade	Second Lieutenant
Second Lieutenant	Ensign	Commander Warrant Officer
Chief Warrant Officer	Midshipman	Warrant Officer
Warrant Officer Junior Grade	Warrant Officer	Sergeant Major
Master Sergeant	Chief Petty Officer	First Sergeant
First Sergeant	Petty Officer First Class	Technical Sergeant
Technical Sergeant	Petty Officer Second Class	Staff Sergeant
Staff Sergeant	Petty Officer Third Class	Sergeant
Sergeant	Seaman First Class	Corporal
Corporal	Seaman Second Class	Private First Class
Private First Class	Seaman Third Class	Private
Private		

*On September 18, 1947, the U.S. Air Force was established as an independent military service under the National Military Establishment. At that time, the name "Army Air Forces" was abolished.

Current Officer Rankings

Rank	Navy/Coast Guard	Army/Marines/Air Force
O-1	Ensign	Second Lieutenant
O-2	Lieutenant Junior Grade	First Lieutenant
O-3	Lieutenant	Captain
O-4	Lieutenant Commander	Major
O-5	Commander	Lieutenant Colonel
O-6	Captain	Colonel
O-7	Commodore	Brigadier General
O-8	Rear Admiral	Major General
O-9	Vice Admiral	Lieutenant General
O-10	Admiral	General
SPECIAL	Fleet Admiral	General of the Army General of the Air Force

Current Warrant Officer Rankings

Rank	Navy/Coast Guard	Army/Marines*
W-1	Warrant Officer	Warrant Officer
W-2	Chief Warrant Officer	Chief Warrant Officer
W-3	Chief Warrant Officer	Chief Warrant Officer
W-4	Chief Warrant Officer	Chief Warrant Officer

Current Enlisted Rankings

Rank	Navy/Coast Guard**	Marines	Army	Air Force
E-1	Seaman Recruit	Private	Private	Airman Basic
E-2	Seaman Apprentice	Private First Class	Private	Airman
E-3	Seaman	Lance Corporal	Private First Class	Airman First Class
E-4	Petty Officer Third Class	Corporal	Corporal or Specialist 4	Sergeant or Senior Airman
E-5	Petty Officer Second Class	Sergeant	Sergeant or Specialist 5	Staff Sergeant

*The Air Force does not have a warrant officer system. The marking differences on the various ranks consist of bars with added darkened areas to designate warrant levels.
**Coast Guard enlisted ranking badges are the same as the Navy's for grades E-1 through E-6. E-7s through E-9s have silver specialty marks, eagles and stars, and gold chevrons. The gold Coast Guard shield on the uniform sleeve replaces the Navy star.

E-6	Petty Officer First Class	Staff Sergeant	Staff Sergeant or Specialist 6	Technical Sergeant
E-7	Chief Petty Officer	Gunnery Sergeant	Sergeant First Class	Master Sergeant
E-8	Senior Chief Petty Officer	First Sergeant or Master Sergeant	First Sergeant or Master Sergeant	Senior Master Sergeant
E-9	Master Chief Petty Officer	Sergeant Major or Master Gunnery Sergeant	Command Sergeant Major or Sergeant Major	Chief Master Sergeant
E-10*	Master Chief Petty Officer of the Navy	Sergeant Major of the Marine Corps	Sergeant Major of the Army	Chief Master Sergeant of the Air Force

Acronyms, Abbreviations, and Slang

All the services use, and would be speechless without, acronyms. For quick reference, many of the ones used in this book are defined below. Other abbreviations and terms are also included. (Many slang words in the list were used largely in Vietnam.)

ADMIN	Administration
ADT	Active Duty for Training
AF	United States Air Force
AGR	Active Guard/Reserve
Airborne	Personnel or equipment dropped by parachute
Airdales	Pilots
AIT	Advanced Individual Training
AK-47	Assault rifle (made in USSR)
APR	Airman Proficiency Rating
AR	Army Regulation
ARCOM	Army Reserve Command
ARPERCEN	Army Reserve Personnel Center
ARVN	(Arvin) The South Vietnamese Army
AT	Annual Training
Black magic	Nickname for the M-16A1 rifle
Boonies	Term used for the jungle or any remote area away from a base camp or city
Branch	Designates occupational specialty for Army officer, i.e., AG, MI, MP, QM, IN (Adjutant General, Military Intelligence, Military Police, Quartermaster, Infantry)
Bubblehead	Diver
Butcher brigade	Nickname given the 11th Infantry Brigade after exposure of Lieutenant Calley's actions at My Lai

*One per each service

BX/PX	Base/Post Exchange—equivalent to nonmilitary shopping stores
C's	C-rations or combat rations
CAP	Civil Air Patrol
CG	United States Coast Guard
Charlie	Viet Cong
CID	Criminal Investigation Division
Comdr	Commander
Commo	Communications or signal capacity, personnel or equipment
CONUS	Continental United States
CPO	Civilian Personnel Office
DA	Department of the Army, located in the Pentagon, Washington, D.C.
DC	Deputy Commander
Deep serious	In the worst possible position, such as almost overrun by the enemy
Desoto	Destroyer naval patrols off Vietnam
Det	Detachment
DMZ	The demilitarized zone once separating North and South Vietnam at the 17th parallel
DOD	Department of Defense
DOT	Department of Transportation
E-1/O-1	Designation for enlisted/officer ranking—entering level
EER/OER	Enlisted/Officer Evaluation Efficiency Reports
Fire base	Artillery firing position often secured by infantry
Firefight	Skirmish between opposing units
Frag	To kill or attempt to kill one's own officer or sergeants, usually with a fragmentation grenade
Frogs	Navy Seals (crack Navy personnel used for water assault, similar to Army Special Forces)
FY	Fiscal Year
Ghost	To take off; be absent, shirk duty
Grinder	Paved drill field—generally used for marching manuevers
Grunt	Infantryman
Gung ho	Hard-charging, truly dedicated to service; also associated with the Marines
Gunney	Marine gunnery sergeant
Gunship	An armed helicopter
HQ	Headquarters
ID	Identification
IDT	Inactive Duty Training
IMA	Individual Mobilization Augmentee (Reservist assigned to an active Army unit in case of mobilization)
IRR	Individual Ready Reserve—does not belong to an active Reserve unit, or hold an IMA assignment
Jarhead	Slang term for Marine
KHA	Killed in hostile action

Klick	Short for kilometer
Lifer	Career soldier
MAC	Military Airlift Command
Medevac	Medical evacuation by helicopter
MOS	Military Occupation Specialty
MTOE	Modified Table of Organization and Equipment
Mudsucker	Mobile Diving and Salvage—Navy (slang for crew members)
NCO	Noncommissioned Officer
NCOIC	Noncommissioned Officer-in-Charge
NG	National Guard
NIS	Naval Investigative Service
NVA	The North Vietnamese Army
OCAR	Office of the Chief, Army Reserve
OIC	Officer-in-charge
OJT	On-the-job training
OSI	Office of Special Investigation
Porkchop	Supply personnel
Psy-ops	Psychological operations
RC	Reserve Component
R&R	Rest and relaxation or recreation
ROKs	Republic of Korea soldiers and marines
RVN	Republic of Vietnam, South Vietnam
Seabees	Naval construction engineers
SF	Special Forces/Green Berets
Short-timer	Individual with little time remaining in service
Sky pilot	Nickname for an army chaplain
SPT	Support
Squid	Sailor
Strac	Ready in the best possible condition, sharp
TDY	Temporary Duty
USMA	United States Military Academy
USMC/MC	United States Marine Corps/Marine Corps
USN	United States Navy
VC	Viet Cong
Zap	To shoot at and wound, kill, or destroy

WORLD WAR II AND THE KOREAN WAR

Before and even after the attack on Pearl Harbor in 1941, Americans did not feel the physical impact of war as their European contemporaries did. Post-Depression America was reawakening. For some, life was returning to normal. For the gay individual, however, it was an era of suspicion and brutality. The general feeling was that such people were not "right" and should therefore stay out of sight.

The gay culture in this country kept well underground, except for the occasional innuendo about Hollywood society and lavender poodles. The so-called gay bars that dared operate in major cities did so in fear of having to quickly close up shop at any time. Los Angeles had a blue law against "masquerading" (for instance, dressing like a man if one was female)—one woman recalls being arrested and jailed for walking down the street dressed in jeans and a plaid shirt.

When the United States entered World War II, men were drafted into the military by the thousands. Many others signed up on their own, eager to perform their patriotic duty. Over 400,000 lost their lives in war-related actions. Gays were a large part of the armed forces of those years, and women got their first chance to be part of the active military.

In fact, it was the first time women were integrated into the military services. In 1942, Congress passed a law allowing women into the Army, creating the Women's Army Corps (WAC). Women in service at the time have told me that a large percentage of all women in the military at that time were gay. The era marked the beginning of true liberation for all women as they joined the work force, entering factories back home so their men could fight.

During World War II, the gay individual in the military was not harassed as greatly as in peacetime. The tendency was to "look the other way." Every willing man and woman was needed for the war effort, and little emphasis was placed on discharge procedures.

The world was at war and the country was at war. It was a popular war with a known enemy. There was honor and duty, and there were medals. We sent our men and women to foreign shores for a cause that was understood and it was a good cause—freedom.

There have been several U.S. military actions throughout history that were considered undeclared wars, and the Korean conflict was one of them. In that undeclared war, the United States and fifteen member nations of the UN came to the aid of the Republic of South Korea. The 38th-parallel border was crossed by the invading Russian Communist–controlled North Koreans, who were later joined by the Chinese Communists. It was a war, once again, removed from our shores, but it was also the first time we were fighting an enemy that was similar to (if not exactly like) the friends we were trying to help.

Although it was not a war supported by the American public—there were many who could not see a difference between the North and the South—approximately 58,000 men gave their lives to this effort. It was an action that required dealing with the harsh elements of the Korean winter, which in itself took its toll on the military.

On the following pages, nine men and two women tell their stories of what it was like to be gay and in the military during World War II and the Korean War.

☆ ☆

"When I finally decided ... what I was going to do, I was very unhappy at home, was even thinking about suicide. But joining the Army was like jumping from the frying pan into the fire."

JAY BROWN

Age 52, U.S. Army, 1956–59, enlisted. Honorable Discharge. Present occupation: editor/copublisher of *Just Out.*

I went into the military in 1956, because it was something guys did. I mean, you graduated from high school and either went to college or went into the military. Since we were too poor to send me to college, I got a job, but not the kind of job I wanted. I didn't have any training or direction at all when I was growing up. We were just expected to grow up and graduate from high school. I didn't know anything, but did read a lot, a lot of romantic fiction, and that fact was some of my basis for going into the military. I read Leon Uris's *Battle Cry.* It was one of those World War II, Marines, gung ho kind of stories. But what fascinated me was the easy sexuality. But it was heterosexual; it wasn't homosexual. Those hunky guys were getting it on with all of those women, so that's actually why I went in the military: I thought maybe I could get a part of that action. I just knew there had to be some "boys" in there that would like to partake of gay sex!

My personal life wasn't going very well at that time, so joining it was something of a diversion for me. When I finally decided that's what I was going to do, I was very unhappy at home, was even thinking about suicide. But joining the Army was like jumping from the frying pan into the fire.

I was called a sissy when I was a kid, still am a sissy. You can imagine how a sissy would fare in this all-male, macho environment. I was always out of step though, I know that. We were marching and it always seemed I would be the last one on the row and my arms would just be hanging there. You were supposed to swing your arms, but my arms didn't naturally swing, making it a conscious effort for me to do it, which consequently made them mad and they were always yelling at me. And that's something else—the military seems to be so dumb about such trivial things.

I worked in a photo lab the last year I was in, at Tripler Army Hospital in Honolulu, which was great. I kept my own hours ... and was surrounded by queers! Everybody—well, I wouldn't say everybody, but a great number of the people in the unit were gay. Like all those orderlies and the women—gay women. It was like being a civilian eight hours a day with no training duties, none of that bullshit stuff, all the military stuff I absolutely hated. In fact, I figured out very early the people running the training had absolutely no idea what they were doing. They were doing this changeover from conventional to atomic warfare techniques, and were usually running around like chickens with their heads cut off.

Private First Class Brown,
U.S. Army, 1957

While I was in Hawaii, my mother sent me a "gift" package—it contained a cake, a radio, and some books—and later wrote asking how I liked the stuff and wondered why I hadn't responded to her. I told her I had never received it. Well, the mail clerk had these wall lockers stuffed full of mail for people who had either just transferred out or just come to Hawaii. I was of the latter group. For some reason, this started an investigation by the CID, as preposterous as it sounds. It made absolutely no sense to me!

I had to get into my dress uniform and go down to their office. I was actually interrogated by the CID people about this package. Well, during the course of the interrogation, one thing led to another and they started harassing me about being queer. Remember, my overall appearance was still sissy. They said things like, the way you're acting, we think you're . . . like, you're kind of funny—I can't remember the exact words. . . . Of course, I knew what they were saying was true, but I denied it and I lied. I was doing everything I could, but they were browbeating me, trying to get an admission from me about having sex with other men. I had to see them three or four times. And all because of an undelivered package—let's be real!

I guess they were trying to get other people implicated, you know, sexually, gay men. I mean, I didn't really know anyone until my time at the hospital. Basically, a large majority of the personnel people, the nurses, male nurses, the orderlies, were all queer—all of them. But dumb me, I didn't know it. I was celibate at the time. Right. Certainly not by choice. I was just too dumb. When they asked me if I'd had sex with other men, I said, "No, I never had in my whole life." Had you ever thought about having sex with other men? "No." What do you dream about? "About women." And they just assumed, playing a hunch, because of my manner, that I was gay. But all those sexual questions!

Gays haven't any rights. . . . At that time, and even now, we are a suspect group. I knew what they were doing was not correct, to ask me these questions, which were totally irrelevant. I had a goddamn package that had not been delivered—what the hell did it have to do with my private sexual life? I believe it was at that point when I really thought this military fucked with me, and I didn't want to have anything to do with it. After several sessions of the good guy–bad guy routine, I guess they figured they weren't going to get anything out of me, and I was let go. Oh, I got the package, but the cake was moldy!

I did have a couple of close friends while I was in; one was a very effeminate man, more so than me, and the other was just a "regular" guy. We had this really wonderful friendship, platonic, brotherhood-type friendship. That was the first friendship I'd ever had with a male. Maybe it was sexual—I don't know. I did feel sexual toward him and it would have been natural if we had made love, but it never happened. Therefore, I did not have any sexual encounters my whole time in the Army.

After I got out in '59, I kicked around for a few years and then went in the Peace Corps, went through the whole training, with one of the very first Peace Corps groups, the India seven. At the end of the training, my name was not considered for selection by order of somebody in Washington, but I never found out who it was. At this point, I believe my release from the Corps had a direct correlation to that fucking interrogation in Hawaii. When I was informed, it was the most traumatic thing that ever happened to me in my entire life. Those bastards! I went into a depression for about six months after that. I couldn't find anything out, they wouldn't tell me who said what, I had no recourse, they just said no, and no reason or further information was ever given to me! I still hadn't even had a true homosexual experience by then, so it had to be the innuendos from my investigation.

I *was* a practicing homosexual by the time I went to work for the U.S. Post Office. And I was making up for lost time. About three months after I went to work for them—you had to be a trainee for a long time—they gave me my own route. It was the earliest they had ever given anybody a route, so I guess I was an exemplary mailman. But that did not prevent me from being interrogated or fired. It brought back memories of my Army interrogation. I gathered the little bout with the CID had continued to follow me. They had a lot of innuendos, outright lies, wrong names, and I had to read this whole stack of about twenty-five pages after I'd been interrogated. The FBI did the dirty work this time, and made a transcript of all the things they had gone over or accused me of doing. I got fired. I was fired . . . for moral turpitude! Specifically, one homosexual act *and* cohabiting with a woman to whom I was not married. *"This Is the Army, Mr. Jones!"*

Then I went to Europe. I wasn't going to come back to this country again. I had had it with the United States. I said, fuck this shit. You got that? And I still feel that way a whole lot. That's why I'm in the business I'm in now, being editor of a gay newspaper. It gives me that freedom the system seemed to take away—the Army, the Peace Corps, and the damn Post Office! When I analyze it, I don't believe the Army gave me any direction. I thought they would but was wrong, dead wrong. All the Army did was humiliate me, treat me like dirt, and take away any future opportunities with unfounded innuendos. They had zero evidence on me and were merely making judgment calls. Destroying one young man's dreams and hopes.

It was a big game. You made it in the Army by playing their game, doing as little as possible and staying out of other people's way. It really didn't have any end to it, any purpose. You played the game. I wouldn't recommend it to anybody, and especially wouldn't recommend it to gay people, no matter what their objective in this life might be. The military doesn't want you. The military encourages gay people to lie and cheat. It's obvious. If you mark the box or you're asked, do you have any problems with homosexuality, drugs, or whatever, and you say no, you don't have any problems, and they say you denied being a homosexual, then that is a lie. It should make us angry that they can take our words that weren't meant at all and change those same words around to fit their stereotypes. See, it's the whole hypocrisy, the double standard, the lying people have to do. It overtly encourages dishonesty. I just can't see why anyone, for any reason, would want to support such a system, I really don't. On top of that, having to give money [taxes] to support it is even more reprehensible.

I don't think there's any need for the military. The military breeds violence and evil. It upholds brutality, particularly under the guise of helping this or that country overthrow dictators and what have you . . . it's just not good for you. Quite honestly, it's simply another form of legalized brutality. That's one thing. Murder. I find it hard to understand what I do in my private sexual life to be reprehensible, yet the military is allowed to use its forces to kill those they feel shouldn't be in power in some foreign country. There is quite a distance between those two examples. Is not the morale affected when a soldier or sailor is killed in some clandestine, covert operation? And they are worried about whether or not I have sex with another consenting adult? I remember this nephew of mine who was the sweetest little boy you could ever imagine, a little redheaded kid—we used to have such fun. One day, my mom told me he had been named paratrooper of the month at Fort Benning, Georgia, or something like that. I wrote back to her and told her it was the most depressing news I'd received in a long time, that this sweet, gentle child was being taught to be a killer. And that's how I feel about it.

It doesn't matter what you do, as long as you still can get out with an honorable discharge. From what I have ascertained, our culture says you can do anything you like as long as you don't get caught.

[AUTHOR'S NOTE: *On March 22, 1990, Jay Brown died of pneumocystic pneumonia.*]

☆ ☆

" 'Garments of shame . . .' "

"MOSS BRENTWOOD"
Age 56, U.S. Navy, 1950–52, enlisted. Undesirable Discharge. Present occupation: administrator, public railway company.

God, Navy was the only way to go. Besides, their uniforms were so damned cute! So, in 1950, I wound up going into the Navy. After the induction, on the train headed toward San Diego, I met a fellow and within—oh, I'd say forty hours of the actual time on the trip, we had come out to each other. Not sexually, but as "sisters." That type of thing. We became very fast friends and remained great friends for years thereafter. We always had one another for moral support. We chummed. We frequently went out together on weekends, liberties, and leaves. Things like that. We operated together. We were able to get into several nightclubs not particularly fussy about ID. We met other fellows and just carried on. We frequented the military YMCA in San Diego a great deal. It was just like a floating whorehouse; San Francisco was notorious, and Seattle was infamous. These were great places to meet people or for little overnight romances, and were always inexpensive places to stay.

The Navy did discuss standards regarding VD and homosexuality, but it was almost like a joke, really. Because of the intimate conditions aboard ship and the frequent at-sea stays that isolate men from any heterosexual relationships, the Navy was concerned that gays could definitely make their way into a situation like that. Perhaps some of the fellows not so inclined would eventually succumb. I don't know. There was always a paranoia on the part of the Navy, I think. Definitely. I always felt it was going to take something a hell of a lot more stringent than six weeks at sea to turn a supposed "straight" man into an easy gay conquest.

I can remember—I'll never forget it—our last night in basic, there was an incident with this big hunky, handsome bruiser, a married man with one or two kids. I was coming through the barracks. The barracks was loaded with all the guys. As I was going by his bunk, he grabbed me, embraced me, and kissed me full on the mouth! It left me limp. He said, "I have been wanting to do that since the first time I saw you." It just blew me away. He was such a bruiser, and had such a reputation, that not a soul in there made a remark or stood up to the man. I said, "Oh, you fool! Where were you when I needed you? Why have you been closeted all this time?"

Other than that specific incident, I was doing quite well, until the spring of 1952, when I was called in in connection with a legal investigation of certain personnel aboard the USS *Los Angeles*. It concerned reported homosexual activities aboard ship. I don't recall the investigator reading any rights to me. I remember I was only nineteen, and terrified, not really being able to have any clear thinking processes going on at the time. He said, "We happen to know that you have been involved in some homosexual experiences away from the ship." He didn't infer that I had been carrying on *on* the ship. He inferred that they had some goods on me. He didn't name any names, places, or anything like that. He just came right out to me and said, "How do you wish to plead on this? As purely passive in the relationship? Or as an aggressive participant?" The only thing I could think of was to lie and say, "Passive." I thought somehow this would come out easier in the end.

I was literally railroaded into this thing. I really was. I wasn't caught in the act. There had been nothing that preceded this that would give a person any warning or hint that trouble was on the way. One by one, they trooped at least twenty of us off that ship. It was a "purge." It was a literal purge.

It was coercion, it was utter coercion. It was apparently a guilt complex—I *knew* that what he was saying wasn't quite right, and yet it was close enough to what had been going on that they indeed had something on me, that possibly they had been in a hotel room right next to me. You know, I was scared. A scared, immature kid of nineteen at the time.

They laid all the cards on the table. Absolutely. Except evidence. There was *no* evidence! They did ask me for names of other people aboard ship. I just said I had always made it a point to keep my business to myself aboard ship, and there was nobody else aboard ship I could honestly name that I knew was participating in any sort of homosexual activities.

Of course, I knew a number of them very well because I'd been with them many times. We had "gang dates"; things like that were going on.

But I gave no names. However, they certainly didn't make any mistakes in the people that left. We were all gay.

It was just that one visit to the investigator, and that was it. I was left aboard ship, I think, for an additional forty-eight hours, in which time I settled things there and packed my belongings to leave. I was taken to North Island, to the North Island brig in San Diego for thirty days. Before I was taken to North Island, I went to see the ship's doctor. I asked him if there wasn't some way I could get out of this. I went to him and I bared my soul about it. He said, "I know that at this point this is tremendously traumatic to you. It's not an easy thing to go through, but there's no way I can help you. Take heart in the fact that I've had this happen to several good friends of mine in the past, and I can guarantee you that within ten to fifteen years you won't even remember this, or it will be so minor in your memories or of so little importance in your life if you go ahead and do this that you'll wonder why you were so upset about it. Most importantly, try to remember it that way." These were encouraging words.

To this day, I still don't think there should be any connection between doing my job and being gay. The regulation shouldn't be. Absolutely not.

It took them thirty days to muster me out, but I was not the only one. Of the twenty that went off the ship at the time, about ten of us arrived at the brig. We were segregated from the other prisoners and assigned what were referred to as green stars. It was like the Jews. We wore green badges. They weren't star-shaped but circular. The badges were worn at all times.

We were set apart, even though we were in the brig with hundreds of other sailors. We received few problems from fellow prisoners. Actually, it was the guards who were out of line for the most part. In fact, one night, one of the guards came over to my cell and exposed himself. He had a roaring erection and said, "Here, baby, how would you like to get down on this?"

I would have loved to, but I was scared to death that it was further entrapment. I was so intimidated, so frightened by the entire "machine"—you know, the process—that it never crossed my mind to fight back. We didn't have alternatives in those days. We were being drummed out of the Corps, literally. We were going to be gone. It never dawned on us that we had a chance to fight, that there was any reason to.

We were all released at the same time. They marched us out onto the grinder along with all of the other prisoners. We had been dressed in the clothes that they had provided for our departure, our leaving the military. Obviously, they had gone to some sleaze shop in downtown San Diego and bought the most flamboyant, colorful, god-awful looking things you ever saw in your life to provide as our street clothes, our "civvies," when we left. Like kelly-green trousers and purple-striped jackets and fake leopard shirts to make us look as ridiculous, as gay or what have you, as we possibly could look. Our "garments of shame."

Over the microphone, the company commander said, "All the prisoners will turn their backs on these ten men." The other prisoners did an about-face, turning their backs on us. The CO went on yelling over the microphone, "These men are being undesirably discharged for having disgraced themselves in the service of their country."

This was the drumming out. It was everything but the slashing of the buttons from the uniform. We were made to look as ludicrous as possible. Then, as though this weren't the ultimate disgrace—his comments—having fellow prisoners, the "murderers, rapists, and thieves," the *real slime* of the Corps, of all people, turn their backs on us was almost too much to endure. With that, we were marched out the gate and left to our own devices to grab taxicabs to downtown San Diego and get out of those god-awful clothes as soon as possible!

☆ ☆

"You know, I never entered the military with the idea of finding other lesbians or having any sort of affairs. . . . I entered the military knowing that I was a lesbian, but also knowing that I wanted to do what was right by military standards and stay there!"

LORETTA "RET" COLLER

Age 57, U.S. Air Force, 1951–53, enlisted.
Undesirable Discharge. Present occupation:
retired speech and drama teacher.

I think it's an innate thing; at least for me it was an instinctive thing. I knew in high school. I knew in grade school. I knew that what I felt was not like everybody else. Many feel they were born that way or knew from the very onset and didn't fall prey to the social pressures—that "it" was not the norm. I was one of those. I realized it was not the commonly accepted thing and if I did anything against the norm, I was going to pay a price. But I was willing to sit on that notion until I found myself in a position where I could do what I wanted and not have to pay that big price. Now, I wasn't quite sure *when* that would ever be or *if* it would ever be, but that was my fantasy.

When I graduated, the Korean conflict was going on, and although I had a good job at Kimberly-Clark Corporation, the big paper manufacturer, it was not a job that would guarantee a great future. Since I was very career-oriented, nobody in our family had ever gone to college, and we were really very poor, on relief and that whole thing, I thought perhaps the service could offer me that elusive opportunity. It would take care of me, so I thought, and give me a lifelong career. The bottom line was that I really went into the service to be a career woman. And I'd have stayed there. I loved it!

It was so long ago now, but once I did sign up, I had to go through a series of questions. I believe this occurred somewhere during the physical. One that particularly stood out was something like, "Do you prefer going to parties with all boys or all girls?" That was one of the questions! I remember I said, "Well, all boys, of course." This is not a turnip here. My mother did not raise somebody with a lobotomy! I knew what I had to say—the questions I had to answer, because once I decided I wanted to go into the service, I knew about those questions—and said what they wanted to hear. Oh, and I do remember one other question that had any indication of sexual preference at all, other than that one, and that was "Have you ever had any feelings for women that you think might not be acceptable to other women?" And I said, "Only my mother."

Airman Second Class Coller,
U.S. Air Force, 1952

You know, I never entered the military with the idea of finding other lesbians or having any sort of affairs or anything. I entered the military *knowing* that I was a lesbian, but also knowing that I wanted to do what was right by military standards and stay there! But, by God, when I got into basic, I thought I had been transferred to hog heaven! No damn kidding! Lordy! But I was smart enough to know that doing anything would be my downfall. And like I said, I really wanted to stay in. There was no doubt in my mind, from the time I raised my hand and was sworn in until the day I was discharged, that that's where I wanted to be. I liked everything about it. I loved the parades, I loved the uniform, I loved . . . I even liked taking orders. I liked standing at attention. I liked getting out there on the field, standing there at parade rest for an hour and a half waiting for a parade. I liked everything about it. I even *liked* KP. I liked everything about it. You would have thought they would have been smarter than to have kicked someone out who liked KP!

I did very well. I did *very* well. I was up at two o'clock ironing my uniforms, and when the whistle blew at 4:30 to get up, man, I was out there and loved it. The challenge was great, and I went for it with gusto. Yeah, I was made squad leader. I remember our trainer was a corporal by the name of Tater, and everybody called her Spud. I have pictures of her and her lover, Powers, who was also there, and Corporal Nichols, who was a dyke, just like they were. They were all affiliated with our flight. Even though there was never anything mentioned, you know, there was that bond that exists that is never acted upon or never mentioned. But the rapport—that was there, and I had that. Actually, once we recognized the bond, believe it or not, we pretty much *stayed away* from each other. In retrospect, I'm sure, it was the survival instinct. I guess we all seem to have it.

After basic, I went to McClellan Air Force Base in Texas, where I spent the rest of my time. They were cross-training me. Then it all came to a stop because I discovered sports, and more women! I was on this basketball team, of course ... I mean, why not utilize my height to my advantage? I'm about five ten, five eleven. And through some of the women on this civilian team I met this gal. As I said, I discovered women. The teams are an avenue. I don't think it's the only one, but I think it's one of the better avenues, just as it is in everyday life. You know, God, we used to go to other games and the stands were just filled with lesbians of all shapes and sizes! But overshadowing it all was the fear of discovery. I still had that caution button going, you know, don't do anything ... and I never did anything on base.

I would stay with this gal over the weekend, and I figured, now, when I put on my civilian clothes and go into Sacramento, that's my weekend and what I do has no bearing on what's going on at the base. So I had this relationship with Marie and there were never any problems, until right around the spring of 1953, when basketball season had ended ... and the OSI started stalking me. My theory is that periodically they'd go through the bases and go on these purges. They would start first with all the women who were involved in athletics and then move from there with any info they had gotten, to snare other women.

They opened my mail. They'd get me up in the middle of the night and take me over to the OSI office for questioning. They'd look under my mattress for anything that I might have hidden, any material, letters, notes, valentines, just anything that I might have hidden that could be incriminating. They'd call me from work or they'd come down and personally escort me back to the OSI office. I was embarrassed being called away from work. I'd just say, "I have to see the OSI," and off I'd go and come back whenever I was released. Sometimes I'd be there ten minutes. Sometimes I'd be there two hours. Most of the time, I would say if I had to make an average, probably forty to forty-five minutes, but their short times were in the middle of the night, just enough time to get me up, awake, out of bed, and disturb my whole night. They asked me things like when was the last date I had with a man, what did I do about my sexual desires, did I know any women who saw other women in a physical kind of sense, did my Catholic upbringing forbid me to masturbate? Hell, my own *mother* forbade me to masturbate!

This whole psychological warfare went on and on. It happened countless times. I mean, we're not talking just once or twice a week; we're talking one or two times a day for about four months! Finally, I went to my commanding officer, who my instincts told me was a lesbian, and as I look back on it, she tried so hard to help me, but couldn't—her hands were tied. Anyway, I went to her and said, "I can't handle this anymore." I had reached the point of breaking, and I knew that if this went on any longer, I was going to end up in a psych ward—I just could not handle it emotionally. I couldn't do my job, you know. . . . They'd come to the mess hall and get me right in the middle of a meal. I mean, they knew no bounds. It was awful.

There was one gal whom they would call in periodically, and she would go over there when she was drunk. She'd volunteer all this information, but never sign anything. When they'd call her back in, she'd be sober and deny it all! They really got pissed off at her. As for me, I just totally denied everything. Well, about the last month that I was being called in, they brought Marie into it, the civilian gal, and said that they knew that I was having this affair with this girl in Sacramento. They knew where she lived, what her parents' names were, what her brothers' and sisters' names were. They also knew about her sister and *her lover*, they knew the times I was there, the buses that I took, how long I stayed, my mode of transportation home, what I wore, for Christ's sake, they knew every damn move I made. It was mind-shattering, it boggled the imagination to believe that they were so concerned about what I did in my spare time, that they would go to such lengths!

So then they started propositioning me. If I would agree to say that I was having an affair with this woman in Sacramento and mention her name, they would give me a *general discharge*. Now, nothing would be done as far as Marie or her family were concerned because they were civilians and the military's not interested in civilians. However, I was threatened with a court-martial if I didn't agree to mention Marie and sign the statement. I could sign and get a general, or not sign, get court-martialed and be dishonorably discharged, which meant I would pay for it for the rest of my life. So I stopped seeing her, for one thing.

When I stopped seeing Marie, it was bad enough, but the whole thing was just terrible.

First of all, you didn't have any outlet. I had no outlet. When you were under investigation, you were pretty much by yourself, so except for Carol, who was also being intensely investigated, neither of us had another friend, because you were just not nice to be around during that time. Besides, no one wanted to be found associating with us for fear of their own careers. Birds of a feather kind of thing, you know, so the people that you had to talk to about it were minimal. Carol and I would commiserate, and that was the extent of it. I was thwarted in that respect, frustrated and angry. There was no way I could tell Marie what was happening and explain to her that my whole relationship with her *was* something of value, not some tawdry affair. And I was angry and feeling paranoid because I didn't even feel safe going off base anymore. So I locked myself onto the base knowing full well that no matter where I went, they would follow me somehow or know where I was going. I also had a fear of incriminating other people and I didn't want to do that.

During their interrogation sessions, they would produce a whole list of names. They must have had a whole goddamn squadron of names. But I denied . . . I really did. I said, "I don't even know them," you know, that was my answer all the time. They told me more than once that I would get a general discharge, which was the same thing as an honorable and carried with it all the same benefits. Of course, the main thing was that there were no negative aspects attributed to it. It was the only way I would be able to get out of there and still be able to hold my head up. All they wanted me to do was sign that statement, and I remember them saying that "Marie's family will not be a part of it." I was worried about my mental and emotional health. I felt I was beginning to crack. I knew myself well enough to realize that I was at a saturation point, and didn't want to end up in any sort of psychiatric unit someplace. But I guess my ego said that I wanted to handle this.

I went to my commanding officer again and said, "I don't think I can take any more of this bullshit, it's just too much, so I'm considering signing that paper, getting a general discharge, and getting released." I was sitting with my hands on her desk, and she reached across, put hers on top of mine, and said, "Well, Ret, (that was my nickname), I think you really need to think about this. Before you do anything, think real hard about the effect it's going to have on your future," and she drew her hands back. I simply said, "I can't think about the future right now, you know, I'm trying to make it day by day."

The next time they called me in, I said, "Well, what do I have to sign?" They surprised me by saying, "Tell us about your relationship with Marie." I wasn't sure what that had to do with my own discharge, particularly since she was a civilian, but I did. I told them all about my relationship with Marie. A day or two passed and they never bothered me. Then they called me in again and said, "Okay, now we need to hear this story again," so I had to tell them again. I left, and the very next day, the major called me in again and said, "I've been contacted by the OSI, and you're going to have a hearing in about a week." I was shocked, and said, "A hearing, what for?" "Well, yes, in order for them to do the paperwork on this and get your discharge, you have to go through a hearing." And I said, "Is that the same as a court-martial?" And she said,

"Yes." To protect herself, she was quite detached and official-acting. It was a pretty sad scenario as I recall.

Once the "court-martial" was in session, nobody read me any rights, told me I could have a defense counsel, or that it was my right to have somebody on that board representing me. I was like a lamb to slaughter. They asked me things like: Did I think that my homosexuality had an adverse affect on my Air Force performance and my military performance? Did I think that being a homosexual in the AF influenced other people? Did I realize that I was a security risk being a homosexual? Those were the kinds of questions, but never anything at all as far as "Is there anything you want to say?" until the end, the very end.

The entire process took about fifteen minutes, including my comments. And when I was allowed to speak, I said, "Well, about the only thing I want to say in my defense is that I don't think I deserve this, to be released, to be discharged from the service, because I feel that my record speaks for itself, that I have never done anything injurious or harmful to anybody else." You know, I was totally career-oriented, and I reiterated to them the fact that I had planned on being a thirty-year Waf and was exceptionally gung ho as far as the AF was concerned. Obviously, all my words fell on deaf ears. I was asked to leave the room for a few minutes while they "deliberated." After about five minutes, they called me back and said, "Well, we've reviewed your case (what could they do in three or four minutes? I ask), and we find that under the circumstances, you should be generally discharged."

Case closed. I was dismissed to get my things in order and get off the base.

It took me that day and the morning of the next day to check out, and about two o'clock the next afternoon, two MPs escorted me off the base. I had fifty-nine dollars in my pocket and bus fare back to my hometown in Wisconsin. However, the corker was that I got an *undesirable discharge*, not a general, as had been expected! *And,* on top of that, the military, the OSI, went to Marie's house in Sacramento, two of them, questioned her parents, questioned her sister, her brothers, questioned Marie, questioned the neighbors ... and if there's anything in my life that I regret, it's that. I wish I had never mentioned that girl's name, because that family didn't understand what was going on. They were Portuguese and had little understanding of the language, let alone what these guys were doing. Those two assholes questioned the neighbors and said awful things about Marie that her parents didn't understand, and because of that, Marie has *never* spoken to me since. And me with this undesirable discharge in my pocket with no explanation from anybody. Just what I needed.

I was pretty devastated. I was pretty numb, but, honestly, I think what I felt was relief that I wasn't going to go through that anymore. However, the down side was that the impact of an undesirable discharge had never occurred to me, *never* occurred to me. I knew it wasn't an honorable, I knew it wasn't the general that I was promised, but the force of it never dawned on me. But I was grateful to be out from under all that pressure and all that investigation. It wasn't until two weeks or so after I was discharged that I realized the impact of *this* discharge. Two pieces of paper arrived in this envelope telling me all the things that I couldn't do because of my undesirable discharge. I could no longer vote. I didn't have any benefits. I could never work for any government-affiliated agency or company. I could not do anything with any state-run organization or state-supported agencies like education or any civil service that had to do with prisons. I couldn't be involved in anything that had to do with security because I could never get a security clearance. I couldn't even work for the post office! You know, all these places where I could never work, the list went on and on . . .

I thought, "Jesus Christ, this is all-encompassing. Unless I want to drive some sort of a diesel truck or an excavating machine of some kind, I am pretty much limited to laying asphalt, or digging ditches! There just is nothing available to me." For about the next six years, I felt like a real loser. I left that base feeling like a piece of shit, with an undesirable discharge in my pocket. I had nothing left that was Air Force. They took every piece of clothing. They took my "li'l Abners," my boots. We wore them for training—we wore them every day, and those little boots were just wonderful. Your feet got all callused and blistered breaking them in, but once you got them broken in, they fit like a second skin. They were high-tops like Li'l Abner wore in the comic strip. So everything I had was turned in, I had no remains of anything military left with me or on me—even my dogtags. And so I really felt—my best description is as crude as it sounds—just like a piece of shit, that I had no ego left, no self-image, no confidence, and no surety of self. I've always been an extrovert with a great sense of humor. I was considered to have this great personality and was always a good mixer, but I found myself being defensive, depressed, and not wanting to socialize.

I wondered what it was all about, you know, what had happened to me. What had I done that was so wrong? I had such high hopes for a military career and had done such an exemplary job, as evidenced by my many letters of recommendation, that I just didn't understand what it was all about. After some unfortunate experiences, it occurred to me then that there was no way *ever* that I could tell anybody I was a homosexual. This is what happened: I went back to Kimberly-Clark, and got my old job back because I told them that I had been discharged under an early-release program. . . . I was there about two months when my supervisor came in and took me into the vice president's office. The vice president said, "Well, we have this letter from the government telling us that you were undesirably discharged, which means that we do not have to continue with your employment, so you're free to go." The same thing happened when I answered an ad in the paper for a government-contract company. I was there four days when they called me in and told me I couldn't work there anymore because of my discharge.

I realized that I felt no strong emotional bonds during that period of time. I don't know if it was a fear of being discovered should I become close to someone, or fear of another sort, of rejection, that kept me distant—I couldn't handle one more devastating situation. Besides my feelings of low worth, it was all pretty damn dehumanizing. You had to be careful, even in California, of being too open about your sexual orientation, so it was even more difficult, like a double-edged sword. It *was* easier, but it was *not* easy. There were gay clubs around, but the club that was open one month wouldn't be open the next—that kind of thing.

I held a number of jobs around LA and Santa Monica, but this just kept feeding my own insecurity, my own lack of self-worth, and my lack of ego. I don't know, but somehow I got the message, I realized someplace, down deep, that the lesbians who had survived had this *something* that kept the survival instinct intact. I'm sure, because I think the women who survive all this are now functioning, contributing human beings, and are not unemployed, in some meal line, and are not on drugs. Yes, I think somewhere we have that gut instinct that says, "You're better than this, you can do better than this, you know you've got the stuff, hang in there." Which is what I did, and I finally found myself in 1958.

I think I started having some success at work and was starting to integrate with the gay community, seeing people on a regular basis. Later, I got a couple of promotions, which helped my feelings of self-worth. But finally, and most importantly, I had come to terms with it. I could look in the mirror and say, "You got an undesirable discharge, so what? Now you've got to handle it." At that point, I was thirty-one, and decided to go to college and, further, decided to go into education. With that decision, I started another whole anxiety trip, because when I applied for a credential, one of the questions at the bottom was about the applicant's military service. If I answered in the affirmative, then I had to list the type of discharge obtained. I answered "no" to that question. I sweated until my application went through and I was issued my teaching credential. But up until last June, 1987, when I retired from teaching, there wasn't a day I didn't labor under the threat of my credential being revoked because I had lied on the application, which is reason enough, or because they had found out about my past. Not that I ever did anything wrong, but I *never* discussed the fact that I was in the military with any of my teaching colleagues.

All those years, I never told a soul about it. Well, three people knew, two of them lovers and one a very good friend. Then, in 1979, I applied for an upgraded discharge, and received it. And you know, it did nothing for me! I did observe that there was a note at the bottom of the new form, "Important Document—Keep in Safe Place." The undesirable one had no such comment! Interesting. But anyway, to this day, I have such a negative attitude toward the government and the military that it's hard for me to discuss it without becoming emotionally upset.

I learned too late that had I the money, time, and the intelligence, I probably could have fought that discharge. It was illegal, totally illegal. With no defense, no reading of my rights, and the fact that I had been lied to all the way down the line, I could have won! But alas, I didn't know all of that at the time. When I got my upgrade, I didn't feel like I had gotten *them*, because after they've *had you* for forty years, it's hard to feel you've *gotten them*. I pay my taxes because I don't want to go to jail, but I'd never do anything service-oriented for this country, and I'm not a patriot. You know, I figure that I gave them all I had so very long ago and they just fucked me over. So fuck them now! I would hope that what I gave *after* I was kicked out of the military proves the value of my contributions as a lesbian. I still see absolutely no reason for that regulation that discriminates against people like me.

I'd like to say to parents, "God, do you realize that this woman, this teacher, this drama coach, who has made all the difference in your child's life, is a lesbian? Are you aware of all the hugs that you have given me and all the hugs your children have given me and all the hugs I've given them? I didn't do anything covert to any of them, but what I did do was educate them, and you saw your kids blossom—under the direction of a *lesbian*. I'm sorry you couldn't have really known me all of those years, so I could have shared what you shared with me, family. Then perhaps, just perhaps, you would have thought differently about gay people in general. But I can tell you this, that I loved teaching your children, and like it or not, I was a positive influence in their lives!" Now, doesn't that say something about lesbians?

☆ ☆

"People in the midst of sex would almost cry of sheer fright. And sexuality seemed to be a compensation for the fear or something to hang on to. I almost became like someone stalking the prey ..."

PAUL HARDMAN

Age 65, U.S. Navy, 1940–46, enlisted. Honorable Discharge. Present occupation: retired.

I was sexually aware from almost the time I could remember, being rather precocious, although it was mostly contemplating and not participating. I remember my mother gesticulating about it and my silly father saying, "Don't you know only sissies play with girls?" Not that the line affected me in my sexual orientation. I had a very early recollection where I realized my father was less than I would have liked. I made a decision very early in my life about my father, because everything I did he assumed was sissy. I learned when I wanted to read, my father criticized reading as sissy. So I wouldn't come home and read, I would go to the library. I suggested to my father I should like to play the piano. Just a little kid—I'm talking between the age of five and seven. No, sissies play the piano. Then I said, "Well, how about a violin?" Then I thought I'd like to be a dancer. All of these things I can see now in retrospect, but of course I had no comprehension of the connotations this would give.

I never was big. When he would complain that I should go out and fight with the kids in the neighborhood and be a man—"make a man of you"—and I said, "I'm too small to fight with the kids," he said, "If you're too small, kick 'em in the balls." I found my best survival technique as a little kid was to outfox them, not to fight them. I tended to use my wits. . . . I would never cry. Years later my mother said it frightened my father to death. I would defy him to hit me, and look him square in the eye. Why I developed that technique I don't know. I was very reticent.

I was being influenced again by the environment. My folks were trying to bring us up as Catholics. But I reached the point with the Catholics of giving up the whole business as total hypocrisy. The moral standards they were trying to impose were inconsistent to the realities of life I was observing, where you explore, and nothing great and outlandish, but nothing happens. It was all mutual masturbation, that sort of thing. No oral or anal business at all—this would be inconceivable at this particular time. I began to understand what my father was talking about. He was intimating that I was a sissy. It was a subtle, constant reality that boys didn't do this. But the reality of it was, all the boys did do this. I began to store it up as lessons that began to have impact a little later. The whole gimmick of my father was "Join the Navy and they'll make a man out of you." He wanted me to quit high school, let the Navy make a man of me—this bullshit, to put it bluntly.

Seaman First Class Hardman, U.S. Navy, 1942

The year before the war and the year before I graduated . . . I joined the Naval Reserve. The Navy mobilized us within a couple of months. I'm talking about March of 1940. I was still in high school—they took me in high school. . . . Then I became aware the education I didn't complete was a crucial factor for anything, even in the Navy, so I wrote a letter to the Navy Department, accusing them of depriving me of my education. Of inducing me into the military . . . which I joined voluntarily, and then providing no opportunity. This created a demand; they set up this coding system over on Treasure Island. We took classes and were issued our high school diplomas when we finished.

I wanted to get away from all of the kids I'd gone through high school with. It was a difficult time, competing with my brother, who was Mr. Perfect. Everybody was supposed to love him, males and females; he was a champion swimmer, tall, got a beautiful tan—I'd get freckles. Well, my brother decided to go with his school buddies, and they went to Pearl Harbor. He didn't get killed, but practically everybody else did. I didn't. I was still here, in San Francisco.

Obviously, I was attractive in those days. Everybody was making subtle passes. Little, blue-eyed, blond—a boy with a tiny little waist. I was the littlest guy on the ship; they had to get special clothes to fit me. And as my grandmother said when she saw me in the military uniform, "Oh, those innocent eyes, what evil they will see." It was a very interesting comment, but I knew what she was talking about. Whether I picked it up instinctively as I grew up, it was trouble. It was confusing for me, who knew very little about the rules of sexuality. There was a presumption in my mind that I was different. That had been sort of inculcated over my growing up. Whether I was or not, I didn't know. But I know that my feelings by definition were different from what everybody else was feeling. But at the end you become aware of something. There was this constant undercut of aggressive sexuality in the military.

There were people in the Navy that were from the old school; they'd been left over, joined the Navy, they were from China duty. . . . Characters, old-timers, guys who could only make it during the rough periods of their life—join the Navy and be secure, that type of thing. It was a time when we got twenty-one dollars a month. . . . Navy personnel were still back in the dark ages with attitudes. Admirals wore these funny hats fore and aft, people had swords, we were on ships that were made for World War I. The Navy itself was an anachronism. But these men were shrewd, and I could sense some of them were being very nice to me. In fact, I got the nickname very early on of being "the cherry." I was very popular because I was a good dancer. And I'd go to the USOs; later on, the girls would want to dance with me. So it made me very popular.

I began to see the line of demarcation. Those who were aggressive and were casing boys were looked at as very masculine. If you were the boy, the catamite—the Navy termed it pogue—they talked about you. It's a Navy word. It's how the origin of the words *pogie bait*, meaning candy, came into being. You give a young sailor some candy and he'll go to bed with you. If you were putting out for someone, then you were supposed to be passive. . . . I knew the technique and I was very, very careful as I grew into the system not to be the one they talked about. I would let them chase me until I caught them. It was complete reversal, and what was actually happening in bed. It was a deliberately calculated defense mechanism. I knew it. I thought about it at the time. I made the decision, no matter what my inclinations may have been, I would never play a reverse role during that period in the Navy.

I was sent all over the place on ships, and I knew the activities. Once, we were at sea for thirty-six days, and don't kid yourself, men don't wait thirty-six days. I don't know how women operate, but it seems to me men are horny every three days. If they can stand seventy-two hours, and these were all young men, they were getting some. I also made an observation that under stress, whether you were dropping depth charges or in some really dangerous situation, whether in the middle of a storm where the waves were mountains or near an island that was blown up, there seemed to be a direct correlation between the sexual desires of the crew and the degree of the fright created. Now, whether it's a survival thing nature does to men, I don't know, but it was an observable phenomenon to me. Men got sexy when they were frightened to death. This became very obvious when we were on an island in the South Pacific. The Navy had a receiving station on shore where people were in tents waiting for other ships. The activity on that island was sexual. . . . I found that people out in the jungle, upon encounter, were anxious for sex.

People in the midst of sex would almost cry of sheer fright. And sexuality seemed to be a compensation for the fear or something to hang on to. I almost became like someone stalking the prey, in a sense a little kid. But I would always look for mature men, like in their thirties, this sort of thing, someone who had been around for a while and you thought would make a play for you and then keep their mouth shut. You never trusted the other kids. And most of the ones that *were* playing were the married men. Almost everybody that was in this condition was married. Whether this is because I selected it that way, or it was the phenomenon, I don't know. But I knew the safe bets were the married guys who were apparently used to something.

I don't think the Navy knows how it works. The smokestacks on the destroyers were hollow, and there is a platform on the top of them, perfect security. . . . There were always places that had security to the location because it required it, yet you had access to these places in the normal course of duty. Aggressive young men find places to do whatever needs to be done. It was more like mutual masturbation and low-level participation. But it was—everybody seemed to be involved in it. From what I observed, the conduct was the same throughout every kind of ship: tugboats, submarine chasers, destroyers . . .

You'd hardly believe it, but one of the techniques, which I outrageously developed, was merely crawling in with somebody and engaging them in sex and leaving them as if nothing had ever happened. You don't say anything; you pretend it never happened. And so long as you never discussed it, it never happened. Now I don't know how the phenomenon is workable; I look back at it now, and say, "My God, that's outrageous." No prior warning, no, and I'm not talking about forcing anybody. You don't even know who they are sometimes because they come in in the nighttime, and maybe they'd leave and take their bedroll and go somewhere else. But it was constant. One of the games that we'd play was called grab ass. Everybody was pinching everybody on the bottom. It was always the topic of a joke. It's something everybody wanted to do and denied.

While I was on this one ship, we had a man who became an admiral and would send for me, using one of his highly dressed aides with their gold braid to come down to the crew's quarters and ask me to go to his quarters. Nothing was going on. Nothing. We talked, and as I look back on it, whatever his fascination, I never was so over-awed with him that I wasn't comfortable with him. But I was never so presumptuous as to take advantage of him. It seemed to be a nice balance which he enjoyed. We would discuss the books that I had read. We would discuss Voltaire, philosophy, or many of the great works; and we would talk about specific things. One day, he asked if I would like to go to the Naval Academy. And I said, well, I didn't have any background in that, which was required. He bought the books, assigned me an ensign, and even relieved me from wartime duties so I could study. But the crew would make fun of me and the ensign didn't like it, and I told him I was being subject to a great deal of harassment because I was the "admiral's boy."

They were harassing me and I couldn't study, nor cope with both. So he set aside a small space in the wardroom passageway, put a desk, chair, and a lamp, where I studied. When we got to Panama, I took the examination and passed with flying colors. He then made a recommendation to Admiral Jacobs, who was then Chief of Naval Personnel—his personal endorsement for me to go to the Naval Academy. I was given some shore leave, and when I came back, the admiral was gone, sent to command a new vessel. I got orders to go on this ship called the *Ganymede* of all things. I knew the plans were to send me on to the winter term at the Academy.

I approached the new commander on deck and asked him about my orders for Annapolis, and he said in front of the officers and crew, "I don't have to talk to the admiral's pogue." That's like calling me a queer. During this time, the business of whether or not I was sleeping with the admiral was so endemic that even one of the officers on the ship made a pass at me, assuming that I was the admiral's boy. I cut him cold and warned him to leave me alone. I wrote a redressive grievance addressed to Admiral Jacobs, and in that letter I expressed I was scandalized that this officer in the presence of other officers and the crew and the men of the ship would make the remark to impugn the reputation of Admiral So-and-so, to suggest that he had made improper advances or that we had actually had sexual relations.

This new commander was sending me out to get killed because he hated me, I could sense it. I felt I had a weapon because I had never done anything, but no matter what I thought, as far as he knew, I was just an eighteen-year-old kid who appeared to get favors from the old admiral. It was inconsistent with what he knew about me (the records were in his possession for my entry into the Academy) to deliberately pick on me, and send me off the ship, when I was scheduled to go to the Academy and it had been already approved. I don't know, I'll have to say the shit must have hit the fan, because special orders came through to send me back to the United States. Pronto!

They put me aboard a ship coming back, and then I was aware of something, on the gay business. There was one lad they kept in chains, and they used to bring him up on the ship for exercise. They would clear the deck; we had to leave a certain part of the deck when they made the announcement over the loudspeaker and brought this one kid up alone so he could walk on the deck, get some sunlight, with chains on his feet and hands. He was a queer. Everybody tried not to discuss it. 'Cause I kept my ears open. I listened, never heard any negative comments; most were sympathetic. Too many of them figured, I think, "But for the grace of God, there'd go I." And it was so endemic. The reason I can say it was endemic is because I was a pre boy, being a pre boy, you know. When practically everybody on the ship is after you, you know. Knowing my own feelings and seeing what they had done to this man, I had to be doubly careful.

I think if you made mistakes, you'd be dead. Because apparently the method the Navy was using, they didn't necessarily discharge you if they were suspicious, they sent you someplace to get killed. Think about that! With me, what was their idea of sending me down as replacement on these particular ships? Because they had a high mortality rate. They could have sent me to anywhere in the world. But that commander sent me specifically on these destroyers that were running the slot in the Solomons. That was a death sentence. There was no escaping their mental mind-set on the subject; they "knew" what a homosexual was.

As an aside, personally, I never associated with the people I worked specifically with, if I knew they were gay. I only went out with other people on the ship that didn't work with me. If you were going to have sex, to put it bluntly, you did it onshore and not on the ship for the most part. If I went into the bar with someone, it was a scene, yes. But to me in those days, it was seamy, it was very seamy, so I stayed away from it. I was aware of it, 'cause the other guys would go, come back and tell stories, and I'd listen, particularly in San Francisco. San Francisco was notorious! I knew they had bars that were restricted because they were gay. In fact, that's how all the sailors and soldiers knew—it was like an advertisement.

I remember all this was filtering through my mind, trying to sort out, who is the queer? There was a negative attitude to that, but if you were the butch number picking up these queers . . . that's okay. It didn't make sense, still doesn't make sense, but I can understand it. But the understanding came much later.

As it turned out, I finally wasn't sent away to die. The commander was directed to send me to my school assignment. However, because I wasn't sent back early enough, I missed the September entry. In the meantime, Congress created a new system, so I was assigned as a cadet with an identical curriculum, set up by the Academy, with the University of California. I had the same program, and since they had this additional need and required more officers than the Academy could finish, it served the same purpose. It was the cream of the crop, to put it bluntly. . . . It was during this time I became aware that more and more people were sexual, and I had to be doubly careful. You were on military duty, confined to the school, couldn't go anywhere, and lived there in barracks or dormitories. We lived in what they called Callahan Hall. You weren't allowed to go anywhere, and only on weekends could you go out.

College was all I was doing. It really wasn't until after the war I first deliberately sought out a place where gay people might be. And the first time I did that would have been in '46. Most of the guys now in these bars were ones just out of the military. At the end of the war I was in my senior year. They offered the commission and I said no. I went on to graduate school with the GI Bill because I was in six years, and even though three of those years were in school, I still got a full six years' credit. So I went to Columbia and got a master's degree and worked on a Ph.D., which I never finished until a couple of years ago.

Ever since my military days, I've been involved in military issues. I've been active with the—what was originally called the Sexual Law Reporter. In those days, we would try cases like Leonard Matlovich's case. We were involved in that. It's now called the American Association for Personal Privacy. We work behind the scene, getting things done without being gay leaders, and consequently, we've accomplished a great deal. It's in that role I work, like I just had this phone call from Cranston's office, on issues dealing with the military as well as civilian. I'm working . . . on a change in the veterans' law, the code that now permits even homosexuals caught in the act—a homosexual act while on active duty— to have their discharges upgraded. That law was passed over three months ago [1988] and has not been disseminated through the Veterans Administration. I'm asking the question with that phone call, why? Who in the administration prevented the information from being disseminated after the law was changed? I got a copy of the law. I'm working with Senator Cranston. I want to know why and who. I won't give up, because someone did it deliberately. I formed the first openly gay American Legion Post—the Alexander Hamilton Post 448. Our oldest member is ninety-seven, from World War I, and was an aide to an admiral. We have a broad spectrum of members.

I do the research on how the veterans lost their rights. And the weird, weird thing is, one of the men who is now fighting us the hardest was a street hustler as a serviceman. Long memory. He doesn't look like a hustler anymore. He's big and he's fat and he's ugly, but he was, and I never tell him I know. The irony of it is he's one of our most hateful opponents. And this is another side of that picture, of being evil to other gay people in order to be in with the boys.

The way the regulation really, really is—don't let it surprise you—the Commander in Chief has absolute discretionary power. When you join the military, you lose your fundamental rights under the Constitution. It's as simple as that. They don't work with the Constitution. It is a military thing. This is why even with the new law that was made, the change was made not through Congress but by administrative procedure—as the administrative bulletin said, out of fairness. It had nothing to do with the Congress. Somebody got it through. An act of Congress could change it. Then it becomes binding on the Commander in Chief.

Half the states in the United States still regard homosexuality as a crime. The Supreme Court, in its supreme wisdom, usually doesn't ask when there are these doubtful questions . . . because whatever ruling it makes would be binding on the states. Like it's similar to slavery; so long as there were enough powerful slave states that considered slavery legal, the Supreme Court would not say it's illegal. Yes, our path is dark.

But think about this—there is an illusion of power that you can generate if you get the propaganda out right. The military does it all the time!

When I think back over my military career, *memorable* is a funny word—probably not the right word. I think going to school, given the opportunity of going to school, changed my whole life. It made everything I have today possible. I make no bones about it. What that admiral did for me—and I never really thanked him, because I was too immature to even know how—was the catalyst in my life. Yeah, he was the catalyst. His belief in me, his interest in me—maybe it had sexual overtones. I don't know, could be. . . . I accepted it as perfectly platonic.

But to me, memorable would be the time I saw all the ships blowing up in the middle of the night, and we're sitting there, and we didn't but were sitting on tons, a million tons, of gasoline. And none of those other ships survived. We were the only ship to survive and were the most vulnerable. They were all cargo ships—like Kaiser coffins, as I called them. That was the most memorable, because that affects life!

The memories of what was hidden, what I could see, when you go through a sexual life, realizing one's sexuality was a pervading undercurrent, constantly living in a hazardous environment of being "discovered"—that memory was ever constant with me. I knew that. And it was a hell of a life to lead. A double life. I stayed away from everybody, almost to the point, I suppose, of being peculiar. I would read, stay by myself, or disassociate; in fact, even be, in a military sense, horseshit, in order to cover up anything that might be apparent. And also being exceedingly good at what I did. I made it a point to know where every line, every water line, every fuel line, was on that ship. When they had to move liquids on that ship, they came to me. I made it a point to know. If you gave me something to do—it was always a desire, or the belief that if you were really good at something, that's a masculine characteristic. Now, this is a naive approach—remember, when you're just a kid . . . They're looking for leadership, and when you're only a tiny thing—I hardly weighed more than a bucket of water—and you don't even shave, something's got to make you stand out. And the thing I did was to know and to be exact on regulations. If they said you folded your towel with the seams inboard, toward the closet, this is the way you folded a towel. There was no other way to fold a towel. The rebellion that I did was to take the system and use it against them, consciously. I was what they called a sea lawyer—it's a term they used. I knew the rules and used them.

Overall, the whole thing was miserable, as a kid not knowing what the hell's going on. I was alone. I was frightfully alone. I didn't make these buddy-buddy relationships. I didn't go out to the bars with them. I didn't trust anybody. I didn't have any long-term relationship going on then at all. I was almost incapable of it. That's the sad part about it. The Navy made me incapable of it. There was—I remember one guy was in tears, who was in love with me so much, but I couldn't respond to it. It cheated me out of my whole emotional life; it trained me not to respond. And that tears you up. You don't realize the damage it's doing, and it ruins a kid's emotional life. I didn't know all the things like these kids coming out today. And so you have to be very self-contained. Since that time, I have established a long-term relationship which has lasted for thirty-five years, and it's been rather habit-forming! But it took me a great while to open up to that opportunity.

One interesting phenomenon occurred when I was on submarine chasers out of Miami in '41, '42, I don't know. We were all called on this big covered pier by this officer, who was telling us not to take prisoners of the German submarines we were shooting at, that even if they were in the water, we were supposed to shoot them. There was an almost spontaneous stamping of feet, and this pier must have been two or three hundred feet long, with thousands of sailors, and the *spontaneous objection*—you couldn't say anything, but they objected with their feet. And that officer was eventually removed, but the callous attitude . . . . You don't mind if they tell you to drop depth charges on people, you shoot at them, but you don't shoot at people in the water or in lifeboats, and that's what this one officer was saying—calloused discrimination.

It was also chauvinistic, but it was part of the time. I don't remember ever having succumbed to the hate propaganda. I could never hate a Japanese. I never hated a German. That's something you saw in the movies. When one guy on the ship went ashore once on an island after it had been captured, and brought back a Japanese man's head, went down in the engine room to try to clean the flesh to get the skull, the crew was appalled at the grossness. Whether the people would be that evil or not seemed to be a product of war. Oh yes, you can shoot somebody if they're coming after you, but I mean the attitude. You're not talking about killing people—like a killing machine. In some of my military work, I recall one veteran, straight man, came to me, cried in my arms because he was remembering watching a buddy being flayed alive in Vietnam. He'd have nightmares. Now, I don't know whether we did things like that. But it was a different kind of war [Vietnam] and it was a war that wasn't appreciated, so whatever pressures got put on those kids was different.

There are many things now that were different from my military experience. For example, I don't necessarily agree with the mandatory AIDS testing. I would hate to see someone given a transfusion and end up with AIDS, because it's not curable. The crime is, they should be spending this effort and even military funds to find a way to prevent it. It's the stigma they've attached to it as being a gay disease which is wrong.

Survival in the military is dependent on many things. You have to have the stamina to play the game and an awful lot of self-discipline. There's nothing wrong with the military, and you can serve honorably in the military, but you have to agree to play the game. They write the rules, and if you don't like the rules, don't join. But if you can play with the rules, it's fine. It's an advantage for both men and women to get an education, if it may be the only way. You can get much more than that, because the opportunities are endless. However, you must give up your gay self to do it, so don't do it with cynicism and think you can get away with it, because you can't.

☆ ☆

"Matter of fact, if we were pulling into port, we printed up all the areas that were off-limits—that listed all the gay bars. . . . So before we ever got to port, we knew where every place happened to be located."

"TONY LANKFORD"

Age 56, U.S. Navy, 1951–54, enlisted. Undesirable Discharge. Present occupation: printing supervisor.

The Korean War had started, everybody, all my friends were being drafted, and I decided I didn't want the Army, and went into the Navy. I liked it. It was a great place for a nineteen-year-old. Basic training was a good experience, and from my tests and so forth, I went to printing offset school at the Pentagon in Washington, D.C. And *that* was a pretty lively place! There were only fourteen of us in the school, and we came and went as we pleased. No restrictions whatsoever. All we had to do was attend school during the day in the Pentagon. I had quite a few experiences there. All you had to do was walk down the street and somebody'd be trying to pick you up. And I must say, I looked pretty fine in my Navy whites! But there'd always be somebody for you—it was fairly open during that time.

After training, I was sent on a cruise to Japan. And even in Japan, well, it was military then, they started picking me up. You always knew where to go. Matter of fact, if we were pulling into port, we printed up all the areas that were off-limits—that listed all the gay bars. There were over two thousand people on board that ship. Wartime complement's close to three thousand. Everything was so quiet and low-key you really had to look hard to find a gay sailor, believe it or not. Oh, you might have your suspicions, but you'd play hell trying to prove it. I do know that those printed lists went out real fast, as I recall. So before we ever got to port, we knew where every place happened to be located.

We went up to the northern island of Japan, met some guys, who entertained us—good food, the whole bit. I'll never forget that place. You walked into the entrance of this hotel and there was a big staircase in front. You walked up the staircase and all these chicken hawks (men who liked younger men and vice versa) were standing around. I mean, if you made it to the top of the staircase, man, without somebody grabbing you, you had to be a dog! You had a couple of drinks, then they would ask if you wanted to go to a room, you know? I went to a room with one guy, came out, had a couple more drinks, went to a room with another guy . . . it was pretty wild.

Ship life had it's advantages, too. They had dividers between the individual showers, but there were no shower curtains or anything and the sinks were right in front, so it was rather cruisy. Then somebody put in a request to have shower curtains added. The joke went around that everybody wanted to do their own thing in the showers. You knew who was doing what when you went to bed at night, because the bunks were stacked four high, on two big metal posts. In the middle of the night, all of a sudden you feel the whole thing start jiggling, and you knew who was doing what! Nobody would make any remarks about it. It was real quiet—well, you do your thing tonight, I'll do my thing tomorrow night—and I don't remember anybody ever saying anything negative about it. It had to be done. When you're out to sea for thirty days, let's face it, you had to beat off as a natural function of the body.

During one of our tours, this marine came up to me and patted me on the ass and said, "One of these days, I'm going to get in there." Well, when I signed for this trip we could take on one of our port calls, he was in it too. So when we got to our hotel, they asked you who you were going to pair off with, and he said, "I'm here alone and he's here alone—we'll room together." We had three nights in this hotel room, with more sex than I can remember. It was super. And funny thing, I can't for the life of me remember what the trip was all about.

My experiences continued across the Pacific and Atlantic. In Copenhagen, I was in seventh heaven! Oh man, super, beautiful men. I mean, you could walk down the street, engage in a conversation with someone who hardly spoke a word of English, and get asked whether or not you wanted a blow job. In Pearl Harbor, it was the civilians that always seemed to hit on me. I suppose it had something to do with the uniform. All you had to do was go down to the beach and lie there for five minutes—pay dirt.

I came back to the States, the East Coast, Norfolk to be specific. There was a gay bar in Norfolk called The Arena, and while most of the people in there were wearing civilian clothes, they were still all Navy. The SPs used to patrol outside. I don't remember them ever coming inside, but I used to worry about getting caught. I'd heard after you got out of there, if you checked into a hotel, that was one of the ways you got caught.

There was plenty of other kinds of harassment and discrimination at that time, as well . . . you know, coloreds. They were always stewards and deckhands. The Filipinos were messboys in the wardroom and stuff. Yeah, and I couldn't believe it. I rode the ferry from Norfolk to Portsmouth, and the coloreds had their own john, and the whites their own. I'd never seen this before. On board, they had their own compartment that they had to stay in too. Yeah, they stayed mostly to themselves. If you got up on topside, like in the evening, they'd be all up on the fantail together. Sometimes they might sit around and talk with the whites, but otherwise you didn't have too much to do with them.

One time, I saw this colored guy I knew from the ship standing at this bus stop. When he got on, he went to the back of the bus, even though there were seats up front. Since I knew him, I got up and walked back there, but he got all upset. The bus driver pulled over to the curb and told me, "White trash, you either sit where you're supposed to or you get off this bus." As it turned out, both of us got thrown off the bus. Those kind of experiences were very foreign to me—it was hard to understand why these people had done anything wrong, that they didn't deserve the same rights as the whites. Of course, this was before I was hauled up on the gay charges, so then it really hit home, and I could truly empathize. And my troubles were about to begin. . . .

While based in Norfolk, I met a lieutenant junior grade in the Naval Reserve who subsequently became my lover. Oh man, it was beautiful. He was beautiful. We were together for two glorious years. Whenever I was in port, we'd get together for evenings and weekends. It was a real good situation—until he was murdered! Ironically, about six months before he was killed, I remember he had loaned me this book—what the hell was the name of it, *Contrafoil* or something. It was about two lovers, and that was how it ended too. And the saddest thing about it all is that I have nothing left except a jewelry box he gave me. Oh, I have the memories, but really nothing else. I'd been out to sea for, I don't know, three or four months—I think I made a Med cruise. Upon my return, we went out to dinner, and he gave me the box. Inside, it had a couple of gold cuff links—that's what I have left. Yeah, those sweet, sweet memories. . . .

His death occurred about three or four months before I got discharged, when he was murdered in New York City. He had picked up a hitchhiker, took him home, and the guy killed him. I was out to sea at the time and got a letter from his sister. But it hit the big-time newspapers and was all over the place, but because I was at sea. . . . Tore me up pretty bad; fact, I was damn close to suicide. I was as close as I would ever come. . . . I knew a bunch of marines and I had access to their guns— I even thought of that. So just as I was getting processed for my normal discharge, I was in the barracks, and Naval Intelligence got a hold of me.

All through the civil murder trial, they had my letters to him and everything, and they [NIS] were dragged into it because he was Reserves, which in turn caused my involvement. *One* week before I was to actually be discharged, I was brought up on charges of homosexuality. They threatened me with a court-martial. I could either admit to it [the sexual issue] and avoid the court-martial or just get a dishonorable discharge, type: undesirable. Yeah, they had everything they needed for a case against me. So at first I was going to fight it and then found out that it just drags on and on and there's no way you can avoid it. I had no representation, no rights, no nothing.

There were a couple of the officers in that barracks who were lawyers, and the one of them told me to go back there—because it just dragged on and on, I wasn't getting discharged, they weren't doing anything—and tell them that I refuted everything I said, that it was under stress and I *was* going to fight it. This was 1954. So when I told them this, all of a sudden, one, two, three, I was thrown right out now! Yeah, well, it was three days later. As soon as they found out I was going to fight it, they processed everything very fast, and out I went.

While I was waiting for all of this to happen, I know I didn't hang around the bars or any of the gay areas for quite a while. After I was in the detention barracks, after I'd been there so long waiting for this discharge, they finally started giving me liberty. Then I went out to Virginia Beach. I used to go out there quite a bit. I mean, I was in holding for four months. So I didn't get liberty for the first two, two and a half months. I couldn't go anywhere.

I remember that about 70 or 80 percent of the other men in there were in for homosexuality. And they were all in and out so fast, you'd hardly get to know them—within a week, they'd be discharged. But for some reason, they just kept me going on and on and on. I assume it had something to do with the scandal of my lover's murder trial. They had us assigned pretty demeaning tasks, like going around policing up the area. You know, like picking up cigarette butts and that sort of thing. They had everybody cleaning up around the area. Some had to do driving duties, car washing duties [officers' cars], *personal* and military, and then if they had any kind of party at the Officers' Club, you had to work as waiters, or bartenders. You wore your dungarees most of the time, but if you were going anywhere, you wore the uniform of the day, whites. . . .

I was in the discharge barracks just waiting to be processed. It was terribly emotional for me, because I was dealing with the loss of my lover as well as all the bullshit they were heaping on me. Sometimes we were called sea pussies or fags by the other sailors we saw. It was damn humiliating. I would have been in exactly four years. I was in the process barracks in June, with a discharge date of June 14, and stayed there June, July, August, September, October.

I liked the Navy, I liked every place I went, and I loved being on board ship. I think the regulation that eliminated me sucks. I just don't believe they can tell you who you can go to bed with and who you can't go to bed with, you know? I mean, after all, you take those officers—they don't tell them who they can go to bed with and who they can't. Personally, I don't give a damn who they sleep with, male or female. Unless you start putting the make on everybody at work. Then you have a problem. I mean you don't do this whether you're straight or gay.

My relationship with that man, over thirty-five years ago, was not hurting anyone. The man that killed him was probably what we would call a modern-day fag-basher. Justice was served: the murderer got prison. But to this day, I still think about my lover, and just this year, I have finally decided to go back and visit his grave. His family blamed me for his death and basically told me never to show my face in their town again. I had the only thing that was his, his high school ring, and, like a fool, gave it back to his sister shortly after his death. I deeply loved him, and if I can get any message out to those who read these words, it is this: True love comes to us but once. This man was my love. I had no control over my feelings because he was a man; it just happened, it was normal. It does not make me less a man. To be punished in the way I was for loving another man was totally inhumane. To this day, I remember this man and the love we had. It's unfortunate that the straight society cannot understand our capability to love someone of the same sex so long and so deeply.

☆ ☆

"My wearing of the Army uniform appeared to be a simple tailor's error."

"JOHN McPHERSON"

Age 75, U.S. Army, 1940–44, enlisted. "Blue Discharge—Section 8." Present occupation: retired teacher.

As of January 22, 1944, I had been a staff sergeant in the Quartermaster Corps of the United States Army for eighteen months and an enlisted man for twenty-eight months. I wore a Good Conduct ribbon. I also had a half-dozen majors' affidavits and recommendations for Officer Candidate School in my files, based on personal daily contact for periods up to six months, which said my character was excellent. My company records carried me as fit for duty, and my last complete physical examination, two months prior, had said the same thing, over the signatures of three medical officers. My military classification, I thought, was chief clerk, as it had been for over two years, but after six months of doing supply clerk work, I'd been assigned to writing military manuals. My company commander had commented to the officer under whom I worked how I was well fitted to the new job and was one of the best men in his outfit.

My problems all started when I was reported for patting a sailor on the shoulder and telling him he was good-looking. That was all, period. He prematurely yelled rape and got the military police. I admitted being homosexual. Even though I had those six "character excellent" letters in my personnel file, it made absolutely little difference, but someone shouting "queer" or "rape" made all the difference in the world.

Without hesitation, I was driven handcuffed from town to camp, and spent a night in solitary confinement. I also spent three days in a stockade. A lousy MP forced me to have relations with him in a solitary-confinement cell. Another MP came in at midnight for the same reason, but he was unsuccessful.

But don't be perturbed. Keep your shirt on. I'm not going to talk about homosexuality in the Army, that unmentionable subject. I'll only comment that there is probably just as much now as when I was in. The crack "There isn't a man (a heterosexual) in the Army Medical Corps" is probably still being made, and still with the same amount of percentile truth. The dozen Army homos I knew of were in after I left.

I was confined to a "sane nuts" neuropsychiatric ward in the station hospital for three weeks. During that time, I saw at least fifty men being given discharges for other than physical disabilities. Forty of them, in round numbers, were from training camps in this country, and ten from overseas. Maybe two of the latter had actually seen combat. In not one single case was there any remedial action whatsoever attempted. In every case, I firmly believe that the men could have continued in active duty, and were no more "mentally ill," "not adjusted to military life," or whatever than three fourths of the men remaining in the service.

I heard stories of violent fellows in the lockup section next door, but I didn't come in contact with any of these so-called violent nuts. We were all the sane and healthy nuts. These are only the people I actually saw and talked to, myself. I want to be very precise: I am not talking about aviators who have cracked up after thirty missions, about tired, worn-out veterans of Guadalcanal or New Britain or Tarawa or Salerno or Anzio. Someone has estimated that around a tenth of the American Army of eight million has, to date, engaged in active combat with the enemy. What I'm talking about is a large number of men who come from the 90 percent noncombat group, and who are sent home under a cloud of semidisgrace. They were politely kicked out because the Army didn't want to have anything to do with them. The Army's job is to fight, and it's the medical department's job to cure men if possible. If they seem incurable, or if the time and cost involved in putting them in fighting trim seems too great, it's reasonable to get rid of them. Searching around for a reason, the Army hit upon psychiatry and "maladjusted personality" as a means to this end. That's all it is.

I also learned I could have gotten out whenever I had wanted to by turning myself in, but didn't. Keeping my nose clean on post, I decided, was the best scheme. Early in '44, a few weeks before I was reported, a new directive provided homosexuals would be discharged with a Section 8 blue certificate instead of a white one as previously given. Too many men, I've a hunch, had tried to get out by letting their hair down, and the "not honorable" angle was to discourage any possible fakers.

From my observations while in the psychiatric ward for those weeks, I found that most of the discharges given were a racket. If the Army had actually supported the "day's useful work" regulation [which provided that no man should be discharged from the service if he could continue to give a day's useful work to the Army in any form or manner whatsoever] and would have applied it strictly, the whole nut discharge ward would have been emptied out. If asked what was wrong with the men I lived with for those three weeks, in most cases I'd have to have said, "I don't know."

On February 25, 1944, I was unceremoniously dumped outside the main gate of camp in civilian clothes, with my Blue Discharge certificate in my pocket. It stated I had poor character and poor health. Other final papers in my possession said that I had never been authorized to wear any ribbons, and that I was classified as a playwright. I wore a yellow shirt and tie, a hat with a yellow feather, and the closest approximation to "hi-yaller" shoes that could be purchased locally. All issued equipment had been turned in, down to four nickel government handkerchiefs. I was left without pride, without self-esteem, and in disgrace.

Army figures in the early 1940s accounted for about 500,000 psychiatric discharges, and "others," excluding honorables, accounted for about 200,000. I'm one of the "others," with a *Blue* Section 8 Discharge. Blue, the color of the certificate, indicates it is neither dishonorable nor honorable. Honorable discharges are printed on white paper, dishonorable ones on yellow. Section 8 is the numbered part of the regulation on the discharge covering insanity. Other reasons for discharges are usually called by abbreviated names, such as "medical," "to accept a commission," "for the convenience of the government," or, in peace time, "purchase." Insanity is always called Section 8; it's worded "habits and traits rendering retention in the service undesirable" and is used as a general catchall.

Legally, I'm only partially a veteran. The first time I went into a Veterans' Reemployment Office, I practically got thrown out and was told I had no right to set foot inside the door. Months later the U.S. Employment Service showed me a list that made Blue Discharges count as veteran status. However, for civil service, I had no five-points credit, was ineligible for any federal job until a year from my discharge date. The review was based upon a semiprobationary, semiparole status. For the draft, I was 4-F, not 1-C; my three and a half years of wearing a uniform was just a simple tailor's error. I was entitled neither to mustering-out pay nor to a discharge pin. In other words, Army psychiatry stinks!

☆ ☆

"General Eisenhower ... [said], 'It's been reported to me that there are lesbians in the WAC battalion. I want you to find them and give me a list. We've got to get rid of them.' And I ... said, 'Sir, if the General pleases, I'll be happy to check into this and make you a list. But, you've got to know, when you get the list back, my name's going to be first.'"

JOHNNIE PHELPS

Age 67, U.S. Army (WAC), 1943–46, enlisted/officer. Honorable Discharge. Present occupation: owner, printing business.

I was an adopted child, not adopted in terms of adoption as it is known today, but adoption in terms of "taken to raise," which is what they did when I was a baby. I was adopted by a couple in North Carolina. My father wanted a child, but my mother was not anxious or happy about the whole situation. So my childhood was not the happiest in the world. I lived under circumstances of abuse. I was an abused child. By her, not him. The best way she knew how to deal with me was through beatings, and she beat me regularly, until my daddy went out and got me a German shepherd. It was my dog, and then she couldn't touch me. That dog could get her and tried on numerous occasions. We chained him to a tree in the backyard, and I was the only one who could go within the reach of his chain. And when she'd get in her fightin' moods, I'd go sit under the tree with my dog and there was nothing she could do. I think she was a little bit off upstairs.

My father was very glad with having me, but needless to say, didn't tell right away that I was adopted. I found out when I was about five or six years old. You know how kids are. "I got something you ain't got." And I had everything anybody else had, or I thought I did. I remember that I said, "Oh no, you don't have anything I don't have. What you got that I ain't got?" And this little girl said, "Well, I have a mommy and daddy and you don't!" Well, I knew that was crap, so I said, "Who you kiddin'? Of course I have a mommy and daddy. That's my mommy sitting over there on the porch." "Oh no. They just took you to raise." So I went over and asked my mom, to which she said, "She's absolutely right, and if I had it to do again, it would never happen!" When my daddy came home, I was, of course, heartbroken. He said, "Look, I picked you out of a bunch." Which was a lie. He didn't pick me out of a bunch, because I was the only one there. But it satisfied me at the time, you know. My father was an exceptional man. He even explained about my feelings after I had my first sexual experience. A man far beyond his years, that's for sure.

Private First Class Phelps,
U.S. Army (WAC), 1945

Phelps in
Talent show
in Germany

I had my first experience with a schoolteacher. You know, I was in school and I was a very young child. I think I was about eight. I mean, I went to school in a one-room schoolhouse, and she even lived with us that year. It happened on the way home from a school play and we were stuck in her automobile. We'd gotten stuck in a rut after a rain, and if you know anything about North Carolina soil, it's red clay. We were stuck there all night. We had to keep each other warm, so one thing led to another. Beyond that experience, my childhood wasn't the greatest, and I was getting in trouble all the time.

I wasn't feeling badly about my feelings, I was just questioning them. And I'd already been in jail by the time I was fourteen. I guess the old saying "Trouble is my middle name" was true. Jail was not a place that necessarily discouraged sexual liaisons between the inmates, so my feelings were only solidified during that experience. All these beautiful young women, and I didn't know what to do about it. Well, actually it was like being in a candy store. Soon, I figured out what to do!

I was also very young. And you know, every time I went to jail, they gave me a lot of bullshit, frankly. So, the first thing they said to me was "If you're good, you won't have to stay here long. You'll be home in six months." But I got better advice from one of the inmates, who said, "If you want to go home in thirty days, be bad." So, they had a punishment detail, what they called "the Ditch." And when you were bad, you worked on "the Ditch." That meant they locked you up at night, and in the day-time you went out and dug a trench six feet long, two feet wide and six feet deep. And when you finished it, you moved it. You filled it in and moved it someplace else. Real progressive training institution, yes. They brought your meals and shoved them through the crack under the door. And if you were any worse than that, they gave you bread and water. Well, it didn't take me very long to end up on bread and water. But I figured out what I needed to do. So, one morning, they came by to let me go to the bathroom and empty my pot. I emptied my pot, right in their face! Two days after that, the parole officer from my hometown came down to visit me, and I got out!

The people in my town put a great store on academic achievement. So after my jail experience, I figured out that I needed to make my own place. And since I had nothing else to do, I achieved academically. I took all of the honors and all of the scholarships and everything else from every kid in that town, which did not enamor me to the hearts of any of those people. I mean, they really hated my guts!

I finished what schooling I needed and later married an old "Navy salt," who basically said that he could change me if we married. . . . To this day, he wears a scar on the side of his face that tells him what he shouldn't ought to have said. And he never really said anything wrong. I mean, it was just my temper. And the fact that he was a man . . . but on the other side of the coin, his temper was a good match for mine! In fact, once I was in the service, I was being held for "lesbian activities," and he showed up to get me out. He literally blew up at them. The personnel that were holding me for the investigation let me go. One of them said, "If this woman is married to this kind of man, there's no way she's a lesbian!" So when I did join the Army, we were still married, although I was still involved almost exclusively with women.

I actually joined the military in 1943. I can't remember exactly. I think that Congress passed the Women's Military Act in December of 1942. And I was in in January. Just that quick. I was a member of the *first* company to ever go through the training. Instead of graduating as enlisted, every-body was graduated as an officer, second lieutenants. We were actually the first three hundred women that made up the corps of officers for the Army.

We wore men's uniforms until the Army could get our uniform stuff together. And it was very cold. We got wet in the morning because, I don't know about everybody else, but my overcoat drug the ground. My body heat melted the snow around my feet because my overcoat closed it in like a tent. That damn overcoat sleeve was so long it covered my entire hand. When I saluted, I had to push it aside to see whether the salute had been returned or not. Oh, and those combat boots we had to wear! I swear they didn't have any in the right size. I always felt like I could stand facing forward and do an about-face and never move my boots, they were so big! Of course, we lost a few women through our initial training, but the guys who trained us did not allow for the fact that we were women at all. We trained exactly like any other military unit. They taught us military history. When they were brainwashing us, they had classes just for that purpose. But I had a ball. An absolute ball. I made it.

The thing I felt most was the fact that I was doing something for my country. When I tell you that I was patriotic then, I was patriotic. Of course, I'm also patriotic today. Gay I may be. But I'm still very patriotic. I'm also very military in my thinking, a lot of it. This was during the time of the Women's Army Auxiliary Corps. I'm not sure of the length of time, but shortly after, they changed it from the Women's Army Auxiliary Corps to the Women's Army Corps [WAC]. I got out of the Auxiliary Corps and *reenlisted* in the Army Corps. I didn't want to be an officer. I didn't like the position—I'd much rather take orders than give them. I didn't like the assignments I got. I stayed in as an officer for probably a year, then I got out.

When I went back in as an enlisted, the war was pretty much in full swing, and I got transferred overseas. And it was on the way to go overseas that I had my first, what I call my "real, down deep, hope-to-die-and-go-to-hell love affair." It started in school before we went overseas. We met there, and it was just something that could not be avoided. It had to happen. But then she didn't come home—she was one of those unnamed, "nonpresent" women who were in combat positions but weren't supposed to be there. Ones who were never recorded. When we landed there on the beach, it was not a pretty sight. We lost a lot of women. She was one of them.

The landing craft had to put us off in water sooner than they expected, because the crafts were receiving direct hits. It was safer in the water than on the landing craft, but she got a direct hit, and I saw it happen. I saw the person I had recently made love to get blown up right in front of me. And I swam, looking. I tried. God, I tried! I wanted to find her, find something of her. And, I guess . . . I guess it's one of those things. I've never forgotten it. I've never forgotten her. She was just never reported as killed in action. I saw it happen . . . I saw her take the hit . . . a horrible sight, still etched on my mind today. War is such a futile waste of humankind.

In that war shows no sympathy, you are forced to go on, so I volunteered to go to the South Pacific as a medic. I saw some very gruesome, frustrating things, I don't know how to describe it. It's just . . . I don't like to talk about it. I can remember working in a hot, steaming, stinky surgical tent for days and having those goddamn Japanese fly over and strafe the whole thing before we could get the wounded to the hospital ship. But I don't even like to remember it. I received a Purple Heart and several other combat medals from the Pacific. The combat ribbons counted for points in determining when someone could come home, so I got out early, but reenlisted so I could go to Europe. And I was in Europe for seventeen months, but by the time I got there, the war was over. We had been sent to Germany as part of the Army of Occupation. I was a military police sergeant, with an initial assignment in Nuremberg.

After the trials, I was stationed in Frankfurt, as the European Motor Sergeant. I was under the direct command of General Dwight D. Eisenhower. When he opened his office door, I looked him straight in the eye. I loved him. He was a wonderful man, very open and sensitive. Many people have said that he was a "soldier's soldier." In the months that I worked directly for him, I found that statements made about the General were pretty much true—he *was* a soldier's soldier!

It was during this time that most of us stationed there had girlfriends: citizens. We had Polish displaced persons who "took care of us" in the barracks. Figuratively and literally. For some of us, not everybody but some. We had our own room, own maid, and we'd come and go in these apartments. It was part of the city that had not been destroyed by the bombings. So we took our girlfriends everywhere.

We had earned our place. I mean, we had earned our right to be there. We had earned our right to have everything, as far as the ordinary GI was concerned. There was no reason why there should be any difference between a woman and a man. If you could do the job, fine. At least, that was the feeling I got. And I was in probably one of the most male-oriented, most visible units. We had what they needed to do the job. So finally, it came down to the fact that they didn't care whether I was a woman or not.

In the beginning, military women were suspect, period. They belonged at home, having babies and children. They did not belong in the military. The only place in the military where women were even vaguely accepted was in the hospitals as nurses, and they were all officers. So the GIs per se felt the military was not a place for women. As the war progressed, and we became more a part of it, it also became apparent to them that there was no reason why women shouldn't be there. But it happened to be a war that we were fighting on both ends of the earth. We did it to the best of our ability. And that was the important thing. There was nothing important about General Eisenhower, me, my platoon, or my battalion other than the fact that they were people that I was perfectly willing, if I had to, to go into combat with and feel safe. I was an American first, a soldier second, a woman third, and whatever else came in line fell in behind, you know. It's unimportant. In fact, I fought *not* to be a lesbian for many years after I knew I was one and knew it was "wrong." I *wanted* to be like everybody else. Of course, I was not winning the battle, but I was fighting it!

While I worked in the office of General Eisenhower, I supervised all movement of motor vehicles within the occupied zone of Europe. It wasn't really a very time-consuming job. It was a title, and I was enjoying all of that. Then one day, Eisenhower got a report—he got a report from somebody—that there were lesbians in the WAC battalion. And I don't know, but I suppose he got the same report more than one time, because I didn't see him as being the kind of person who would take somebody's nitpicking word. The General called me in and gave me a direct order. "It's been reported to me that there are lesbians in the WAC battalion. I want you to find them and give me a list. We've got to get rid of them." And I just looked at him and said, "Well"—you know how you talk to generals. I said, "Sir, if the General pleases, I'll be happy to check into this and make you a list. But you've got to know, when you get the list back, my name's going to be first."

I think he knew, but I don't think he wanted to know. I think he wanted me to rat on everybody else and then keep quiet about myself, which I wasn't going to do. His secretary at the time was standing right next to me, and she would have had to cut the order. She just looked at him, and she said, "Sir, if the General pleases, Sergeant Phelps will have to be second on the list, because mine will be first. You see, I'm going to type it." He sat back in his chair, looked at us, and then I said, "Sir, if the General pleases, there are some things I'd like to point out to you. You have the highest-ranking WAC battalion assembled anywhere in the world. Most decorated. If you want to get rid of your file clerks, typists, section commanders, and your most key personnel, then I'll make that list. But when I make the list, I want you to remember that we haven't had any illegal pregnancies, we do not have any venereal disease, we have never had any negative reports, and we have always served and done our duty, just like we're supposed to do. As a matter of fact, since this unit has been here, it has received Meritorious Commendations on a regular, six-month basis. Now, if you want me to get rid of these women, I'll get rid of them, but I'll go with them." He just looked at me and said, "Forget that order. Forget about it." That was the last we ever heard of it.

There were almost nine hundred women in the battalion. I could honestly say that 95 percent of them were lesbians. We were exceptionally trained, exceptionally good at what we did, exceptionally experienced at this point, and that's what was needed in that place, at that time. Now, I'm not saying that they would have kept us forever under those conditions, but I'm saying at that time and in that place we were needed, and so they didn't point the finger too much and get rid of too many experienced people. I think that's what the whole thing boiled down to. The need justified the situation—our being there in such great numbers.

The occupation continued and I was still working at headquarters. I witnessed the comings and goings of the big guns—you know, Patton, Bradley, and so on. In fact, someone asked me if, because of my closeness to the General, I was aware of any liaison between him and his lady jeep driver. I was cognizant of things going on in headquarters, but you know, what he did in his private time was his business. He never asked what I did, and I never asked what he did! All in all, I was there for about seventeen months total, when you include the trials. I wanted to make the Army my career, but my enlistment was up, the war was over, the cleanup was pretty well being handled by the German citizens, so it was time to go. I tried to reenlist but could not pass the new physical.

When I got out, I didn't realize just how fatigued I was, mentally fatigued. The longer you're in under those kinds of conditions, the harder it is. The longer you're in, the harder it is to get out of that military stance. And suddenly, you're back out in a civilian world that thinks you're some kind of a hero. I can't say you're a "nut," because they don't think you are. How can you be, when they've given you all these honors for having been there? You were a hero in the eyes of those back home, no doubt about it. You know, those were the days when a European ribbon was worth a cup of coffee, but those days don't exist anymore. I think that's why a whole lot of us ended up in psychiatric hospitals after the war was over—with what they called battle fatigue. They didn't take the time or spend the money to put us back into civilian stance. If they had done that, I think that they could have avoided an awful lot of problems. That's one thing I can look back at and feel could have been handled in a much better way.

During my lengthy stay in the VA hospital, I became hooked on drugs, so I came out of there as an addict, basically. Once, I even tried my hand at suicide, but obviously was not successful. The military medical community didn't care about our mental pain and were highly responsible for our drug abuse, which was the problem. I mean, I didn't attempt suicide, or didn't consciously attempt suicide. But of course, when you're locked up for three years, you kick. At the end of the whole time, the only thing they could say to me was "You've got two problems. You've got to admit you're a lesbian and stop shooting dope." Which I already knew.

They were not well staffed in the neuropsychiatric section at that time. I don't want to label them by saying they didn't care about the patients. However, most of us were just locked up and forgotten about. God, they even had veterans in there from World War I, the Spanish-American War, and all the way back. I mean, this was like the dumping grounds!

After I got out of the VA hospital, which was in the early fifties, I had many more ups and downs, even a stint in jail, but finally got myself together, tried to get a hold on my drug *and* alcohol abuse problems, and formed a relationship with a woman that I was with for ten years. When I left her, I lived alone for a year because I wanted to get to know me. (I moved out because one day I realized I was the only lesbian in the house!) So I busied myself with political activities. In the mid-seventies I was called in to help protest the witch hunt on the USS *Norton Sound*, involving several women assigned to the ship. They were called the *Norton Sound* Eight. As chair of the Lesbian Rights Task Force in California, I was the obvious person to head the operation. However, my political days are now long gone. But it was a good feeling to help at that time—all those lesbians.

As I have matured and gotten a better look at life and how the military now operates, my attitude has changed. I think a woman that is openly gay would be out of her mind to enter the military. She'll have no stay in the military, and if it doesn't ruin her life, it'll certainly put a black mark on her career that she'll have to carry the rest of her life, so why do that? Anything she could get in the military she could get on the outside, if she worked for it.

Today, I think about the modern Army and I think about women's issues. I think about all of the picket lines and the actions we did over the years to gain progress for women's rights. I think about young women today and what is here for them, and that all that has been gained is not necessarily guaranteed without great work. They weren't old enough to know what was going on—but they just accept that these things are here, believe they are rightfully theirs, and don't realize how easy it would be to lose what has been gained. I think that the young women in the modern military are only able to be there because *we* were there. That's how I feel about it. It's my comparison of the current political atmosphere. I have no way of knowing whether I'm right or wrong.

I would go into the military again. Absolutely. For myself. Under the same conditions and circumstances. But I wouldn't join the peacetime Army. Absolutely not. It's a whole different atmosphere now. I think the gay military person, man or woman, is more prone to push harder and get more done than the nongay. But during peacetime, there is a greater effort to focus on paper pushing, and witch hunts for gays. Even though they are probably the best soldiers, the pressures are just unfair and unjustified. It's a time of greater vulnerability. No one should put up with that in order to perform a particular job, no one! Gays are also more alone within themselves and within the service—that should also not be. The straight GI has a mother, father, sisters, brothers, *wife*, and possibly *kids* to come home to, and he's going to do everything he can to protect that. The gay soldier cannot share whether he has a partner or not, so, yes, they end up much more alone. If not and he admits to such a partner, the chances of being thrown out, become the only option. No, it's just not a good career choice.

Personally, I think the moral fiber of the mission would be far better served if they said, "Okay, you're gay. So what? Do your job and do it well." And if the person in question does the job well, they shouldn't be messing with you. And that stupid reason about treason is a joke! The facts hold that most of the people who have given secrets and have been tried for treason have been male heterosexuals. Absolutely. Forevermore. Forevermore. And they will always be. I just can't support it anymore—too many human rights are being trampled, and that does not nurture the inner spirit.

I have come to a place in my life where I realize I must be a woman before I can be a human being. And my sexuality is only a very small part of that metamorphoses. I made it to this place, but not with the same attitude I had during the war. I am quite satisfied with my life now, and I recognize that the military did serve as a catalyst in all of it. Through it all, it helped me find the peace that I needed. I know I'm a good woman, a strong woman, and a loving woman. That's enough.

☆ ☆

"People were being discharged for being gay.... They were put in the brig ... marched to the mess halls separately, so everybody would know they were queer."

CHARLES S. "CHUCK" SCHOEN

Age 65, U.S. Navy, 1942–63, enlisted/officer.
Dishonorable Discharge. Present occupation: self-employed.

It was 95 percent patriotism. After all, it happened to be 1942, and right after Pearl Harbor. I was seventeen, my home life wasn't that happy, and it was wartime—a way out for me. That's really why I went in in the first place, as an enlisted sailor.

I had been sexually active before I joined, so I could tell that some people were interested in me on board, but I ignored them. But I was fairly active in San Francisco before the war ended. We had a great time when the ship was in port in that city. It was pretty wide open! In fact, a "capital." I played it cool and was very cautious about talking with people and accepting a time out with just anybody. Not that I could detect any better than the next guy, but I tried to analyze a person and say, "Okay, this is the guy to go with—he isn't one that will turn me in."

Discrimination was a strange bedfellow. I had an occasion to view it up close and personal. During this time, while a member of the EO [equal opportunity] organization set up for the Navy, I observed that this organization was *all* male and that there were also *no* blacks in the group. The Navy was very prone to blacks being messmen for officers, until the early fifties. Of course, looking back, it certainly was very unfair. I was stationed in Norfolk, which was a segregated town at that time, and I became very aware of discrimination. The blacks were treated unequally, but *I* even fell into that group by unconsciously treating them with less respect, as if they were some sort of lower-class citizens. So it was not a good time for *most* minorities in the service during the war years, never mind anything about the gay situation.

Petty Officer First Class Schoen, U.S. Navy, 1950

When the war finally ended, I decided to stay on in the enlisted ranks until 1958. By that time, I had reached the rank of E-7, or a chief petty officer. I was encouraged to go for my commission, and was commissioned in 1958. I was assigned as a limited-duty officer in electronics. But in the early fifties, before I received my commission, I became a staff member with G-5 [intelligence work]. This was during the McCarthy era, when I observed a great many people were getting discharged for being gay. It wasn't until after I got commissioned that I found out how those people were really treated. They were put in the brig . . . marched to the mess halls separately so everybody would know they were queer. The marines in charge of the brig were completely unjust and cruel to them. Physically cruel . . . and verbally. When this group was in the mess line, guarded by a bunch of big, burly marines, of course peer pressure caused other people in the mess hall to call them names and so on. It was a pretty sad situation. As one who knew what it was like to be gay, I still couldn't jeopardize my own career by speaking out against those clowns. So I remained silent. The price one pays for silence is overwhelming! But you know, there has never been a great love between the Navy and the Marine Corps anyway, so it just followed suit that if they had a sailor in the brig, much less a "queer" sailor, those jarheads were going to get their best licks in whenever they could. They seemed to be particularly mean to the Navy boys. I saw occasions where the marines were on the gate duty and were very critical to the sailors coming on and going off the base: searching their cars, making them show proper ID, wait extra long periods of time, and just letting all that authority go to their heads— the little bit that they did have.

As a newly commissioned officer, certain social duties were expected of me. As a method of career advancement, I was required to attend dances, be an escort. Some group in New York would sponsor a dance and want five officers from a ship to come over, and as junior officer I was selected most of the time. So yes, I had to participate. I looked at it as an unpleasant part of my duty for a couple of reasons. One, as a non-Navy duty and two, because I didn't necessarily enjoy carrying on small talk with some straight woman. But as a junior officer, I had to do what the commanding officer wanted. It was part of getting along, and the political aspect of promotions in the Navy was tied very closely to such "requests."

One day, not long after I had made junior grade or O-2, I was called in by the NIS, which is the intelligence arm of the Navy. Apparently, they had been observing me for a while and had signed affidavits from different people that stated I had engaged in homosexual acts. At that time, I denied it, of course, but with what they had, the commanding officer recommended a court-martial. For some reason, I was transferred to Chicago, to the Great Lakes, for about three or four months. Then I lost my job. Then I got arrested in Milwaukee, by civilian police, for indecent exposure. It was like all these things were coming down at one time. The civilian police dropped the charges but sent the information back to my command, so my commander called me in again. The NIS was there too, with all their information. They finally said, "Well, this time we're gonna push this commanding officer so they will court-martial you." I was under quite a bit of pressure.

Again they presented me with names of people I knew, and said that the affidavits were from people that had sex with me and three of them had agreed to testify. "We can't find a couple of 'em anymore," they told me, "but since we have enough evidence to try you, we don't care." But they had those three that made an agreement with them. Let me tell you, I know exactly how they made those agreements. Hell, they intimidated them to agree to those kinds of things in order to receive speedy discharges for themselves. They even tried to get me to give names. God, they were such lowlifes, such worms! They got those "witnesses" when they showed my picture in Norfolk to different people: "Do you know this person?" Someone who would identify me would then be pressured into making statements to save their own butts. Once they got onto me, they just played it cool for a while until they got the necessary affidavits. I feel, in retrospect, I panicked, and decided to resign, in lieu of a court-martial, under other than honorable conditions.

It was pretty devastating. I went to the naval hospital for an "infection" while I was waiting for my discharge. I was in the hospital for about two weeks under observation, and they claimed it was for hepatitis or something. But during that stay, I recall being looked over quite specifically by a couple of psychiatrists. It was like a cover-up in the hospital, so that no one else was aware that it was a psychopathic-type ward. The psychiatrist asked all these questions about my "mental problems" and about my homosexuality. I was feeling pretty low and was totally disgusted with the whole system, especially when I thought I was pretty damn loyal to the Navy for nineteen years and shouldn't have gone through all that demeaning bullshit in the first place. And particularly so close to retirement. Would you believe I had eighteen years, nine months, and twenty-seven days in by that time? Boy, they really know how to fuck someone over!

When they decided they were going to process my "resignation," they took me to the executive officer, who said, "Well, okay, Chuck, I'll have you work over here," to which I said, "You can take your job and shove it. I'm sorry, Commander, but if you're going to force me to resign, I'll be damned if I'm gonna do any work at all!" So he finally said, "Okay, let's not make an issue out of it. Call in every day, that's all." Since I knew enlisted people were put in the brig for being gay and had to wait for what seemed like forever, being an officer at that particular point was an advantage. We weren't treated quite like that. I felt a little better that the people who knew I was being discharged for this were very sympathetic. In fact, I never found one person that was nasty about it.

When I got that discharge paper, my "forced resignation," I remember this captain, an O-6, who told me, "Chuck, you know, you can still go out and start a whole new life again, so don't worry about it. I know of people that have been discharged and have gone out and started new lives again. Don't make this a personal thing that is allowed to defeat you—it's not the Navy way." At that point I'm not sure just exactly what the Navy way was, but it was obviously one that did not include gays. I still don't know how my personal life, my sexual preference, had any damn thing to do with the Navy way and the completion of mission. It's still a complete mystery to me!

I think there was an awful stigma attached to my discharge. I would have stayed in the Navy thirty years even under the pressure of hiding. It was something I enjoyed, or I wouldn't have gone back in nineteen months after the war ended. It was a very comfortable place for me. I determined that I was going to stay in thirty years; I *liked* the Navy. It gave me a position of leadership, and that's saying a lot, because as a high school dropout, I never thought that was a possible goal for me. I think I gained a lot of friends. It was good for me, until . . .

Once I was out, I started checking into some electronics jobs and found out that most of the things I was qualified for were all classified positions. I couldn't afford to go through any kind of a security check again, so I found a job selling hardware. Then I started working for a wholesale hardware company, after which I got into selling stage-rigging equipment. Finally, I decided to go into business for myself. I just went out on my own and got into a drapery and upholstery business. During that initial period of time, it was pretty rough, with my feelings of near worthlessness. But once I got it together, I survived fairly well. As a matter of fact, I worked much better once I was able to be openly gay, and had a lover that I could share my life with without living in fear.

So now, one of my goals in life is to do all I can to see that gays *are* accepted in the service. I believe there are millions, probably four or five million gay people, gays and lesbians with honorable discharges, who have served without being detected. The military can't detect them all. But there is still that unfortunate half out there, or less than half out there, probably a hundred thousand or so with "bad paper" that still should be upgraded. There's no question. The reason for discharge [being gay] is ridiculous. It needs to be changed.

I've worked diligently to change that regulation. I joined a group in Los Angeles called Veterans Care and, within a year, started my own group in Sebastopol. To date we have over 160 members in the northern wine country, which is supposedly the "redneck country" of the Bay Area, but we've got great support. We work heavily with the AIDS network. Our national goal is the acceptance of gays and lesbians in the armed forces so they can serve honorably. We also help the upgrading process for discharges when nothing else is connected with the bad paper, other than the fact that the person was gay. We continue to educate on veterans' rights, pensions, and so forth. I feel it is extremely necessary to lend support to those with bad discharges—to change or prevent those discharges because the psychological feeling associated with it can be so debilitating and harmful to the human spirit, but more particularly to the gay spirit. Yes, that is our goal, but more importantly, it is a personal goal of mine. I hope to see these changes within my lifetime.

☆ ☆

"It happened immediately. When we arrived in Norfolk, they called these people to different offices, before they even left the ship."

RICHARD TEATS
Age 53, U.S. Navy, 1951–56, enlisted. Honorable Discharge. Present occupation: credit manager.

When I joined the Navy in 1951, I had a lover who did not want me to join. I knew I was gay, obviously, but got in, went to boot camp at Bainbridge, and did quite well. I got letters from him every single day, but I did not write him. I couldn't write because I was not going to give the Navy any chance of doing anything to me. I figured they might open my mail, I didn't know what would happen, and I was not going to let anything happen. Everybody, my friends, were saying to me I would not be able to make it. I was too "fem," was such a small, tiny person, had jet-black hair, that they thought they were going to discover me immediately. Therefore, with my appearance not being the most masculine, I wasn't going to allow anything to happen and would not allow my lover to write anything in a letter that would implicate me in any way in case my mail *was* opened.

After basic I had gone to Norfolk for the Corpsman's School [for pharmacists or hospital assistants]. Well, that's when I started making contact with gays–Norfolk was a very gay town. Oh yes, it was a very gay town in those days. There was this old saying they had on the local signs for the grass, DOGS AND SAILORS KEEP OFF THE GRASS. There was also the "great white way," which was just on the other side of Portsmouth as you came into Norfolk. It was nothing but bar after bar after bar, where everybody used to pick up whatever they wanted. It was pretty freewheeling, to say the least.

Seaman Second Class Teats, U.S. Navy, 1955

Around 1953–54, I decided I had to leave the medical field because I couldn't stand the sight of blood and I couldn't stand giving a needle . . . so I went aboard ship. I went aboard a transport carrier, a troop transport carrier. The first time I arrived aboard ship, the bosun's mates saw me and said, "Ah, here comes a tender one. We got one now." I remember saying, "You think so, don't you? You're going to have a surprise—no dice." They sort of protected me after that, because I was so small and petite. I was able to get into their group, learn their lingo right away, and started acting like them, you know, real tough, even butch, masculine, and everything else. I figured if this was the way to be, then I'd be that way too. Self-preservation. And I was aboard ship long enough to become the chief yeoman for the admiral and captain.

During the Cypress rioting, it was the first time a ship was ever brought into Norfolk at midnight since World War II. We were told we could make one phone call, were not allowed to say where we were going, and that we would be gone maybe a year. Once we left the States, it took us six weeks to get over there, so ship life was extremely active. The things going on on board ship were unbelievable! I had some of the cutest little yeomen working for me. They used to get dressed and have every pleat in their uniforms perfect, right. Most of them had their uniforms specially made, very form-fitting. You just knew what was happening, what they were doing, and they didn't care whatsoever. It was wild! They didn't care; the Navy did not care, or so it seemed. They would go down below-decks, at night and visit the marines; we always had a complement of marines, especially to run the brig.

After we came back to Norfolk, they had a list of every single person that had done something on that ship, who they had done it with, and everything. It was amazing the amount of evidence they had gathered. It was quite clear they had informants within the ranks, either as plants or as "forced" laborers for their side. I had a personnel officer who said he was going to turn me in because he knew I was gay, and I said, "Go right ahead, because you turn me in, and you're going to come right along with me. As long as you don't have proof, there's not a damn thing that you can do!" He was champing at the bit to testify against me, because he could not stand the fact I got along so well with the captain and admiral. This was particularly grating to him because I was only a third classman and he was already a first classman going for his chief's papers.

I found the events that followed our return to Norfolk to be sad and disheartening. I became personally involved in the discharges that took place once we berthed. They shipped me back to New York and had me working in one of the offices on shore discharging all these people caught in the gay mess aboard ship—150 discharged. It all happened like a grapevine effect. It went right down the line. Nothing was said the whole time they were over there, which was seven months, to any of these people. Nothing was said until they arrived in Norfolk, were called up, and all the evidence was handed to them.

It happened immediately. When we arrived in Norfolk, they called these people to different offices, before they even left the ship. When they left the ship, they left with their bags, ready to go to the brig. They put them in the brig, right on shore. When many of those who did not get caught saw this going on, they were really shocked. But for the grace of God, there go I, and so on were certainly some of the thoughts entertained. They saw their own buddies being taken off the ship in handcuffs, oh yes—steel-cold handcuffs—and put into the brig. It was pretty severe, taken in a paddy wagon to the brig like common criminals.

If they wanted to deny it, they were given a trial. If they did not deny it, they were automatically given an undesirable discharge. There were some that chose a trial, yes. About two dozen of them went that route. Without a doubt, in those days you lost. . . . I mean, that was it. When you were charged with homosexuality, that was it. I don't care what you did, you still got booted out, because there was just no way you could prove you *weren't* a homosexual. [Technically, there is no way to prove one is heterosexual either!] Witnesses would come forward the accused didn't even know. I know these witnesses were not valid. The military was coercing them, forcing them, paying them, special duties. . . .

The average time in the brig was six weeks, for the most part. The gays were placed by themselves in a separate section of the brig. Heavens, there was no way they wanted to mix this "scum of society" with their regular, everyday murderers and rapists. After all, those fellows had some pride! I do recall one of our group did commit suicide while he was in the brig. He was maybe twenty-one, twenty-two years old. A young fellow, for sure. I remember clearly because he was afraid his family would find out.

Yes, he was absolutely petrified they would disown him, turn their backs on him, so he took his own life. I guess he felt there was no way out. But 150—that was the ultimate disgrace, probably some of the best service members they had. Lives crushed without retribution, a waste of our most precious resource: young, strong, intelligent, sensitive, and dedicated men. I had a severe feeling of guilt while I was doing those young sailors' and marines' paperwork. I'll never forget how that affected me, the total lack of human compassion.

I had a feeling the whole time I was in the military service, they were looking for the gays. I don't know why. Oh, I was aware of the regulation, but it was something more. It was just a feeling, like around every corner they were trying to catch you if you were a homosexual, or trying to prove there was something different about you. It's like my locker. My locker was always neat and clean, everything in its place, and they used to make comments about it. It had nothing to do with whether I was gay or not. I was brought up to be neat. But they would think right away, because I was so neat, I was gay. I *was* gay, but so what?

I was a professional the total time, from attitude, work habits, and procedures to the complete separation of my sexuality from that of my time on duty. The only person I had sex with was my lover. He would either come down to visit me, or I would go up to our place. We never stayed in Norfolk, always left. That was it. I refused to have a relationship with anybody else. When I was aboard ship, people would come up, pat me on the fanny, and say, "Oh, isn't this nice and tight." I'd absolutely ignore it—just went over the top of my head—or laugh it off, just so they would get the idea, well, no. No thank you, asshole! I wasn't about to get caught, and besides, I had something I wanted to prove to my father. My father knew I was gay, and I was going to prove to him I was man enough to be in "this man's Navy."

I've never used my GI benefits. I've never felt a need to use them. And as far as the VA hospital is concerned, I wouldn't go there either, for the simple reason they're a bunch of butchers, and even though you did serve your country for four years, and you feel that they do owe you something, they really give you nothing. And it wasn't just the basic sailor that received so little, but the other minorities received even less. . . .

I'm glad I had my experience in the Navy. It helped me see just how unjust the system can be. I've learned to live my life better because I was able to survive that stifling atmosphere. It made me strong. It showed me I was a survivor of the first degree. I may have been less masculine than the rest, but it did not stop me from being a success.

☆ ☆

"Otto's been my lover for the past thirty-six years. We met in 1952. Then I went into the service in 1953. He was in the Marine Corps at that time."

"JIM TEE"

Age 56, U.S. Army, 1953–55, enlisted. Honorable Discharge. Present occupation: librarian.

My parents emigrated from Japan, settled in Hawaii. We were ten siblings, I was second-to-the-last out of ten children, five girls and five boys. There were two generations of children in the family. The girls all left home by the time I went to high school. Some of my sisters I didn't even get to know because they were already gone. My father was a heavy drinker who used to beat me. And God, my mother suffered from depression. So it wasn't a typical family, as such; it was dysfunctional. My sex drive began at an early age. From eight to about thirteen—boys and girls. By age fifteen, I had made an exclusive sexual choice and went only with male companions.

During World War II we were not involved in the internment. In fact, none of the people in Hawaii were involved unless they were part of the intelligentsia. If you owned your own business, if you were any person of authority or influence, then those people were sent to the internment camps. But the rest of the people were not bothered. My oldest brother was in World War II, and my other brother and I were drafted into the Korean conflict. I was terrified to go because I thought for sure I would be killed in the war. I went to Korea and he went to Germany.

That thought made no mind to the Army boys, so off I went to my basic training. It was wonderful being surrounded by all those men in basic training, but gee, I didn't quite know how to explain it. It was like having a field day, I suppose. Having that many men around, exclusively. But it wasn't hard to concentrate, because they kept us pretty damn busy. I knew I was gay, because it was *before* I went in that I had had several gay sexual experiences. I pretty much realized that the gay lifestyle was what I wanted to pursue.

The year before I went into the Army—right after I graduated from high school—I understood somewhat what it was like to be gay. I really didn't understand it totally. When I went to Honolulu to go to school at the University of Hawaii, I realized what it was all about to be gay for sure! I was seduced by an older person and I was introduced to gay life—the bar scene and so forth. . . .

Otto, "Jim's" lover for the past thirty-six years (U.S. Marine Corps, 1954)

"Jim Tee," 1954, Hawaii

During this time it was pretty active [sexually] in Honolulu. Yes, it was very active. And I went to school, but I never completed school. I just spent my whole time cruising. I guess I was in "Crusing 101!" Anyway, at that time I met Otto. He was at this party, and was in the service. As a matter of fact, Otto's been my lover for the past thirty-six years. We met in 1952, and I was drafted into the service in 1953. He was in the Marine Corps at that time.

I met him at this straight party. I was invited by a friend of mine who also, somehow, knew Otto. So he invited him to this party. On the way back home, I talked to the friend of mine, David. And I said, "You sleep with Bob, because I'm going to sleep with Otto!" And so we ended up that night in bed together. Then I didn't see him for about three months. Otto's duty in the Marine Corps was a radio operator, so he flew to Japan and Korea frequently. He flew to Japan regularly and then to California. Then three months later—I used to work at the pharmacy as a soda jerk, in Waikiki—Otto showed up with a friend of his, and that's how the whole thing really started. Our relationship began in earnest at that point. We maintained our relationship during my two years in the Army. And when

I was sent to Korea, he came to see me once. But the rest of the time we were writing letters.

When I was in Korea, we lived in a small outpost. This was right after the war ended. We lived in a small military compound—I think there were about two hundred men. And I usually associated with only those men that were in my tent. I suspect there were gay men in the company. As I look back, I recognize people who were gay. Being Oriental, I spent a lot of time by myself. I couldn't get rides in any of the military trucks that passed through because they thought I was Korean. Even in uniform. Somehow, they thought that I had either purloined a uniform or had just found a uniform. It made me feel very debased.

The Koreans have hated the Japanese, because of the Japanese conflict. Actually, I could just blend into the Korean population because we looked so much alike. Except for my uniform. But they didn't know if I was Japanese until somebody told them or *I* told them. So if I kept my mouth shut, I was pretty much safe. But as far as the Americans were concerned, I looked no different from the Koreans. So they acted accordingly.

I was the only Japanese, yeah. I remember the master sergeant coming to me and saying that he wanted me to give instructions to these Korean locals that had refused to work for them. And I remember going up and speaking to the Koreans in Japanese. Boy, you could just see the sudden change in their faces! They were shocked, because they hated the Japanese. See, they were forced to speak Japanese for thirty years, you know? They understood Japanese, obviously. They thought I was Korean at first. I could see the difference in their faces. And there was one man who answered, surprisingly, and the other men kicked him, so they still refused to work. I thought that was a pretty interesting situation.

Anyway, I did have two liaisons while I was there. But those were very brief incidents. The rest of the time, we were just forced to live life as everybody else. You know, pretend to be straight. I don't remember any pressure put on by the guys in the military for me to act straight or to go out and carouse and chase after women. I never felt that kind of pressure.

Once, while I was on R&R in Japan, I met this full colonel. I was in Tokyo and was walking around the Imperial Hotel, looking in the windows, when I happened to look up, and there was this colonel—who was also looking at me. And before we knew it, we were in bed. What could I do? What could I do? Of course, we were both in uniform at the time. It was as shocking to me as anything else. We went to another place, another hotel. He was married. I mean, he was gay, but he was married. It's still fresh in my mind. One of the things—the next morning, we just put on our uniforms, had breakfast, and said good-bye. That was it, nothing more.

On my second R&R, I went to Kyoto and stayed with Otto for seven days. It was a pretty solidifying time. Well, he was gallivanting around.

He had a lover in Japan and a lover in California. Yeah, all over the place. He said, "Well, you can love three people at the same time." You know how those marines are. Gay or straight, they think they are the horniest and the best. I put my foot down and said, "No way!" Otto was six years older than I—he was about twenty-five, twenty-six. I don't know. I don't think it bothered me *that* much. But still, he must have gotten the message and realized that it was real important, especially when I got jealous.

When I was first out of the service, Otto and I moved to Long Beach, because it was the closest place to the Marine Air Force Station in El Toro. We set up housekeeping there and I remember his marine friends calling up and commenting that Otto had a "houseboy" because I would always answer the phone. So I think Otto got worried that these guys were suspecting he was probably gay. I think it was an unspoken disapproval by all of his buddies.

Since the war was winding down, there was added pressure from the administration, and more time for paper pushing, which allowed them to sit around and think about such things as a person's sexual orientation. The McCarthy era didn't help. So Otto got out, but I really think he would have made it a career, retired, if that hadn't happened. He was a marine through and through, you know. He was one of those military men. Nothing against marines, but military men! I mean, he enlisted at a very young age, about seventeen, was in World War II, the Korean War, and except for a short period *between* World War II and the Korean War, he's always been in the military.

Nowadays, everybody talks about gays. They read in the papers and everything. But if someone's going to be gay and open in the military, I think it's going to be very difficult. Because no matter what you say, people aren't *that* tolerant of gays. Especially in the military. However, I think that gays can be just as effective soldiers as anybody else. I mean, that rule about being gay and being ineffective is not valid, as far as I'm concerned. And this has been proven many, many times by people who are gay and have not been discovered.

☆ ☆

"I was so cute and tender, some guy was always coming on to me."

ARCHIBALD "ARCH" WILSON

Age 65, U.S. Army, 1943–46, enlisted. Honorable
Discharge. Present occupation: retired, currently
Commander, American Legion Post 448 (Alexander
Hamilton, 99 percent gay membership).

I was aware of my sexuality by high school. Yes, definitely by high school, but, of course, denying and suppressing it all the
while. But some of the first repeated experiences were at church with
another young active guy in the choir. He was, of course, homosexual
and knew how to go about it. Another guy I knew became a minister. We
were regular sex partners. And then another couple like that were very
religious but, of course, screwed up. Pent-up. They were also regular sex
partners.

The war was on and I knew I couldn't stay in this place. . . . I'd just
turned nineteen and everybody was going. I didn't want to be left out. I
knew I was going to be drafted, so I volunteered. There was a guise of
patriotism, but I won't pretend that it was, purely. It was also not wanting to be left out and be made to look inferior. I was always a little
weakling. I was proud when I passed the physical and guys bigger than
I were 4-F'd.

Once in, I did notice it was all quite segregated. Blacks were in separate units. When I was in the Quartermaster Corps and in firefighting
school at Fort Lewis, Washington, they even had black squadrons. There
were a few whites. The officers would always be white. They had some
segregation in dining halls and johns—latrines. No Asians. I think they
were in concentration camps during this time.

But observations aside, I began to look for more types like me. I was,
of course, surrounded by men all the time, but having little opportunity
to do anything about it. The attractions, of course, were very powerful.
In fact, by the time I came out of the service, I was pretty sure that was
the direction that I was going to go.

I had to have been in awhile, over a year, before there was any chance
of a real encounter. Over a year. And there were very few encounters,
very few.

I went to Europe as an infantry rifleman and replacement. A basic foot soldier, a buck private. The atmosphere was very relaxed and there was a lot more open carrying on, and I had lots of experiences then.

We hit France the day Roosevelt died—at that time—in "40-8" boxcars. I had a wonderful experience with a married man alongside me on the straw, lying in these boxcars made in World War I. They carried either forty men or eight horses. So they were "40-8s." They're still in operation. Here we were, together all night, going into Germany, and when we got up in the morning, we had to get back into our pants. It's broad daylight, everybody was dressing, and one guy yelled, "Hey, those guys don't have any pants on!" The captain said, "Oh, maybe they were just having fun!" Everybody broke up laughing. . . . Phew, that was close!

Private Wilson, U.S. Army, 1944

The Army occupation was a ball. But it proves my point—with the end of the war, luck. And then all of the military hierarchy— Everybody was interested in getting out. *They* were interested in getting out. Everybody couldn't wait to get out. There was no vigilance that I was aware of. Nobody was reporting anybody. Nobody cared if you were gay or not.

I didn't have many problems, except that I was always small, and, when I was younger, I was cute. Some of the older guys, even the married guys, would get horny. Often straight guys would be married, and try to attack a guy on a troopship going to Europe. One actually tried to rape me! He was a married man from a farm somewhere in the Midwest. Down in the hold with the lights still on, he got me somehow over to his quarters—some pretext. He was wrestling me on the bed, just trying to get my pants off; he was crazed—actually trying to rape me. I was screaming. I said, "Stop! Don't! Stop! Don't . . ." A straight guy! And then there were other straight, married guys who'd kid about getting me into bed with them and so on. I was small and tender and all that, but nothing ever happened.

I had an encounter with an American from New York while on the ship returning to Seattle. Then there was an encounter with a British soldier, who was straight, I'm sure. The New Yorker was gay. With the New Yorker, meeting in the john was it. He cruised me and I didn't know how to cruise. But they knew how. Of course, I was a pushover, and so we'd get together.

Even so, you had to be cautious. It governed your life. My buddies had me swearing and everything else. We all picked up crude swearing to be just as butch as the other guys. I pretended to be interested in women and go along with the jokes, and all the comments that go along with it. I was always cautious to the point that most of my liaisons took place outside. It's true of most of the guys that they were always too afraid to repeat ... afraid of having a relationship. If an apparent relationship developed, they were so threatened, and would break it off. They'd keep distance.

However, I do remember, in one of my first posts—two guys were caught in bed together. They'd come in from the same hometown. They'd been lovers. They were caught in bed together. Their lives were made miserable. Everybody talked about them and jeered. They were ostracized. They were called the Gold Dust Twins. As I recall, they were never reported, so they didn't get discharged. They had to suffer through this with basic training. I don't know where they went from there. I hope they escaped for themselves. I couldn't jeer. I couldn't make fun of them. So I was silent. No, I really felt sorry for them.

I also remember there were two others that had asked me to go out to have a "queer quibble" with them, but I didn't know what they meant. These two were cute, laughy, having so much fun. They were camping and carrying on with everybody, yet *they were accepted*.

The two who tried to hide and sneak in and out of bed were caught and made fun of by the men, but these other two little guys, who perhaps were only sisters and never did get together sexually, were just open and talked and camped. They never had any problems. I was amused but still afraid of them. I had to give them distance. I thought they were charming, and you know, I think both couples were in the same damn unit!

Before my final discharge from Fort Bragg, especially when the war was over, the whole atmosphere was relaxed. In the Enlisted Men's Club, the john was very active and guys would meet in there to have sex. If not right there, out somewhere, out in the fields, in the pitch-dark. You could have a new experience every five minutes. The pace—I'd never seen anything like it before in my life. Maybe it had gone on in other places, but I didn't know it. At Fort Bragg, guys were doing it. And doing it a lot!

Not all were gay; some were just getting their kicks. Some were, as I say, obvious, though at the time, they had to be real effeminate for me to say obvious. I didn't know they could be butch as hell and be internally obvious.

During this time, I can remember having repeated incidents with one guy. He'd get me to go into town, and we'd check into a hotel. We liked to be in a bed, so that happened several times. I can also remember riding trains to and from furloughs, and these trains were loaded with military. I'd score any number of times on these crowded trains. Everything was crowded all the time, wherever you were going—troops changing stations and civilians trying to get around. I had several interesting experiences on the trains.

However, the whole regulation and how it affects you makes one more aware of the total picture. I thought I had to be superior—to prove myself and be extra good, an extra good little Boy Scout. Do everything better, faster, cleaner. I was perhaps superior because I couldn't relax. I just had to prove myself all the time. Good behavior was the code.

I feel I *was* superior. I really do. I was afraid to look like a sissy or a coward. I was scared to death. For example, in basic training, crawling through the mud, under the barbed wire with my rifle and helmet, with shots going off overhead, I *was* scared, really scared, but I didn't dare show it. There were some straight guys—spoiled, big, straight guys—getting discharged because they were so emotionally immature. I remember a guy panicking at the gas mask drill. He really started carrying on—sobbing and blubbering. He was about forty and couldn't take it. He got himself discharged because he broke down like a baby. I had so much contempt for him, it made me even tougher.

The gay soldiers I worked with didn't respond this way. As a matter of fact, I saw it many times. Some of the best soldiers I knew were gay. It may have been compensation, caring what the hell they did, and pride. They were just less likely to be slobs.

The military experience liberated me. I got the hell away from my conservative background and had some chance to live a little more freely, even under the constrictions of the military. I had to find my own person, and I sure as hell had to provide and fend for myself, which was very hard at nineteen. It was a different time; needs were different then.

Nowadays, unless it's the only way a young gay person can get some technical training, I say, "No! Keep the hell away from the military. Don't put yourself into that pot of boiling water. Uh-uh!" The risks are too great. If you're going to live and have a relaxed, happy, normal existence—it's the worst thing to do.

Overall, I hated it. I really hated it. I was so unhappy the whole time I was in—at least 90 percent of the time. It's funny, but after all I put up with in the Army, I'm deeply involved in the American Legion here in San Francisco. It's quite a changeover. But maybe I'm really getting active in causes. In fact, I guess I'd like to be known as a gay activist. Being commander of an American Legion post that is basically made up of gay veterans, as the Alexander Hamilton Post 448 is, is a great way of achieving that goal. It seems to give me a quiet peace, particularly in light of what the American Legion represents and "our" fight to eliminate the military regulation against gays. It's all rather incongruent, don't you think?

PART TWO

VIETNAM

Although military advisers were killed in Vietnam as early as 1959, the so-called "ten-thousand-day war" officially began in 1961. And despite the approximately 58,000 military casualties, the war itself was not recognized by Congress until the late 1980s, when a war memorial was erected in Washington, D.C.

This was not a popular war. It caused dissension and division in the United States and abroad. In contrast to World War II, and even the Korean War, the enemy was not identifiable. Indeed, the enemy often was not visible. Many atrocities were committed during guerrilla warfare—by both sides. And the cause was less apparent—a great number of Americans felt we were interfering in the South Vietnamese right to self-determination. The conflict had originated between old enemies in a country that was far away and unfamiliar. Many young men of draft age left the country, preferring to live in Canada or other foreign countries rather than be sent to fight a war they thought was not right, a war that was not theirs to fight.

Gay men and women served in all branches of the military during the Vietnam War. They faced the same traumas as their straight comrades and suffered the additional pressures of being gay and trying to hide their sexual identity.

It was the era of Kent State and My Lai, but it was also an era of unity. Violence and brutality against homosexuals had escalated steadily since the McCarthy period of the 1950s, and gay people were tired of being considered second-class citizens. The time had come to stand up and be strong together. On June 28, 1969, the Stonewall incident in Greenwich Village, New York City, marked the beginning of an era of pride, visibility, and unity never seen before in the gay community. San Francisco, Los Angeles, and New York City became meccas of gay identification. Gay men and women were out of the closet and had little intention of ever going back. The pendulum swung precariously to the left as a new age of wild, carefree sex began.

In the interviews that follow, twelve men and six women tell their stories and describe the varying degrees of acceptance they found in the military during this tumultuous period.

☆ ☆

"I definitely didn't want to become part of the infantry ... to be sent to Vietnam ... I was chicken. ... I was a sissy."

CAL ANDERSON

Age 42, U.S. Army, 1968–73, enlisted. Honorable Discharge. Present occupation: Washington State Representative, 43rd Legislative District.

I was born and raised in Seattle. I have two brothers and one sister, and her name is Gay, which gives me all kinds of fun things to do. It gives me all these great stories around her name, you know: "Are you gay?" "No, my sister is Gay"—that sort of thing. I was probably quite young when I realized my gayness, somewhere as a teenager. I always knew I would grow up in the gay lifestyle, but I didn't have any traumatic experiences or anything. During high school I'd always been a pretty straight kid. Not a jock by any stretch of the imagination, but a pretty straight kid. And short hair, a crew cut. A friend of mine finally talked me into growing my hair out so I would look more like a regular person, so I started growing it out. I had a nice head of hair—not long or anything, it was still fairly conservative—and when I was notified that I would be drafted, the first thing that came to my mind was they were going to cut off all my hair.

I didn't go to college, but got drafted in 1968. I remember I was working at the King County Democratic headquarters at the time. I wasn't a screamer, but it was obvious I was gay. Well, I was active politically, was the secretary to the county chair, and had friends in high places. I was so naive—hell, I was only nineteen years old. During the physical examination, I was so naive about it [the ramifications of the "homosexual" question], I thought if I checked "yes" on homosexual tendencies, that the next day, the *Seattle Times* would carry the headline "Cal Anderson's a Faggot." And so I checked "no." And given history, Perry Watkins [see page 248] checked "yes," and it sure didn't keep him out of the military.

If you've ever seen the phenomenon of a preinduction physical, it's a cattle call. It's three hundred or more men in a room lined up for these physicals, and it's pretty spectacular, I mean, 'cause you've got three hundred naked men in one room. Doctors went down the line, having each one turn his head and cough. Exactly. Can you visualize this? The line in front of you all bends over at the same time so they can go down and do the *other* examination. It's pretty hilarious. I mean, it would make a wonderful part in a Mel Brooks movie, or like the scenes from *Alice's Restaurant* for sure. But on a serious note, it's very dehumanizing. I mean, you really get the sense you are only a number.

Specialist-6 Anderson,
U.S. Army, 1968, Vietnam

Even in this naked situation, there were those you could tell were gay, that were, you know, in our own little way of just kind of knowing, or maybe it was wishful thinking. I remember calling home and saying to my folks, "Well, they got me; I'm going to Fort Lewis." Which was nice because it was the last time they had basic training in Fort Lewis, so at least I was close by. At the same time, I had a relationship, my first serious relationship, with this guy who lived in Portland. We were lying in bed the night I got my final okay, and both of us were crying our eyes out because here we had this great relationship and had been seeing each other for several months, and we realized my going away to the Army certainly was not going to help it.

In basic, there was abuse. I mean, we were verbally abused for sure. They would use the words, "You dirty rotten faggots," or . . . they would sometimes single people out if somebody was going a little bit slower in throwing the grenade or stabbing somebody with a bayonet, which certainly didn't help people who were actually gay. I did pretty well. I mean, I became an expert in the rifle, both the M-14 and the M-16.

During basic, I kept thinking of the Vietnam situation. I was scared, too, because I definitely didn't want to become part of the infantry, and so originally enlisted for school, in an effort not to be sent to Vietnam carrying a rifle. I was chicken. On top of that, I was a sissy and didn't think I would have been as good as I was with the rifle. So I was originally going to go to teletype-operator school and then switch to court-reporting school, so I went to Georgia first. Then I decided to get out, not do any of it, tell them I was gay.

I told the first sergeant and the company commander, but the company commander probably thought I was just trying to get out (and wasn't really gay). The first sergeant was real nasty about it, and said, "We're gonna get rid of you, we don't want your type in the Army." In the mean-time, I went to my classes for a while, thinking I would keep myself occupied until they processed my discharge. However, I did such a good job in this training group, managing the records and everything—yeah, dumb on my part—it was becoming comfortable. I finally asked the first sergeant, after a couple of months, about my supposed discharge. It's like they had all forgotten about it. He told me I would be discharged for the good of the service under other than honorable conditions. I thought, "Well, that's pretty drastic," but by this time I was kind of fitting into a niche, kind of enjoying it. In fact, life became pretty good, whereupon I was sent to court-reporting school. I was to become a court reporter, thinking, you know, that's going to keep me safe, I'm going to be in a courtroom, doing this court-reporting stuff, and it worked out great. I went to school in Rhode Island, the Naval Justice School. It was all-service for court reporters and legal clerks. At that point getting out of the Army was no longer an issue for me.

I mean, it was heaven for a gay person because there were folks from all the services: Marines, Army, Navy, Air Force, Coast Guard. A great school, all very professional—it wasn't any of the "kill or be killed" sort of stuff. I graduated from the school, first in my class, and got my as-signment to Vietnam. But while I was at school, I was involved with a couple of guys. One was this Navy guy who was married in the straight sense, who definitely liked to play around, but was very, very cautious and very scared. I was still having my relationship with my friend from Portland. As a matter of fact, he came and visited me a couple of times when I would get a weekend off, but I think we had also realized it was going to be real hard maintaining our relationship as we knew it.

Once all my schooling was over, I called my folks. It was really kind of funny, because I said, "I've got some good news and I've got some bad news." They said, "What's the good news?" and I said, "Well, I finished first in my class." They said, "Isn't that wonderful! When are you going to Vietnam?" And I said, "Well, that's the bad news." So I went to Viet-nam, was assigned to the 23rd Infantry Division . . . and was assigned to the 33rd Company. . . . Next thing you know, I'm carrying a rifle, killing people or being shot at myself. But that was before I really got settled in with my position.

When we first arrived, we could hear a lot of stuff. I'd made up a fantasy in my mind that we really weren't in Vietnam, and then that first night as we were lying in our beds, we could hear the shelling and every-thing close by—it was a realization that you *were* in Vietnam. We were given a little bit of in-country training, everything from tactics as far as shooting in the jungle to staying away from the natives, like how to avoid sexually transmitted diseases and stuff like that. They showed the grue-some pictures and all.

Once I got things set up, I found if you're court reporting you don't have to do guard duty. There were only twenty-some-odd (no pun intended) court reporters in the entire country, so we were kind of special; they protected us. Not just from getting killed, but I think they wanted to have the trial perfect, so I thought, well, this might not be bad. However, division headquarters was very far north, and that did scare me. We got rocketed and mortared. We were situated about a mile from the Viet Cong. Being that close to possible death, I think the people were a lot more tolerant of each other, and most of the people kind of looked out for each other. There wasn't a lot of fear of getting caught, exposed, or kicked out of the Army for any particular infraction.

This headquarters had an outer perimeter of about ten miles square, so it was like a large city. There were several NCO clubs around. They'd bring in these acts from Korea, Korean performers, sometimes American performers, and Bob Hope was great! You could be entertained by a pretty good act or one that was really bad—it was hit and miss. I think gay people really enjoy tacky things, so it wasn't too bad. In fact, there was occasionally a real tacky Korean group, and you would follow that group around from club to club because it was so hilarious. There was this one Korean boy who sang Elvis songs—he was a riot. Of course, they thought they were wonderful. There was a group of us (all gay) that would follow them around. That was basically the only way you could have parties. There were never any officers present which we knew of, not in the public light anyway—we were all enlisted, except for some of our conquests!

We had a game where we'd have four or five gay guys go together, spot somebody in a club, and if you were interested, you would bet on . . . who would get him first. I had the award for getting the highest-ranking officer in bed with me. He has since become a brigadier general! In fact, it was always the ongoing joke that I received my second Bronze Star for landing the general-to-be in bed. It was pretty funny, we had a good time of it, and nobody did anything they didn't want to—trust me. I'm sure the whole process has gone on for a long time. I mean, it's just like a mating dance, two dancing around, then they would pair off. And then there would be the report the next day; the phone would ring, you know. There were a couple of people that got beat up. There were also straights who would have sex with somebody gay, for convenience, and that happens.

I stayed with the 33rd Company for the whole time. I was the judge advocate's court reporter. We had many, many rape cases, rape of Vietnamese women. Men were prosecuted but rarely convicted. There was only one conviction in the entire time I was there, of an American soldier raping a Vietnamese woman. It was what we called the gook rule or the dink rule, which was the derogatory term for a Vietnamese—well, they're just a gook, they're just a dink. Therefore, they're expendable and you can rape one. The one conviction we did get was overturned. The judge was asked by the defense counsel to instruct on the phenomenon called mistake of fact. This little four-foot-whatever Vietnamese woman that had been raped by this six-foot-something guy—and at a point she stopped struggling. And so the defense attorney wanted the judge to say, well, it was mistake of fact. This soldier thought because she stopped struggling that she was acquiescing, and the judge refused. He said that's ridiculous and I won't instruct, and it got overturned at the appellate level. It was rather universal. So from my observation, it was not only seeing the destruction to a lot of young soldiers but of the Vietnamese people as well. It was tragic.

I was also associated with the My Lai trial. Lieutenant Calley was in the 23rd Infantry Division, so the investigation took place under that jurisdiction. Captain Ernest Medina was his commanding officer. They did the initial investigations—under Lieutenant General Pierce—and I was involved in part of that in Vietnam. When I came back to the States, the trials were going on down in Georgia. I was transferred down to Georgia to be one of the court reporters on the Medina trial. It was more than four months of trial. But the actual evidence gathering in Vietnam was just that. The trial of Calley also took place in the States. During the investigation in Vietnam, they had Vietnamese interpreters interpreting for victims from the village of My Lai, and at one point they were going through some of the pictures—some of the pictures of the massacre that appeared in *Life* magazine and were extremely gruesome—and this interpreter broke down and started crying, because part of his family were in those pictures, but he was not aware of their deaths at the time. It was real, real tragic.

Overall, I think they were very complete in their investigation when it finally was done. There was a lot of effort to say, but this happens all the time, that these people [Calley] are made scapegoats because ... that Lieutenant Calley was being made a scapegoat simply because he got caught. And my attitude on it was, no, this doesn't happen all the time. Two-year-old children aren't thrown into ditches and shot. Little old ladies, seventy, eighty years old, aren't thrown into ditches and shot. We don't do that. Unfortunately, a lot of people in the hierarchy and a lot of people along the line tried to make excuses for Calley, saying that he was a victim of it all. I just didn't buy it. I think his mentality was below average ... I don't think he had the proper training. If they'd been a little bit more careful, he probably wouldn't have been an officer. He wouldn't have been in a position to lead troops into battle and to encourage them to do that kind of killing.

The courts were down on drugs as well as insubordination. There was a lot of abuse of drugs and of alcohol. Alcohol was extremely cheap. You could buy a gallon of vodka or a bottle of gin for eighty cents! A quart or a fifth or whatever, yeah. You would go to the NCO Club and you could have a double shot of Courvoisier for fifty cents. I think it lent itself to alcoholism, but it also lent to people blinding themselves to the conditions, and it calmed some soldiers down and let them participate in things that they maybe wouldn't do back home, like heavy sex with other men. Oh yes, of course, and there were also people who went totally berserk in the war. Probably the saddest case was a trial I handled as the court reporter, where a fellow had gone from one barracks over to another to get a Coke from these guys, a simple Coca-Cola, and he asked and they said no. Well, he went back to his barracks, got his rifle, came back, and killed those three guys—over a Coca-Cola. God, over a Coke! I saw people brought to trial because they had set up mines to blow up their officers—it was pretty crazy.

Actually, *Apocalypse Now*—even though it is incredibly bizarre—is probably one of the best depictions of what Vietnam did to people, the craziness . . . yeah . . . where they would go in and napalm an area so they could go surfing, where they would go in and wipe out areas, where they would turn the music on, things like that. That did occur, and people who weren't in Vietnam just bristle at the idea that it could be true. I think *Platoon*, although it was more of a marine-type film, and *Full Metal Jacket*—from my experience at the court level, after seeing things and reading reports, those films were pretty true to the experience.

It's funny what we do to survive under those conditions. No matter where I was in the military, even before Vietnam, you develop . . . . Everyone starts to know everyone, and you make your connections—networking, yes, exactly. It's not the kind of networking you do at the gay chamber of commerce or a women's group, but similar. So when we formed our little group, it was through this method of networking. And it was amazing, the grapevine and how word would get around on who conquested who. Yeah, most of them were one-timers. A few times there was somebody that would be around for a while, but usually just passing through, which was basically the way things happened, with people having to come through the area because it was the division headquarters.

Our group was very close-knit. I was assigned to a fairly small office. And one of my friends—his name was Jack—was pretty good at getting around. He really liked southern guys, for some reason or another, and this one time he met this guy from Texas, and they were seeing each other rather regularly. One morning, Jack came into the office and had the other guy's shirt on, obviously, because of the other guy's name tag. I think the name was Johnson, and he held a different rank as well. I said, "Good morning, Sergeant Johnson," and he looked at me and said, "What do you mean?" I said, "Look at your shirt." Oh, he just about flipped out. He got on the phone, called the other guy, and said, "You've got my shirt!" He flew out of there like a house afire. They'd gotten dressed in the dark, no doubt!

Actually, I got caught once . . . in the act, yeah! I'd been there for quite a while, in Vietnam, met up with this guy, and for some reason or another, we decided to go up in these bushes. There we were in these bushes, having a good time, until along came these three guys. I looked out and saw six big combat boots, and this one guy was saying, "What's going on in there?" Well, it was perfectly obvious what was going on. . . . So I went out, doing up my pants, and said, "What's the matter?" My idea of the best defense is a good offense, put them on the defensive, whatever is proper . . . I said, "What's the matter, can't a couple of people be alone without somebody else butting in?" This just shocked the shit out of him, and the guy asked for my name. Since it was rather dark out, I knew he couldn't see my name tag, but I looked at him and noticed he was a staff sergeant, an E-6. I said, "What's your date of rank? You're an E-6, I'm an E-6—what makes you think that you can start interrogating me?" I told him I was Specialist-6 Anderson, I worked for the staff judge advocate general, and if he wanted to talk to him, we could go right then. So at that, the guy became totally flustered and left. By that time the other guy had come out of the bushes, too. Fortunately, he gave a wrong name or something.

I thought it was over, nothing was going to happen. This was war and no one's going to pay attention to this. Well, unfortunately, this guy—the E-6—went to his company commander, and that one came to my company commander. I was working in my office—this was two or three days later—and one of the guys I worked with, a straight man but a really good guy, came in and, out of the side of his mouth, told me everyone knows *everything.* I just said, "Oh, shit." I was told I could expect to be called in by the company commander. Well, to say the least, I was beside myself. I ran down and got my hair cut. I was going to look like a good little soldier, get my hair cut, get my uniform pressed, and get my boots shined like mad. I mean, this was the jungle, and I'm shining my goddamn boots! But I was determined I was going to look perfect. On the outside perfect, but on the inside I was a mess. Being very familiar with the legal process, I thought I would be court-martialed, lose all of my rank and my medals. Everything that I'd worked for would be out the window.

Sure enough, I got called in by the company commander, an armor major, the macho type, but he was really good . . . a real jock. I reported in, stood at attention, and saluted. As I said, "Specialist–Six Anderson reporting as directed, sir"—whatever—my voice cracked, and I said "sir" in this high-pitched voice, and thought, "Oh shit, I'm only compounding this." He was sitting at his desk, ordered me at ease, and said, "I'm not going to read you your rights. I just want to talk to you. It was reported the other night you were found in the bushes having sex with another man. Now, I don't care what people do on their own time, but the Army doesn't feel that way, so in the future, be more discreet. That's all. Dismissed." And that was it. I said, "Thank you, I appreciate your understanding." I nearly fainted once I was out of his sight. I had very little contact with him, but maybe he looked over my record. Maybe he talked to my boss, I don't know, but it took a load off my back for sure.

They knew I was gay, most of them—I imagine almost everyone did— but there's a difference between being gay and getting caught with somebody else, especially by straight people. I went back to my office, and this warrant officer said, you know, the day may come when this will be accepted in the military—which I thought was kind of prophetic, given all the stuff that's going on currently—but it's not accepted now, so cool it. I prefer to look at it like, God, he's a good worker, so what? I was very clean cut. I was Mr. Soldier, Soldier of the Month and all that. I was an E-6 in under two years. When I was in Vietnam, I received two Army Commendation Medals, two Bronze Stars, on and on. I would complete records of trials before the judge left town, which was just unheard of. Yeah, I was really good. I hope that was a big part of his decision. Well, I was a lot more discreet from then on. I sure didn't go in the bushes or anything.

After that, I would use the courtroom! It was locked, but because of my position, I had a key. If I met somebody, we'd go back to the courtroom. It was air-conditioned besides, so it was nice. I always had a fantasy, if I ever got caught again, especially in the courtroom, that the prosecuting attorney would point to the judge's bench and say, "Right where you're sitting, Your Honor, was where the dirty deed took place. See those spots? Stains, stains of degradation, my God!" My friends teased me about it for a while, and would say, "Honestly, in the bushes, Calvin. That's really tacky." I would have to say, "Well, this is war—you got to do what you got to do!"

There really wasn't any overt hateful kind of attitude. Even the straight guys I worked with were just very good people. They were actually kind of curious about my being gay. In fact, my first date, conquest, or whatever you want to say, was with a marine, who was supposedly straight. But they have a saying in the Marine Corps of—God, I hate to say it—"Fuck me, suck me, but don't kiss me, I'm straight." That's their attitude, and it was kind of like, well, you got to take care of your buddies. This was war. This was war—there weren't any women around, what was a boy to do? In their case, it's about being super macho and, well, this way I'll establish my manhood if I'm here and there'll be no suspicion that I'm gay. I mean, the slogan is they want "a few good men." Then again, don't we all? But I think the pressure is more on the Marine Corps because of the attitude. The marines have always been the real macho guys. So there seems to be more pressure on them. They got exposed to a lot more, were on the front lines, so I wouldn't doubt that they were more crazy, kind of like what was depicted in some of those movies.

There were many guys, marines, who used the old story of "I was so drunk last night, I don't remember what I was doing," but, trust me, they were *doing it* real good! I found that "I was so drunk last night, I don't remember what happened" also meant, let's not talk about it. Even if you'd go out and have sex again, you wouldn't talk about it. You wouldn't say, gee, that was good. Given the nature of Vietnam, with people coming and going and all that, you didn't have a chance to really build up any long-term relationships. Usually, the maximum you were going to be there was a year. Marines were there longer because of their particular mobilization patterns.

There was this one guy, about six foot five, I believe, just huge, amazing, and really good-looking, that I liked. We had this bet at the NCO Club, and I asked him to come over and join us at our table, and it wasn't very long until his knee was up against mine and the connection was made. It was just that feeling again, but everybody in the straight community thinks that we all know each other—that gay people know other gay people. Oh, wouldn't it be nice if you could just tell? But there was also some truth to it, because you at least have an inkling that this person is approachable. And so I think in Vietnam, though, it was probably a little bit easier simply because there wasn't a huge stigma on it. You had an excuse, and if necessary, the "I don't remember" routine was always an option.

This guy and I went back to my room. The barracks were set up . . . actually just partitioned off, with those tacky beads or whatever, strips of plastic that you hung in the doorway, so you had some privacy but not a hell of a lot. We were being very quiet, but at one point he lost his balance, fell onto the floor, onto a wood floor. Well, imagine a six-foot-whatever guy falling out onto this wooden floor—the sound was deafening! This was a case of one of those herculean efforts where the adrenaline flows in your body so quickly that you can do anything. I remember reaching down with *one arm* and yanking him back up into bed—putting him under the covers, straightening them out, and lying there so very still, waiting to find out if anybody was going to come down the hall. Well, sure enough, somebody did, somebody came walking down the hall, but turned around and went back. Nobody said anything. They probably thought, oh, Cal's at it again. As soon as everything settled down, we got out of there. But lifting him up with one arm, I was great!

Overall, the military experience was a very positive thing—it was good for me. It instilled discipline, both personal and otherwise. Yes, a good experience. Being a politician, I'm always very careful not to distort my military record like some politicians have done. You can win a Bronze Star for valor, which is going out killing people or getting almost killed yourself, or whatever; then you can do it for meritorious service as well. Mine was won for meritorious service. I think the fact that I'm a veteran, and a Vietnam veteran at that, says a lot to my constituents. You know, it's funny, because in a couple of instances, it's worked against me because of people who are in the pacifist community. Well, they have to remember that I was drafted originally, that the reason I enlisted in order to go to the court-reporting school was to avoid being an infantryman, and that sort of thing. And that I was very much against the war. And on top of that, I did try to get out because of the regulation against gays. But I realize now that that was stupid. I did as well or better than others during my military career, but that still didn't mean I was for the war. Others protested the war in many bizarre ways, like trying to blow up their own officers and people mysteriously getting shot. Yes, I'm sure many soldiers who were shot, and officers especially, were shot by their own troops.

Regarding my ability to serve, the recent report by the Defense Personnel Security Research and Education Center in Monterey really showed there's no reason to exclude us, especially if a person is out. If they're out, there's no way to blackmail a person. It's just not a big deal. A second report by the same center concluded that gay men and women are actually better workers. I think I worked harder and performed better. And by the time I was out of the Army, I had four Army Commendation Medals, two Bronze Stars, a Good Conduct Medal, and so on. I had done an excellent job. All of my evaluations were excellent. Yes, I was good, and I feel the fact that I was gay contributed a great degree to that kind of excellence. It's obvious not all of us are goody-goody two shoes, not all of us are wonderful people, just like all straight people aren't wonderful. If that pressure [the regulation] were taken away, I don't think it would affect how well we perform, only that we would be even better than we are now. Can you imagine, under the pressure-filled situation in the legislature, if I had to devote my energy to hiding who I am? And not being able to talk about my personal life, always having to hide that? If I had to use that energy, I wouldn't have any energy left to get the regular job done. If you removed that pressure on gay people who want to serve in the military and they no longer had to hide, they probably would be even better soldiers, sailors, and marines than they already are now.

After I returned to the States and was finally discharged, I was extremely grateful for being able to make it out of Vietnam in one piece. In fact, one of the saddest things concerned that issue with my dad, who was extremely proud of me. . . . He wanted to parade me around the local neighborhood taverns. One of the saddest things occurred when we went down to this tavern called The Nineteenth Hole. There was this father there whose son hadn't come home—I had gone to high school with him— and the tears just welled up in his eyes, because it could have been his son that he was talking to in the tavern. Now, you multiply that by all those kids killed in Vietnam, all those boys and girls killed over there, and it's pretty sad. I'm really glad they finally put a memorial up to the war. I don't know if it's sufficient, but it is very necessary, because not only does it remind us . . . serve as a memorial to those people but it also reminds people, let's not get in there again, let's not have an El Salvador war, a Nicaragua war.

I know that being a member of the military builds credibility. It shows that you're part of your country, proud of it, and all that stuff. I was drafted, and I'll admit I sure didn't want to go to Vietnam. No one in their right mind would have wanted to go into a war zone, especially because Vietnam was a real pretty country and it got ruined. You know, it had a wonderful history. I mean, a very sad history, with the French and the Chinese and so on, but it has a rich history. Beautiful buildings and architecture and all that, but tragic. But now, in looking back, you know, it gives me a real appreciation for the refugee group.

Basically, I'd like to be remembered for not being just one of the guys, but there was something a little bit more, you know, the effort to do more, to serve the whole community, and to help highlight the fact that gay men and lesbians are part of that whole community. That we can function at the same level or higher than everyone else, that we can excel and we can make a contribution, and that we shouldn't be prohibited, prevented, from making that contribution, that we can serve in the military and come out first in our class and win a war and serve our country, that we can be elected to public office and serve our country and our neighborhood. And that we really bring stuff to our culture. But at the same time, right now it's much too difficult, the pressures, to be in the military. And that's too bad, because there are people in our community that would be excellent, but in good conscience I just couldn't tell them to do it, knowing that they had to hide it, because that energy to hide should be channeled in more positive ways. It just wouldn't be worth it in that respect. It's too bad, and the military loses.

Not long ago, the executive board of the party was invited to the governor's mansion for lunch, and our spouses came with us. Eric, my partner of five years, came with me, as he does to a lot of official functions. It's important that people see us as a couple. Anyway, the dining room at the governor's mansion was set up with round tables, and Eric got to sit with the governor, at the governor's table, and I was at a different table. When the governor was leaving lunch to go back to his office, he came by my table and said, "Gee, I'm sorry you and Eric didn't get to sit together." Now, the recognition that we're a couple and having that come from the governor of the state was very flattering and a very positive sign.

If it's possible for gays to be out and open, do it. There is a great need to show people they're in contact with gay men and women every single day, that we are just like them. But because we're hiding, they don't know. It's important that we be as open and honest as possible. I know there are some people that just can't do it because they think their moms would have a heart attack, and I can understand that kind of thought pattern. But what I'm saying is that if it's possible for you to be out, then do it. You're going to be helping this straight society realize more and more that we are everywhere. Let them know you, let them see who we are—we're every father, mother, daughter, son, and neighbor. It is important for understanding. This is particularly true and necessary for young people, because we don't simply turn eighteen, twenty-one, or thirty-five and then become gay; we're there and we need to show that to people as much as possible. The military should be honored to have our many numbers among their ranks. We are indeed just like everyone else, except that some of us are a bit better than that.

☆ ☆

"I tried to tell them about sex with women, but they weren't interested in that. They never are, and they never include it in the statements either."

VERNON "COPY" BERG, III

Age 37, U.S. Navy, 1969–75, officer. Dismissal-to-Honorable Discharge. Present occupation: museum-quality painter.

You always heard jokes, but it was always about somebody else, and a "homosexual" was so far beyond our experience at that point . . . I mean, we had never knowingly met one, we'd never seen one, you just heard it as the butt of a joke. So it wasn't something that was internalized. I went through high school and into college with an active sex life, with no trauma associated with it at all. There were no bad experiences; I just had good experiences. As a matter of fact, we would double-date with the women and then go home and have sex together, and I continued that kind of a practice—having sex with women, too—even into the Academy, and that lasted right up until I graduated in 1974.

I graduated from high school in '69 and went to enlisted boot camp and then to a year at the preparatory school before I went to Annapolis, the Naval Academy Preparatory School. So I went through enlisted boot camp, through the year of preparatory school, through four years at the Naval Academy. And then, after graduation, I was sent to a special missile battery school in San Francisco and picked up for a flag staff, and served as an assistant chief of staff to Vice Admiral Turner in the Sixth Fleet. *If* I was unqualified to serve, any one of those screening processes would have eliminated me, but having graduated with honors from each of them, I felt I had something left to offer the military, whether they wanted it or not.

While I was in attendance at the Academy, I became a public affairs spokesman. I made the financial appeals and gave the speeches. So by the time I did graduate, there was almost nobody involved with the military, the Navy league, those groups around the nation, and the public affairs offices up and down the east coast especially that didn't know me on a first-name basis. My case came as a shock to most of these people. However, I had left some indelible impressions. In fact, I guess I had made such a good impression on Admiral McKee, the superintendent of the Academy, that he came down to my trial and testified that he considered me to be in the top 10 percent of the class for activities and performance. He said that he would have no difficulty serving with me in combat, that it would be fine with him. It still amazes me that he came to testify. . . .

Ensign Berg, U.S. Navy, 1974

There were a lot of very bitter feelings at that time. And '69 was a terrible time to be in the military to begin with; we were withdrawing from Vietnam, and the anti-Vietnam sentiments were at the height. . . . I kind of missed it. My father was in Vietnam in 1969, and so I had personal experience through his letters, but that was all. And as a Navy chaplain, he had a terrible time. He won a Bronze Star. He was in combat all the time, and his job was basically giving last rites to people who were dying. That's all he did, yeah. By his own words, "It was very traumatic."

My class had the highest attrition rate of any in the history of the Academy, I think. As soon as they could get out, they did. They had a big problem with the gay issue around this same time *because* of Vietnam. There were an awful lot of guys who'd march in and say, "Hey, I'm gay— send me home." So the military had a very bizarre policy for a while: that if you came in and said you were gay, you had to be able to prove it! That boggles the mind when you consider what the implications are, but they really did require proof for a long time because of people trying to use homosexuality to evade the service.

The military attracts a kind of person— Most of the people in the Navy are from the Midwest and from the South. They've never seen an ocean, they've never been to sea, and they join the military to get away from home. They wanted to get away from wherever they used to be, but it also attracts a kind of personality which tends to be rather self-isolated. They were not socially active to the extent that they had to study hard enough to be able to get into school to begin with, so they didn't go out a lot, and they didn't have a great deal of travel experience, and so the Academy was a peak experience for them. That was the highest point in their lives. But they also tended to be a person who— They kept their own counsel; they were masculine or they wouldn't have been in that environment, and that kind of person just didn't share feelings. They didn't talk about things, especially anything about gay feelings.

During my Academy years, I didn't know any midshipmen who were gay, so I suppose my relationship with Lawrence was monogamous. He was the first person that I had sex with that I actually knew on an ongoing basis. And I didn't meet other people. I didn't really know how to meet other people. In fact, throughout my training I never had any sexual liaisons with anyone at the Academy. But at any rate, he came over to Italy and got a job on the same ship I did, as a civilian, teaching on board. That didn't last long. He came over in June and I was interrogated in June. His arrival had nothing to do with the investigation. It was just a remarkable coincidence. He got swept up into it and he lost his job at the same time, but it was not because of my relationship with Lawrence that I was questioned. In fact, it all happened rather quickly. I graduated in June of '74 and my trial was in January of the next year.

I don't know how my name got into the investigation. There was a confidential informant, and because I was not court-martialed, I was not allowed to confront the accuser, so I never did find out who it was. But somehow my name ended up on a list and the Naval Investigative Service called me in and said, "We're here to talk about your homosexuality." I said, "What homosexuality?" And they said, "Come on now, Mr. Berg, we're not naive," and they produced a list of names, dates, and places that was astonishing in that it was so *inaccurate*. It was a lot of people that I had known, or knew of, or had met, but had never had any activity with—professors at the Academy, other midshipmen at the Academy, other officers in the Navy. My best guess is that it was just a major fishing expedition, that they had caught somebody who gave them a list of names. . . .

They were trying to corroborate and get more information. And at the time, I made the decision that I essentially said, "Yes, it's true, I am gay—what are you going to do about it?" There were two guys—good guy, bad guy—and one of them ganged up on me and the other one then left the room. It was very, very predictable, the routine, but it was very frightening at the time, because I'd never been through it before. I was twenty-three, I guess.

I felt very strongly that I needed a position of credibility, and I said, "That's not all true, but I'll tell you what is true." I gave them a statement about my sexuality, and I was discharged based on my own statement, but I felt—I *still* feel—like it's very important that they understand that all those other accusations were *not* true. There's an assumption on the part of military investigators that all of us know each other and that we all communicate on some unknown underground network, and that if you're gay you, by definition, know everybody else who is. And it's just not true. We're not that superhuman and we don't function that way, and it's certainly not so in the military, where it's "forbidden" anyway.

The investigators wanted to know what kind of sex I'd had with what individuals at what age. They wanted to know a sexual history. So I admitted to having had sex in high school. I admitted to having had sex with other people while at the Academy, and I specified that they were all civilians and that it was experimental. I tried to tell them about sex with women, but they weren't interested in that. They never are, and they never include it in the statements either. It doesn't serve their purposes. You have to be able to support your own case.

By the time they sprang this thing about a sexual investigation on me, it was a complete shock. I was totally unprepared for it. There was really nobody I could talk to about it. Nobody could give me any legal advice. The lawyers assigned to the staff were all on the side of the staff. They're there for the good of the Navy, and they always advise you to resign and go home. Their advice is to be very quiet about it, take your lumps, and leave. Oh, they're very nice about it, you know, they're very polite, but they always tell you exactly what you should do from their position, you know, what's best for them. And especially since I was on the staff of Vice Admiral Turner, they wanted it kept quiet; they didn't want any publicity, they didn't want any problems.

After I signed my statement and volunteered to resign, instead of removing me from the ship right away, they *promoted* me. My boss had been slated to go on a vacation and he wanted to be able to take that vacation, so he left, and I assumed full responsibility for my staff activities after I volunteered to resign, and we went to sea and I took charge of the whole operation. So the *greatest responsibility* I ever assumed in the military was *after* I volunteered to resign, after I stated that I was homosexual, which the court picked up on, and the court was very supportive in saying that if I was such a threat, I should never have been allowed to do that. And the very fact that I could function, even given that everybody on the ship knew about it, was enough that they could support our petition.

I was sent back to the United States very quietly and came back to the Norfolk area at the same time that Matlovich [see pages 151–55] was beginning his case. They left me there almost six months without doing anything, up until January 1975. I had to go in to work and sit at this desk every day, all day. And it was made more complicated by the fact that I had been robbed, which I still think might have been a setup. They stole all my luggage. They took everything I owned as I was leaving Italy. Now, you can think that it was Italians and Italy's just not a very safe place for luggage, but it's also a remarkable coincidence that all my documentation, service records, papers, and pay records were all lost at the same time. I didn't get paid for almost six months because they had no pay record. I had to buy all new uniforms so I could go to work every day, sit there, and do nothing.

During my trial, they produced an accusing witness, an enlisted man who had not been under me but I had worked with some, and he accused me of making a pass. There was no sex, there was no accusation of sexual activity, but that I had indicated to him that I wanted to. There's an old maxim that one witness is no witness, because both sides got him to say exactly what they wanted him to say. He was utterly destroyed by the experience. When he didn't do exactly what they expected of him, they turned on him, really destroyed him. He wasn't prepared for it. I think very few people are. I mean, it was intense media scrutiny. It was the front page of the paper every day for two weeks. It was television cameras. It was people from the Pentagon, who flew him over here and flew him down and told him what to say. He had a bad time, and then when he didn't say exactly what they wanted him to, they sent him right back where he was, but he was castigated for the whole thing.

I testified for eight hours over about three days. It made *Time* magazine. At any rate, they overreacted, I mean, massively overreacted. They issued parking tickets. They had first-come, first-served tickets that you had to get for parking to be able to come in. They had special seating. They had special press rooms. They brought in all kinds of typewriters and telephones to set up to handle the media. They were going to be ready for this thing. And as a result, it became a self-fulfilling prophecy. The thing just mushroomed. It skyrocketed way out of proportion. It was a big circus.

When Admiral McKee came down to testify . . . they wanted to know if he would serve with me in combat, and he shocked them by saying, "Yes." They did not want to hear that. I think the accusing witness was their undoing . . . the prosecuting attorney just drew it out, and he wouldn't really accuse me of anything . . . and they couldn't find anybody else. Nobody who'd ever served with me would say anything. They brought in some Navy psychiatrist who had never met me, and he said that homosexuals were a bad idea in the service but couldn't speak to the specifics of the case *because* he'd never met me.

They had a statement from me saying that I had sex with Lawrence. They had a statement from me saying I'd had sex prior to my entering in the Navy, and they could have discharged me based on that statement all by itself. That's why I say that the whole hearing was a circus. It was unnecessary, completely unnecessary, and most of what went on was more than unnecessary; it was counterproductive. The three best witnesses in the whole trial were Admiral Mac, who gave splendid testimony; John Money, the doctor from Johns Hopkins, who gave kind of a historical overview of the entire Western civilization; and my father.

Commander Berg, my father, testified at great length about how he felt that I had a sense of moral integrity that was stronger even than his own, that I'd always been a good son and a good officer and had served well, but he also branched out in his testimony. . . . He talked about Vietnam. He talked about openly gay combat marines that he had known, and he testified that he knew of still-serving, active-duty officers in the ranks of commander, captain, and rear admiral who were gay. And he said on the stand, "You'd better be careful who you criticize, because you may work for somebody who is." It made the front page of every paper in the country, and I personally feel because of that, he was passed over for promotion and forced to retire. He got cancer that same year and died four years later.

He was utterly destroyed because of his truth. And he was angry about the fact that many people accused him of betraying the professional confidence of those who had come to see him for help. My father said many months later and in some jest but certainly with a true sense of irony, "The only thing I was talking about were people who had made passes at me. I wasn't talking about professional confidence. I was talking about people who had indicated that I was attractive and that if I was interested, they were willing to have sex with me."

He used to tell me that he had friends that he knew of who were gay and served very well. He also made reference to admirals and generals that he knew were gay. They were his friends. They were his comrades. He'd worked with them, so it made rather good sense that they would be the people who would confide in him, talk to him, or approach him. Of course, that all died with him. It never got into the trial and wasn't part of the testimony, but he got tremendous, tremendous criticism from other ministers. His own church denomination wouldn't back him up, so he quit the church, quit the Navy as a commander, moved to the Outer Banks off North Carolina, and died there at fifty-three, a man destroyed by speaking the truth.

If a young man has a suspicion that he's homosexual and wants counseling and goes to either a doctor or a chaplain, they are obligated by regulation to report him and have him discharged . . . so that the one person that you would go to, to try to sort out your feelings, is the very person who's going to turn you in, so that there's almost no such thing as professional confidence in the service. There are individuals in the service, chaplains and doctors, who will not do that, who feel that their allegiance is equally to the individual, and who feel that their personal integrity is called into question. My father was one of those professionals. May he rest in peace, knowing the world now knows his truth.

When the trial was over, they voted against me, voted for my discharge, and gave me a fully dishonorable discharge. So that was the end of it. Since Lawrence was there taking notes through the whole thing, we used it to write the book *Get Off My Ship*. It was based heavily on the transcripts of the trial.

Later, the trial decision was overturned and I was given an honorable discharge, but what I really wanted was reinstatement. So the very next day, they gave me this honorable discharge to take away the sympathy of the court. And sure enough, when we went before Gerhard Gesell at the U.S. district court, he said, "Well, you've got an honorable discharge—what more do you want?" And so we had to say, "I wanted to be able to serve." He decided the case on the merits itself. He essentially told the military that they had to come up with a reason other than my homosexuality to justify the discharge and sent it back to the Pentagon at that point. By that time, Reagan had been elected, and we decided to terminate the litigation because there wasn't any better law to be made out of it, so after five years of appealing the case, we settled out of court. I received a cash settlement and had to sign a statement saying that I would never attempt to reenlist, which by that time was fine with me.

Through it all, I had no difficulty with the public aspects of it. The television and newspaper coverage and the speaking and even the trial itself were all things that I'd done before. . . . The personal aspects were a little worse. You know, dealing with the family and making sure they understood. And the uncertainty of it was very unsettling, you know: What do I do now? Where do I go from here? How do I pay the rent? Little things like that became very big concerns, and I literally moved to New York with no place to live and no job, and just sort of made do after I got here. Lawrence and I moved to New York together but separated shortly thereafter. So I started cleaning apartments, painting houses, and anything I could to earn money. Then I went back to school. I got a master's degree in design from Pratt Institute and studied drawing at the Art Students League.

Now I'm a painter full-time. I always did cartooning and football posters. I did a lot of artwork at the Naval Academy, and it's one of the things that helped me gain recognition while I was there. I did portraits of Admiral Mac and that kind of thing. In fact, there are a lot of pieces still there. Presently, I'm represented by a gallery in New York, museum-quality paintings. I sell virtually everything I do. I go to Europe twice a year and have a house in the Hamptons, two dogs, and a station wagon. It's a Volvo too. Yep. And I've been with the same guy for eight years now.

The military gave me a tremendous amount of experience in public speaking and interacting with other people, which served me well in my trial and has served me well since then. They made a gentleman out of me, and I've been able to maintain that. The only thing I regret are the circumstances under which I was terminated, you know, told to leave. If that had been different, it would have been a wholly good experience. We were the first—Matlovich and myself. I mean, it's astonishing to think, but sixty thousand people were discharged between World War II and my case, and nobody ever said that they wanted to stay in. It had never happened before, and so when Mat and I stood up and said, "Well, wait a minute, there's no reason for us to be discharged," it was a big turning point.

I think the biggest turning point, apart from our lawsuits, was the inclusion of women. When women were allowed into the service and then into the academies and then onto the ships, and people could see that they could function and they could be in that environment and that sexual indiscretions, even in those circumstances, could be dealt with . . . I think most commanders imagined their ships were going to sink if women came on board, but that didn't happen. And quite honestly, I think women and homosexuals are two categories that fit that concept.

Today, I am aware of the controversy surrounding the military's mandatory AIDS testing program. However, for once, I personally feel that testing is very good, because there's a lot you can do if you know you're positive now. The medications are all very effective in asymptomatic HIV-positive people, of which I am one. I am taking medication and I'm stabilized, and hopefully, for the unforeseen future, we have prevented it. And my lover has AIDS, yet he also is on medication and responding very well, because we both started medication very early. But so long as the military in their testing knows enough to counsel these people, protect their confidentiality, which is a severe problem, and offer medical treatments, it's a very good thing, and I think more people should be tested.

I think there are many more things that create controversy than the mandatory AIDS testing in the military. For example, I found out recently that the Red Cross has an investigative agency and they routinely investigate and report people, and yet most of these investigative agencies are considered secret so that they don't even report to Congress. They're given funding every year, but they're not held accountable for what they do with it. And my personal opinion is that most of the investigators involved in these agencies, like the NIS, are only out to justify their existence so they can keep their jobs and keep getting paid.

Gore Vidal once said that he was on the top of a very small heap, and I feel that way—that in certain circles there are people who remember, but it's very small circles. I mean, I know very well that anytime I write a letter to the editor of the *New York Times*, it gets published, and that's something. I know that if I ever speak out in public about the Pentagon, they know about it, and that's something. They've got a big file on me. But beyond that, very few people remember.... But the lawyers at Lambda [which help in gay issues] are aware of those court cases, and there are precedents in court and there is interaction between the cases. And all of that is cumulative. It helps. It all adds up toward one goal, and that's basic human rights and understanding between people. A lot of people think we're different, but I think we're a lot more like other people than we are different from other people.

☆ ☆

"So here we were in this huge auditorium, and this fat, ugly master sergeant yelled, 'Boler, get up here. You say here you're queer. Ya' want to suck my dick?' I said, 'No, God no.' 'Then ya' ain't queer,' booming out. I can still recall it to this day!"

JEFF BOLER

Age 46, U.S. Air Force, 1963–78, enlisted/officer.
General Discharge Under Honorable Conditions.
Present occupation: computer sales and owner of
Mustang restoration shop.

As far back as I can remember, I've always been interested in guys; even like when I was five or six, I can recall times when I always had the urge to do something and didn't know what to do and didn't have the guts to do anything. Of course, my best friend and I would have circle jerks or whatever, where you beat off together; in fact, before we were even able to climax, we started that stuff. Oh yeah. We did that a lot. I knew some other boys that I was interested in, but I wouldn't pull mine out because I was embarrassed . . . I heard that theirs were real big. It's not that I had many full-blown experiences (no pun intended) during my early years, but I knew I was gay. However, that didn't stop me from applying for the Air Force.

Now, when I joined the Air Force I told 'em I was gay. I marked a box that said, "Do you have or have you ever had homosexual tendencies?" When I enlisted in Jackson, Mississippi, in 1963, they went through all this BS about "tell the truth, fill out all these things, but whatever you do, tell the truth." Well now, I could just see me getting found out, and I wasn't going to get caught in a lie, so I checked the little box. They said, "Well, you say here you have or have had homosexual tendencies. Have you ever had any . . . you know, did you ever suck dicks and do all that stuff?" And I said, "Oh no, never—that's dirty." But he said, "Well, have you ever done anything?" I said, "No, but everybody has tendencies when you go through adolescence." He says, "Well then, I don't think that's what they're talking about here. What it means is, have you ever done or do you regularly do anything?" And I said, "Well, no, I've never done anything, but I have had a desire to do something. I've never done anything with a girl, either; I've had a desire to do that, too. You don't have a little box for that." I could not understand that, because in my religion that was wrong. I can't even remember anything in religion about sucking dicks! Anyway, they changed the box that I had checked.

Off I went to basic, and of course you're scared shitless anyway—it's the first time I've ever been on an airplane. I guess it was my whole flight [group of recruits] and probably a couple other flights. Anyway, they crowd you all in these old hot buses right after you get off the plane and take you to the final destination. Then they yell hellfire and brimstones. You know—we're gonna find out if you misrepresented anything here; you are, I mean guaranteed, you are out. So the little box came up again: Do you have or have you ever had . . . Yes. Bigger than shit. And so we're still in civilian clothes, have our hair and everything, and of course, I always had a flattop back then—in fact, I had shorter hair, shorter than the military—so I didn't have much to lose one way or the other.

Captain Boler, U.S. Air Force, 1977

So here we were in this huge auditorium, and this fat, ugly master sergeant yelled—back then weight wasn't a big hassle like it is now, but you could be fat *and* ugly—"Boler, get up here!" I went up to the front of this auditorium, to the source of this booming voice, to see why he wanted me. He said, "You say here you're queer." And my God, I turned 147 shades of red. I just crumbled, and I could feel the tears—it was in front of all these guys, and of course, everybody up there. I was sure they were probably thinking, "Oh, here's a good one" or whatever. I don't know what they were saying. But oh God, it was horrible, the most traumatic experience I'd ever had at the time. I said, "That's not what it says; it says, do you or have you ever . . ." And so he went through this questioning. He said, "Do you suck dicks?" Everyone laughed. His voice just boomed in this huge place to the point where you could hear it echo in back, and he continued, "Ya' want to suck my dick?" I said, "No, God no." I mean, even today, if I were dying I wouldn't; you could kill me first—never in a million years. He said, "Then ya' ain't queer," booming out and echoing off all those damn walls! I can still recall it to this day. Oh God. Every eye was on me, totally. Oh God. I said, "Oh fuck, they're gonna be beating the shit out of me tonight." There weren't but three queers in the world, and if ya' ever found 'em you were supposed to beat 'em up, right? (Once again, they changed the box I had checked.)

I was still this dorky-looking kid with glasses—precontacts. After we got into training, nobody ever said a word though. At least I don't think so. They might've mentioned it, but I managed to erase it from my memory. After that I only got in trouble a couple times. My mom had sent me this neat cordless electric razor, but they told me that I couldn't use an electric razor back then, you know, like they were trying to turn us into real men, and I guess real men didn't use such things. They forced me to use a straight-edge blade. Well, believe me, I managed to take off the first four layers of my face! They sent me to the dispensary and then let me use the electric razor, no problem. I was the only one in line that was allowed to use an electric razor.

The other time, they put soap in my mouth, which put me in the doctor's care at the dispensary. It started during an inspection. They were inspecting lockers, and see, I was perfect. I never got caught doing anything wrong in my life—well, hardly ever. Whatever the directions were, if I knew the rules, I could play the game. Tell me the rules so I know what they are, no sweat, I can follow directions—I ain't no dummy. Anyhow, they were inspecting lockers and pulled out this guy's bar of soap, and he said, "There's a hair on this bar of soap. You been cleaning your ass with it?" I sort of giggled, and he said, "You think that's funny?" So he took the soap and scraped it across my teeth and made me swallow it. Well, I started choking, and then they had to send me to the doctor.

After basic and tech school I went to Georgia. While there, I was in the communications center working with the plant 55 switching system, which was Teletype equipment. I did my job, but did very little in a sexual way. I never really had any great uncontrollable desire to do anything. Yes, I had desires for certain people, but it was usually an emotional attachment, all except for this one fellow. We had what I might describe as a quickie.

I mean, when I woke up and somebody was lying on top of me, kissing and all that sort of stuff, I knew it was Burt. He'd been doing all this groping, and I was hot to trot, I mean ready for anything, I didn't care what. Then his roommate came in. "Hey, what's going on in here?" Burt said, "Aw, Jeff just passed out on the bed over there . . ." After a while I wandered back down to my own room, I think crawling. Next night, I did the same thing he had done the night before, cuddled to him and started snuggling. Well, he pushed me to his waist, so I went down on him. He rolled over on his side, started to pump, and I couldn't handle it. I gagged. I mean, a toothpick would have gagged me; used to—it doesn't anymore. I put my hand around it and realized he didn't have much anyway, but a lot more than *I* could handle, though. He came in my mouth, which was all right with me—didn't bother me at all. Then he pretended to roll back over and fall asleep. I got up and went on down to my room before his roommate came in, 'cause I didn't want a rerun of that! It was really my last day there. Then I went to a new duty station.

I hadn't planned on becoming an officer, but the opportunity came up and I went for it. And all this while, I was still looking for a real queer. I knew if I went to the school in California I could find one. If they're anywhere in the world they're there. I'd be true-blue the rest of my life if I could find just one. All I needed was one—preferably under three-hundred pounds. Everyone told me there were "fruits" everywhere in California. But in the two years that I was there, I only found one! It took me two years to find that one, and I looked hard. Well, this all occurred around 1968, during the height of the Vietnam conflict.

So I left the enlisted ranks, was commissioned in 1968, and then transferred to Florida. . . . I got a new car, and was feeling pretty sharp. I was driving around the city in this big "Queenmobile" when I saw this kid. He waved, so I went around the block again, stopped by, and said, "Do you need a ride or something?" He said, "Yeah," so he jumped in the car and after a respectable time started playing with my crotch. I went up this little side street, stopped, flipped up the steering wheel, and he proceeded to give me a blow job. . . . Then he tells me about the Cactus Room, a gay bar. I mean, I'm still looking for the fruits, so next day at 3:30 sharp, I'm at that bar in my silk and sharkskin suit. You always dress up for dates, right? So here I am in this suit—it didn't work in California, but perhaps in Florida I'd be lucky!

I'm looking good, I mean, all gussied up, and ready to find my one queer. There was one parking spot right in front of the Cactus Room. I found out later it was there because the straights wouldn't park in it because it was in *front* of a queer bar, and the queers wouldn't park in it because they didn't want anyone to know they were *in* the bar. Me, I didn't care; I'd decided that I wasn't gonna live in total fear all my life. What I didn't know was that during the day it was a *straight* bar. The queers didn't come out till night. I didn't know that; they don't put that in the training manual. It's off limits, but they don't say what time. Well, I knew there were queers there, 'cause I'd seen one the night before. I knew I wasn't mistaken, but still no queers in sight. Finally I said, "Last night this kid told me this was a gay bar." The bartender said, "It is, but not during the goddamn day!" I said, "Oh, you've got hours. It's like you got duty hours—you can't be queer until after dark." He says, "Listen, you take yourself out of here, get something to eat, put on some cutoffs and a T-shirt and come back after ten tonight, and I'll introduce you to everybody." I said, "Fine." I went home, changed my clothes, and waited forever until ten o'clock. Nope, couldn't wait till ten o'clock so about nine-thirty I was there. When I returned, he had already told everyone about this Air Force pilot that was coming back. I wasn't a pilot, but he didn't know that. I was in the Air Force, and when you're in the Air Force, everybody flies planes. I was really very important, so they thought.

They introduced me around to everybody. . . . It was nice 'cause I'd found others like me—other queers. I'd stay out all night; then the next morning I'd come in, change clothes, and go to work, but usually I'd gotten in somebody's bed somewhere along the way. If I didn't have a trick from the bar, I'd been known to pick up a gate guard on the way back, 'cause they were a little queer anyway. . . . I was extremely brazen. The "authorities" never said anything, but I'm sure they knew. I would take guys home on many occasions. I would sign them in at the gate, bring them over to the Officers' Club, or we'd end up at my BOQ [bachelor officers' quarters]. Once I came out, I was extremely conscious and very butch-acting. Nobody thought I was gay, supposedly. Anyhow, I made a conscious effort of looking straight. My dad even noticed it. He told me he thought the Air Force had really turned me into a man—little did he know! I never got in trouble, and I never hid it.

One time, in fact, I went into the Cactus Room . . . still in uniform. I just stopped by the bar. It was actually early enough that it wouldn't be that much of a gay bar, but it was late enough for the gay bartender to be on duty. These two guys came in and sat down at this little booth thing right behind the bar. The bartender said, "Two sergeants just sat down behind you, and seeing an officer in here has just blown their minds—they're scared shitless!" So I said, "Well, we'll have a little fun." I'd had a couple of drinks by now, right? And with drinks I got guts, I got balls; without drinks, forget it. I turned around, went over to their table, and said, "Sergeant, what are you doing here?" And they just slid under the table. Just literally slid under the table. Scared them to death. 'Cause obviously, nobody would be there in uniform, and it was earlier than the queers would normally have been there anyway. . . . It was pretty damn funny! The only reason an officer would be there in uniform would be to check up on somebody for an investigation. I let them suffer for a respectable amount of time. Normally, you didn't wear your uniform off base much anyway; it just wasn't real popular, with what was going on against the war effort at home. I was quite aware of that, but looked cute in my uniform and was proud of it. I finally let those fellows off the hook, and later we actually became good friends.

Then I was transferred to Vietnam. They needed people in cinematography over there real bad to film the war—anything that happened in the Air Force was documented on film. . . . It was all much more accurate when it was done in that manner. It was strictly documentation. This wasn't for public release. I'm sure that all those documented flights are still in some war archive. I was in a plane that was shot down, and we had a crash landing. The landing gear was badly damaged, so we landed on flat tires, and the body of the plane dug into the ground. Thank God no one was hurt. For my contributions to the war effort, I did get a Bronze Star and an Air Medal. I felt pretty proud of all that I had done. And believe me, some of our flights were extremely hairy.

That's probably why there was so much drinking and drug abuse in Vietnam. People were trying to numb themselves to all that was going on around them. The death, destruction, dank and damp really could get to the most hardened soldier. People just didn't pay much attention to what you were doing. So everybody drank a lot, including me; I drank a lot. I didn't notice much concern about whether one was gay or not. It may have been there, but I didn't see it. Sex in general was pretty free. In fact, I don't think I ever met a marine I didn't fuck. . . . I wasn't heavy into kissing, but most of 'em didn't seem to mind. I *was* a good kisser. A lot of marines said, "Suck me, fuck me, but don't kiss me—'cause that would make me queer." I heard that a lot. Yep, that was it. That "makes ya' queer"! You know, they were shooting at ya'—what the hell. I guess that's how they justified their sexual activities and maintained their "straight" outer shell. That super macho image and all.

Everything seemed so open during those years. One time, I found a friend between the barracks passed out, just lying there. I tried to wake him up and pick him up, but I was in no condition to do much of either. So I undid his pants, and went down on his peepee. After a little bit I quit and zipped him back up. This occurred right out there in front of everybody—anyone walking by could see what I was doing. It wasn't concealed at all. It was wide open. Another time, I gave this guy a blow job right in the barracks with others sleeping all around us. There was all this bouncing up and down, you know, pretty audible. Finally, the guy in the upper bunk just said, "Would you stop making so goddamn much racket!" All this noise was going on and nobody gave a shit.

Not too long after that, I got transferred to Thailand and was made commander of a small detachment. I did a good job of that and they were real happy, because we did a lot of good documentation. . . . I made several trips to Saigon, and would get laid solid on every trip. Like I said, it was all open wide.

Transferred once again, I ended up in Texas, and received some super outstanding OERs, but at this same time, my troubles began peripherally when one of my friends was picked up by the OSI. He had sent a message to another friend of mine to get a hold of and warn this Sergeant So-and-so at Offit Air Force Base to watch out for some things coming down the pike. He was at the time a SAC general's lover. The OSI had *another* letter from this sergeant at Offit Air Force, and it was a little incriminating. So my friend was trying to tell both of them, the sergeant and the general, to watch their p's and q's. Since my telephone number and name were on his desk, the OSI later called me in about that. But nothing came of it. That was the first time, the first thing on my OSI record.

There was a lot of sexual activity, but I had connections, friends that worked with the OSI. It allowed me to get the inside scoop on what might be brewing in investigations. Well, I got a call from the friend at the OSI office, and he said, "Hey, I saw your name come across my desk, and it's in association with something somebody had said about sexual activities." But by then I was getting outstanding OERs, the colonel thought I was great . . . I did all this extra-duty stuff, which was outstanding, and they loved the results, which made me the favorite guy. The colonel and the general, everybody thought I was the greatest. It was well known everywhere. I could do no wrong then. When this problem came up, I just called the military personnel center and said, "Don't you have any assignments for me? I've been down here for three or four years, and it's about time for a change." They said, "Well, how soon do you want to leave?" And I said, "Next week." They said, "You know that job you had in Thailand? Well, they've taken on some additional things; they put television in the fighters. And there are also some morale problems that need to be straightened out. The place is falling apart and we gotta have somebody; we needed 'em there yesterday." So, sure enough, I was out of there in a week.

My secretary protected me when the OSI came to talk to me. In fact, she told them I had already gone to Thailand, which I hadn't at the time. Every civilian and every straight person totally protected me, totally. After a couple of weeks of being in Thailand, the OSI called me in and asked all these questions, and I told 'em, "I don't admit or deny anything." But see, like I said, in Southeast Asia they weren't that concerned with it. You know, they had other fish to fry. My God, the drug deals were totally out of hand. I mean, while we were sitting there people were passing drugs behind the guy!

By then the drug situation had gotten significant. They were carrying it out by the tons. You could buy double handfuls of pure heroin for ten bucks, on the streets—even more open than the time before when I was there. This was now '73 or '74, toward the end of the war. We closed down Thailand. While I was there we had already pulled out of Vietnam, and when Vietnam fell, we did the documentation of that. I was involved in the final phase of that operation.

Well, anyway, I told the OSI, "Listen, I don't know what you're talking about, and regardless of what it is, I've been on enough court-martials to know not to say anything to you. If you're asking me about somebody else, fine. If you're asking me about me, I don't care what it is, I ain't answering your questions." So they didn't bother me. Nothing was ever said again. However, after they left me alone, I became fairly active. I fucked everything that moved. I was notorious. Marines, Green Berets, everything. If it was male, I had it. I didn't lose a lot of sleep over it one way or the other—I don't think most people even noticed.

After Thailand I came to Hawaii. . . . My colonel called me in and told me that they'd inquired of him about me and any kind of involvement in homosexual activities. He was sure that they'd be contacting me shortly; he was just letting me know that they were putting everything on hold until it was all squared away. I was doing a good job and was straightening out all the messes, but it didn't give me any immunity. They referred me to a lawyer with the air defense counsel for the Air Force. I was very honest with him and told him everything, and he said that he would do his best for me and wouldn't sell me short; he was honest.

When they finally got around to bringing charges, everything on my charge sheet was false. Nothing was true. They had picked out this huge amount of stuff, intercepted my mail, talked to my landlord, talked to everybody in Hawaii that I knew, talked to people back on the mainland, and basically harassed my friends all over the place. I was relieved of the command, and they froze my security clearance. And I was assigned as a special assistant to the wing commander. It cost me about six thousand dollars, but I had an attorney from town who worked together with the air defense counsel fellow. I was very open with both of the attorneys. We could have won against their charges, but it was going to cost me a fortune, way more than the money already spent. And I would never be able to go anywhere else in the military [promotions] because of the black mark. I'd never get any further. I could've stayed on for twenty and retired, since I had the enlisted time, so even if I didn't make major I still wouldn't have been RIFed before my retirement date. I had thirteen years in at the time.

It just went on and on and on. I felt like I was wasting the Air Force's money and I was going to be stuck there doing nothing for years. It was driving me crazy. I couldn't get transferred, couldn't do anything, and was going to be stuck in that spot forever—there was absolutely no future. They said, "You're gonna do nothing for the rest of your Air Force career, and we'll keep finding evidence until we get you out on something, like drunk driving, a parking ticket, or something. Sooner or later we're gonna get you." So finally, after about two years, I decided to resign. They said, "Well, you'll get an honorable discharge and nothing will show on your record about it." They never proved anything. I was never formally charged, so what could they put on it anyway? But you never know what those fools are going to do. For example, from my past court-martial experiences as a participating court member, I had observed that the guilty always got away with their crimes and the innocent were always prosecuted to the max. I couldn't believe it. There were these huge drug dealers, and these *real* guilty ones always had immunity to testify, yet some kid that smoked one joint in his entire life got prison or a bad conduct discharge. It was unreal.

I was able to secure a job in sales during this time, and when I found a job that paid as much as I was making in the Air Force, I made the decision to leave. I told them that I was unwilling to sit there for the next couple of years just waiting to get out. I said it would be nice to have retirement, but I didn't feel like all those years of sitting were worth it. It was unfair to the Air Force, unfair to me, and I was certainly capable of doing a lot more. So I resigned, got out, became a civilian, and started selling computer equipment to the government, immediately! The only catch was that I didn't get my honorable, but a general discharge under honorable conditions.

I guess, other than my final two years, I really enjoyed my Air Force career. And I think it's still sexy. I was very successful in the Air Force. I mean I did a very good job. A lot of people where I worked knew, and nobody cared. The vast majority of the people didn't care—it was quite all right, and they were *straight* people. There was never any problem.

Someday it'll probably be all right, but not right away. If the AIDS thing hadn't come up, change would've been a lot closer. I think that polarized everything again. Anybody that had anything against it and had something to say had a platform to stand on and shout about it. So they've got a "good reason" now: "AIDS is an obvious punishment for all those queers. They deserve it, because what they have done all these centuries has been wrong and totally against God's will."

I simply had one small goal during all those years. I don't feel that I did anything wrong. I was just looking for somebody for years and years. I've been looking for a long time. I was stupid, but I was chicken, too, and I was very shy. I have a friend now, and we've been together for ten years. I've found it easier to have a relationship with someone when you don't have all of the sex and other things giving you problems. Off and on, I'm happy. A lot of those feelings relate directly to the fact that in July 1988, I tested positive for AIDS. But you know, from ages twenty-five to thirty-five, I lived a very full, wonderful life and I don't regret it, even if I have contracted this horrible disease. I did everything in the world, you know, I had new cars, lived in nice houses, and had many, many tricks. But up until I was twenty-five, I'd never done anything sexual except for playing with "it" with my hand. And since age thirty-five, I have been relatively inactive on the sexual side.

I'm more settled, and I have stopped drinking. I really had a reason for drinking. I never had a lot of guts without a drink; so I'd go out and have a few drinks so I'd have more guts. In the past, I was sometimes so drunk that I'd even fall asleep on top of a gorgeous guy and not remember a thing. It was terrible. But when I came out, I was looking for that *one* guy, and if I had found him I would probably still be with him today, and we'd have gone through years and years and years. . . . I just wanted that one person, that's all I was looking for, one person to settle down with and never ever stray. I love people now that I don't have sex with—now I don't consider love and sex as synonymous. In the past, I wouldn't trick with anybody that I didn't think there was a sincere possibility for a permanent relationship. By coming out, and by not concealing or holding so much in, you can move forward and experience life more fully, good, bad, or indifferent. I did that.

☆ ☆

"I met Perry Watkins in Korea, when he was doing 'drag' for the Army. He used to give drag shows all up and down the peninsula. I can remember him saying, 'This place is wonderful. I can get a dress for so little you wouldn't believe!' "

JIM DRONENBURG

Age 40, U.S. Navy, 1971–81, enlisted. Honorable Discharge. Present occupation: accountant.

I couldn't afford college, so in 1971 I went in the Navy. And trust me, if there's a special place in hell for military recruiters, I hope mine goes there! He was quite impressed with me, or that's what I thought. I didn't know that I was just grist for the mill at the time. I was interested in electronics, aviation electronics. He didn't bother to tell me that—without my glasses I'm legally blind and he knew that—with my eyes, I couldn't get it, nor could I get nuclear, nor could I get almost anything else that was interesting. I found that out after I arrived in boot camp and they said, "Well, we're not letting go of you, but those areas are closed to you." I really wasn't interested in much, but there was this interpretive specialty. I didn't know what that meant, but I had the idea it was something along the lines of the U.N. translators and I thought, oh, nice. Okay, Japanese, Hindustani, or Norwegian. And they said Korean it is. I was lucky because we've got a massive military presence in Korea and speaking Korean, more often than not, you were either sent there or to one of the two "language pools" here in the U.S.

Language school seemed to attract a high proportion, in retrospect, of gays. Why this is, I don't know, but on the proportions I observed when I was there for my second tour, they couldn't have done any better if they'd opened the proverbial hairdressing school. There was always a large gay presence there. Most of us wouldn't acknowledge ourselves. On my first tour, God knows, I didn't know enough to acknowledge it.

We all tended to go to the same places. Basically, in Monterey sexually it was one-night stands. That's all that I was ready for. I'd heard about settling down. I'd heard about lovers, but I wanted no part of it. We were going up for security clearances, and I was acutely aware of what would happen if I were found out. So I didn't want anything that would cause me problems, particularly a full-time lover. Monterey was not as gay as San Francisco, but it was still quite gay. There was plenty of opportunity.

I received my top secret clearance, and after a tour at Fort Meade, I was sent to Korea for a year, and Korea, basically—and this goes for both tours that I was there—was decent sexually. And nobody cared that you were gay. Korea was an alcoholic factory, always was. I was regarded as more an odd bird out that I didn't drink than perhaps for not whoring around. By and large, it was considered the only thing to do, to drink. For most GIs, that was the only thing to do. Now, I will say this—I was an ugly American in that I don't particularly like Koreans for bed partners. If I wanted an anorexic twelve-year-old, I could get an anorexic twelve-year-old. The Koreans are generally smaller, much slimmer, flat chested, hairless. I still remember my first kiss, like a river carp! But there was a place in Seoul, it was on one of the bases (I assume that it's still active), where people could meet, look each other over, start a conversation, or swing down the hall and *then* start into something more than conversation. The old USO was particularly good in that respect. It's long since torn down, but it had facilities and you could identify other gays there, and more often than not you'd drift into the shower, and somebody would drift with you. So that worked out well. It had a door that opened with a marvelous creak, so you could tell if anybody was coming.

I met Perry Watkins in Korea, when he was doing "drag" for the Army. He used to give drag shows all up and down the peninsula. I can remember him saying, "This place is wonderful. I can get a dress for so little you wouldn't believe!" Yes, girlfriend made to order! I can still remember one time we were out front of this bar, and Perry said, "I'm going to try to walk straight for a night," and he managed maybe three steps, and we all collapsed laughing because Perry was just not known for that. We had some really great times over there.

When he did a drag show, he was always billed as a straight woman singer. Nobody ever figured it was a drag show. They just thought this woman named Simone was a *real* woman on all the publicity stills, and you never saw him. He played it straight until the last number, and I think it never varied. His last number was "If My Friends Could See Me Now," and he proceeded in an evening gown to do a strip into a miniskirt and a halter, and from there into a bikini. And with the last bars of the number, he turned his back to the audience, still in his bikini . . . *If my friends* . . . slip out of the bra . . . *could see* . . . flip off the top . . . *me* . . . slip off the wig . . . *now!* . . . turn around and bow. Wearing nothing more than a very skimpy bikini bottom, he would then field questions from the audience.

That man did more to raise consciousness than anything I can think of, and it was due to his professionalism *and* the fact that he was gay all the while! But he wasn't without a touch of irony. He did this one number, "Always Someone There to Remind Me" with a baby doll, an illegitimate baby. He came out pregnant with this doll halfway through, and he was always able to find out if the base chaplain was there and almost always leave the doll in that poor embarrassed chaplain's arms—the implication being, of course, that this is the father. And they weren't gay audiences. Perry was considered a favored person, a darling, as it were. Talk about improved morale!

After a second tour of Korea and another at Fort Meade, I went back to the Presidio in Monterey to take intermediate Korean, where I made the mistake of having sex a few times with an E–2. About six months later he decided he couldn't get out of the military fast enough, so he said, "I'm gay. You want to get rid of me?" And they said, "Hey, you're gay, you're going to name everybody you know before we let you out!" And I was one of the people named. It triggered a major witch hunt, which netted some of us, but not many. But that some was a good two dozen.

They had people there—intelligence boys—basically grilling every-body, and if I hadn't had interrogation training . . . . That's what it was like—it was worse than an enemy interrogation. Of course, they were just after information; they didn't really care. I realized in the early stages that all they had was two people saying I was gay, but hearsay was enough to strip me of my clearance. I said, "Well, I can't be in any worse trouble regardless," so I became openly gay and went to the Gay Rights Advocates on Castro Street in San Francisco. I was dumb, but I wasn't stupid. I hadn't signed or said anything. And a couple of us went up, but I was regarded as the only case that really had any promise. It was a major story about then, the witch hunt in Monterey. It hit the major papers, and then our commander literally locked himself in the security vault and wouldn't come out. Obviously he was giving no statements.

It was hilarious, because people that basically wouldn't speak to me before, except to be civil, came out and clapped me on the back, and I'm talking straights here—atta boy, Droney, give 'em hell. Everybody in Monterey knew me. And the other thing was being out. I figured I could use this. It was June when the whole thing started, September when I left my class, and around January they'd sent me up to Treasure Island for my hearing. I was up there for two or three months, and then they sent me back down to Monterey. The final appeal came through in April of '81—and I was discharged, honorable. I was accused of homosexual acts and I said, yes. I didn't think that I had any business being kicked out simply because I was gay. If I had denied it in the hearings, I would have been denied my clearance forever and a day, which meant that I would have been scraping barnacles on a ship somewhere, and I couldn't see that. It wasn't anything I was trained for, and I probably couldn't have kept my rank for the simple reason that I would have been useless. And I said, "Well, the hell with this, I'll fight openly because everybody, including me, said I had a good case as an open gay."

I was a loner, but I was still popular. I had contributed to morale and to the well-being of those around me each and every place I'd been. That wasn't a problem. So we said, "Well, let's fight this openly." Aside from its being a negative presence, most people don't remember my case, which

I'm just as thankful for. What else can I say? I believe my case was used as a negative precedent in the Hardwick case, which, of course, failed. I have no way of knowing how much of that failure was due to me. All the time my case was in court, I was going to school on the Navy's GI bill, please and thank you, and they'd also given me, just the year before, $12,000 in a reenlistment bonus, which they didn't bother to take back. I worried about that, but if they tried that, they wouldn't have known much about contract law.

We went to federal court. I left at the federal court level, went to the court of appeals level here in D.C., and I got Justice Bork, Judge Bork. And in one respect, it was good because my case was quoted. Judge Bork used privacy, and I like to think I played a small part later in getting Bork shot down in flames. So, you know, there are some small jollies that come to you if you wait. Gay Rights Advocates funded it for the most part, but basically I've been poor as a church mouse. Going to college took most of my nest egg.

There are times when I wish that I had just gotten out and kept my mouth shut. But then I'd have to live with the fact that I could have done something and never even tried. Looking back on it, this is much better than that. When you're at the last judgment, it's not did you win that will be asked, but did you try to fight. You should still work for success on the theory that change will come or the job will be finished sooner or later, and just because it won't be finished in your time, that's no excuse for you not to keep plugging at it. So that's basically it. I won't say I haven't any regrets, but I think I have fewer than if I hadn't done anything.

It was funny, but last year at the Renaissance Faire, a person came up to me and said, hi, I'm so and so, and I didn't remember him, but he knew me from Monterey. I'd become rather a legend in the translator circles. Apparently I was the best the Navy had ever produced and all that good stuff, which, of course, was not the truth, not even near the truth, and in all self-deprecation I told him so. But it was still nice to know that I was a legend, and rather a favorable one, in my own time.

☆ ☆

"This little room ... [this] padded room ... I spent the night in there. I had to lie on the floor, bare naked. They didn't even give me a mattress."

ROBERT FUCCI

Age 42, U.S. Air Force, 1967–70, enlisted.
Undesirable Discharge. Present occupation:
librarian.

I was afraid of everything. I wasn't afraid in the sense of coward afraid, I just didn't want complications, and I grew up with a feeling of never wanting to ask a question because I never wanted a negative answer. As I matured, this became part of my gay life. But when I was young, I was a wallflower, the kid who knocked over the soda, the one who spilled the jelly beans. . . . I'd been trying to get in trouble since kindergarten, but I never got in trouble, couldn't get in trouble. It was, don't you understand, I *wanted* to get in trouble. Punish me, do something, you know, let's have some interaction this way. No, they found the books [porno]. They blamed somebody else. They found some way to fix it. I mean, it just didn't work.

When I got in trouble in the Air Force, I had this idea somewhere in the back of my mind, well, it makes no difference, they're going to bail me out. Going AWOL . . . It was really more than AWOL, because we were gone almost a month and a half. But God, I was such a good guy that the colonel didn't even report me AWOL for two weeks! No, thirty days, but finally he sent his lieutenants out for two weeks to check every bar in the city, every night, seeing if they could find me, because they just couldn't believe it. They thought I had been kidnapped.

I should have known from all my past experiences, though, that I was just too good a fellow to ever get in trouble. In fact, in the ninth grade, I found myself with the best-looking guy in class, both buck-assed naked, behind the school playing with each other. I mean, anybody could have— anybody could have found us while we were having mutual masturbation. I think it was at that time that the light dawned on me about my sexuality. I sat down and said to myself, "God, here's something I actually could do from beginning to end. Here's something I could be, and wanted to be good at it. Not the physical thing but the concept, everything, I wanted to be true. If I was going to be homosexual, because I hadn't heard the word *gay*, then I'm going to do it to the best of my ability, be the best at it, not hide in the shadows!"

The Vietnam conflict was hot and heavy, and my number finally came up. I got my I-A in the mail not two weeks later: "I-A, report for induction, you're ready to go." They sent me for my induction physical for entrance into the Army. Well, at that time, if you went to Vietnam with the Army, it was almost guaranteed that you weren't coming back. My dad's not an important man, but he's always been very helpful in politics in Yonkers; he knew this wonderful retired general, who wrote a letter to the draft board stating, "Here's a wonderful young man who's willing to join the Air Force for four years. Why draft him for two years into the Army?" Well, they thought that was a wonderful idea, so I went into the Air Force. When I went to sign up, I didn't tell them I *wasn't* a homosexual, I just didn't fill that in. I left it out.

Airman Fucci, U.S. Air Force, 1967

"Air Force, here I come!" I stepped off the bus that had delivered us to our basic camp, right into this big puddle of mud, and should have known from that minute on, it was going to be downhill. . . . I kept getting in a lot of trouble. In basic training they all picked on these poor straight guys that had lisps. Every guy picked on these two wonderful young men that just happened to be in the wrong place at the wrong time. It was pretty sad.

The problem seems to be, whenever you get a lot of straight guys together, they talk about gay sex and conversations of a similar nature, more than gay people do. I've often found, I mean, with gay people, unless they're getting really campy, they don't talk about everything done in bed the night before, where with straight guys, that's *all* they talk about. They'll even talk about a blow job and make a big deal out of it. You know, *they're* the ones that grab ass in the showers or the ones you can hear masturbate in the middle of the night, but, hey, they're all true-blue, all-American, straight guys. Trust me, every guy that I went to bed with in the military *was* straight.

After my basic they tried to make me into a carpenter. Now, I came from a line of painters. I could have understood it if they had tried to make me a painter, but they didn't. They tried to make me a carpenter, and then as soon as I passed all the tests for carpenter, they put me in a temporary duty slot in the drafting section. Reason? I had gone to college and had taken some drafting, and since they knew about that, I was moved once again. I spent the whole time either surveying the flight line, which never moved but we surveyed it anyway, or taking little names and numbers off of survey maps so they could be fixed. That was my duty.

Then I fell in love with this nineteen-year-old boy. His name was Donald—you never forget them. He was wonderful, from Tennessee or something, a real cowboy. I got an apartment in town, and we lived together, slept together, but *never* had sex together. For four months I slept right next to this guy, never touched him. I want to tell you what the word *frustration* means! It was horrible. I used to write how I felt and then give it to him, wait for a reaction. Now, of course, I expected him to beat me up, but he didn't. He said, "Oh, that's very nice." It was no problem to him! He would walk around naked, take showers when I was in the bathroom—oh, what a bastard he was. He would bring his girlfriend over, and get girls for me. It was a horrible four months, horrible.

Meanwhile, I had to keep up my assigned barracks room, and they gave me a sergeant for a roommate. One night, I ended up staying in my room because of an early assignment the next morning. This guy was there. We knew each other on a casual basis. He asked me how things were with Don. I said, "Well, you know how it is." He said that it must be pretty frustrating feeling the way I did about him and not being able to have any sex. It probably would have changed my whole life had I not spent that night there. He basically told me that he "might be able to help me out." I was shocked, but to me that meant sex. I was right. He said, "Do you want to come up here or do you want me to come down there?" I was a little worried here. I said to myself, "This guy's a sergeant, I don't know him *that* well, sure he's been in the room all of this time and we're supposedly roommates, but who knows what his story might be." It was beautiful. He came down and we had sex all night, hot and heavy sex for me for sure, because it was like frustration city up until that point.

I had a lot of friends in the barracks. And before I knew it, guys were knocking on my door in the middle of the night, wanting to come in. I finally got my own room again. Nobody wanted to be my roommate, but plenty of people wanted to come and spend the night—they just didn't want to live there. Every time I had sex, every time somebody knocked on that door and came in, or somebody wanted to be my roommate for a while, or whatever the situation, or made friends with me and then we would end up having sex, I was always astonished, always. Yes, these were military people, lots of them, always in bed. Most of it just had to do with oral sex. There wasn't a whole lot of screwing going on. It was humorous to me that this guy on the first floor who *was* gay, but who kept saying he *wasn't* gay, was catching all the flak. He kept running around trying to be this macho man but obviously wasn't, and people knew that he wasn't, so he got the brunt of everything. Nobody really ever said anything to me. I never got hit or punched. It was unbelievable to me that I could be having sex so much without any repercussions.

I had sex, without exaggeration, with 99 percent of the guys in my barracks. They would come to the room as long as nobody knew about it. I got the whole gamut of usual excuses: I was so drunk, I didn't know what happened last night, you must have taken advantage of me; or if they woke up in my room, I only did it because he promised me favors, or money—every excuse you could imagine. I remember this huge, macho man, "Big Chevy," who used to ride around town with a gal on both arms and half a dozen more in the backseat. Every time he used to drive me anywhere, he'd make a point of telling me about his conquests. He'd say, "Oh yeah, I humped a girl in that apartment, and I had another one last week in that house." Well, once I screwed him in front of half the guys in the barracks, only I was so drunk I didn't find out about it for two weeks. Drinking had become an important part of my life at that time, so I was drinking very, very heavily. In fact, it took me two years after I got out of the Air Force to stop drinking.

Of course, when you are in the military, you drink. Most people would probably say it was because everybody else was drinking. There weren't any major programs against it at that time. It could get out of hand quite easily. The environment supported it. You know, cheap drinks, activities that were tied to drinking—it was hard to escape. I used to get up in the morning and have the other half of last night's beer, which I kept under my bed—this is like nine o'clock in the morning—buy a six-pack, take our ten o'clock coffee break, splitting the six-pack. Lunch, another six-pack. Afternoon break, another six-pack. Then I would go to the beer garden at four o'clock and drink all night. There were no restrictions. As long as you were there for work in the morning, they didn't care where you were the night before. I was pride airman, so I did my job . . . and did it very well, thank you, even with my rampant personal life. I took care of myself. I always did my job, tried to help everybody else. It was easy to keep my act together.

I was riding high and having all the sex I could possibly have wanted. Guys were making bets when a new airman came into the squadron of how long it was going to take before that person ended up in my room. I could have taken all that as derogatory, but none of it was ever meant that way, so I didn't. However, I was only really safe, and I found this out later, in my squadron. On the rest of the base, I had quite a reputation. My roller coaster ride began to get a little crazy, as did my drinking. My real trouble began when some of my buddies and I got quite drunk for several days and went AWOL. No one even came to look for me. We were gone about thirty days!

I decided to turn myself back in. They came right away with handcuffs, the whole big deal, and brought me to the jail. It's the only night I spent in jail, and I wouldn't even have spent *that* night had the first sergeant heard about it sooner. We were given permanent dorm guard, and they took away one of my stripes and fined me three or four hundred dollars. I could not believe that was all I got. I guess that is what set up the rest of my problems.

I think it sent a message to me that I could do whatever I wanted to do and there would be little or no punishment. So it was like, just enjoy today. Let's have a party today. Who knows what's going to happen tomorrow. Other homosexuals were being thrown out. I knew this—it was the word on base. People would point out guys that got court-martialed and say that they were kicked out for being queer. This was happening. It was like a witch hunt. Now, with this, any sane person, even a gay sane person, would say, "Hey, it's time to roll in the carpet, you know, go under cover." But no, not this one! Guys were trying to protect me, lie for me, even guys who weren't my friends, but sooner or later you knew these people were going to start saving their own asses.

I was soon aware of just how much was known about my activities. When I came back from being AWOL, they had already started a file on me. The OSI was sneaking around every corner. They called me in to ask me questions. I was staying off the base more and more, because I was getting flak from everywhere. I was getting kidded a lot in the barracks, not so much about being gay but about being in trouble. Then, for some reason, I was taken off of my job, my security clearance was pulled, and just all kinds of stuff, little stuff, started to happen.

Paranoia started to set in. Then I began having hallucinations, probably partially from the drinking, or maybe from not drinking as much. I had cut down a certain amount because I had to pay attention to what was going on around me. While at a friend's house, I had three episodes of hallucinations. The medics were called, and they took me back to the base. They strapped me onto this stretcher and stuck something in my arm. I floated through almost eleven days, and they never took me off the stretcher for three of those days. They put the stretcher in this padded room, no bigger than maybe eight by eight, with bars, which could have been a jail for all I know. This little room was one of those typical padded rooms one might see in the movies. I spent the night in there. I had to lie on the floor, bare naked. They didn't even give me a mattress. Finally, they gave me a set of pajamas, some little scuffy things for my feet, and a tag. I later found out that the tag meant I was dangerous.

I saw a psychiatrist, who gave me all these stupid blot tests and all that asinine stuff. When he was finished testing, I was sent back to my room and given a roommate, a guy who was an alcoholic and checked in every year for his drinking problem. This guy was a military policeman, so finally, I told him, right out, I said, "Well, you're just here to spy on me." I really had it bad, paranoia plus. But it gets better! The next guy they stuck me with was a kid who had just gotten back from Vietnam.

And to compound my problems, I fell in love. Jerk—here I was in the nuthouse, with another nut, and fell in love. And all he did was continually hold on to his damn guitar. Oh, he played it too, but never talked to anybody . . . but he'd reach into the air and grab things. There were some real wing-ding people there. And since this was the height of the Vietnam period, a lot of the people were just trying to get out of the service.

Once you got into the dayroom, you were with the real wing-dings, the guys who sat in the corner playing with themselves or banging their heads against the wall. There was another guy who kept ripping his clothes off and throwing his food all over himself—not a pretty sight. *One Flew over the Cuckoo's Nest* had nothing on this. And I'll tell you, I was there for fifty-four days, and after about thirty days, oh my God, I began to fit in . . . I just felt very comfortable. It was like being in a cocoon. . . . As for myself, they never really labeled it a nervous breakdown; they didn't label it anything. I only later found out that the very last sentence on my medical report said, "This man is not a homosexual." The psychiatrist said that I couldn't possibly be a homosexual because I had too many "other problems." Now that was rich! They tried very hard to find out what made me tick, but in the final analysis, I was normal.

Finally they told me that I could go back to my base, and within a week of my return, I found out that every single person I had ever spoken to had been questioned, that the OSI had pictures I had taken of these nude boys in Puerto Rico, had pictures of me walking around the base talking to other people, other known homosexuals, heaven forbid. I mean, they had a complete history of my life almost from the day I was sworn in. This one agent had more pictures of me than my mother did. He wasn't too crazy about me. But what was the difference? I didn't care at this stage. I got in contact with my congressman—I just wanted out of there. It wasn't bad enough that I was a fag, I was a *crazy* fag.

I was finally charged with associating with known homosexuals. That was the charge, period, and they said that I would get either a medical, because of what I had just gone through, or a general discharge under honorable conditions. And oh, how those bastards lied! A colonel called me in to read the charges and make his last statement. He told me they added the evidence regarding the nude pictures and decided these were more *pornographic* than just nude photos, and they also included my "known" homosexual *activity*, not just associating. These two charges changed the face of the discharge and made it an undesirable discharge. . . .

The OSI kept telling me that they did not want homosexuals because of this big security risk stuff. I said, "Well, how can you blackmail a person if everyone already knows that this person is a homosexual?" Now, if I were in the closet, had a top-secret clearance, and the Soviets decided to do something, I could understand that, but first of all, I never had any big-deal security clearance. I was just a little airman in an office with no access to any big damn secrets, and what I did know they wouldn't have wanted anyway. But even if I did know some big secret, I would never have committed treason, you know. Just because I was gay didn't mean that I would have sold out my own country. It's like they, the military, thinks gays have no conscience, no ideals, and no loyalties. But on the other side of the coin, if everyone around me already knew I was a homosexual, who was going to blackmail me? So I couldn't understand that concept. In fact, it's sort of the same reason why the regulation should be abolished. If everyone knows, who gives a rip? If someone is out of line, there are regs for that. Why throw out everyone just because they are gay? Dumb, really dumb!

They also gave me this garbage about, "Well, you know, it hurts the morale." I felt quite the contrary, it boosted morale. Let's be logical about this. If you stick a bunch of guys in a place where there are no women, or no access to women, what do you think they're going to do? They're going to beat each other up, beat themselves off, or they're going to beat each other off. Those are the options. And since I didn't see that much fighting going or single masturbation, I would assume that they were doing it with each other. Yes, I did have sex with consenting adults. As far as I was concerned, they happened to be in the Air Force, were adults, and I repeat, they consented. I mean, you know, it may have been wrong in somebody's eyes, but damn it, nobody forced anybody to do anything, that was for sure. There was no violence. I didn't need to advertise. It was like this chemistry occurred, an unspoken aura, what have you. Many people may assume you're gay, but sooner or later they will know you're gay, and so it just happens. No question. But understand that I didn't have sex with every single person I met in my life, nor every single military person. However, there were plenty of opportunities.

I was disappointed that the service wasn't as strict as I thought it should have been. They only became strict when they wanted to or when it was to their benefit. I was let down. I think my experience truly affected me. I had returned to civilian life as a totally different person than when I had left, and that was very unnerving. Still is!

Sometimes I felt that my patriotism got in the way of my understanding, if you follow my reasoning. I felt what I did in my free time was of my own choosing. I was, and am still, a very patriotic person. My sexual orientation had nothing to do with that patriotism and the essence of what I did. I mean, my undesirable discharge purely had to do with my sexual preference, nothing else, because I was a good airman, by their wording. I received accolades from them for being such a good airman. I was an asset, in their words, to the United States Air Force and to my country, which I was proud of for all the right reasons.

They certainly lost out, because I was willing to be a good military person and do my job to the best of my ability. In fact, I feel one of the better periods in my life was the first couple of years I spent in the Air Force. I really enjoyed it.... The last few months were sheer hell, affecting my whole adult life, and *that* was not necessary.

☆ ☆

"Our first sexual encounter was in the backseat of a Corvair up at this man-made reservoir ... I saw fireworks, you bet, no doubt in my mind. As a matter of fact, it was the first orgasm I'd ever had."

DARLENE GREENAWALT

Age 43, U.S. Army, 1964–68, enlisted. Honorable and Undesirable discharges. Present occupation: nurse.

I was raised in Missouri, and adopted into my aunt's family when I was six. They had three young boys. Well, my natural mother let her sister and her husband adopt me. And *that* turned into a dysfunctional family. There was child abuse and incest. My stepfather was responsible for the incest. In fact, I'm doing work right now on that. One always looks back and thinks it could have been one hell of a lot better.

It seems like the day I had finished high school, my mother had this Army recruiter sitting in our front room, I mean, literally! Obviously, this was a surprise to me. We never discussed it ... I think it was just a way to get me out of the house and let them feel good about it. Yeah, the recruiter went through her list of questions, which were all fairly simple except the one about whether or not I was a lesbian. And I said, "Well, what's a lesbian?" I didn't know what the term meant.

I thought a lot about why, you know, and what I was supposed to do now. Did I really have a choice about the military? Growing up in an atmosphere of abuse, I just kind of accepted things as they came along, so I went into the Army "as planned" in 1964. I missed my brothers a lot. And it's funny, because when I went into the service, they started acting out. They didn't have me anymore to take care of them.

In fact, I personally feel that my leaving *caused* them to act out. As a result, I have two brothers in prison—one with a life sentence, one on death row—and the youngest one is kind of a hillbilly. I never knew; my folks lied to me about their whereabouts. When I was in the military, I kept asking about the boys, and they'd say, "Well, they're so and so, married, living happily ever after." I never questioned that, until one day my dad told me one of my brothers was going to be put to death. But then, that's another story, for another time.

Going through basic was almost an exercise in rote memory. I just always did everything anyone told me, so it seemed to follow suit that I would operate that way in that eight-week situation. I'm sure that's how my first affair occurred in the military, just doing what I was told. She was the leader of our troop. She had actually enlisted at the same time, but they had chosen her as a recruit leader.

Private First Class Greenawalt
after gas mask drill, U.S. Army, 1965

She really bothered me. It was rather confusing, because I didn't know what I was doing sexually. My only contact with sex, of course, was with Father—darling Daddy—so I didn't really know. . . . In other words, when someone asked you for something, you gave it. That was my role . . . that was my role in the family. I didn't have a right to say no. I didn't have any boundaries. It really scared me. It scared me a lot. She kept trying to come to my bunk at night, take me to the showers, and do all this kind of stuff. I knew it was more comfortable than male sex. I related better. It felt more natural. I mean, I didn't have a great point of reference at this time. I didn't give a lot of forethought to it, but knew I liked it and wanted to continue doing it. Even with those feelings still going on, she was still a real problem for me. I didn't sleep many a night, trying to figure out what to do next if she came to my bunk.

She *was* rather horny. I'd like push her away. I said, "Now look, if I'm understanding this right, the recruiter asked me if I 'was' and I said I 'wasn't,' and I know that they throw people out, so why are we doing this?" Then I realized that whatever we did, it was all a big secret. We had to do it in secret . . . we couldn't share it, and since I knew that secrets were usually no-no's, that they were bad, that was probably one of the reasons they'd throw you out for doing it. And that woman did end up getting thrown out before basic was over. She made a pass at the cook, and the cook took a butcher knife after her! So they decided she wasn't real compatible with military service. Personally, I would have been a whole lot more concerned about the cook and her knife-wielding ways.

I went on to Fort Sam Houston for Medical Corps training. And while I was there I dated this fellow for a while. . . . It was like a brother-type thing. He kind of took care of me, you know. I'd never been treated like that before, so it was a new experience. I was sent on to Fort Riley, and he continued his tour at Fort Sam Houston but wrote to me a few times. He was the one responsible for introducing me to my first real lover. He had asked her to look me up when she went to Fort Riley, and that's how Charlie came into my life.

My position involved special assignments—airport transports and things like that. While I was at Riley I received a Good Conduct Medal and a Medal of Valor for saving someone's life. I feel it was something anyone would have done, but anyway, this guy was driving across this railroad track, was drunk, and a train hit him. His car rolled and caught on fire. I was the next car back, pulled him out of his car, and basically saved his life. It was a good feeling to be recognized, even though it was still something I didn't feel was unusual.

Anyway, after Charlie and I met, we started identifying gay people. The old seasoned veterans, the recruiters of the gay world in the military, like my sergeant, used to tell me it was easy to spot Charlie and me. I guess we never thought of ourselves as being obvious. I knew that I was terribly attracted to Charlie because she was real ... well, she was a farm girl just like I was. She was from Iowa, so we had a lot of things in common. I mean, we liked to skid cow pies and play out in the farmlands. We liked the same things. We became very close, and one thing led to another. Our first sexual encounter was in the backseat of a Corvair up at this man-made reservoir. This happened about three months after we had been going together. Even though that Corvair was small, we couldn't wait! I saw fireworks, you bet, no doubt in my mind. As a matter of fact, it was the first orgasm I'd ever had. It felt great, something natural to me, comfortable. She felt the same way—it was just as good for her. And from that point on, we were never apart, went everywhere together. If we dated, we dated with two men because of appearances. Some of the older veteran lesbians had gotten us aside and advised, "If you want to survive, this is what you need to do"—make good cover.

We were doing our own thing, but there was another side to this story. Several of the lesbians in the barracks were picking up on me, and since I had no "boundary" lessons when I was growing up, the "ask and ye shall receive" syndrome was still in place. I had several sexual encounters, but I wasn't the instigator. They would come to me and say things like, "Come on, I want to show you my apartment off base," and then the old buttons were pushed. They wanted something—okay. I would try to tell Charlie, "They don't mean anything. I'm just doing it because they want to." That took me a while to realize where those feelings were coming from, but I didn't have the insight of what the abuse in my home family had ingrained in me. So I didn't know what boundaries were. This caused a lot of conflict between Charlie and myself. She couldn't figure out why I wasn't faithful. Well, I didn't know what being faithful was all about.

Due to the environment, my inability to be faithful, and a whole bunch of other things, alcohol began to become a problem. Charlie had a hell of a time with me. She's had to carry me out of the bars on her shoulder, and she got so mad at me. God. But when I was numb, I didn't have to figure out all those things that were going on at that time. It may be hard to believe, but I was able to function very well on my job. I never missed a lick on my job. Working in the hospital wasn't the easiest job, with or without alcohol. My emotions were being pulled in so many ways—and the Vietnam wounded didn't help.

About that time, I went into a coma. I think my body just said, "I can't deal with this on a metaphysical level anymore!" I couldn't deal with it, I was burnt out, and my body just shut down. Every day, I mean, I was confronted with missing legs and forlorn looks. There were those young people that I'd sent over to Vietnam as medics, that had come back looking very old, disillusioned, traumatized, bitter, and basically destroyed. It was not a good time in the nursing field. I mean, it was real traumatic. I was on overload.

Even though we didn't go to Nam, we didn't escape the training. The women went through the Vietnam training too, you know. We went through the tunnels and the whole business. We had to understand how the landscape was in Nam. I remember when we were crawling through the tunnels, it was really scary. I felt as traumatized as if I were really there. I mean, it was real serious business. We didn't just go, "Isn't this a nice picnic, yeah, I'll crawl through that tunnel." I mean, they made sure that it was an emotional experience.

My patriotism was quite high at that time, but the experiences were so gut-wrenching. I mean, I was dedicated to the military. There was nothing that I wouldn't do. Charlie and I, our relationship, wasn't number one. It was the military. Whatever they needed, we were there. Charlie, in fact, was stationed at the hospital. She was on the OB/GYN ward when I went into the Med/Surg ward as wardmaster, so we worked at the same hospital. We used to sneak down to the linen room and give a hug once in a while. That was about the extent of our on-duty relationship.

I was actually discharged at Fort Riley. I finished my first enlistment there and received an honorable discharge. This was in 1967, and probably not a good time to get out, because the Vietnam conflict was really heating up at that time, and everyone in the medical field was greatly needed. But I had finished my three-year enlistment, and then Charlie got out two months after I did because she was two months behind me. I was still drinking, kicked around for about sixty days, and decided to reenlist. Charlie wanted to stay out, so she did not follow my lead.

When I re-upped, I went to Leavenworth, and felt that I needed to turn over a new leaf. I was going to be faithful to Charlie and live happily ever after, right? And then the girls started coming on to me again. And again, as far as I knew, I never did anything to solicit sex from any of those individuals. It was like I was in demand, if you can believe that!

Most of that action, the attentions were coming from the sports teams that I associated with on my new base. Yeah, yeah, because ball-team players were pretty aggressive—they simply came on to me. I was on a couple of Army-sponsored teams, basketball and volleyball. The teams were important in that it was always an excellent place to make lesbian-type connections.

I made my connection the first night I walked into my new barracks at Leavenworth. I walked in, put down my duffel bag, and this gal said, "You play basketball, don't you?" Those were the first words out of her mouth. And I said, "Well, yeah, I do," and the next night I was practicing with the team (they heard about me from my previous base, when I was in on my last tour). A member of my new team, an officer, started having some of the team members over to her apartment after games for *more* fun and games. Of course, alcohol was involved, and I was still involved with alcohol but was trying to control my use. She must have known my weakness, because she definitely plied me with liquor. There was this game called Twister, where you lay this sheet out and get all tangled up with the other player, and that, you can bet, was her favorite game. I think I could figure out why. Needless to say, I was invited over several times.

It was quite obvious that she was using her position for undue influence. Definitely. You were not supposed to fraternize, so you felt pretty special if you were invited over to an officer's quarters. In this particular person's case, she was expecting her guests to put out for the privilege of being with her. She was really pretty much of a lowlife as far as I was concerned. In fact, she started getting angry because I finally decided this was not the way my relationship should go with Charlie. I turned the lieutenant down, and she sought revenge against me.

It just so happened that when I recognized something was right, that was the end of the wrong. So I was real firm, no matter how drunk I ever got. All of a sudden—I was an E-5 at the time—I found myself on extra details that noncoms weren't supposed to be assigned, like picking up cigarette butts at 6:00 A.M. There weren't any more smiles. There weren't any more cutesy invitations to her apartment. That was all over, and the shit just started piling up on me. What could I do? I mean, you know, I couldn't go to my commander and tell, because she would probably deny it, and besides, I would ruin my own career if I did. It was a no-win situation, and she knew it best of all. So I let it go.

About that time, I'm sure the officer had disclosed her "suspicions" to the CID. Charlie and I began to be followed, and I was given even more extra details. She was also doing this to our friend Karen as well. I mean, we went to Kansas City on the weekends to the gay bars and came back and did our military stuff during the weekdays. God, it was ironic. In my job, I was about to be promoted to E-6, yet in the barracks it was a total switch—you know, every time I turned around, she was degrading me. This goddamn officer. I mean, you don't put somebody with that rank on detail. That's just not kosher. She had us on detail one day trimming the lawn edges. We weren't professionals, so we accidentally left the edges too long and the border too deep. Well, she came along, tripped on the "incorrect" work, and sprained her ankle. It was, no doubt, because her nose was so damn high in the air every time she saw us that I was surprised she didn't break her neck. I was *really sorry* to hear about her injury! Because of that, we got even more details.

I was also standing more inspections in the barracks than usual, getting reprimanded for having short hair—my hair was short but always looked nice. She'd come up, put her nose right in my face, and say, "Curl your hair." And trust me, *she* wasn't feminine at all! She was as butch as they come. I don't know how she could justify her actions, and doubt that she did, but it was getting pretty old. At the same time, the extra details, the little "How come I'm doing this?" routine, was starting a lot of conversations. All the privates were starting to laugh at me, you know. It went on for about three months.

The CID began to get further involved. They'd pull me out of work, and I had to say, "Well, I guess I have to go, Colonel." I mean, I was working for this colonel, and every time I was pulled in, which was often, it was very embarrassing. There were usually three or four men in suits. I was never given any rights, never represented. I didn't have a female person present, except for the officer, and she didn't offer me any support, because it was obvious that she was on their side. One time, they said, "Well, we need to search your car." I took them to my car, opened it up, and they searched it. They found nylon panties in my trunk. I used them to polish my car. However, they felt the pants were concrete evidence of my sexuality. I'm not sure what they thought the substance was on those panties!

About this time, I totally became a basket case and remember going into the hospital, real upset, so they put me on tranquilizers. I was just losing it all over the place. And I think at one point I said, "Charlie, I can't take it anymore." (It took me about eight years before I could even talk about this. . . . It comes back sometimes.) But I just said, "Charlie, I can't take it anymore. Please go in and help me out of this." So she went in and told the commanding officer that she was my other half, that we were lesbians, and that this needed to come to an end. Since she was a civilian, it validated what they had been looking for, but they also could not do anything to her, thank God! That basically finished my stint with the interrogations. But you know, oh God, before she went in for me, it was happening on a daily basis. Yeah, they were really putting the pressure on me. And I think they were trying to make me break because they couldn't find anything solid. They didn't have any love letters from Charlie. They didn't have anything that really could hang me. And at the same time, that damn officer couldn't hang me because it would incriminate her. But I think they knew they were getting close with me, yeah, somebody knew something. So it was pretty intense, and I was cracking. There was no way I could keep my integrity with all that was going on.

Everything in my life was suffering. I remember being really quiet. I wasn't nurturing my patients anymore. I mean, people were usually scared when they came into the dental office where I was working, and they needed me, but emotionally and mentally I wasn't there for them. I became isolated and introverted. I wasn't giving anymore. I could tell they knew something was going on, but I didn't want to disclose it in my workplace. And I think it was the day before I knew I was going to get drummed off the base that I told them I was leaving.

At the very end, in 1968, one year after I had begun my second enlistment, I signed . . . I don't know what I signed, but I remember signing a lot of papers. At that point I was so drained and emotionally spent that I didn't have any thought much at all. I just wanted out. They said, "You want out? Sign here." I signed all these papers and *then* they read the conditions to me. I could never come on a military base again, and my rank had been stripped, which really hurt. I think Oregon slugs have a better self-esteem than what I had at that moment.

I remember turning in my uniforms, dog tags, and getting my rank ripped off me. . . . I set my uniforms and stuff on the supply sergeant's counter and laid my dog tags alongside them, and she kind of turned around and walked away, so I put my dog tags back in my pocket (she was one of those veteran gays who had survived). She was obviously trying to say she was sorry in a quiet, unassuming way. It was a pretty hard, *damn* hard time, especially when they escorted me off the base. They had one MP in front of my car and another one in back of me. I was given only a few hours to gather my personal things. I drove my little car, stuffed with all my possessions, off that base, and believe me, it was real yucky. Nobody spoke a word. They said that I didn't have any rights, my rank was demolished, I didn't have the respect of the military anymore, and that I had to turn in all my medals. It was as if I had never existed, and with my emotional level at ground zero, I was not sure I wanted to exist beyond that experience, anyway. Then the bastards gave me an undesirable discharge. That was never mentioned when I was told to sign all those papers! Today, I have nothing except the dog tags I stole. I hung that damn discharge on the wall and threw darts at it.

I definitely was drowning my sorrows in alcohol by the time they kicked me out. Every step that I've taken since my discharge I've done in fear. I was really a good person in the military until that one day, and then I was nobody. So I've always felt a little bit less than everybody out here, and it's taken me a long time to get where I am. I held a lot of factory jobs. I couldn't cope with decision making. I was mentally devastated, actually. I couldn't do a lot of complicated tasks. I worked in production factories making butter dishes. And then I finally got up the courage to work in Hammond, Indiana, as a medical assistant and did a fine job. It renourished that nursing part of me. And then I started venturing out.

Once I began to feel good about my abilities again, I applied for a lab tech position, and they turned me down and said, "No. With your discharge, we're afraid you're going to recruit the females in the lab, and we can't have you working here." And at that point I decided never to tell anybody about my undesirable discharge again, until I went to work at the VA hospital as a registered nurse. I was afraid it could be used to blackmail me, so I told personnel about the Army and what had happened and had them check through all their legal books to make sure that it was okay that I work for the VA hospital. Since they couldn't find anything about it, I was privileged to work there for some time. It was a good way to validate my nurturing abilities that I thought I had lost.

At this point I still live in constant fear of this discharge. Right now I'm director of nurses at a nursing home and I'm in a pretty powerful position, and nobody knows any of my background, so I'm still keeping secrets. (If they read this, who knows what might happen!) So it's still scary for me that if they do find out, I'll be in the same boat that I was in in 1968—thrown out. So I'm still not safe. I don't feel safe. I'm involved in a metaphysical-type church now. I'm also presently in group and private counseling, trying to resolve my feelings involving self-worth, esteem, and my devastating military experience.

I'm leery, and except for my work, I'm isolated. I went into isolation about two and a half years ago because I was dealing with my family and the process needed to resolve the issue of incest from so many years ago. Yes, just a whole series of things happened, so I went off by myself, am still by myself today, but I'm coming out a little bit better now. You can't turn that [emotional] trigger off, especially when you open up the hurt. I'm not covering that hurt with anything, so I'm wary to experience my emotions through counseling, and that's a toughie. You know, you've got to be tough, but it feels pretty sad, going through all this healing process.

Even after everything has happened, I'd do anything to maintain my freedom. But if I were ever asked to go back in, I'd go, "Whoa, wait a minute. I'm not going through *that* again!" I'm still very patriotic. I would still fight for my country. I would fight only if I were given the respect and honor due me as a human being, nothing more, nothing less—the same respect given to the straight soldier. But unfortunately, the military isn't able to accept me under those terms. And I now realize, it's their loss, not mine. Therefore, it is not a good place for gays, even though there is no reason for their regulation against us. And because you're always hiding, it's not good, much less healthy. You're always under stress because you have to live in secret all the time.

But there's one positive thing that I can say about my experience, and that is that they didn't destroy me completely, although they certainly tried. They didn't take my dignity. I left with my dignity because I had finally set my boundaries and made people respect those, no matter what the consequences were. It was hidden from me for a while, but when I found it, I realized it was still there and still intact.

When I look back, it was so unreal, like a nightmare, like my family. It was all one big nightmare. Did it actually happen? I went from an alcoholic mother into an abusive family into an abusive military family, almost like a circle unbroken. But now, after several years, I will not allow those things to abuse me again. I value myself too much now. It took several years to understand that value and to get myself together, but I've done it and feel good about that. But through it all, I still wonder, will the fear ever go away?

☆ ☆

"They weren't going to have a goddamn Green Beret come up as a queer, uh-uh, that's armed forces; someone said that that's Air Force stuff ... those guys were queers anyway, oh God."

JAY HATHAWAY
Age 40, U.S. Army, 1971–76, officer. Dismissed Under Conditions Less Than Honorable. Present occupation: part-time teacher, doctoral candidate, and editor of gay periodical *Among Friends.*

I had had plenty of foreign travel because of my father's work with a petroleum company. I had plans of a military career at an early age, and undoubtedly the travel helped solidify those feelings. This was my goal in life: to attend a hotshot private college—and to pursue four years of a military career, which I knew little about. My father thought that going into the service was a good thing for his son. I think he was looking to me as, "This is my son, the military man, the future commander, every man's son, isn't this wonderful."

I knew that being gay in the military was taboo. When I joined the service, I think every person in any branch of the service has filled out the same form. They ask you somewhere in your medical history, "Are you now or have you ever been a homosexual?" I'd been to bed with men and suspected very deeply that was what I wanted, but when I saw that question, there was no hesitation—I lied. I nevertheless wanted to participate in sexual activity with men, wanted to meet other men that wanted the same thing, and thought I could keep my activities under wraps.

Once in the ROTC program, which was around 1966–67, there were a lot of protests going on toward the Vietnam conflict. I found myself getting more and more unhappy because I realized that I would be forced to get involved in this war, even if it was against my personal feelings, once commissioned. I was going to fight a war in a foreign land that I didn't want to have any part in because of those feelings. The recognition of the antiwar movement on my own, and my beginning to understand what the war meant for me as a person—not even for the country but just for me, Jay Hathaway—made me realize I didn't want to go to Nam. I didn't want to be a casualty, a victim of someone else's war.

As it turned out, my grades were not low enough to flunk out of college, but they were low enough to get me into the infantry. Yeah, being a second lieutenant in the infantry in 1970–71 wasn't the best choice, and everybody went everywhere else, but Hathaway got the infantry. So I thought right there, I said, "Vietnam, here I come," kind of like Robin Williams in *Good Morning, Vietnam*. I reported to Fort Benning, Georgia, for infantry officer's basic course. They lined us up and said, "You second lieutenants will not be going to Vietnam." In fact, they even had a special assignment for me. They said, "We have a job that would send you to the Defense Language Institute in Monterey, where you would take Italian for six months, return to Fort Benning, Georgia, for your jump wings, and finally to Fort Bragg for six months of Green Beret training. How does that sound? Then after which we'll send you to Germany."

Lieutenant Hathaway,
U.S. Army, 1974, Germany

My decision to say yes wasn't based on being brave, it was based on the language training and going back to live in Europe again. So while I was in my final phase of Green Beret training, oh my God, I met this private, E-1, who came from Puerto Rico. This became my first sexual encounter in the military. I was in my billet when I noticed him: one of those furtive glances that you have looking down the hall, cruising but not really cruising, when someone's looking right at you and you have to say, "Well, where have you been all my life?" It turned out that he was in my life for about four months while I finished my training.

It seemed we were fairly obvious. We were supposed to have had private pup tents, but mine was never private! I got told to cool it, because I think they may have felt something sexual was going on, but I don't know for sure. I suspect not. The military can be profoundly stupid on things like that. You could be having sex in front of them and they would say it was just two boys having fun. Their mentality sometimes, you know, if you give them an orange they'll see an apple.

After I completed my training, I told my friend good-bye, left for Germany, and was assigned to the 10th Special Forces Detachment Airborne, Europe Headquarters. At that point, like a fair number of healthy twenty-one- and twenty-two-year-old males, I was thinking of sex an awful lot—however, I was thinking of sex with men—but they kept me simply too busy to do anything about it. We did air exercises in Norway, the Middle East, Italy, and France. We climbed up mountains, down slopes, did mountain rescue, parachute rescue, and basically accomplished more things than John Wayne could ever have possibly done. And doing it quite well, thank you. I wasn't a macho troop like the rest of my unit, but I held my own quite well. So they didn't give us enough time to think about sex. We did, however, drink a lot. When we came down out of the mountains, our heads were out of the sky. So it was a good excuse.

About 1973, I began to make quite a few enemies rather rapidly, particularly when I became part of the staff. The most obvious enemies were those of higher rank and who had no personality, other than that of an orange. I had nothing in common with them. They might have been my superiors in terms of rank, but they were idiots. They were people back from Nam who wanted to turn Vietnam into a big fish tank, a parking lot, or at least a nuclear waste zone, and I found I didn't like them, and our post was small enough that I had to see them nearly every day.

I had to see their faces, they had to see mine. I thought they were ugly, they thought I was ugly. They thought I was a leftist, I thought they were fascist. They thought I was a commie, I thought they were motherfuckers. So we developed a real sparring attitude. They began to distrust me in general. I was known as a communist outspoken queer, even though they didn't know really that I was gay at that time. They just assumed that I was a communist, and all communists, you know, are queer, and all queers smoke dope. It was that kind of logic. That set it up. I was also the youngest officer by many years. The next officer who was anywhere near to me in age was almost ten years older. In this situation I felt more comfortable with those my own age, and they happened to be enlisted. So it only seemed natural, in this isolated situation, that I began to fraternize with some of the enlisted.

The problem one faces in this kind of unit is that one can only go by the book, and fraternization was against the rules. That was not helping my overall situation. One time, this sergeant who really disliked me . . .

got real drunk, stood up on top of one of the beer tables in the NCO Club, and said, "Hathaway sucks the dicks of all the enlisted guys." (*He* was enlisted, but I believe he was excluding himself!) Of course, I was immediately relieved of my job. I was told that any accusation, any accusation from any source at any time, is grounds in and of itself to deny me access to my vault, to my documents, to my work station. I was ordered in front of the post commander. He said, "We have an accusation that you're a homosexual. It's being investigated by CID, and you are not to go to your work station at the vault until we find out what's going on." I was quaking in my boots because it was true, it was quite true that I was gay, but I thought nobody knew, least of all this person. However, nothing was found in the investigation, so he later called me in and apologized.

About three months after that incident, I was in the NCO Club again, and the shit really hit the fan. People were getting drunk, calling me faggot, calling me queer. . . . Some of them were standing on chairs hooting and hollering. At that point one of the field grade officers came in and said, "Okay, this is it," and cut off the alcohol. Then he said, "Hathaway, you're to go home right now, and the rest of you people just continue with your party." Well, I didn't go home, I stayed there, because damn it, I wanted to stay there, and *that* almost got me court-martialed. Of course, this alerted the commander, who said something to the effect that "where there's smoke, there's fire." And unfortunately for me, although he didn't know it at the time, I had become very sexually active with a number of soldiers on the post.

I had been there almost five years and my tour was almost up, so I began throwing caution to the wind. I wasn't much into the psychological mating or lover relationship. Life was too frenetic, too much going on here and there, so it just didn't work for me. I'd gotten confirmation that I was going to be released from the service in August of 1975. At that same time, many started coming forward to tell of their knowledge about my activities, and the rumors began to get very sickening and painful. There were even some officers that started calling me queer out in the open. In one respect, it was making it easier for me to leave, but it did not remove the pain caused by these comments that were aimed at me. I didn't want to deal with them anymore. I just wanted to get out of there alive. But I couldn't go out quietly. No, not me.

This guy caught my eye about five days before I was to ship out, and he asked me up to his room for a "good-bye drink." I had seen him around and was somewhat interested in him, so I thought, "What the hell, why not?" One thing led to another and we were literally in each other's pants, when his roommate walked in and saw us in this rather obvious situation. He left very hurriedly, and I said, "Oh God, that's the last thing I need!" The next afternoon I got a call from the adjutant, saying that the commander wanted to see me.

It was short and sweet. He reviewed my rights and said I was accused of violation of Article 125 of the Uniform Code of Military Justice. And I gulped a few times and said, "Sir?" He said, "We can resolve this right now between you and me by signing the papers you see in front of you, which basically state that you resign for the good of the service under conditions less than honorable." And I said, "What does this do to my benefits? I've been in for five years, I planned on going to school. What about my benefits for that?" When he said that I would lose all benefits, I declined to sign the paper and opted for a court-martial. When that became public knowledge, literally the whole shit hit the fan.

It took eight months from the time I was accused to my final dismissal. During that time the military pulled out all the stops in their attempt not only to accuse me of sodomy and of being a homosexual but, in my opinion, to literally drive me insane. They used sleaze tactics—you know, if they couldn't get me on sodomy, they were going to get me on drug dealing or something like that. I found myself turning to Valium the doctors were giving me, but after a couple weeks I decided that was not appropriate. I couldn't think straight. It made me depressed, not psychologically but physically—I was drooling at the mouth.

I was outraged that the military could spring this kind of charge on me *four days* from being discharged. . . . I would have been out of their hair for life within a couple of days, but they didn't want to see it that way. I was assigned to sit behind a desk and do nothing else. It was not house arrest, but it was an assignment without a function. I was assigned to the S-1's office, which is administration, and as such I did nothing for those eight months.

My phone was tapped. I was also followed, shadowed by military intelligence, which resulted in an attack one night in a place not too far from where I was stationed. It was known that I had been in a very sensitive intelligence position within the unit. I was getting an intense amount of pressure from all sides. They wanted me out of Europe because it was their belief that I would give "secrets" to the other side.

The unit had gotten a nickname throughout Germany as the "Gay Berets" as a consequence of my court-martial, and on top of that, our unit was under scrutiny from the Pentagon for misappropriation of government funds, which was none of my doing. However, my case was good in that it was one more thing the Pentagon could use against the unit—this homosexuality—but along with those two charges, there was also a question of how some weapons got into the hands of the Red Brigade and some allegations in relation to misappropriation of vast amounts of government property. The government made me their whipping boy or sacrificial lamb for the Pentagon, covering their own butts at the same time by implying that, "Gee, if you take this person off our hands, we'll be all right."

I was given a series of sanity tests, neurological tests, where pins were stuck in my head—every time a pin went in, blood would drop, and they didn't even bother to clean it off of me. I went in for another battery of verbal tests, but fortunately—and *not* to the perceived view of the military—in essence I was a normal human being. Then, on top of all this, the military contacted my family against my will. They did not need this kind of crap, at least not the way the military presented it to them.

The whole philosophy was obviously to put me in as bad a light as possible, even though they had no real charges. You see, our unit, and particularly most Green Beret outfits, were very right-wing organizations. For example, they hated blacks, Jews, and any other minorities, so what was new about gays? As I see it, they could have drummed up charges even if I had been a member of any one of these minority groups. You know, when I think back on my unit, I realize just how extremely prejudiced they really were.

It was profoundly disturbing to me that there were no blacks; there were no "fucking niggers," as most of these men preferred to call them. Most Green Berets were from the South. I would venture that it had something to do with the legend of the dashing soldiers portrayed in all those old southern-theme movies. Of course, that does not dismiss my opinion that they were also desperately lacking in the brain department as well. They are a lot like the Marines in that respect. I never really saw anybody who was other than white, Anglo-Saxon, and Protestant in the Green Berets—neither from the lowest ranks to the highest. Those few blacks that were present were treated like dirt, like scum. In fact, there seemed to be a similar opinion about them that was not unlike the one they held for me.

Asian ancestry was pretty bad, too. Many of these guys had just gotten back from Nam, so any Asians that came through the unit were seen in that same context, as "slant-eyed gooks." They were prejudiced toward anybody who, in their personal view, took a broad approach toward what mythologically or practically we would call the American way— discussion and compromise. There was one way; it was their way, and if it wasn't done their way, then *you* were wrong. That's all there was to it. There were men there who had people like *Hitler* as their idols! I found these men to be despicable, and they should never have been allowed to wear the uniform. I personally don't care much for the military, but I found it rather disgusting that we would leave certain aspects of our national defense to those who viewed the whole system that we operate under to be anathema.

It may be no coincidence, or rather it may be a big coincidence, that George Patton was stationed in Bad Tolz, the same unit, the same post where I was. And it was from that post that he wanted to lead an attack on the Soviet Union in defiance of Eisenhower. And to make it even more coincidental, this post, during the war, was the SS Officers' Academy, and was now where Special Forces were located. . . . I'm not attempting to exaggerate. It was frightening and I didn't like it, but there was obviously little I could do. As a member of the Special Forces, it was very unwise to make too many political statements, and particularly not when you're being court-martialed. The collusion between these two [being politically right and fighting as a member of the Special Forces who he felt had nearly Nazi mentalities] in terms of attitude regarding right and wrong sets them off in a universe which was quite different from mine. For example, when I moved in as a green second lieutenant, I put up antiwar posters in my billet. I was told to take them down, not because they were illegal but because "we don't like them, boy." Therefore, I was a communist, or worse yet, I became known as a liberal. I'd never lived in an environment where you were physically threatened because you were liberal, let alone living in fear for your life for being gay.

I can speak from specific experience as the S-2. My job was to approve security clearances for personnel coming in, so I had firsthand information on the "Army's best" that were being rotated into our unit. Talk about crime—being gay couldn't hold a candle (as a military no-no) to what I was instructed to pass clearances on for those joining our unit. We had people in Special Forces who had dossiers with backgrounds of drug dealing, homicide, rape, and even murder. It seems to me those were pretty heavy crimes. Some of the crimes occurred in the military, some just before entering the military, and some many years before entering the military, but they were there. These people, in my opinion, were a little unbalanced, but you know, they'd gone to Vietnam, they'd purified themselves, were strong men, were clean, and could come back to defend the motherland. But when they came back, they were still rabid, mean, angry, vicious men. As I said, while they were ready to turn Vietnam into a nuclear waste zone, or at least pave it over as a parking lot, I was saying get out of the damn country. But I'm not going to say that they fought and their ends were glorious. Yes, they fought well (that's to their credit), and they fought honorably, which was also to their credit ... but that says nothing about the goals for which they were fighting, which I think were *not* credible. . . . People will probably think that I'm totally mad ... but if you're going to have an empire, you have to have an army. How can you have an empire without an army? So we have an empire and we have an army; it seems one follows the other. So I think, why have an empire? If we get rid of the empire, why have an army? Well, we're going to be invaded by the Russians. . . . Okay, fine—end of discussion, at least from their point of view.

I feel my observation about this unit only increased how deeply the total court-martial proceedings affected me. It was one of the most painful times in my life, because I didn't totally understand what was happening. I didn't appreciate the extent to which an institution would pull out all the stops for one person. I'm not talking about the Russians, I'm not talking about the Pentagon investigation. Their whole goal was to make me appear like a psychological, blithering idiot, a total incompetent, or one oversexed queer that went around screwing every male that walked free. When that couldn't be proven, they started doing the psychological things. I remember that sense of desperation I felt, where everywhere I turned, the military tried to smear me. If it wasn't with drugs, it was with booze. If it wasn't with booze, it was with unauthorized talking about military secrets. And if it wasn't talking about military secrets, it was my homosexuality. And when the whole trial came to a conclusion, the ACLU attorney said he'd never seen a case where they railroaded an individual quite as unfairly as I was railroaded. Every shred of evidence we submitted was rejected.

We questioned what was really on trial, who was on trial and why, and what it all meant. Was it sodomy, was it Green Berets, was it Special Forces? At the time, we were a bit befuddled, and I think part of me still is, but I'm sure part of the trial was to use me as an example, a lamb to their slaughter, to show that these were things that one could not do in the military and get away with it. You can't fraternize with enlisted people, and you certainly cannot be accused of fucking them, especially if they're men.

We introduced evidence to show that officers fraternized with enlisted females and the government said, "That's okay because they're females." We introduced evidence that the prosecutor admitted under oath in front of the jury that he was guilty of heterosexual sodomy—defined in the sodomy statute as anything other than vaginal intercourse. He admitted in front of the jury that he engaged in oral sex with his wife and his wife engaged in oral sex with him, and then he said, "Yes, that was sodomy, but what this man is accused of is disgusting. It is not sodomy, it is homosexual." Then the judge made the comment, "I'll state for the record: This is *not* a trial about homosexuality. This is a trial about sodomy. You keep the distinction in your mind, because I am." Of course, then we tried to use the argument that the military was guilty of sex discrimination, because had I been a woman, I would not have been charged with sodomy at all, as the judge so aptly put it.

One of our attempts, therefore, was to argue that heterosexual sodomy would never be tried, whereas homosexual sodomy would be, and the judge said, "You're right, and in my opinion, I do not perceive that the prosecutor committed a crime." The bottom line was that there weren't going to be any fucking queers in "this man's Army," no intelligence people who were queer, no fraternization, and that I was going to be used as their example to drive that message home to anyone else who might be thinking about doing the same.

We called every active officer in Special Forces, Airborne Europe, to testify either on my behalf or against me, and figured that we cost the government *over a million dollars*. On top of that, I got paid for my own court-martial, which permitted me to take home over ten thousand dollars. I was dismissed. I received a discharge under less than honorable conditions. It was supposed to be effective the moment the judge said it was final. However, it didn't take effect until the last military court of appeals had ruled, which took six years, so I got my VA benefits all the way through that time. I was even paid for six months after the court-martial, until they tied up the loose ends. This was in addition to the money that I had made from the court-martial proceedings. It seems that it was a poetic but bitter irony. They were going to kick me out for being queer so that I would lose all my benefits, yet I was able to complete all my educational goals, with some money left over, for going through the court-martial. I guess that is why I still contend the words *military intelligence* should never be used in the same sentence.

They were so concerned about their image. You know—if you have an army full of "pansies," then Mom isn't going to want her son to join up for fear it might rub off. I could go on and on about all the threads that were coming together during my trial—the drugs, the end of the war, and of course, Matlovich coming out in the Air Force [see pages 151–55]. They weren't going to have a goddamn Green Beret come up as a queer, unh-unh, that's armed forces; someone said that that's Air Force stuff—Matlovich—those guys were queers anyway, oh God.

I got a little crazy at the end, after the trial itself. I slammed open the door of the adjutant's office and said, "I'm not leaving until I've had my say. You kicked me out of the service—there's nothing you can do to me, you fucking asshole!" I was screaming at him; then I turned, went into the colonel's office, and repeated my act. I said, "You're a bunch of motherfuckers!" I was very angry. I'd done nothing wrong. I was so angry—so angry because I felt totally out of control, or better yet, I had no control over any of the process. I was accusing him of being a bad American, using buzz words that I knew he wouldn't like—a rotten soldier, unqualified to hold the rank of a captain, and a shame to his unit. His ethics and those of the unit were that you didn't lie, steal, perjure yourself; you helped a fellow person in distress, and you didn't lead them down the wrong path. But this man had misled me several times with information that was inappropriate. I berated him and said, "You call yourself an officer? How can you? You're an absolute disgrace as an American citizen. You don't deserve to be wearing a uniform." These things were intended to really get at him, because he was proud. In fact, his sense of pride was really like the screen portrayal John Wayne made in the film *The Green Berets*. I mean, the guy had a huge poster of John Wayne in his bedroom, for Christ's sake! I think he was very taken aback by the bitterness with which I reacted to him. All he could say was "Whatever you do, don't be so angry as to tell the whole world of what you know Special Forces does to protect the free world." What he had done with that statement was take the wind out of my angry sails and put his burden of national defense on me, so I told him to fuck off. I just flipped him the bird and walked out.

I felt badly about the men who were truly my friends. The sad point to all of this was that some of those friends were hauled before the colonel and ordered not to associate with me. They were ordered to stay away from me, and to their credit, they disregarded that order and would actually sneak over to my house in the evenings to sit and talk. Unfortunately, two of them actually got bad efficiency reports because of this, for not obeying orders. Their careers were probably adversely affected by those reports, which undoubtedly decreased their chances of advancement.

My road has been a long one since I was dismissed. As I reflect on all that happened, I still considered myself a good soldier. I did my job and got great officer efficiency reports, except for the time when I was court-martialed. My performance was rated high, as high as you could get. As far as I am concerned, being gay was and is not wrong, so that's how I received the low reports, not because of my work. I also should say that I wasn't always the one seeking out sex during those four or five years. I mean that people who were either bisexual or gay (no, I wasn't the only gay in the unit) would come up to me and ask what I might be doing any particular given night. Sometimes there would even be a straight guy who would just want a blow job but all the while made it very clear that he "wasn't gay." And those were other Green Berets! It was not limited to enlisted people; there were officers as well.

You need to know that the whole ordeal changed my life forever. The court-martial completely altered my life, altered it one hundred percent! It made me angry at arbitrary authority and therefore, decidedly, an individual who wanted to "question authority." That's on a real basic level. It also threw me squarely on the side of individuals who wanted to rectify a bad situation. . . . In some small way I now want to contribute a little more of me to the unshackling of gays and lesbians wherever I am, in whatever community.

Presently, I publish a bimonthly gay and lesbian paper called *Among Friends*, and I'm on the Governor's HIV advisory council. With my VA benefits I was able to finish my master's degree, and I'm now working on a Ph.D. in German history. I also teach history on a part-time basis. I'm getting to the point where I want to learn more about this process that causes people to work so feverishly and "religiously" going about the task of excluding gays. I have a need to know why. What I'm learning and what I'm discovering about prejudice against gays, blacks, women, and other minorities still surprises me—how cruel man can be to others for things that these people have no control over. I'm sorry, well, no, I'm not sorry, I was born with this orientation, no doubt about it!

I know there was great personal growth. I grew up real fast. . . . As a result of the court-martial, I began to discover some inner strengths that I didn't know I had, one of which was perseverance, and what at first I thought would have been the end of my life turned out to be a magnificent new plateau for beginning again and reassessing my own position in life. I was in some ways and at some times almost killing myself psychologically, with many periods of doubt and self-hate. There was a tremendous sense of low self-esteem. What I felt to be correct, proper, and worthy of goal seeking had been crushed and stomped. They were basically sending me a message that I was no good, and for a while I believed it. But fortunately, they never destroyed my soul, so I have been able to survive.

I can only hope for a change in the military's attitude, so other gays will not be caught up in the same psychological and physical turmoil that I was forced to go through. The gay spirit is a strong and resilient one, as evidenced by the many who have survived such travesties. We have a lot of work to do, but supporting each other is one of the first steps. We need to make a powerful statement of community by our very presence. We must be able to show this majority, this straight society, and in particular the military, that there is nothing wrong with any of us. And we won't go away. I hope that will someday come to pass, when the fact of our "okayness" is recognized and accepted.

And finally, just maybe in my case the real long-term up side will be for me to realize and appreciate not only the ability to heal myself but the ability to help others to heal, or at least let them see that they can help themselves to heal.

☆ ☆

"There was one "lady" marine, a lieutenant colonel, who walked the corridors of the Pentagon with more swagger than any of the men, and a colonel who walked with his military uniform coat pulled over his shoulder like some queen."

ALYN W. HESS

Age 49, U.S. Army, 1963–65, enlisted. Honorable Discharge. Present occupation: landscape architect. Retired because of AIDS.

I had an older sister named Adele, who was my best pal, and in the process of coming out I realized that that's probably part of why I was gay. Something seemed to happen whereby I liked my sister extra well. I was always such a little guy, and I liked to jump rope. I didn't mind playing with the girls because I'd been doing it for so long. Obviously, I was called "sissy" from a very early age.

I knew for some time about the fact that I was different from other kids. I didn't know what the difference was when I was in school, and of course, in such a little town, my mother and dad could easily shelter me. I was one of the class "twerps" in terms of weight and size. The older guys beat some of us up once in a while. Once, they beat me up, rolled me in the snow, mud, ick, and the mess ... it wasn't fun.

One of the other twerps became one of my best friends. I wanted him to invite me over to his house, because I'd heard that he and his brother took baths together, so I wanted to join in on the fun. I also understood that he had a "big one" and his brother, Glen, probably had one too, but damned if I ever got to have the chance to see.

My first sexual exploits were nil, to say the least. The thing that really got me was when I was in college and got a hold of some works by Plato and Socrates. Somewhere in the reading I came across the word *homosexual*. That's the first time I'd ever heard the word or even seen it written down. It was like a big old Chinese gong. It reverberated through me and upset me for several days. I thought, my gosh, I wonder if that's me. Maybe it *is* me.

In 1962, my college days were halted by the draft, but I really wanted to be drafted. It was a way of getting out of my hometown, because I couldn't see another way out. While filling out the necessary paperwork, the recruiter caused me to reflect on my past by asking if I had ever had any homosexual experiences. I said, "No," and I hadn't. I hadn't even masturbated at that point. It was silly, but I immediately remembered my first encounter, which occurred during my senior year at college. But I hadn't really labeled myself at this point.

Private First Class Hess, U.S. Army, 1964

It all happened when I went into this notorious public toilet in the basement level of the courthouse.... Finally, someone ... I turned around and realized he was motioning toward me, so I turned around fully. I couldn't do anything, so I walked right over to this man's stall. I had to take a crap, so I sat there, and he stood in front of me. I was getting embarrassed and started getting a hard-on. Stupidly, I played right into the situation, because they always say that if you mean business, show it hard. And I was. He unzipped his pants and pulled out his dick. I went, "Gosh, what does he want me to do with that?" My, my, my, would you look at that big, black, wonderful thing, so much bigger than what I had—mine was so dinky. He said, "Suck it," but I just couldn't do anything like that, so I grabbed it with my hand and kind of felt around on it. After that I got up and stood in front of him, and he proceeded to suck on my dick, but again, I didn't know what the heck that was supposed to be doing. Then he jerked himself off. I said, "Jiminy cricket," as all this white stuff started coming out of the end of his dick. It clicked that that was what I had when I had a wet dream. After he had left, I went back to my car, sat down, and had my own wet dream.

Recollection aside, I did get into the Army, and basic went fairly well. After basic several of our same platoon ended up in advanced training as draftsmen, artists, and illustrators for the missile school. We had all these artsy people in the same place, and such a faggoty barracks you could not believe. They put "our kind" in the Army band and in Special Services. And . . . all in one barracks—so we wouldn't contaminate anybody else, I'm sure.

During my first leave from advanced training, I went cross-country to Oakland. I walked around, got myself a place, and found the YMCA, and you know how those places are. During the night, this stranger, with alcohol on his breath, worked and worked and worked on me. I hadn't ever had anybody truly induce an orgasm while they were right there. He was relentless, and continued to work and work until I just couldn't hold back anymore. Finally, I erupted for what seemed like forever. It was so strange to me—though it didn't seem like it was anything I wanted to do, it nevertheless felt glorious.

The next day, I went on in to San Francisco. I was wearing my uniform but couldn't make contact with anybody. People were doing things that I should have known were passive, but I was too stupid or too naive to catch on to them. I stood out like a country bumpkin. It was not my most memorable trip to California.

When I got back to Texas, I was transferred to Washington, D.C., to the headquarters of the Army—the Pentagon. I was assigned to the "Army War Room" in the Pentagon, under the deputy chief of staff for military operations. This was *the* place where they truly ran all the military operations for the Army. In fact, one of my personal assignments was to plot the first bombing runs into North Vietnam. It was the very nerve center of the Army. Kennedy used this room when he was handling the Cuban missile crisis. It was exciting.

As I became more comfortable, I was amazed at how many gay people were around the Pentagon. There was a Wac, a beautiful redhead, who was a secretary. They always tried to pick the prettiest and the best to go to the Pentagon so that they could show off. They sent some very talented people there too, and what I was so surprised about was that most of them were in the same barracks. Some of these people would scream around . . . they were so far out: "Oh, Barry, I'm pregnant." They'd act like dizzy queens . . . they were such screaming ninnies. . . . There was one officer whom we called Miss Crystal or Lady Crystal. He would review the guard with his uniform jacket thrown over his shoulders, and we would start to giggle. It was so silly for him to mince around in front of the group doing guard duty at night . . . you could hardly keep from laughing because he was so effeminate.

I couldn't believe what I saw. There was one "lady" marine, a lieutenant colonel, who walked the corridors of the Pentagon with more swagger than any of the men, and a colonel who walked with his military uniform coat pulled over his shoulder like some queen. Frank Sinatra he wasn't.

Even as obvious as many of the military personnel were, there wasn't any great pressure to eliminate anyone. There was a bit of concern when Walter Jenkins got caught. A right-hand man of President Johnson's for years, he was caught in the "tearoom" of the YMCA. He had been caught but good . . . had somebody's dick in his mouth . . . sucking off an old, black janitor. We later found that out, because the fellow worked in the Army-Navy building. That was one of the biggest personnel bombs dropped while I was there.

However, I was more interested in the active gay life in D.C., so I got a gay guide listing places to visit in the area. I walked into this gay bar cold turkey. I thought "Oh gosh, what am I going to do when I get there?" I was terrified to walk in, but I knew this was where I had to be, and so I opened the door, walked in, and just stood there. I didn't know what the hell to do. There was an empty table nearby, so I sat down and waited. This fellow, quite handsome, winked at me, then came over and joined me at the table. It ended up we worked in the same area of the Pentagon.

One thing led to another, and we left the bar for his place. It was so wonderful to have somebody kiss you who wanted to kiss you. We became friends and then lovers, after a lengthy period of time. One day, I was so embarrassed by one of my friends, who politely told me, "Pull up your collar, your hickey is showing!" Here I was, finally in a comfortable relationship, and there were very few that could be told about it. I couldn't come right out and say, "Hey, I'm gay," for fear of being removed from the service. Even with all the obvious ones floating around, it was not a good move in one's career to speak the unspeakable.

In fact, there was this one guy that they *said* was gay. He was just a goofball, kind of a silly old farm kid. Maybe he was and maybe he wasn't, maybe the others just wanted to pick on him, but they let him get out [of the service]. He didn't get released until he had spent a couple of months mopping floors and doing other menial tasks . . . real degrading.

Even though it may not be evident at this point, I didn't honestly like being in the military. To begin with, I was psychologically torn up during basic training, because it was so rough and I had never been treated that way. Here I'd gone all the way through school, with my parents protecting me in our little town, and then off to a brilliant college that had challenged me intellectually . . . and then, wham!—the Army makes you feel like you are nothing . . . trying everything they could to break me down.

The military's a tough road and isn't for everyone, especially a gay person. Whatever a young person chooses to do, if it has to do with the military, and that person happens to be gay as well, *never* check the box asking to positively identify homosexual activity. The Army is so homophobic! Butch it up a little bit—it doesn't take that much. If you had witnessed what I saw swishing and flouncing down the halls of the Pentagon—the bull dykes and old fairies—honest to gosh, anybody can get through the military. Now, I'm not saying all my times were bad, but if I had it to do over again . . . I think not.

The Pentagon was my best assignment, but not enough for any career. I loved the summers, where I could sit in the center courtyard for lunch and cruise to my heart's delight. The Navy boys assigned to the Pentagon wore their whites and knew just how to have them tailored so everything showed off magnificently. It was beautiful, but do it again—never.

[AUTHOR'S NOTE: *Alyn W. Hess died March 31, 1989, from complications of AIDS.*]

☆ ☆

"You always lived in absolute terror. . . . Talk about Gestapo."

RUTH HUGHES
Age 48, U.S. Air Force, 1958–65, enlisted.
Honorable Discharge. Present occupation: youth health care coordinator.

I became aware of my emerging sexuality during puberty. I couldn't define it. I couldn't tell what it was. I knew I had an attraction for women or girls, but that was back during the forties and fifties, when homosexuality was not a subject one talked about. I would have these yearnings, achings sort of, to be with women and girls . . . to be close and touch them. I couldn't really tell what it was, except that I felt love. I'd think, "Oh, I feel warm all over—I like being in the presence of women." I think I actually became involved with the same sex around age thirteen or so. I was close friends with this girl, and we both became aware of our sexuality, so we experimented. We did dry humping. However, it wasn't until I was in my advanced military training that I had my first serious relationship.

During my formative years I was a rebel, but I would never have spoken out about my sexuality. Back then, I didn't know what the word *lesbian* or *gay* meant, even though I had a copy of *The Well of Loneliness*, and every good lesbian knows about that classic. However, after finishing high school and having little sexual experience, I pursued a military career, not knowing what would happen or how all these feelings would be sorted out.

Initially, my reason for pursuing the military was based on a family pattern. Several family members had been or were in the service, but I also feel the reason I went in was because my hometown wasn't big enough for my mind. I knew that I was a pretty unaware person about a lot of things, but there had to be more out there. I couldn't stay in my hometown—it was too small for me.

There was a certain amount of patriotism forming my decision, but it's not exactly the word I should use. I do, however, feel I'm a patriot. I truly respect and love my country. As an observation about patriotism, I was in England, attending a party given by a good friend. I was the only American there, and a woman came in with the American flag wrapped around herself. I had this incredible *rush*. What she had done was disrespectful. I said to her, "You know, you must take that off. You shouldn't do that—it's the flag."

Ruth Hughes, 1987, San Francisco

Overall, I *was* pretty gung ho in the military, but it was also the true awakening of my sexual urges. I think I was at my first permanent station when I met *her*. I remember noticing her because she had a warm face and drove a sports car. Every time I'd see her I'd think, "Oh God, there she goes." Of course I was aware of the regulation regarding homosexuality, because we were told about "queers." I mean, we were told that the homosexual was criminal, dirty, and the worst thing you could be. However, as for me, I still couldn't define it. All I knew was that I saw this woman and *liked* her. I would feel all fluttery. I mean, literally. Every time I saw her, my heart and stomach were fluttering, I got nervous, and my hands would shake. We finally got together on one of the many camping trips we would go on just to get away and be with "our own kind." The funny thing about those trips, which actually saved me later in an investigation, concerned how the women would pair off. There was never any physical touching, kissing, or whatever until each paired off in separate tents. No one knew what the other couple was doing. Well, let me tell you, I *know* what we were doing. It was so intense and was what I had been reaching for all my life.

You always lived in absolute terror. I felt I was careful in both my work and love life. There was that absolute terror of unannounced investigations of rooms, lockers, and so forth. How I survived I'll never know. Anyway, we were a hot item for about two months; then she got with someone else. Since she had whet my appetite, the rest of the time seemed to be a blur of women.

The service became an awakening for my sexuality as well as my racial awareness. At home, racial discrimination was never a problem, but it occurred in the military shortly after boot camp. I was going to my new assignment for advanced individual training at a school in Texas, and rode a civilian bus. I felt proud and cut quite a figure. I had my uniform on and my first stripe. Along the way, in Lubbock, Texas, we stopped at this little café. I'll never forget seeing this woman—the waitress—with that beehive hairdo. She had red hair—just like in *Alice's Restaurant*.

I was the only black military person in the café. This waitress took everybody else's order. I said, "I would just like toast and orange juice." She never said anything—she didn't make eye contact with me. Thinking she had not heard my order, I repeated, "Oh, miss, excuse me. Can I have orange juice and toast, please?" Without looking at me, she said, "*You* have to go in the back. You'll get served back there." So I said, "I don't understand." I remember this rush of feeling humiliated because of her tone and also for being singled out. When she talked to me, the whole place got real quiet. I said, "Oh . . . oh, I guess I'm in the wrong place." Then—*then* I started to remember, "Well, hmm, I guess it's segregated, and this is Texas-style discrimination." I went around to the back where this waitress had directed me to go and remember thinking, "I'm not eating anything that comes out of this place." It was filthy. It was the back door, like telling me to go back to the garbage cans to eat. I quietly went back to the bus and sat down. I felt *humiliated*.

Then something strange and wonderful began to happen. When people got back on the bus, they started handing me breakfast. An old woman gave me orange juice, a man gave me toast, an egg sandwich and coffee from another. They didn't say a word. For the rest of the trip, all was quiet.

I think about that now, and it makes me feel warm inside; to think about the humanity of it all. It was their way of saying, you know, "This is the only way we can rebel against this." Those people had a sense of humanity. I think my uniform had some effect on them too. I'm sure those people had a sense of patriotism, and it obviously drew on those emotions. And basically that was it, but it certainly made a lasting impression on me. I was getting used to this different attitude—minority, lesbian, whatever. . . . Things were starting to fall into place. I became a more aware individual—doing my job, and expressing my "minority" activities in secret.

No matter what we would do, though, it seemed investigations still happened with great regularity. It left an unforgettable memory in my mind. In one case, involving a friend of mine—talk about Gestapo—without notice, simultaneously, the investigators came to our base and went to her girlfriend's base at the *same* time, the *same* night. My friend was absolutely terrified. I remember it so well. They kept her—can you believe it?—under guard for a month. I mean, under *guard*, in the barracks. They took one of the supply rooms and made it into a brig. You weren't supposed to talk to her, but I was talking to her all the time. You were supposed to stay a certain number of paces behind her when escorting her anywhere. How degrading!

When they had the "drumming-out" ceremony, she had to put on her full-dress uniform and stand at attention in front of the commanding officer. Then, of course, the CO and the first sergeant cut the uniform buttons off and ripped the epaulets off. I know this all sounds like something from the 1800s, but it really did happen. My friend was shattered. The CO said she *had* to do it. It was awful, so humiliating and degrading.

My turn was about to occur, which came during one of my leaves. I went to visit my sister, who was also in the Army, and brought my lover with me. My sister asked if we were lesbians, and I said, "Yeah, so what?" She said, "Well, I can't have it in my home," and immediately wrote a letter to my military command telling them that I was a lesbian. She wanted to "help" me. Shortly thereafter, I was brought in for interrogation. I was preparing to transfer to my new station in Hawaii, and I was told, "You are not on the manifest and are to report to Building 313 tomorrow." I just *knew* what it was all about. Believe me, I prepared myself for the worst. I went out and bought red fingernail polish. I mean, I did the absolute stereotype of what would be acceptable. Everything. The next morning I was ready, but instantly thought, "Shit." I had really been sexually active, and just maybe they would get me, too. Yet even though I was afraid, and had a "sordid" past to protect, I performed magnificently.

Promptly at 8:00 A.M. a staff car, with two agents and a secretary, was there for me. Like I'm this criminal. I was in *supply*, for God's sake. One fellow was nice, the other was mean—just like you would expect. The one who was mean was real big. I'm only five foot three and a half, but this sucker was over six foot four. He said, "Get in the car!" In my sweetest voice I said, "Oh, thank you very much."

I was *nervous*. I had no representation, which was probably to my benefit, because it was illegal for them to deprive me of my rights. The big mean one threw something down on the table and said, "Look at this!" It was the letter from my sister. I said, "What is this all about? What's going on? What's the matter?"

Now for the plan of attack. I crossed my legs and pulled my skirt back. I thought—I'm ashamed of myself but I thought, "I'm gonna get through this! I'm going to survive. You people aren't going to do to me what you did to my friend." I was actually *flirting*. I flirted with the good guy. The other guy said, "We want to know about the people on this list." They had this incredible list of names, addresses, and telephone numbers. Not just people I had been sexually involved with but *all* the women I knew. It was *only* women. I played cat and mouse. "What is it that you want to know about them?" "Have you ever seen them do anything unnatural?" "Unnatural? What do you mean, 'unnatural'?" Then the big guy jumped at me. "Well," I countered, "I certainly don't mean to upset you, but I don't know what you're talking about." He said, "Don't act dumb!" "I *don't* know what you mean! Tell me what you mean!" He continued, "Have you ever seen any one of them kiss each other or do anything unnatural?" I said, "Well, you'll have to tell me what you mean by 'unnatural'—I don't know." The list was three pages long.

I was there two or three hours. They kept asking me questions and I kept playing dumb. Finally they said, "Look, there's a flight leaving at four o'clock. Cooperate, and we'll get you on it." "Oh, okay, fine, you know, this isn't going anywhere." They said, "Just take a lie detector test." "Oh, absolutely, I don't have anything to hide." They went out to set up a lie detector test, while I had time to think about it. When they came back and said the test was ready, I said, "You know, I don't really know about those people. I could be getting myself into trouble. Maybe some of those people have done those things—those 'unnatural' things that you're talking about. I really don't know." This guy—the big one—played it beautifully. He said, "This is— Aw, shit, you're disgusting." He walked out and slammed the door. The other guy just smiled and said, "I guess you can go now."

I was so frightened after that experience that it must have been four or five months before I socialized with *anyone*. I was really afraid. Later I thought about their comments—"Are you doing unnatural or natural acts?" It was strange how we really submerged our sexuality.

You know, because of the fear this type of experience instilled in me, I can say that I learned, certainly, a sense of discipline, developed an acute awareness, but also developed a sense of pride. It came from a sense of community pride and integrity. No matter how terribly we were harassed, it was still a home. I wasn't ready to go out into the world— so it was a way for me to be out in the world but have a sense of protection. I was able to be responsive and responsible to my comrades and superiors. It gave me a real sense of pride and a sense of structure.

There are some people who can benefit from being in the military, from being in a place where those parts of a person are really nurtured. I am a pacifist, so the idea of a military career is something abhorrent to me now.

In the final analysis, I can't emphasize enough that we lived in absolute terror of being found out. It would have been a terribly overwhelming experience. The devastation would have been excruciatingly demoralizing. It just isn't for everyone, the military. There is too much one must hide in order to stay in undiscovered. It's not worth it.

☆ ☆

"She starts trying to kiss me and I'm frightened, you know? But I felt like I couldn't move from the waist down, and so here I am lying in my sleeping bag and this woman is trying to kiss me and I'm flailing and trying to keep her off. . . . Then she starts touching my breasts . . ."

"JANICE"

Age 53, U.S. Army, 1960–62 and 1963–82, officer. Honorable Discharge. Present occupation: retired nurse.

As children, we really didn't have much exposure to boys, period, in our adolescence, and the girls, including myself, had crushes on the nuns. There's hardly any little Catholic girl brought up with the nuns that doesn't want to be a nun. I felt all along that there were two things that I wanted to do in life. One was to go in the military—in the Army particularly—and the other one was to be a nun. Well, obviously, I had to do the military first because becoming a nun would be a lifelong commitment.

I was always attracted to being on the ground—die with my boots on type of thing. I didn't want to be in the air. I'm afraid of airplanes and just didn't want to die in one—that's a terrible way to put it. Some things just attracted me about the Army. We had the recruiters come—all three services—when I was in nursing school, and I liked what the Army recruiter had to say. Everybody else liked the other two because their uniforms were prettier.

Once I finished my degree in nursing, I went in the military as an officer in 1960, when I was about twenty-three. However, I was only in a year and a half. I got an early out because I went in the convent. The Army tried to put me in the Reserves during that time, so I wrote them back and told them I didn't think they'd let me out to go to Reserve meetings. I never heard anything more about it.

When I think back on that time, you could draw parallels between the military and the convent. I see a lot of similarities. The structure, the uniform, and you go where you're told. You find a lot of ex-nuns in the military. But I guess the call to the military was stronger, because I only lasted the first year, which is called the postulancy. The thing that it really taught me was to love women, to appreciate women. They were such beautiful women. Everybody got along beautifully. My postulant mistress was a doll for that year.

I went back into nursing, and then I came back into the Army fairly shortly thereafter. This was at the time of the initial buildup in Vietnam, so there was a real need for qualified nurses. I didn't get sent to Vietnam but did have my first sexual experience with a male. Another Army officer. We just dated. And it was pretty satisfactory. I decided it was about time I did this—I was twenty-six or twenty-seven, or whatever I was. And then I went on to have several more male relationships. In fact, I had an affair with a priest. In secret of course. Very secret. We would swear off that we weren't going to do this anymore. I'd go to confession, and he'd go off somewhere to confession. And then he'd take me out again, and we'd go way off driving somewhere where we could dance, drink, you know? We'd drive all around the parking lot. . . . He was happy being a priest—he just couldn't leave women alone. We had a lot of fun. We really did adore each other. As I said, he'd run to confession, and I'd run to confession.

Eventually, my time to find out what real women were like was upon me. An old nun friend of mine introduced me to this other friend of hers. She said that this gal liked to camp. Once I met her, this Margaret says, "Let's go camping," so we did go camping in this fairly remote area. We sat there with a bottle of Southern Comfort (it's awful stuff—I have never drunk it since), and this woman is on one side of a picnic table and I'm on the other, and there's a fire and we're talking away, drinking this Southern Comfort. . . . Then all of a sudden she says to me, "Why don't you come over and sit on this side of the picnic table with me near the fire?" It was getting chilly so I said okay. Then she put her arm around me, and I thought, "What is this?" And then I said to myself, "Janice, you can handle anything." And that's the last thing I can remember until she was dragging me into the tent.

Whether it was from fright or what happened, I know that I was not able to get into the tent under my own power. It was like my legs were paralyzed. So she was helping me, dragging me into the tent, and I mean I was like paralyzed from the waist down. I would imagine it was from fright. I don't think it was like a blackout or anything. We didn't really drink *that* much. I wasn't a big drinker. She starts trying to kiss me and *I'm frightened*, you know? But I felt like I couldn't move from the waist down, and so here I am lying in my sleeping bag and this woman is trying to kiss me and I'm flailing and trying to keep her off. I'm turning my head and all that. Then she starts touching my breasts, and I said, "Nah! I don't want any of this! What are you doing?" I thought she was going to kill me—I mean I was very frightened. I said, "If you're going to kill me, just do it and get it over with." It was the closest thing to rape that I'd ever felt. That made her sit back. She probably had too much to drink too. She said, "Oh, I'm not going to kill you, for heaven's sake." Then I said, "Just let me go to sleep," or something. Then she said, "If you'll let me lie beside you with my hands on your breasts, I'll let you go to sleep." And I said okay, because I knew I couldn't get out of there. And it felt kind of pleasant. Well, by morning, I was *terribly* upset. I mean, I was in an anxiety reaction about what had happened, but believe it or not, she stuck by me and taught me the ways of lesbian love.

I was performing my duties and all that. Nobody knew. But I had gone on leave at some point, and while I was there I wrote Margaret a couple of love letters. For details far too involved to mention, she sort of lost it mentally, and when someone cleaned out her place, the letters I wrote to her turned up. Guess who was called on the carpet? This was like my first time, and was I scared! My immediate supervisor called me in first and told me. I thought, "Oh my God." I was a captain at the time, but I was still shaking in my boots. "Go see the chief nurse at one o'clock." The conversation from the supervisor was "We ask our men to resign for this, and you'll probably be asked to do the same thing." She didn't make any judgment about it, but she said that the letters were very incriminating.

So I went to see the chief nurse, who was a straight woman. She said, "I showed these to the chief of psychiatry, whom I know on a first-name basis. And he said these are definitely homosexual in content." I said, "Well, I did have an experience with this woman," but I said I had been going to see a civilian psychiatrist about it, and I said, "I am not a homosexual." And I sincerely believed that at the time. The psychiatrist did too, because he said, "I will have Dr. So-and-so check with your doctor, with your permission." I said, "Fine." Well, I'll tell you that was money well spent on that woman psychiatrist, because she told them no, I was not a lesbian. Whereupon the chief nurse called me back into her office, handed me the letters, and said, "It's all over. It's okay. You got the good word from Dr. So-and-so." I took those letters home and burned them. And let me tell you, I breathed a big sigh of relief.

From that point on, I felt a particular need to be careful. I got involved with another officer, who was so closeted—I can remember her saying to me, "We're not like those other lesbians. We're not real lesbians. We just love each other." We lasted for a short while. The military just wasn't real conducive to long-term relationships—at least not gay ones.

Then I met this other woman (while still with the closeted one) that I had been attracted to all along, who worked at the installation. She was a civilian. *Very* masculine-looking. She was sort of like my mentor, because my lover was so closeted and secret that she hid it from herself and from me—that type of thing. This mentor woman told me all about lesbian life, sort of took up where Margaret had left off, and eventually pointed out that I was a "fem" [meaning feminine in looks, actions, and so on], and that's all I could be, that there were fems and there were "butches" [meaning the opposite of feminine in looks and actions] and all that stuff, and that there were places where gay people congregated called gay bars. I had never gone to one at that point, but I certainly learned a particular view of gay life from this woman.

We'd meet at the tennis courts and all kinds of funny places. My current mate couldn't stand her because she was so obvious, so I'd meet her somewhere else just to "learn my lessons." I was trying to figure out why people were lesbians. Well, she had a bad relationship with her mother, so I decided all lesbians were women who had bad relationships with their mothers. Of course, much later I found out that this didn't hold true.

Well, my career went on with no more frights. I felt that I was really bisexual and was encouraged by my then lover to be that way. "It's okay if you go with a man. That's not being unfaithful. Besides, it's good cover." I also had a lot of traveling to do, but she didn't want to go with me. She had been in the military but was retired. She didn't want a committed relationship anyway. She realized it wasn't too practical with me traveling around. It seemed the minute I landed at a place, I would find me a lover within a week. I don't think I was ever single more than a week. Serial monogamy, you know. I went to Europe and I had a lover there—in fact, we lived together the whole time I was in Europe. But when I came back from Europe, I got myself into trouble. We were caught in a gay bar. I didn't go to gay bars in any area where I was stationed. I never did.

Some people led charmed lives, no matter what they did or what their rank. They just got away with things. Not anything illegal, but if I tried some of their tricks, pow! Somehow I wasn't so lucky. In this one particular case, I was not actually in the facility yet, so I went to this gay bar, but had mistakenly put the military stickers on my car and didn't know that they sent military police around to the parking lots of the gay bars to look for military stickers.

This was back in '69. . . . So I stopped in. Actually, it was a very innocent thing. I knew there was this bar out there, so this friend of mine from Europe said, "Let's stop for a cold beer." It was a real hot day. I said okay. We pulled into this place, and I saw the name and thought,

"Oops, I think this is a gay bar"—if I remembered the book or wherever the heck I learned the name. And I thought, "Well, this is okay." So we went and sat by the bar, and there's all these fruits hanging around—decorations. Pineapples, pears—everything, fake stuff. She said, "Do you think there is any significance to the fact that all these fruits are hanging by the bar?" I said, "Gee, I don't know. What do you think?" But when the bartender's boyfriend came and kissed us good-bye, we knew for sure! A few minutes later my name was paged on the loudspeaker, by rank, my full rank—Major So-and-so.

I went outside to the military police personnel, and they asked, "Are you alone?" And I said yes. They put me in the military police car. I kept saying, "What do you want?" But they wouldn't tell me. The next thing I knew, they had her out there too and put her in with me. "What are we doing here?" She got very haughty. Finally, one of them said, "Ma'am, that's a known homosexual hangout."

They took us to the base and unloaded us in the jailhouse. We were sitting on this hard wooden bench in the jailhouse, and the officer of the day came and essentially bailed us out. We immediately called our supervisor—who happened to be a lesbian—and told her we were caught in a gay bar. So we had to report in and see the chief nurse—sounded like a rerun! She interviewed us each separately to see if we were lying. Finally, she said, "We'll let you know." Well, they didn't let us know, and we were afraid to ask. We thought, "My God, are we going to get kicked out of the service for this? Here we're majors, we've got quite a number of years—about ten—I mean, we're career people."

I found out later that the officer called in was one of the most obvious dykes—later to be my lover—that you could ever see in your life. She looked like a man. But she had taken care of the commander when he had had a heart attack. Anyway, he thought the world of this woman. And I'm sure that he knew she was a dyke. So he called her in. Apparently, she was his confidante about a lot of things. He asked her, "Do you think those two are lesbians?" And she said, "Oh no. Not on your life." This is what she told me later. So she supposedly saved our careers. You *know* I kept my nose pretty clean after that.

Again, my lifestyle should have been obvious, though. I always had a woman living with me. Now, this is the one that supposedly saved my career—she was really masculine-looking. And I lived with her on and off for five or six years. Chased me all over the country. So that would be the most obvious-looking dyke for looks, if people were looking for a stereotypical dyke. But after some time, I wasn't attracted to that extreme kind of appearance anymore.

As the years rolled on, networking worked real well for me. That's right. Networking. I had friends in the Pentagon. If I was going to another assignment, I'd call up one of my friends and say, "If I go to so-and-so city, who should I be looking for?" And they'd say, "Colonel So-and-so, Major So-and-so." They'd give me the names. So I knew. And they would tell them if their friends were there, "Hey, she's coming here." So you walked into a place and everybody knew each other. We protected each other. When we needed an escort someplace, gay men and women would escort each other. I recall a lot of the lesbians, and some of the gay men—one of them was such a nellie, he was really so effeminate . . . but many were pretty obvious. I mean terribly effeminate or masculine. I mean, if anybody didn't know about us, they would had to have been deaf, dumb, blind *and* stupid. There were dykes in the Army Nursing Corps that were VERY obvious and really didn't make any bones about it whatsoever.

I'd heard about the witch hunts. I'd been told personally about them, but I never experienced a witch hunt. I was aware that these did and still do occur with enlisted people. In the old days, when we had the Women's Army Corps where all the women lived together, they would have the witch hunts. One gal would report that someone had made a pass at her. They'd get these young kids in and frighten them—they'd confess to everything. Tell who their sexual contacts were. Get everybody—lots of people—in trouble, sometimes even officers. So we were taught early on never to mess with an enlisted woman. And I never did.

Back in the sixties, when I first came in, the system encouraged lesbians, because you couldn't be married. Well, you could be married and stay in the Army, but you couldn't get pregnant, and they wouldn't particularly station you with your husband. So there were a lot of discouraging factors there to being a heterosexual on active duty. There was a large contingent of lesbians. Of course, I didn't even know about it at the time, but there were a lot. Obviously, we didn't have babies, we remained single. They didn't have to worry about husbands—whether we'd get married or not. In many instances, a woman who was not a lesbian would get the name and not the game—usually given by some disgruntled male!

The poor male nurses have had the reputation of being gay for years. There was not an opportunity for equality with the women for a long time. They got their right to a commission later on in the history of the Corps. Nurses were lesbians. But all kinds of military professions have gays in them as well, so it's not that it's particular to the Medical Corps.

We were never harassed. As officers, we were never . . . very rarely. I remember in Europe there was a nurse who was what we called a slut. She was a very explicit heterosexual who went with married men and slept with everybody and their brother—black, white, whatever, enlisted. But, boy, she thought there were lesbians in the nurses' quarters, and she went to the chief nurse, reported this, and got them all in trouble. And we got the word, "Watch out for her." It was years later that I found out what she did. It's not just some person whose morals might be questioned at that time—but what about the sexual adventures and how she carried on. And they were criticizing lesbians and gay men. Really!

We always did what was expected, dutywise. And it was expected that you would attend a majority of the social functions. You were indirectly—or directly—rated for your ability to participate in social functions. When you're in the military, you're on duty twenty-four hours a day. Social functions are a part of the duty also. You were expected to drink like a lady and a gentleman and hold your liquor.

I felt that the military actually supported drinking and alcohol. Very definitely. Oh yes, happy hour—a quarter for drinks. Sure. Happy hour practically every night. Drinks at half price. Maybe they were a quarter or fifty cents. For every hail and farewell, you were required to show up, have a couple drinks, mill around, and be social. No wonder alcohol abuse was running rampant. We never heard of drugs in those days. That was just not a thing in my generation. I never knew anybody that smoked pot or anything like that, but yes, there were a lot that had drinking problems. Some nurse did a study on it for her doctoral thesis. And boy, was that suppressed! I read it. A very heavy alcohol abuse problem.

In 1982, my career ended with an honorable discharge and full benefits. I retired as a full colonel, an O-6. I was very pleased by my achievements over those twenty years. When I retired, I was given the highest peacetime award—the Legion of Merit. It's the highest award you can get for somebody not serving in a war. I also received the award under that, the Meritorious Service Medal, and was awarded two Army Commendation Medals. Of course, getting the Legion of Merit was a big highlight—it was a great honor.

When I look back over my twenty years and what I have contributed, no amount of medals, citations, or letters of appreciation could ever replace the loss I felt to my total commitment because I couldn't be honest with people. You found yourself developing a close friendship with a straight person, and they were talking to you about their romances, their boyfriends, whatever—the intimate details—and you couldn't discuss that sort of thing with them in turn. You couldn't talk about your relationships, and that put—for somebody as open as I was—that put a lot of pressure on me. I'm not a very private person, and yet for twenty years I was forced to hide that part of me. Sure, I could have gotten out sooner, but once your investment becomes so great, it's difficult to walk away from it. To me, it was a tremendous personal loss. We are all human beings. Loving is only a small part of our person. Yes, it was a loss not to be true, open, and honest, for fear of military revenge. And I resent that.

As for my overall professional endeavor, I thought it was a wonderful experience. I loved it. I feel very fortunate in life that I had a job—or two jobs, officer and nurse—in which I loved both, loved what I did. I had a lot of power and I used it wisely. And I liked having the power in those commands, but I wielded it in order to gain benefits for my patients and staff. I didn't wield it in an unkind manner.

And probably, if I dug way down deep, I would have to say that I owe all of this to the fact that I *am* gay and that that gayness made me more aware and sensitive of the task at hand, and not dysfunctional nor ineffectual—a detriment to the completion of the military mission, as the military would lead you to believe. It also made me the kind of person I am today, more accepting, understanding, and cognizant of a world steeped in bigotry and bias.

☆ ☆

"... they grabbed us, put us in handcuffs, and locked us in a room without clothes...."

FLORENCE M. JANISCH

Age 46, U.S. Navy, 1961–62, enlisted. Undesirable Discharge. Present occupation: printing and graphic arts.

I have no idea about any association with anything or why I'm gay. I've just been gay for as long as I can remember. I was never brought out by an older person. It's simple: I've always been gay. As I recall, my first sexual experiences came at an early stage with a girlfriend who played an integral and intimate part during my formative years. She was a big influence in my life, and I even finished high school because of her. She went into the service and became a nurse. I decided there probably were some great benefits or she wouldn't have joined, so I joined up too. Quite honestly, it was a quick way of getting out of my hometown. I lived in a very dumpy small town of three hundred people. Shit, it was so small, everyone knew everyone's business. What with one store and one post office, it wasn't a difficult task. So in July 1961, I became a Navy boot.

I was on the recruit regimental staff, was the Protestant flag bearer, and did very well. I enjoyed the pressure, just loved it. During this time, everybody was so paranoid, no one would even discuss "the subject." Since we filled out a questionnaire upon entering that asked us about our sexual experiences and explained what would happen if they found out we were gay, everyone was really sort of afraid to come out to anyone. No one was sure who could be trusted. I mean, you could tell some of the other women were gay, but nobody was ever willing to admit outright that they were lesbian. When I went to Hospital Corps School, it seemed to loosen up a little bit, but still people were pretty guarded.

I had met Sue while I was in school. We were in the same barracks. After we got to know each other, we were too paranoid to do anything on base, so we'd go off base whenever we could, which started the development of a close physical relationship. It was such a sensual, heady feeling, something I had only toyed with when I was younger. Sexually, we couldn't stay apart but didn't know what to do about it. Rumor held that our best chance was to admit we were lesbians and we'd get quietly removed from the Navy, or so we thought.

Hospital Apprentice Janisch,
U.S. Navy, 1961

At this time the Bay of Pigs crisis was heating up, and everyone was extended for an extra year. After finishing Corps School and being on duty for such long hours, the idea of facing another year, trying to hide everything else that was going on in my life, proved more than I could bear. So what did we do? We left the base, absent without leave, and were gone for eight days. Although our sexual exploits for those eight days were unbelievable, so passionate and fulfilling, I began to think about our actions and decided this wasn't the right thing to do. "I'm not a deserter," I said. Well, she agreed to do whatever I wanted, and we returned to the base.

When we got back, I mean, they literally grabbed us. We had gone back voluntarily, yet they grabbed us, put us in handcuffs, and locked us in a room without clothes . . . they took our clothes away. I mean, it's pretty silly to lock us in a room *together without clothes*, don't you think? There wasn't anything worse, except to slap us in the face! I felt like an evil villain or some dirty criminal. I don't remember how long we were there. At this point in my life, I've rather blanked most of it out. I do remember they put us through all these psychiatric tests.

The Naval Intelligence Service questioned us separately, but I don't think the fact that we were gay had come out yet. They just wanted to know why we had left the base. I said, "To get away because I was going crazy." I guess they didn't believe me because they raided our lockers and confiscated our belongings. I had an original classic gay novel entitled *Women's Barracks*, in my locker at the time. Knowing the mentality of the NIS, it didn't take much for them to assume that I was one of those "disgusting, dirty, unnatural" kinds of women. They had taken everything we had, for Christ's sake. In fact, I had this real expensive radio that I later saw in one of the officers' quarters.

Once they had cleaned us out, the course of questioning changed. They asked if I had ever had a sexual relationship with a woman. I didn't quite know what to say, but I remembered that rumor about stating you were a lesbian, and that would be your ticket out of the service. After all I had gone through, I wanted out, so I proceeded to tell them I *was* having a relationship with Sue. Then things really changed—the questioning, the attitude, everything was completely different. They gave us lie detector tests, which she passed and I didn't. One of the questions—"Have you ever had oral-genital contact with a member of the same sex?"—almost made me choke. Their manner of questioning was disgusting and degrading. "Have you ever fucked your girlfriend with your fingers, and do you prefer a dildo?" "What's the matter with a real penis—too much for you?" They pressed on and on with the sexual aspect, like they were probably getting off on it themselves. They put me through a psychic evaluation and told me I was immature. They tried to convince me I was immature because I was gay. And the real corker—if I were mature, I would realize being gay was something one should know was abnormal, and be ashamed of without any question.

We were restricted to the base, and of course, everything was made public. When we would walk into the cafeteria and sit down, everyone else would get up and leave. It seemed we had some terrible disease or were like lepers. It was a terrible time, but thank God, we had the support of each other. There was no one else to talk to, no one else to count on—we had to cling to each other. After the response from the others in the cafeteria, we decided to stop going, because we didn't want to face anybody. It was just part of the torture, so to survive, we ate off the patients' trays in the ward where we were still working.

As a continued part of the punishment and torture, we were put on twenty-four-hour duty, so we'd hardly get any sleep at all. We'd work our regular job, on our regular floors, and then be on duty all night in the delivery room. This went on for a couple months, while they were continuing our investigation. There was no rhyme nor reason to it. They would tell us we were needed and to get our butts over to the hospital. I mean, one night I might be able to sleep six hours or so, the next night I might get one or two.

It was a no-win situation. I mean, there was no way to come out with anything logical at that point. Everything was very degrading. It was like one of those old war movies, when the traitor was being prepared for the drumming out of the corps, and all the other troops were standing by ready to cheer the ouster. They told us we were to receive undesirable discharges because of our confession and for having been absent without leave. They even dickered with that, too. They wanted a list of names, other gays I knew on the base. The funny part was, the only women I actually knew that were gay were officers. I mean, now, what good would *that* have done me?

The final drumming out was sort of . . . . My mind goes blank because everything was . . . there was so much pressure. I remember standing in line with maybe four other people. The officer in charge did the same to each one of us, one at a time. He ripped off my stripe and all my buttons. The whole thing was so horrible, so traumatic, I can't even remember if Sue was there or not. All I do remember is that I was standing there with a bunch of strangers. I had gone into the service with such a sense of obligation, duty, and patriotism, and it was like, what did I do to change all that?

I felt worthless when I came home, because I had been degraded to a point where my self-value didn't exist. I ended up getting a job in a mushroom cannery, because it was the only thing I could find with the kind of military experience I had. When I tried to use the service and listed the type of discharge I was given, the employer wouldn't even consider me. It was pretty damn discouraging for a long while. I felt like I was still being punished and didn't know what I was being punished for in the first place. It took a long time to rebuild a sense of self-worth.

The pressures of my ouster and the bleak outlook for employment caused me to turn to the bottle. I drank heavily for about four years, to the point where I became an alcoholic. I drank so much, I don't even know how I became pregnant. It was just a case of being drunk for a very long time and finding this one person who was halfway decent to me, regardless of what had happened to me in the Navy. I felt I had nothing of value to repay him with, so evidently gave him myself.

After four years Margo finally left me and got married. To this day, she has never gotten over how the Navy made our total relationship out to be a dirty, sick, unnatural union. My life spiraled downward, and I was at an all-time low. From the time of my discharge, my days and nights blended into one drunken fog. However, once I found out I was pregnant, something snapped, and everything seemed to turn around. It gave me a sense of duty, a sense of obligation. I had something to live for, knowing I was now the one responsible for a soon-to-be-born infant. If I hadn't conceived and had my child, I probably would have killed myself in a car accident or something like that, from all my drinking. So I quit. . . .

I worked three jobs while I was pregnant, and didn't ask anyone for anything. I paid for everything myself. When my son, Jamie, was three months old, I got a job with a company where I worked for fourteen years, and I've been working for my present company eleven years. Even with my work record of today, I'm still paranoid about someone checking into my Navy background and finding out about my undesirable discharge. I guess it still hangs heavy over my head.

The whole thing has changed me. . . . I can handle things that other people can't, get through things, get through tragedies, and come back, even after they stomped all over my emotions, all over what I thought was natural and right. I'm a survivor, and for what it's worth, the military helped give me that stiff upper lip. I talk of it now as an experience, a part of growing up, just something I went through, because I do feel it helped me to be who I am today. Once I got past the stigma of being a freak, of being cast out, and of getting over those hurdles, I can look back on it as a training experience. I look at people today, and they don't have that sense of obligation or sense of duty. I've always been a responsible person and I think that's why I've gotten to where I am, and I've done it all on my own. I think surviving was enough. The way the world is today, I don't owe anyone anything. I've gotten here on my own.

I still have strong feelings when our flag goes by and want to stand up and salute it. The Navy destroyed a lot of my youth, joy, and innocence, but through it all, I've never lost my original patriotism; I put my flag out on Flag Day. I realize that half the government is corrupt and most of it's bullshit, but it's my country, it's all I've got, and I'm going to stick behind it. And the Navy says there's something wrong with me because I'm gay, and they can still feel right about giving Ollie North full retirement after what *he* did! I guess that's the bullshit I was speaking of earlier.

Be that as it may, what is most important for you to understand is that I've made it—I'm a survivor. No one, not even the U.S. Navy, can ever take that away from me.

☆ ☆

"If I would have been killed in action, I could have been a hero and no one would have known that I was queer."

ROBERT "JESS" JESSOP

Age 50, U.S. Navy, 1961–67, enlisted. Honorable Discharge. Present occupation: registered nurse. Officially disabled because of AIDS.*

To this day, I remember the stab that I felt in the pit of my stomach when filling out my application for entrance into the U.S. Navy, as I came to the question "Do you have homosexual tendencies?" After looking around the room to see if anyone noticed that I had just gone pale, I checked the "No" box and thought about the absurdity of the question. Who, in 1961 (outside of a few freaks in California), would have been crazy enough to answer in the affirmative?

I had spent most of my twenty-two years up to that time trying to conceal my homosexuality and prove my masculinity. I saw those two aspects of my nature as being in conflict with one another. My very decision to join the Navy was in part motivated by a desire to demonstrate my manhood to myself and to the world. Surely no one would call me queer if I was defending my country. Surely no homosexual could make good in the military, could he?

I postulated that if I could do well in the Navy, I'd somehow put my homosexuality away forever. I set out to be the best sailor I could possibly be. And I didn't do too badly, either. Actually, it wasn't all that challenging. I made the honor roll in all three schools that the Navy put me through, advanced in grade as fast as the regulations would allow, and was selected as the most outstanding hospital corpsman at the Naval Air Station where I served for three years.

All these successes in a very masculine environment should have made me feel better about myself. But I knew that deep down inside I was still queer and that no matter what level of excellence I might achieve, if anyone ever learned my deep dark secret, I'd be disgraced and drummed out of the Navy. There was never a day when that thought didn't cross my mind, when I didn't feel like the world's greatest fraud. Each day the dishonesty of living a lie produced a little more self-hate.

When my four-year enlistment was up, the Vietnam War was just be-

---

*Parts of this interview came from a letter given by Mr. Jessop to the author.

ginning to escalate. Incredibly, I felt a "duty" to stay in a little longer because the need for hospital corpsmen was so great. Out of that sense of duty I volunteered for assignment to Vietnam with the Fleet Marine Force and extended my enlistment for fifteen months to cover the tour of duty.

That period was the most enlightening, provocative, painful, introspective, and change-producing time of my life. It was enlightening because I came face-to-face with the cold, hard realities of the death and destruction that are inherent in war. I saw what monsters it made out of the men who fought it, who lent their bodies as weapons, and who perpetuated the daily agony. I saw more effort going into covering up behavior that didn't fit the American image of bravery and righteousness than was going into living up to that image. I saw what happens to men who are placed in a situation where they must commit genocide in order to stay alive.

Hospital Corpsman Jessop,
U.S. Navy, 1962

Ironically, combat produces bonds between men that can be formed in no other way, and I'm sure that many of the marines that I served with loved each other a great deal. Though I never heard any of them use the word *love* to describe their feelings for each other, I know that in the midst of so much chaos and death there was an intense need to express love, affection, and tenderness as counterbalances. In such settings a hospital corpsman becomes physician, nurse, psychologist, and father confessor. I enjoyed the role and nurtured it and the men who seemed to need nurturing.

Not surprisingly, a number of very close and affectionate relationships evolved out of those times and situations. There were quiet, intimate talks late into the night, sometimes expressions of fear and self-doubt. Occasionally there was touching—a head on a shoulder or a chest, or maybe even a massage if the situation provided enough privacy. Though these were intensely erotic situations for me, there was never any overt sexual behavior.

Yet even in that situation, homophobia (a term I had yet to learn) raised its ugly head. Someone who was uncomfortable with the touching and affection that was observed reported it as homosexual behavior, and immediately I became the subject of an investigation by the Office of Naval Intelligence. As the news of the investigation raced through the company, I became socially isolated. Oh, how marines fear the accusation of homosexuality, whether directed at them or at an associate. Even if my buddies held no personal disdain or fear of my rumored homosexuality, they knew how severely the military dealt with queers, and they knew of the military's policy of guilt by association. I understood their withdrawal and forgave them.

Alone and without counsel, I stonewalled my way through the investigation, lying about homosexual tendencies and my love for men with whom I'd shared fear and foxholes. A few marines testified as to my good character, the excellence of my work, and my contributions to the morale of the company—as if such qualities were incompatible with homosexuality. However well meaning, they seemed to be saying, "He's a good man—he can't be queer." For once, the stereotype seemed to be working in my favor.

The investigator concluded that there was insufficient evidence to bring formal charges against me, and the matter was officially dropped. But the damage had already been done to formerly nurturing friendships. Further, I had internalized even more homophobia. Instead of feeling betrayed, I believed that I was guilty of betrayal—betrayal of the respect and trust that marines had placed in me when they had come to me for comfort from the daily terror of war. It did not occur to me that it was indeed my gay sensitivity, my innate nurturing ability, and my softness that had made it possible for them to establish a special (and nonsexual) relationship with me.

Full of guilt and self-loathing, and with no vision of how my sexual preference could ever be compatible with an open, honest, and moral life, I wanted only to die. When the next firefight came, and I stood up and ran through a hail of bullets (ostensibly to get to wounded marines), it was really a suicide attempt. If I would have been killed in action, I could have been a hero and no one would have known that I was queer. The five marines who had trodden the same ground moments before me had all died. Why not me? Instead of getting hit, I crashed through a bamboo thicket almost into the lap of a North Vietnamese machine gunner who abandoned his weapon and tried to flee. He ran into one of my own company, and while he was trying to separate himself from this marine, I became swept up in the madness of the moment.

I watched myself pull my .45, as if watching an actor on a screen, and put three rounds through the head and chest of the now unarmed Vietnamese. It mattered not that he threw his hands up to his face in a last desperate plea. I didn't hesitate.

I was brought back to reality by the screaming of the wounded marine I had "rushed" to save. Because I'd spent the extra time it took to kill another man, I was now forced to watch as a grenade slowly rolled under the shoulder of this severely wounded comrade. For a split second that felt like hours, I waited for the explosion. I had no way of knowing how long the arming pin had been removed from this rocket of destruction.

The explosion ripped at the man's back. Because of his flak jacket, his torso remained whole, but his arm flailed grotesquely at his side, attached only by a thin thread of skin and muscle. I tried to inject him with morphine to numb the excruciating pain. He was in severe shock and didn't know where he was. He was crazed. He would sit up with a jerk after each ammo burst from the continuing firefight. He was dying, and I knew it. To this day I can feel the pain of that moment. Had I not wanted to destroy my own life, could I have saved another? God, the guilt I feel is still overwhelming.

As senior corpsman with my company, I had always instructed the corpsmen under me that they were noncombatants—present only for the care of the sick and the injured whether American, Vietnamese, friend, or foe. I had strongly and repeatedly discouraged hospital corpsmen from engaging in combat. And now, after months of such teaching, in the span of a few minutes I had gone back on everything that I stood for. I had gone from suicidal ideation over my own homoerotic feelings to homicidal behavior. But worst of all, I knew that I had been in part motivated by a frantic need to establish my masculinity. All this because of homophobia, self-hate, and my own inability to see homosexuality as compatible with masculinity and self-acceptance.

When the firefight was over, the effect was amazing. The worst act of my life brought praise from all sides! Men who had steered clear of me since the investigation were now slapping me on the back and shaking my hand. The company commander and two other marines wrote me up for a Silver Star (the Navy's second highest award). But I vomited. I wondered how I could ever live with myself. That night I cried alone and wished there was someone else queer enough to hold me. I wondered if anyone would ever understand the conflict and anguish I was feeling.

After a few weeks I wrote a letter to my command declining the Silver Star before it was even offered. This was a very small first step toward the atonement that I knew I must make.

I soon returned to the States and was honorably discharged. I was so emotionally involved with Vietnam that it took me two full years to actually join the antiwar movement. By then I felt that I had fought on the wrong side.

I believe that it is very important that the American public never be allowed to forget that its gay and lesbian members have made (and continue to make) a valuable contribution toward the national defense. By doing so as a community, we expose the military's grand lie that we are not fit to serve.

In order to serve in the U.S. military, lesbians and gay men must live a lie and be in constant fear of exposure. That is destructive to the gay spirit. If they are found out, the personal and civil liberties of these individuals are reduced to nothing. They become nonpersons and are booted out, usually in disgrace and often with less than honorable discharges. That is destructive to careers as well as feelings of self-worth and self-esteem, not to mention personal dignity. Such is not an environment conducive to productivity or mental health.

The military not only oppresses and stifles its lesbians and gay men but it continues, by its internal policies and public statements, to perpetuate the image of unworthiness of our brothers and sisters. It seems to me that we are long past the time where we should be spending our energies trying to convince the military that we are worthy to serve. Rather, it is time for the military to start demonstrating that they are worthy of the incredible sacrifices we have made on their behalf in order to serve the land we love.

[AUTHOR'S NOTE: *On February 20, 1990, Robert "Jess" Jessop quietly passed away.*]

☆ ☆

"My sexual awakening came about so naturally. We didn't discuss our first attempts at making love. It was just ... so natural. I was not fighting it ... I didn't realize I was doing anything wrong."

CHERYL MARDEN
Age 42, U.S. Navy, 1966–68, enlisted. Undesirable Discharge, upgraded to General. Present occupation: unemployed.

I was born in a boxcar, somewhere in California. We spent our first years in California, living on welfare, until we moved to Wyoming. My mom was sent to prison for reasons that I never knew, and my sister and I were then adopted by a family that already had three grown children. They were taking in kids for extra money, so we were appointed to them by the court. It was a very bad situation—we were surrounded by abuse and alcohol and constantly moved about. Twice we landed back in one of those shacks. Believe me, it was not a good life, and the military seemed to be my only salvation, my way out of that hellhole.

I also knew from all I had been through that there was something missing in my life, a certain longing for comfort, something female. It was not to be gotten from my adopted mother, who paid more attention to all the men and women who continually flowed through our home than she did to me. After visiting the recruiter in town, my mind was made up as to what I had to do.

In 1966, I joined the U.S. Navy. It was there that I had my first lesbian experience. We met for the first time in boot camp. My sexual awakening came about so naturally. We didn't discuss our first attempts at making love. It was just . . . so natural. I was not fighting it, but then, I didn't realize I was doing anything wrong.

She had come from Illinois, and when we got our first leave, we went to her hometown together. I met her family and was comfortable—in fact, elated. For once in my life I felt like I really belonged. They were the farming type, one big, happy family that took to me like one of their own.

After boot camp we were still quite involved, but I was sent to the Great Lakes area for my Medical Corps schooling. We continued our relationship by long distance and plenty of spicy letter writing! As I felt from the beginning, it didn't seem that what we were doing was wrong, but soon my eyes were opened about how the military felt. I was doing well in the school, even though the love of my life was far away. I truly excelled in the program, finally being a part of something so important. I never thought about what was going on sexually, only that it was a natural feeling and nothing else, until word started to filter down about certain witch hunt procedures.

Hospital Corpsman Recruit Marden,
U.S. Navy, 1966

Soon there was word out about being careful, so I decided to cover my activities by putting up with the advances of the men at my base. It was a game with the men, and they were so willing to be manipulated. They were like warm puppies, you know. I was definitely not intellectually stimulated by them, but it was a game, and they found me attractive. I had a few lesbian friends, but due to military pressures, it was in my better interest to be seen with men, so I started dating the guys in my new unit once I transferred to Bremerton.

Meanwhile, I was further alerted to the fact that the military was specifically searching out lesbians. I was never blatant about what I was doing with women. It was always a certain look, or a certain feeling when I would meet another woman. Somehow, people think it's automatically a given that we can tell one another from the straights, like there's some kind of mark on our foreheads. If that were the case, why is it that the military can never identify us and always needs to force frightened young sailors or soldiers into naming names for them?

Anyway, I got frightened and decided to cover my tracks. I ran a number on my soon-to-be husband, but he was thrilled when we tied the big knot. After we were married, he certainly tried to show me who was the boss; he was so chauvinistic. He would grab my medical work and do it for me. It was getting a little old rather rapidly. I would pray for my duty days, when I was on call at the hospital, so I could sleep in the barracks, just to get away. It shouldn't come as a great shock that our marriage lasted about six weeks. After that I really started my other lesbian relationships.

Not surprisingly, shortly after our separation, letters I had received from one of my old lovers came to light. It started a witch hunt that involved another lesbian. She was interrogated, and because of threats by the investigative personnel, she implicated me. Suddenly she was gone, kicked out, transferred, I am really not sure, and, like, one day I was enjoying my duties, and two men from the Naval Intelligence Service came to my nursing station.

They cornered me and questioned me all day long. Like, "Have you touched another woman's breast?" "Have you kissed another woman?" I said, "Oh sure, my mom." The NIS was not amused. I thought they were originally there to give me a commendation. . . . I was blown out of the water. There wasn't any indication that this was what they wanted. Yeah, and they had my letters to the woman in boot camp. Then, after the interrogation, believe it or not, I was promoted. I was really concerned. I was still allowed to take care of the female patients, which was confusing to me. On one hand, they were saying, "No, you can't because you're a lesbian," and on the other, these same officials were allowing me to work on the ward. So why didn't they provide protection for the female patients, if I was such a terrible person?

Even though I was promoted, it did not stop the interrogation. I was called in several more times in the next two months. When it was all over, I was told to turn in my uniforms, given fifty bucks and a bus ticket back to Rock Springs, Wyoming. Before I was given the undesirable discharge, I was questioned at all hours, at all times. No matter what they tried to say, I continued to protect my friend, Cathy, who was strictly a platonic friend at the time. They wanted names, and I was not about to give in to their threats.

Cathy had been hurt in an automobile accident and was in the ward—which was how I met her. She received a medical discharge and was gone before they were through with me. Since she left before me, my whole support system was dissolved. Once that happened, the NIS really got to me. They were relentless in their questioning, and believe me, it destroyed me and my self-confidence. Everything I had earned to that point was taken away. Pure and simple, it wiped me out.

I was darn proud and believed that I was doing my country a service. This was during the height of the Vietnam conflict, and I was taking care of men who were wounded. . . . I was blown away with my discharge and the way they handled it, taking my uniforms, everything I had ever earned, as if none of it mattered. They robbed me of my dignity, my personal pride . . . and I was only twenty years old. To this day, I think I was punished unfairly. Probably my futile attempts at establishing successful relationships and my drinking problems were because of all that happened to me in the goddamn service.

I originally went in for the long run, the twenty years, the retirement benefits, and only served a little under two years. I liked it. In fact, I loved it! The discipline—I rejoiced in the military. I was fed three squares a day, given plenty of responsibility, which I relished, and was a go-getter from the start. I prided myself on being a supersharp sailor every day of my enlistment. The Navy chose to ignore all of that.

I would not advise lesbians to join, because there's a concerted effort to witch hunt us, then and now. One of their main concerns is that you're a threat to national security. Did I have secrets? No. It's the military, and you have to abide by their rules. No deviation—no *deviates!*

My life has been a living hell ever since I was forced to leave the service, but recently, when my undesirable discharge was upgraded to the next level, I was able to use the facilities of the veterans' hospital, and thank God for that. Just recently, I spent a year in the alcohol abuse program in the VA hospital in Roseburg, because I was half dead from drinking.

As I look back over my past, I shouldn't have gone down without a fight. It buried me. Fight the damn thing, because we have no rights the way the regulation now reads, but we'll never gain any if we continue to let the military walk all over us, the way I let it walk all over me while I was serving. Still, I'm not bitter. Before, I was and was obviously torn up by it. Now my feelings are probably due to the passage of time, because it's kind of okay. What I went through . . . it happened . . . part of my past. However, if my sad life as an alcoholic, my many attempts at suicide, and my failed relationships are any evidence of what the military can do to a young and impressionable sailor like myself, please, all you little lesbians, don't go into the military!

☆ ☆

"I went to Camp Eagle, which was the holding company ... I look up and see across the runway a fighter pilot standing ... a direct hit ... there goes his plane ... I saw this person get blown away ... my very first sight ... of the war in Vietnam."

BOYD MASTEN

Age 45, U.S. Army, 1968–70, enlisted. Honorable Discharge. Present occupation: Assistant Director of American Youth Hostel Association, New York City.

We were sent to Fort Ord for AIT. At Fort Ord, all the way along, you're a college graduate, you've been drafted, let's make you an officer. No thank you. I was treated with a little bit more respect in many ways, so that I was not ... I was not fucked with. They very clearly knew from the beginning I was a teacher.... I think in any basic training the most common term was *shithead,* but at the same time there were more innuendos than blatant names like *faggot, queer,* or anything to that effect, but they were all the way through the entire basic training. Then there were a couple of times I know were very clearly sexual innuendos made toward me by staff sergeants or people within the company, people who clearly picked out who I was in terms of my sexual orientation as being different.

There were thirteen of us who were held back, held back because we either wanted to go to OCS, didn't want to go to OCS but were picked for it. Basically, they never threatened, but they'd say things like, "Well, you're on your way to Nam, we're going to send you, why don't you go for it?" Again, no thank you. But finally, they shipped us to Fort Benning, Georgia, for NCO school. We had no choice on that one, so we were at noncommissioned officers' school in Fort Benning. This was a fast track to Nam, no question, no question about it. We were thirteen very diverse people—it was a new kind of close-knit feeling that I liked, sort of a fraternity.

Then I was shipped out. I spent six months in a company in Nam, with the 101st Airborne, the 3506. I went to Camp Eagle, which was the holding company, in country. I get there, the sirens go off, I'm told okay, this is the bunker. We run to the bunker, I look up and see across the runway a fighter pilot standing ... getting into his plane, when a direct hit comes in and there goes his plane. I saw this person get blown away. That was the very first sight, in a way, that I saw of war in Vietnam. That happened, right there. And the shrapnel! We got hit close to where I had just been standing. It was so hot, I had left my fatigue shirt lying on top of that bunker, and I came out to find it was shredded to pieces. Yeah, that was my welcome to Vietnam, and believe me, it opened my eyes. I thought I was going to die right then and there—it was frightening.

As luck would have it, my assigned company needed somebody to do all their records. I made up an entire years' worth of records and books so we could pass an inspection. I was entrusted with American money the officers and sergeants used at payday to play poker—totally illegal. There were people who were, as time progressed, court-martialed because of what I would call asinine reasons, things like they didn't— One of my vivid memories was of an American Indian who had been in the field for three months, came back, showed up at formation late, and didn't have his fatigue uniform starched and pressed—he didn't get back in time to have the mama san give him a clean set in order to make formation. Would you believe some asshole got so mad, he had him court-martialed! Reason: He was being surly and didn't do anything about his soiled uniform. Well, the way they did it was incorrect, but I know the story because I typed his papers. . . . On top of that, there was also a lot of discrimination against blacks in the company too. You know, job assignments, the way they talked to them—just basically cannon fodder.

Boyd Masten, 1988, New York City

Other discrepancies occurred as well. There were people who received Purple Hearts who were injured in the kitchen, doing KP. I saw all of that. I typed it. I did the records. I typed up the letters—"We're sorry to inform you that your son died honorably"—and I knew what was going on, and a bunch of other bullshit, lies, just more and more crazy things that happened in a combat situation. The amount of parents today that cherish the letters sent to them, that their son died in valor and glory . . . the knowledge that's come out today on what really happened to many of the men that died—it's not pleasant, it's not nice. And unfortunately, many of them, as you see in movies today, didn't die very well, didn't die honorably. They weren't heroes. American accidents, military screwups, where you bomb your own people, you know.

I was also assigned to this medical holding company while I was there. I took care of that company at nighttime, with a lot of crazy, crazy men who came back and were just loony tunes. They needed drugs. They needed drugs to keep them down, and that's what they got. I remember this one guy just walked into the commanding officer and said, "I want to go on leave, I'm going on leave, going back to Chicago." The commander said, "No, you just can't do that, you just don't come in here and tell me that." So the guy walked out, came back with a .38, and killed him.

I left Vietnam purely "by accident." I had cut my hand with a knife, and without the proper medical attention it became infected and as swollen as a football. They were going to fix it there, but for some reason it was too complicated, so they shipped me to a hospital in Japan. When I was getting my hand injury repaired, lying next to me was a professional football player who had both legs amputated, one of which was not necessary except that he wasn't attended to, so he got gangrene and had to have it removed, too. He had not spoken in like three months to anyone. . . . Here I was having my goddamn thumb repaired because I sliced it while peeling an apple, and that man gave his legs to a war without reason. I feel it was not as much of a total waste and a futility, as it was, what in the hell were we doing! It's the kind of experience where you say, this is totally fucked up, *totally* fucked up. Whoever thinks the military had their shit together—I mean, from the very start of it, you lose respect instantly.

Although I felt I may have appeared different from the other men, I don't think there was a question in any one of those particular friends of mine, if I were to ask them today, if I ever saw them, what they thought about my sexuality. I don't, at this point in time, don't know what they would say. It was never an issue, never brought up; there was never a confrontation. At that time survival was the important issue.

It brought a lot of feelings to light in terms of who I am. . . . "If you're going to be smart, you're going to keep your mouth shut and hands to yourself. And there will be a time and a place for a different form of who you are, but this is not it." I think there was a very clear indication from a couple of sergeants and people above me that they knew very clearly, and they were very protective of me, but it's taken many, many years to relate that to what's going on in my life and who I am. The Vietnam experience, to me, was the one solidifying period of time in which I had to honestly be who I was and put my objectives together. It changed me. There's no way you can have been in that experience and not have been changed.

I now work with the Gay Veterans Association. The mission has been camaraderie and finding out that we exist. The purpose is to say we served honorably, and that we're entitled to certain veterans' rights like anybody else. There's no reason for us to be discriminated against, so right now we're a service organization, very clearly a service organization. We're entitled to medical benefits, educational benefits, but specifically, we're entitled *not* to be discriminated against.

In the last two years, I have developed some very strong opinions, and the military helped me clarify those, because I see, hear, and now understand what people are saying about clandestine operations. What are we, fools? Of course not. For example, I think that man North is as much of a demented problem as we can get within our military structure. To have this man become a hero is one of the major complications and problems of how we see ourselves and our perspective. I believe North should have been given prison, lost all his military benefits. Who are we to excuse this kind of behavior? But there's a lot of hostility out there still to this day on what the military stands for. There's a lot of ignorance.

If you're in the military, you're under the control of the military, so you have to understand what the rules and regulations are and why they're there and what they're for. That doesn't mean you eliminate people simply on that basis, of sexual preference, because let's go back in history. Alexander Hamilton— Stop right there. You shouldn't have to go any further—one example is all you need. He was respected enough by the Continental Congress to become treasurer. It's a frustrating situation. We need to let people know that we do exist and we are honorably discharged veterans, and if you were dishonorably discharged for a reason other than misconduct, then we have to do whatever is necessary in order to become recognized as an honorable veteran.

One of my most devastating emotional experiences was Leonard's [Matlovich, see pages 151–55] funeral. His belief was that somebody has to be there. There have to be reasons to go back and identify who we were and what we did. He deserved to be horse-drawn to the Congressional Cemetery. He deserved the service, and Leonard would have been proud that the Air Force finally did something right. They finally did it. They had to be forced to do it, they didn't want to do it, but they did it right. It was a moment that drove the point home for me. It was a moment which said, "Okay, now you have to recognize that here was someone who did stand up for his rights." A gay veteran.

Veteran's Day, three years ago, was the day we got to march as gay veterans for the first time in the parade. Walking from the tomb of the Unknown Soldier, with Leonard leading the way—and I was carrying an American flag—it was like there was a perspective back there in my head. I could see this group marching across, coming into the assembly area, being the last people in the parade, carrying this huge flag. It was one of the proudest, most deeply moving moments of my whole life. I was going to be recognized as a gay veteran.

☆ ☆

"When I was in the military they gave me a medal for killing two men, and a discharge for loving one."

LEONARD MATLOVICH

Age 44, U.S. Air Force, 1963–75, enlisted. Honorable Discharge. Present occupation: Gay spokesman, activist. Officially retired because of AIDS.

My father was career military, so I usually tell people I was born in Georgia, raised in Alaska, joined the Air Force in England, and came out of the closet in Florida. So, I've lived all over the world. I came out at thirty. Up until that point I had been celibate.

One of the main influences for my going into the military was the Vietnam War. It was just beginning in '63 and I was—for so much of my life—afraid that there wouldn't be a war for me to prove my manhood. My father pleaded with me not to go into the military. He wasn't too keen on the idea.

I questioned that I was "different"; therefore, I had to prove that I was just as masculine as the next man. I felt Vietnam would do this for me. It may have also been a secret death wish. As I recall, I felt my life was miserable, growing up as a gay closeted person—and that maybe it *was* a death wish, a suicide wish. I'm sure that was the real reason for going into Vietnam so many times. I received the Purple Heart when I was wounded stepping on a land mine, and received the Bronze Star for actions in combat. But the suicide wish was not to be.

I was continually falling in love with straight men and continually getting hurt. I hadn't even hugged or put my arms around anyone other than family members until after I was thirty. It was a lonely life, not knowing other gay people.

I knew the military's attitude about gays, because I grew up as a military brat. It was just common knowledge that a homosexual couldn't serve in the military, but I never really knew the reason why. We'd always hear about So-and-so getting thrown out of the military for being queer. I can't even remember my father talking about it, but the kids— my friends—would talk about it. I had an absolute commitment to this country as a patriotic American. That's another reason I went in. I feel America is a divine country—we're truly better than the average bear.

During my first few years in the military, I invested incredible time and effort into relationships that were purely platonic, and was constantly getting hurt. I remember the first person I told that I was gay. He was my roommate in Florida. I was convinced beyond any reasonable doubt that he was gay, but he really couldn't handle it. One night I gave him a massage, and the next time I offered, he got upset and said, "No!" It made me have terrible nightmares, and I know those nightmares were probably about having sex with a man. I finally broke down and couldn't take the suspense of not knowing for sure if he was gay or not. I came so close to touching him in a romantic way. I told him about my feelings for him, and five minutes later he packed up and moved out. Literally. In five minutes, he was gone. That's the closest I ever came to committing suicide, because it made me feel so dirty. I felt, "Well, God, if that's the way everyone reacts when they find out I'm gay, what good is life anyway?"

Technical Sergeant Matlovich,
U.S. Air Force, 1975
(drawing by "Copy" Berg)

During these early years of service, I was always able to work and control my sexual feelings. I was in such horrible emotional pain, yet I still managed to do my job and do it well.

I didn't know anyone else that was gay. I'm such an old-fashioned person. I wanted "love, marriage, and the family," the whole nine yards. I was always looking for love, not just sex. I was merely seeking a relationship.

I had almost ten years of service in and knew something had to change. In the race relations class I taught, occasionally we discussed homosexuality. A captain in the class said he and his wife had stopped at this bar in Pensacola, Florida, but didn't know it was a "homosexual" place. He noted that every time he went to the bathroom, "fifty people would follow him in." I didn't know differently, but I knew I had to find out. I finally mustered up the courage and went to the bar myself.

I was like a yo-yo. I took two steps in and turned around and ran out, built up some more courage and went three steps, and so on. I was terrified that when I finally entered the bar, all the men would be wearing dresses. My stereotype of gay men was that they were always propositioning young boys. I had read about a gay man who was beaten to death with a candlestick holder because he'd propositioned another man. I was terrified that when I got inside, all those stereotypes would be there.

When I finally turned the corner and walked inside, I only saw ordinary-looking men and women sitting at tables. You know, there weren't even any young boys walking around. Moreover, *one* person could hardly get into the bathroom, much less two, or fifty. That night a million pounds left my shoulders. For the next few months, I went there on Friday and Saturday nights just to walk around and observe people. I was mesmerized. I decided that I had to get out of the Air Force. Why should I stay in the military and be unhappy when I could get out and be happy like all these people? I had found what had been missing in my life.

I was forming a plan. If there were some way of being open about my sexuality and remaining in the military, I would have done that. However, the final straw that pushed me over the edge was my two dogs. My supervisor wanted to switch my training assignments and send me out on the road for two weeks at a time. I was forced to put my dogs in the pound for two weeks each time. I decided there was no way I was going to put my dogs in the pound every time I turned around. How could I get out of such assignments?

So the dogs gave me the impetus to get out. When I told my superiors I was gay, they said, "Look, forget this whole thing. We don't believe it. You can't have a Bronze Star and Purple Heart and suck cock." My first sergeant said that he could not understand why the Air Force was going through this bullshit, referring to the fact that I was gay—and possibly skirting the issue—and that if they left it up to him, he'd get rid of me. He'd keep me in, and within six months I'd be gone. It was my biggest fear, that somehow they'd succeed in doing that.

My supervisor finally got around to relieving me from my job, saying, "Your very presence in the military will cause a collapse of morale and discipline." And then he put me in charge of barracks full of young airmen. "Two and two doesn't equal four here," I thought. They were trying to set me up. The first sergeant would go in on inspections and get people up out of bed in my presence. A lot of guys sleep in the nude, and he was trying to claim that I'd stare at them and make them uneasy.

Ironically, it just so happened one of the sergeants in my unit used to give nude swimming parties. Straight nude swimming parties. I told my lawyer about it. When my lawyer called him in and said, "Do you think homosexuals should serve in the military?" he said, "Absolutely not! Under no conditions!" He was then asked, "What about people who give nude swimming parties?" and the guy said, "What I do in the privacy of my home is my business and no one else's business." My lawyer's response was quite specific: "Exactly. That's what this is all about. The right to your private life."

After a while I was discharged, and my lawyers went to federal court, where they decided to hear the case but felt I should be discharged anyway. We lost at the district court level, although the judge didn't agree with the ruling. He said that the military really should reconsider its policy. The case went forward to the U.S. Court of Appeals, but it was sent back for reconsideration because the court of appeals wanted to know why—at that time—the Air Force had an exception to the regulation. As it turned out, I won the case on a technicality. The court awarded me $160,000 for back pay and promotion. I settled for the award and an honorable discharge.

It was all very rough on my mother. Before I was discharged, I called home and spoke to her. After stuttering and stammering for a while, I finally told her that I was gay and what I had done. She said, "God's punishing *me*, that's why you're that way. . . . You haven't prayed hard enough, you haven't seen the psychiatrist yet." Finally she said, "Your father will throw me out when he finds out you're gay, and he'll blame *me* because you're that way." My mother grew up Catholic in the South, from Georgia, and she just had all of her old prejudices. God forbid what religion has done to people. My father found out when he read it in the morning newspaper. At first, it was a terrible shock, but he's been the big champion throughout this whole thing. He's been great.

Then I really started living. However, to this day I have never had a long-term lover. On the wall I have a little sign that says STARFUCKER. Well, there are more starfuckers, those who would take advantage of one's position, than there are starlovers. I remember this type of person seemed to come out of the woodwork. I was in a bar in D.C. one time, and was introduced to this guy who I thought was the most beautiful man on earth, but all I got from him was "attitude." Of course, I was introduced to him as Matt. I got the message real fast and went on my merry way. About twenty minutes later, he came up to me, put his arms around me, and said, "Oh, I didn't know who you were"—and la, la, la, la. "I know who you are *now!*" Yeah, starfucker.

Yet I have no regrets and would do it again. Of course, there are things I would do differently, because hindsight's always better than foresight. I loved the career I had, and am proud I was one of the few who survived. In fact, the headstone I had erected in the Congressional Cemetery was for that career. I wanted to honor those gay veterans who are basically unsung. I chose the heading that reads, "A Gay Vietnam Veteran. When I was in the military they gave me a medal for killing two men, and a discharge for loving one," because the military can honor death and heroism but discharge for love. It just doesn't make any sense.

I didn't know I was going to get AIDS when I erected it. That's why my name isn't on it. I had planned on being around for a long time. As I said, I basically put it up for gay Vietnam veterans—lesbian and gay— as a reminder, because we really didn't have anything. Then I decided, since it was so expensive, I would just be buried there. My father thought I should add on the tombstone, "Mission Accomplished," because it would make the public aware of the contributions of gay veterans.

When I think of dying, if there had to be a disease, AIDS is the right disease for me. If I had gotten leukemia or cancer, I would have just died and that would have been the end of it. AIDS is a very political disease. There is and will be a lot of good coming out of the AIDS crisis. A lot of battles. There are many silver linings in the AIDS crisis. Medical research will be catapulted two or three hundred years into the future. If there's any one singular word to describe the lesbian and gay community's reaction to AIDS, the word is *love*. The reality is that before we meet, the only thing we really have in common is our sexuality. For this kind of love to come out of such a narrow beginning shows that we are truly a people of deep compassion, love, and caring.

Now that I'm coming to the end of my life, I don't think about relationships anymore. I have love all around me. It's a different concept, more fulfilling, more real. There for a while life in the gay community was a candy store. Well, it ain't a candy store anymore. I think it's much healthier now.

In all that has happened, I was one domino of many dominoes. There isn't going to be a single court case to change everything. It's going to take a slow process, like one domino falling against another. We should stop putting our efforts in the courts and put pressure on the Congress. The courts are ultimately simply nine people in Washington, D.C., that take five of the nine votes to make a change—but that can change in *both* directions. If we change Congress, then we've accomplished a great deal.

And it's coming. We just ain't tolerating anymore. We're not tolerating the way we used to. I have my dignity, my self-dignity. Some of us may be two dominoes, some of us may be one—that's all. I did what I could do.

AUTHOR'S NOTE: *Leonard Matlovich, 44, died of AIDS June 27, 1988, and, according to his last wishes, was buried beneath his headstone in the Congressional Cemetery in Washington, D.C.*
As his father said, "Mission Accomplished."

☆ ☆

"Having people kill themselves at the age of eighteen or nineteen or twenty years old just simply because of the person that they loved—it's crazy."

"PAT RICHARDSON"

Age 49, U.S. Navy, 1958–61, enlisted. Honorable Discharge. Present occupation: social services.

I felt like it was the thing to do, and I was very patriotic. It was accepted as okay in my family, you know, we had people in every war. Civil War, Spanish-American War, World War I and World War II, every one of them. It was expected that you fight for your country and be patriotic. . . . We were a middle-class black family, heritage Afro-American, American Indian, French with English. . . . It was also one of the best ways if you couldn't go to college or go away someplace. Certainly that was a way to be able to enjoy yourself and be respected at the same time—respected by your community. You're doing something that's taking care of the country.

I lived a lot before I went into the service. Since I was from New York, I used to go to the Village as a teenager. One could drink there when you were eighteen. Basically, there wasn't a big deal made about it. I was going to lesbian bars when I was fifteen or sixteen. It was very frightening, very scary. They were all Mafia-owned, everybody knew that. Everything had to be done in some kind of hidden way. Like you would walk into a bar, and even though it was a gay and lesbian bar, you would hear the waitress say, "None of that, girls." It certainly was not very free. It was a terrible era of social control. McCarthy's era was happening at that time, so everybody felt a need to be very careful.

It was also a very tough time, with people being very different then, as opposed to today. People were extremely into roles, and there wasn't any way that you could just strike up a conversation with somebody without your being accused of messing with somebody's girlfriend. It was very heavy and wasn't inviting at all. It was like, "We're going to beat you up if you're not. . . ." That whole role-playing stuff. It was separation. Basically, either you were totally accepted or you weren't.

Absolutely, I was aware that I had to change the way that I lived. I was very aware that I had to make some choices. The choices had to be community-approved. There wasn't any doubt in my mind. I realized that I could not have relationships that were very visible, because you'd get thrown out. It just wasn't worth it, losing all that time and energy. So when I finally went into the Navy, I had lived a lot, and knew there were many things that could not be said. I lied when I was asked the question about homosexual activities.

I noticed in my particular company there were lots of lesbians. I don't know—it's like you know who's who. You sort of feel it, you understand it, there's a general sense that one gets from your experience, and I had had plenty! When I was in, either you were totally and absolutely into a particular group or you were not. I was not. I was not in the group that was totally out and practicing. Being black, I was very aware of racism, and it was one of the biggest things during that time. People were not particularly friendly to black or brown people. The racism was extremely noticeable. It wasn't at all hip. That was a more blatant form of the separatism.

People made comments. I had white women who would not even begin to acknowledge my presence and they refused to sleep in the same barracks as blacks or other minorities. It was just really horrid, and certainly was exceptionally hard to figure out which one was which. Clearly it was racism, pure and simple. After all, it was only '48 when Truman made the decision and made integration begin in the military. It was only a few years after that that I was experiencing, still, a really heavy-duty hatred. Because that's how the United States was.

I remember when I went through boot camp at Bainbridge, Maryland, it was bad. All over. Maryland was really awful. I had a drill instructor who was from Georgia. I was on the drill team and had this experience of going out to do a drill at Annapolis (or somewhere around there) one particular holiday, and while we performed our routine, people made ugly comments about us being women in the service.

"Look at all those queers," or "Look at all those whores." You were either a queer or a whore. No doubt about it. Of course, there was always some kind of talk about what we were, whether we were niggers or whatever. After our performance was over, we walked into this old-time diner to get a soda, and everybody just stared at us. It was a pretty tense situation. I felt extremely vulnerable at that moment. I recall the manager saying, "I can't serve any of your nigger girls in here." The drill instructor got very angry and broke her drill stick over her knee. She could not believe that people could be so cruel and treat other human beings in that way. I guess she thought that northerners were a bit more humane than those in the South. Being a longtime career Navy woman, she had been removed from that kind of racism after leaving Georgia. But I remember it was scary being that close to people who hated you. You just didn't know what the hell they were going to do to you. Obviously, after a while, it became crystal clear that either way I went, I was not going to be in good shape.

There were other things. I mean, they were in my barracks—there were lots of women who were acting or practicing lesbians. There was a whole group of people who had somehow or another identified themselves to each other and were accepted. I was not one of those people. I think that part of it had to do with my being black, and part of it had to do with not knowing other ways. . . . But yes, it was done very openly. But my new base had a lot of squealers in the bunch. When I got there, twenty of my barracksmates were pulled out and rousted out of the Navy. They just kept disappearing.

I didn't know until after about ten people had left. Then the information got back, because they had sent some people who were very good friends of mine back home, and so you know at that point your mail was all censored. Mine was, anyway. The word did come back, and altogether twenty women were put out. I doubt seriously whether all those women knew whether or not they were lesbians. I think that, basically, they thought they were being friendly with each other. . . .

Mine wasn't the only barracks that was hit. Again, this was the early fifties, and there were witch hunts all over the place. But it wasn't only for lesbianism, it was also for those involved in radical politics—whatever that was. If you weren't a Republican, you were considered some kind of a crazy woman. There were plants . . . spies. . . . There were Reserve enlisted or Reserve officers who just came into our particular situation and were somehow explained away. They dressed a certain way, looked a certain way, and acted like magnets to those who were unaware. In other words, they were the people who were supposed to identify and attract these other people—baiting. And they did. It was really heavy-duty. People were constantly being found to be "unfit" or whatever other labels they wished to apply to them and were put out. I don't know how many of the twenty women were actually given dishonorable discharges, but a great number of them were. Others went out with bad conduct discharges and some, but very few, got general discharges under honorable conditions.

I was almost unconscious. You know how you get to be sort of numb? I did have friends and also dated men. Shortly after this particular action occurred, I got married. In fact, I was a Navy wife for eleven years. But even though I finally got out of the service, I was very cognizant of what was going on through my continued observations. Part of it, again, had to do with the psychological part of you that says, "I don't want to be a bad person, I don't want to be a crazy person." At that time lesbian and gay people were seen to be pathological. Marriage was probably a cover for me at that intersection in my life.

Certainly, most people did not understand at that age, eighteen, nineteen years old, that it was *not* bad. However, if you're told that you are sinful, illegal, and sick, as they put quite often in their presentation, then what was your protection? Unless someone else is there to give you some support, to say it's not you, it's them, what are you supposed to do? A lot of it was very difficult for many of us to deal with, to deal with the realities of the consequences. They wanted to embarrass your family, to disgrace your family because you had broken their rules. I think that a lot of people had no idea of what was going on for them and certainly did not put it into context of this being an acceptable way to live. People committed suicide because of those kinds of actions by the military.

One of my friends had been kicked out, gone home, and been rejected by her parents and then, with nowhere else to turn, took her own life. She could not understand why what she had done was wrong, nor why everyone, especially her parents, had rejected her, so she took what was thought to be the only option—suicide. It got back to the press. . . . It was pretty heavy. I know for a fact that people were set up for that purpose, seek and destroy, to hell with the consequences. A lot of women, like myself, got married in the service to protect their own sanity and their own reputation, not knowing that it was okay to be who you were. That just didn't come out. You were never given any kind of support for being yourself. It just didn't happen, no matter who you were. You had to follow these very rigid guidelines. . . .

During that time I also drank an enormous amount. So did most of my friends. It seemed that one of the ways you dealt with the constant contact with same-sex situations was to make yourself oblivious to it by altered states of consciousness. I have no idea why they continued to practice that craziness. It excited them and gave some people something to do. It was also in the whole scheme of things, the social control issues were there. How does one control this and that and the other? . . . Seeing people experience . . . people being persecuted because of who they were makes you older a lot more quickly than most people. Having people kill themselves at the age of eighteen or nineteen or twenty years old just simply because of the person that they loved—it's crazy. It isn't the person who loves who's crazy. It's the entire system that people continue to support that's crazy, knowing full well that it has no basis for its continuation. It's just strange. . . .

There was an enormous amount of guilt that was carried around. An enormous amount of sadness and persecuted people who tried desperately to fit in. There were problems with role identification—people just couldn't explain it any other way, their attraction to another woman. . . . You were suspect for so many different things. I don't think, for example, that my marriage was a conscious kind of a thing. I think for many of us we just wanted so much to fit in, do something good and right, to actually be the perfect kind of person that everyone had thought or talked about. You always had those kinds of ideals, those kinds of goals. To grow up and be the perfect person.

But my God, it was so sad to realize the lives that were lost, truly lost. Whether it was suicide or substance abuse, you know people just lost themselves. That form of social control, one that made a person sick because of the person they loved, it was just one of the saddest things I could think of, and that it's still happening is even sadder. There's obvious research that supports our right of participation in this life just like everybody else, without any apologies as to who we are. It doesn't come down to just a sexual attraction; it comes down to being a full, conscious, spiritual, psychic, physical experience.

I found myself able to relate fully, and that's what's most important. People go around saying, "I prefer . . ." or "You have a preference . . ." and so on. It misleads people into thinking that you wake up one morning and decide to be heterosexual or homosexual. That just isn't so. My feeling is that we need to be real clear about our lives being fulfilled in the most useful way, by being who we are and who we can be. It's okay for people to be heterosexual, but that isn't anything. In the black community sometimes people, either heterosexual or homosexual, will ask you, "What are you? A gay black? Or are you a black gay?" meaning, how do you identify? Do you identify as black, or do you identify as gay first? My response usually is that I have never gone up to another person and said, "Are you a heterosexual black, or are you a black heterosexual?" It's such a schizophrenic kind of a reaction or response. It's like you can't separate yourself from the whole being. It's sad that people want to make a way of gauging your loyalty.

So, as for my military career, I finally just said, "I can't deal with this any longer," and I left. And as for a young gay joining the service today, I think I would probably say, "Don't do it unless you want to put up with a lot of crap for the time that you're in there." It's unhealthy not to be yourself. When I left, I had to finally say, "I'm sorry. There is no way that I can be who you want me to be. I have to be myself." Some people are never able to find themselves. I was lucky and got out administratively unscathed. But on the other hand, people have to do what they have to do.

Unfortunately, I don't know if the regulation will ever be removed. I just can't imagine that all these people would become conscious at the same time. I don't think so. It could, if we put a little logic into the system and follow rules because they actually made sense. I would think that that might be useful. In terms of what is for our future, I believe that we are eventually going to win this struggle. I can't say that it's going to happen in four years, ten years, or by the twenty-first century, but I know that there are people who are committed and dedicated to making the changes happen. Whether it's in New York, California, or in Arkansas, I'm sure that it will have a unified, uniform response nationally.

You know, it's very hard for me to compare my being black and my sexual orientation. I don't feel very comfortable comparing those kinds of issues. Black people, it is true, have no way of hiding themselves, under any circumstances. However, I think that any oppression, any kind of bigotry, all of them are equal to one another, but it's not a comparison, it's not comparable. But I guess that I'm a principled, thoughtful person who considers every single thing that I can in making decisions, and that I work very hard not to be bigoted.

Recently, I was at the Congressional Cemetery in Washington, D.C. I was selected to speak on behalf of the National March Committee about our rightful place, as gays and lesbians, to serve alongside our straight brothers and sisters without prejudice or bigotry. And after that speech I was one of the first people to place a rose on the area that is going to be designated for the lesbian/gay unknown soldier. For that single moment, my sense of honor, pride, and patriotism shone brightly. I was proud—proud that finally, after so long, those thousands and thousands of lesbians and gay soldiers, quieted by so many hostilities and wars gone by, had at last been consciously recognized as "being there."

☆ ☆

"When I went out on a cruise with the USS Constellation . . . *I was introduced to the Connie girls, a group of gay guys."*

JIM WOODWARD

Age 38, U.S. Navy, 1972–74, officer. Deactivated, Honorable Discharge. Present occupation: county administrative assistant.

I avoided any kind of social relationships with females and really any kind of social relationship that would be the normal socialization during adolescence, and basically postponed my adolescence until well into college. During my junior year, one of my classmates came out, was the first person to come out on campus publicly as being gay, and that brought things to a head for me. I did make a decision—I would never lie about my orientation—but was not ready to come out and join him at that time.

My father was clearly concerned. He noticed that I was never dating and sat me down when I was seventeen or eighteen and said, "Why don't you go out? It's not natural. You should go out and you should date." There was not a lot of affection. It's not an affectionate kind of household in terms of physical touching. It was more of a respect, support, and loyalty approach. It was a Yankee, a very classic type of Yankee family. Little emotion but a lot of free thought and respect for one another.

I knew I was going in the military anyway. The papers included the security questionnaire with the questions, and I truthfully answered the one whether I had any homosexual relationships with a "No," and I truthfully answered the question of whether I desired to have such relations with a "Yes." It all got folded up and stuffed in an envelope without anybody looking at it. I went to naval officer candidate school. I recall a lecture we received about gays. He talked about it with a great big grin on his face ... something about how you might find in the shower, one day, one of your mates that seems to be getting a little bit too happy with all of the sexual organs there. He said, "If any of 'em makes an approach, you just grab him by the whatever and take him straight down to your commanding officer, and we'll take care of it!" The mentality, yeah. It was this Marine Corps major—what an ass!

Toward the end of my training, I was determined I was not going to leave Corpus Christi without having had my first sexual experience.... I got to know this civilian guy and spent a night with him, lost my virginity ... felt great. He was a very shy, gentle, slightly effeminate guy, and he enjoyed it as much as I did. We wrote a couple letters after that ... but no long-term relationship. The light had already gone on. I knew that I was gay. I had known for nine years what I wanted, I had just never had a physical experience. It wasn't that I was entirely unable to get it. Part of it was just like everyone else who gets raised with puritan traditions; just because you want and have the sexual feelings doesn't mean you have sex. But, oh, it was fantastic. And all we did was rub bodies.

Ensign Junior Grade Woodward,
U.S. Navy, 1973

Later, I met a lieutenant commander physician from the Balboa hospital. He invited me to go Christmas shopping with him and a few friends ... they invited us over to have treats, some brownies. I took a couple of bites and said, "Somebody put too much of something in here." They all giggled and laughed. And after a few minutes I started to feel funny. I was wasted. I went home that night with a hospital corpsman and had the best sex of my life.

When I went out on a cruise with the USS *Constellation*, there was nobody in the squadron I knew who was gay, but I did, within a couple days, recognize a seaman I had seen at a bar, and made contact with him. I asked if there were any of us around, and he said, "Oh yeah." That's how I was introduced to the "Connie girls," a group of gay guys. The highest rank was a second-class petty officer, and for the most part they were really flamboyant queen types, relatively young, mostly first tour. I was the only officer that associated with them at all. There were a couple of senior petty officers who took me aside and said, "Why are you associating with those people? You've got something going for you. You're an officer, you're mature, and so forth. Why do you associate with those immature little twerps?" I said, "Hey, at least those immature little twerps have the balls to stand up and be who they are." I just couldn't understand how somebody would be so paranoid as to destroy their lives by staying so deeply in a closet.

I had a streak in me that just wouldn't allow myself to be put down. I saw myself being as good as anyone else, and if they couldn't handle it, then it was their problem, not mine. And I wasn't about to let it become my problem. There was one night when a group of about half a dozen of us were headed back to the ship, and there was another group of enlisteds standing close by that started calling us fags, and believe me, I was ready to rumble. You do things out of character when you're on a cruise . . . there's an energy on a ship that makes you move. It heightens every sense you have. If you are prone to violence, it's going to make you more violent; if you're prone to be sexual, you become more sexual; if you are intelligent or duty-oriented, you become even more oriented in that direction. There is an intensity that's increased and you do things—or at least I did things that I would never have dreamed or believed that I was going to do. I don't think that I would have expected to be involved with the Connie girls. But I was. I would not have danced with a man in a bar where the shore patrol came on a regular basis. But I did.

One night, I was dancing with this sailor and limboed down toward my back, and he shimmied down on my face. All of these other guys who were not gay were sitting around going, "Oh, oh, oh," and "Gross." I just loved it, loved the heck out of it. The clincher was, this was not a gay bar. We usually took up two tables or so. Trust me, anybody who was at least on their second tour in the Navy would have known what was going on.

It was on this cruise when it became crystal clear: the blatant, open, institutionalized, active homophobic harassment and oppression. At that point I'd been in since July of '72 and this was August '74. Two years. I decided if this was the way the military was going to be, it was wrong, and somebody had to change it, and it shouldn't be up to the E-2s or E-3s to do it. It had to be the people with the college educations and the ability to do something on the outside, who would be able to live their life without the military if that's what it came to. Those who would be able to fight effectively. I felt these were the ones who ought to do it.

In the beginning, I wasn't sure what I would say. I had this fantasy I'd tell my commander about my orientation and say, "I just want you to know because I'm aware the NIS has been informed. I figure you are gonna find out anyway, so I want you to find out from me." It was something along those lines that I actually said when he called me in. He replied, "Well, I would recommend that you resign. You know we can't keep you in the Navy." So I said, "I'm not going to resign." And he said, "I want a statement from you." I went back and wrote a statement which essentially said, "This is to inform you I'm homosexually oriented, and I'm telling you this because of investigations of people with whom I associate and because of my background investigation for a top-secret security clearance. I will not resign, I will not be court-martialed, will not be discharged." And I wasn't. The Navy would be depriving itself of a competent officer for no good reason. However, he processed me through very quietly, left me on all billets, and was processing me for an administrative discharge. I, in my letter, requested an administrative discharge *board*.

It took about a month and a half for them to get everything done. I had one commander who really irritated the hell out of me during the wait. I was bull ensign, and as bull ensign they give you bars, big bars. It's kind of an honorary type of position. I was getting down to the last week or so and was still wearing the bars. This commander kept putting the screws on me to give the bars back. When you start getting short [end of enlistment], you can get 'pussy' [bitchy, even pushy] with assholes, no matter what their rank. One day I said, "You'll get your fucking bars back—get off my case!" I was telling him and everyone else, "Hey, I take no shit for this. I am what I am. I take no shit."

The code on the paperwork was: separation to inactive duty, active duty obligation complete. They weren't *discharging* me; they were *deactivating* me, like some frigging battleship. Effectively, as far as the Navy was concerned, it was the same thing as a discharge, because they wouldn't have to deal with me. But legally, they weren't discharging me, and there is a big difference between discharge and separation to inactive duty in terms of the perceived value and loss. If you're discharged, you clearly lose your career; if you're separated to inactive duty, you are still in the Navy and, technically speaking, can continue in your naval career. I said, "I'm gonna fight this. I'm gonna stay in."

That was 1974, and I've been fighting that battle in court all the way along. I signed some things and didn't sign some things. I talked to the commander and told him I wanted to challenge my separation, and he was much taken aback; at the time, it wasn't something anybody had experienced before, really, and they weren't prepared for it. "You want to what? You don't stand a snowball's chance in hell." It went to the same court of appeals that made the Matlovich and Berg decisions. After reviewing it, they said it should be reconsidered on the same basis as the other two cases, and the Navy was ordered to say *why* I was not retained.

The Navy came back and essentially said . . . I was retained, since I wasn't discharged.

The Navy argued that I was simply deactivated as a part of a poor standout [not performing well]. There was no poor standout; it was a bold-faced lie. My brother, who was a legislative aide to Congressman Gerry Studds on a postcard subcommittee, put in an innocuous request for separation from deactivation records from the Navy, and there was only one ensign ever deactivated. The statistics showed very clearly there had been no force reduction. Then they offered to settle if I would drop the fight. I said, "Well, my costs may be a quarter of a million dollars." And they said, "I guess we will continue the court fight, then." It still goes on . . . and so far, my costs have amounted into the thousands, eighteen or nineteen at this point. And I did wind up being discharged, 'cause I was not promoted. Since I wasn't drilling, it ultimately became a discharge, you know, with no way to rate me on promotions. Technically, I had to be passed over two times before they could take action, but two times and you're out! We then feathered that into the lawsuit by saying, "Here it is guys; we've been telling you." What they did inevitably led to a discharge, essentially disenfranchised me from my career.

Once I got my priorities squared away, it became a constructive part of my life. It's an important part of my life. It's something I have not given up on. For five years after I got out, I coordinated a military counseling program at the gay center here in San Diego and probably was involved in about one third of all the discharges for homosexuality that went through the Navy during that period. During my case, I probably gave the Navy its wording for the definition of a homosexual act. They couldn't seem to come up with a definition, which was holding up my discharges, so I called them up and said, "What's going on?" And they said, "Well, people have to demonstrate they understand what a homosexual act is." And I said, "Well, okay, how is this?" And I gave them "mutual genital contact for the purpose of sexual gratification," and they used "bodily contact for the purpose of sexual gratification." So I've been fairly heavily involved in the total case.

The mere fact that someone is gay—that does not cause an impact. The impact occurs when you deal with it and in the way other people deal with it. The fact that you're gay has no bearing. You may have a lover back home you worry about, just as somebody who is not gay will have a lover or a spouse they worry about. It may detract from their work; on the other hand, you may sublimate to a point where all you ever concentrate on is your job. And I think that may be what makes gay people better career military than nongay people. I mean, that's been observed even by the Crittenden report conducted by the Navy on itself in the mid-fifties.

I also have a real problem with the mandatory AIDS testing in the military. I think the people who made that decision made it out of homophobia. The case of Danny Abata came first. He was a second-class hospital corpsman and had AIDS. In the medical workup he had given interviews, made statements, and told them he'd been involved in homosexual activities. He was in the hospital, sick with full-blown AIDS; the Navy decided they were going to discharge him for homosexual activities. They blew it. I mean, they didn't know what they were in for. The medical authorities at the Balboa hospital were incensed that they had this person, bedridden and literally on a gurney, and were taking him down to the naval station in San Diego to stand for an administrative discharge board. As soon as the 11th Naval District commander got wind that he was going to have cameras watching this sick sailor being wheeled in on a gurney to stand a board hearing for discharge for homosexuality, he forbade the media from coming on the base and also put a stop to the whole proceedings. Finally, on his deathbed, about to die, Abata asked for a leave home to Texas so he could die—to visit his family. And they denied it. So he said, "Fine. Discharge me for being homosexual." They did; they went through all the discharge processing, and they handed him a bus ticket. Great compassion!

In the final analysis, being gay and being in the military are not incompatible, even with the military's antigay policies. I would say they should go in with their eyes open to the homophobia; they can be subjected to investigation at any time, and they should go in with a clear decision in their mind as to how they will conduct themselves. They'll be faced with a decision of lying, leading a double life, or telling half-truths and getting by, hoping they don't run into an asshole. If they are under investigation, are they going to remain silent and simply withstand the scrutiny, heat, and harassment? Are they going to stand up as a test case and fight it, with the knowledge it may be decades of their life before it is solved, if ever?

The gay man or woman who joins the military needs also to address . . . to consider this is not just a job, it's not just an adventure, this is deadly real. There were people getting killed every year of Reagan's administration while serving in the military, and potentially killing, and those who have killed. This is not a game, this is not *Rambo*, it's real blood and fire, real agony and death. I think a lot of people who have been in the Persian Gulf have had reality slap them square in the face. And this country doesn't understand nor realize what our military is doing right now; they don't realize that we have people in the military, particularly in the Navy, who are on a war footing, and if you join the military, you better damn well understand that you, too, can go to war. The government establishment has a lot more control over what gets where first than we do.

I am hoping we will get a president who will issue an executive order lifting this idiotic policy and all of the cases will become moot. He'd order the military to settle up; that's what I'd like to see. The O-7–8's, O-6's, E-9s, W-1–3's, with twenty years in can make a difference. They can go to

Congress, the Pentagon, and the President, and show them their records. Show them twenty, thirty years of exemplary service, with ribbons all over their chest and gold braid all over their hat, and say: "I commanded thirty thousand men and women. I am gay. I was gay then. It didn't make any difference in the way I handled myself, and my record is here to prove it. I knew plenty of gay people who were in my command, and if there was any shit one way or the other, it was gonna get dealt with."

This is a bullshit rule, and it should be changed. God, if we could get even a half a dozen people to come forward, even in total anonymity or total confidentiality; talking to the President and telling him he's got a very bad rule on the books, it could be changed without a flutter. President Ford changed it for the civil service without a ripple. And it can be done for the military, too.

AUTHOR'S NOTE: *On March 29, 1989, the United States Court of Appeals for the Federal Circuit affirmed the lower court's decision. In September 1989, Mr. Woodward filed a petition for writ of certiorari for hearing by the Supreme Court. On February 26, 1990, the Supreme Court refused to consider Mr. Woodward's constitutional challenge to the military's policy against homosexuals.*

☆ ☆

"They ... told me, 'We cannot be responsible for you after you leave this base, and the Bangor police may be arresting you because of this ... and charging you with sodomy.' That was really the most scary ..."

DAVID A. ZIELINSKI

Age 45, U.S. Air Force, 1962–63, enlisted.
Undesirable Discharge, upgraded to Honorable.
Present occupation: owner of beauty shop.

I was very much in love with my best friend, and he wanted to go in the Air Force. At the time, I didn't think I would be able to go on without him. It wasn't because I didn't have any independence of my own, but I was just so mad about him that I went with him, signed up, and we were gone within a week. I knew that my sexual orientation would be a big factor as to whether I wanted to go in the service, or that I could use it if I didn't want to go in. We had to go through a physical. I don't know if the doctor at the induction center was a psychiatrist or not, but he asked a couple questions about whether or not I was gay, and I basically denied it. I know I also filled out the forms and said that I wasn't.

After I got to basic training and we went through the initial ugliness and verbal abuse, I never really got to like it, but I did start to accept that it was going to be a way of life for a while. Nothing actually went on during my basic training at all. We were given such heavy doses of salt tablets in July that I don't think I could have gotten a hard-on if I had wanted to, to tell the truth. It's something like saltpeter. Anyway, I don't remember having one during that period of time.

Shortly after basic I was having a sexual relationship with another guy who was in the Army. I really did like him, and I suppose he probably fit a father figure for me very well, because he was twenty years older than me, but he was very kind. . . . It was my first time away, and I don't know, things changed. I just didn't want to be there anymore. I figure the initial shock of it all had begun to wear off, and I realized it wasn't a place where I really wanted to be, Joe or no Joe (my reason for going in initially).

As I said, I was definitely aware of the regulation against homosexuality. My best friend on the base was a real screamer and we had some real wild times together, which, as I look back now, was probably my way of hoping they would catch me so I *could* get out. I wasn't very careful at all. A guy in my barracks had just been turned in by somebody in Germany that he had had an affair with years before, and he was like four months short of his discharge, but they kicked him out anyway. So I was really aware of what could happen, but it never seemed to bother me.

Airman Basic Zielinski,
U.S. Air Force, 1962

I had my liaisons, mostly with people downtown. It was a very closeted atmosphere, because Bangor, Maine, twenty-five years ago, was the end of the world. One time, I went home with a man who was a major in the Air Force Reserve. I thought I would share the fact that I was also in the military, and he practically came unglued to think that I was in the service and he had just had sex with me. He was scared to death! That was how paranoia reared its ugly head in those days.

Toward the end of my first year, I finally decided to go in and tell someone about the way I felt, so I could get the discharge procedures started. It's strange, you know, I felt I was a pretty obvious queen, but the military can certainly look the other way when it wants to. No one seemed to suspect me. Finally, I went to the chaplain and told him, and he recommended that I go to a psychiatrist. I had already, in the past, filed for a relieve of guard duty because I just couldn't see myself carrying a gun, not to mention shooting a Russian per chance one came upon our shores. It was a SAC base. I decided that it was absurd. Maybe it's because I was never a violent person. I just said, "I'm not going to be shooting anybody anyway," so they relieved me of that duty. And I also think it was things like that that helped me decide consciously against the military in general and made me realize this was not my cup of tea. Not that it was so gruesome or anything—it was just that I was not interested.

The chaplain could do little for me except report me to the CID. And they did question me a lot. They didn't really want to believe me, because fourteen people before me had already tried the same thing. They wanted me to give them names. I knew that if I did give a name, it could not be anybody in the military. I did not feel it was my place to make a decision for those in the military, because that would be out for them, too, and they were my friends. I finally gave them the name of a civilian in town. Of course, the CID has no bounds, and they went directly to this man to find out if what I had said was true. They asked him, and he said yes, he had been to bed with me. It's so funny, because the CID has no jurisdiction over civilians, but they always present themselves as if they do. However, I guess it solved their curiosity about me.

I was called in a few more times for the gruesome details, or at least that's what it seemed like to me. They had a confirmation about me from the guy in town, yet they seemed to have this unnatural interest in my sexual activities. They asked me what we did, you know, like, "Did you take his penis in your mouth?" It was crude-type stuff, things that people would ask who are *not* gay. They also told me, "We cannot be responsible for you after you leave this base, and the Bangor police may be arresting you because of this . . . and charging you with sodomy." That was really the most scary . . . well, it was all scary, but I think that was one of the highlights of the scary part, because I thought, "God, are they going to be arresting me when I get off base here?" They gave me an undesirable discharge, and I knew that it would ruin my chances of ever working for the state. . . . I probably could have dug ditches, though. I was very young at that time, so my thoughts probably weren't very rational.

They literally escorted me off the base, and left me standing outside the gate. I was told I could never set foot on a military installation again, and if I did, I would be arrested. Pretty heavy stuff for an eighteen-year-old to comprehend. I got downtown and sweated out waiting for the bus to leave. Then I watched along the bus route. I thought maybe the police would even go so far as to pull the bus over. I worried until I got out of that goddamn state. So that was really very scary, that part.

I went as far as Chicago and stayed with my friend Ron, who was still in the Army. I was very happy for a short period of time, but then my parents encouraged me to come home. Besides, Ron said that he would come to Oregon when he got out, and after he did get out, we lasted for maybe a year. I was young and wild and I knew that I couldn't stay committed at such an early age. My parents really liked him, got to know him. In fact, they've liked all my boyfriends—all eight hundred!

When they encouraged me to come home, I never told them that I had gotten an undesirable discharge. I just said that I received a medical discharge, and of course, they seemed to accept that. It never affected our relationship . . . I've always been pretty much myself. I feel that people should accept me and like me for the person that I am, not necessarily for being a homosexual but just for the way I am. So once I got settled at home, and with the support, emotionally, of my parents, I went to beauty school. I never had to deal with that rejection that the military was trying to lay on me. Soon after finishing school, I was able to buy my own shop. I have been able to live my life as I have wanted to, without that guilt and feeling of low self-esteem that so many of my friends used to express to me.

About seventeen years later—in fact, just a few years ago—a friend was telling me about this board where you could get your discharge papers upgraded. At that point I had owned my shop for several years and could see no real benefit to having this done. However, for what it was worth, I thought it still might be a good idea, because one never knows.

I had to make a special trip to San Francisco, where the board was to be held. I had my lawyer go over the case with me the day before the actual board met. I looked at all the information and realized that it brought back all those memories of so many years in the past. I was *still* scared. It was an amazing scenario.

The worst part of the whole thing was that I actually felt like they were interrogating me. *Again!* They asked me if I knew before I went in that I was gay. Well, girlfriend, I lied then and I lied again. I said, "No, I didn't know." I told them that I was very young when I joined and that it probably presented a problem with me. I had felt a need to be with somebody in some kind of a relationship-type situation, and perhaps I was seeking out more of a companionship-type thing or something, which we all do anyway. . . . The thing that sticks out in my mind through this whole new interrogation thing—and a lot of it was probably trivial bullshit—was that they were most concerned about whether or not I had ever sought out anybody in my uniform. They wanted to make sure that I wasn't out walking the streets in my uniform, trying to pick up other guys. This is a big deal.

There are plenty of military people around, men and women, who probably only get half their uniforms off before they commit "the act." So why is there so much concern about a gay person doing the same? It makes no sense to me. The way the military carries out its double standard system has always been a mystery to me. Anyway, that was really their big concern after asking me all their embarrassing questions: that I had not defaced the whole United States by walking down the street, trying to pick up another guy. After I got out of the place, I really felt quite good about it. I felt like I had passed the test ... I think I really displayed a lot of personal worth.

When I got the upgraded honorable discharge in the mail, I mean, it didn't do a thing for me. I never felt any different. I didn't throw a party or scream from the mailbox to the house, "Oh, I've got my honorable discharge. I'll be able to work for the state!" No, I guess it was merely the fact that I had completed their test. And my own worth was something they could never take away from me, and I knew that. This is not to say that those many years ago, the CID didn't try to make me feel like a nothing. If I *had* used my discharge paper in those early years, who's to know what might have happened—I may have ended up as a ditchdigger, or a dishwasher.

I think that the short period of time I was in the military, I did get something from it. I mean, it wasn't a total waste. I learned more discipline than I had probably ever had in my life, because I was always getting away with murder at home. So there was some positive points, but I simply realized it wasn't for me. For some people it's fine, but I am an independent individual, and the military just doesn't cater to that kind of personality.

One thing that sticks in my mind from that experience involved the people I worked with on the base. I was in the clothing sales department of the base exchange. When those at my clothing job found out I was being discharged, it was more like a disappointment, because they liked me as a kid and felt that I was going to have this gruesome life ahead of me for being gay. My lieutenant had a long talk with me before I left and told me that he thought it was going to be a long row for me to hoe. I knew he meant my gay life, you know. When I was trying to get my papers upgraded, he wrote me a wonderful letter of recommendation that I still have today. So, yeah, I guess there were a few positive things that I remember from those 356 days in the Air Force, so many years ago.

PART THREE

POST-VIETNAM YEARS AND THE PRESENT

Vietnam marked the end of any major military involvement for the United States. The country has been involved in isolated incidents in various parts of the world, but nothing as all-encompassing as the four previous wars.

The emphasis on an all-volunteer force has changed the face of the military. Its modern dependence upon space-age technology and computerization requires a more educated individual to fill its ranks. Advertising campaigns have been aimed at recruiting both the high school graduate and the college graduate, yet not all military branches are able to meet today's enlistment quotas. If this trend continues, the military may be forced to change its direction and requirements. The current thaw in the Cold War and the new awakening of democracy in the Soviet bloc countries may force further changes in military attitudes about the size and competency of our armed forces. It may decide to reconsider the gay men and women who already possess the skills required of able service members.

The situation for gays today has changed 180 degrees from the free-wheeling days of the seventies. The devastating disease AIDS has taken a huge toll, robbing our community of a large portion of our young men. Their absence will be felt in the arts and sciences, in the fields of politics, education, business, and technology. With the resurgence of violence against gays, many have gone back into the closet. The great strides gained in the seventies seem to have been halted and even reversed by this disease of the immune system.

Yet the gay spirit prevails. At this time we know the disease can be stopped with safe sexual practice, proper care, and education, and men and women in the gay community are uniting to battle the enemy. We have gone into the lion's den and have taken control of our lives. Sexual transmission of AIDS in the gay male community has been significantly reduced, and at the time of this writing fewer new cases are being reported. As a community, we have begun the process of building long-term relationships. Many are seeking stability similar to that guaranteed to heterosexual couples by demanding legal protection and health benefits for permanent relationships.

Seven men and six women tell their stories in this section, which covers the military from the end of the Vietnam War to present-day active duty. Many chose pseudonyms out of fear of discovery—a fear that has heightened as the administration tries vehemently to remove gay service members identified in the peacetime military. Several individuals—Perry Watkins, Joe Steffan, and Miriam Ben-Shalom—have gone forward with legal cases.

This is the era of standing up and saying, "Yes, we are gay and we are proud." This is the time for change. Indeed, it is the time to demand change.

☆ ☆

"My position as an officer in personnel required me to work with the CID. It was really tough, because as a gay person I was obligated to do the paperwork on the military members or rings that were reported. I was like two people but was forced to do my job because of the assignment."

"JAMES"

Age 32, U.S. Army, 1976-present, enlisted officer. Present occupation: Chief Warrant Officer 2, Personnel.

While I was on leave in Indianapolis from my officer basic school, my brother convinced me to go to this gay bar with him. Actually, he was working there at the time. I was leery at first, but I was certainly curious, so I went with him, went in, and sat down. This guy came by the table, asked if he could sit down, and did so. He started fooling around, doing something . . . he started rubbing my leg. I don't remember everything that he said. I wasn't aggressive enough, I guess, to push him away, 'cause he waited for me to push him away. Then, believe it or not, right there in that bar, he gave me a blow job. I decided to leave but did give him my hotel number. He called the hotel, and by the time I got back, he called again. I don't know if he apologized or something, but he asked if we could have dinner later on in the week. I had dinner with him; then we went back to the apartment and had sex. I liked it. I didn't think anything of it. I mean, I liked it. . . .

After my experiences in Indiana, I was transferred to the Presidio in San Francisco, and felt it was time to seek a separation from my wife, whom I had married a few years before. Our relationship was deteriorating, sexually and otherwise. She decided not to go to San Francisco. It was a good time for both of us to mull over the situation. Of course, the toughest part of our separation centered around our daughter. We felt we could work that out, and so far it has gone along fairly well.

While I was in Indianapolis, I met this captain, who was also being transferred to San Francisco. So when we got settled, we decided that it was time for us to explore San Francisco, the bars and so on. In November 1984, I met Ron, and we moved in together the following April. He was prior service but was now a civilian. We have been together ever since.

My actual feelings toward men began a few years before truly acting upon them. I was serving in Alaska when I first noticed my tendency toward liking men. But then, that's where I met my wife, and got married 'cause it was the "normal" thing to do. During all this time, I was in the enlisted ranks. From 1976 until 1984, I traveled all over the world and piled up plenty of awards, medals, citations, and promotions.

I was what you would call an exemplary soldier. I received two Meritorious Service Medals; a Defense Meritorious Service Medal for my four-year term with NATO; two Army Commendation Medals for the in-and-out processing of trainees in the training brigade; and two Army Achievement Medals (full impact), one for one hundred percent on the skills qualification test (total job knowledge) while enlisted, and the other for shooting competition among NATO members. It was this record that impressed the supervisory staff, and they in turn encouraged me to apply for the warrant officer program. I was accepted, and commissioned in 1984.

My position as an officer in personnel required me to work with the CID. It was really tough, because as a gay person I had to do the paperwork on the military members or rings that were reported. I was like two people but was forced to do my job because of the assignment.

Things were going well until a friend of ours had his house robbed. It was a robbery that involved the FBI. Since Ron and I were friends with this man, the FBI assumed we were gay because most of the people interviewed were gay. To make a long story short, the CID got involved with the local police of Sausalito and the FBI, and things started coming down on me. They initiated elimination proceedings against me. I decided it was getting a little too sticky, too nasty, so I contacted the gay advocates and out of my own pocket recruited my own attorney, one whom I could be totally truthful with, honest with, and who would know how to react. He was gay and also an expert in military law. During all of this, there were never any rights given except by the CID. The FBI never gave a right, warning, or anything. They never even provided a sworn statement, never provided anything in writing during the whole course of this to anyone.

Being a homosexual and being in the military is not a crime. Why CID gets involved I do not know. It's a crime to regulations, but it's not a felony. They are only supposed to investigate felonies. They twist it around and find a loophole. They're saying that if you're homosexual, then you've committed sodomy; and sodomy is a felony, by the military. And if you are homosexual, then the possibility exists for you to have committed sodomy on a federal installation, which is punishable by imprisonment. I think the military is more homophobic than society is in general. Everything I hear about homosexuals in the military is: "It is just not appropriate; they do not fit in. . . . It would disrupt the military spirit, the Corps. . . . After all, if Johnny knew that I was gay, he might not want to spend the night with me in a foxhole for fear I might do something. . . ." The mentality that believes if you're homosexual, you immediately want to have sex with all the men, whether it's in the showers, gym, sauna, or the foxhole, is totally absurd.

The CID continued to pressure me in many ways. Because my lover and I owned a company, and I was performing work—one of the provisions within CID is that you have to get permission to work off duty—they leveled charges against me for failure to get permission to work off duty.

Since my wife and I were still close (she was not aware of my relationship with Ron at this time), I called her and told her about the basis of the investigation but didn't tell her anything else. She didn't say anything but did write a very nice letter with signed attachments and enclosures, and the general court-martial authority dropped the case, but I was still flagged. I was flagged for the whole year, and when they did not lift my flag, I filed an Article 138 [complaint against superiors] which gave them ten days to lift the flag, drop everything, or I would file a redress against them. They signed a suspension lifting it and dropped everything. They tried to reassign me, solely for the purpose of reopening the investigation, but that didn't work. They tried everything they could, legal and illegal.

I immediately responded. I told off my supervisor with heated, nasty conversation to the point of yelling, blurting, standing over his desk, letting my anger get the best of me. All I wanted from him was a sworn statement from anyone who had proof of my sexuality. He basically said that policemen don't lie and that their telling him was good enough. Even today he has it in the back of his mind that they were telling the truth; no matter what's on paper, they were right and I was wrong.

Because of this bullshit, I've been denied continuation from active duty; no reason was given. . . . Along with the elimination procedure, they suspended my security clearance, which I was not aware of until recently. And it had been suspended for the last year. . . . So technically, because of policemen lying, my active career is probably over. Yeah, September of 1988.

The military is continually worried about gays and their seemingly endless sexual adventures, but I would like to cite another example of the military's basic head-in-the-sand approach to what is truly right and what is probably very wrong. A full colonel, a commander, in charge of CID agents in several western states, was requiring sexual favors from female officers under his command, and the secretary was literally having sex with him in his office, during the duty hour. He was exposing himself to the women, touching them, pinching them—you name it. They (*not* CID) investigated and found all the charges to be substantiated and accurate. The government and military decided to court-martial him, but a pretrial agreement was made, and he was allowed to accept a lesser charge. The bastard received a *five-thousand-dollar* fine and was allowed to retire with full benefits. But in the misplaced objectives of the military, he was only doing what was "normal" and after all, how would all that screwing around decrease morale anyhow? Bottom line here, folks, *he was a heterosexual.* Lest we forget what is right and wrong, it's okay if you are straight but not okay if you are gay. I'm sure there is a moral in there somewhere.

I think the military might be a little more lenient with the Medical Corps. Although these people *still* couldn't do what that colonel did and survive like he did, the Army may look the other way a bit more. Because of the Army's need to retain qualified medical technicians, surgeons, dentists, and so on, it is more accepted. I am aware of many times when it's been known that a certain Dr. So-and-so or Nurse So-and-so is gay and they just let it go by. It doesn't interfere with the Army's mission, and they can still do their job. So with the Army traditionally always being below standards for medical people, they don't go after them or put them out as fast as they do otherwise.

I always wanted to retire with twenty years under my belt, then say, "Hey, look, I served twenty years, am gay, and had nothing negative reported about me, even though everyone knew!"

I won't be able to do that now.

☆ ☆

"They wanted me, and told her I was the head honcho in this whole mess and that they felt it was like a Mafia operation. I was even charged with threatening to kill somebody."

BARBARA BAUM

Age 24, U.S. Marine Corps, 1985–87, enlisted.
Dishonorable Discharge (changed to Bad Conduct),
six-month prison term. Present occupation:
construction field.

I had several problems growing up. I was physically beat on by my brother for years. My whole family life was difficult. Everyone drank a lot. I began drinking when I was quite young. I would take my mother to the liquor store because she didn't drive. We'd go to the store for a bottle of vodka or something, then she'd buy me a six-pack. That's how she'd butter me up—then we'd all be happy.

As for my brother, there was no hiding the physical abuse. I would be scarred and scratched up, with black eyes, fat lips, and all kinds of stuff. I know my father had to be aware of it, but never did anything to my brother. This went on for years, to one degree or another.

Then all of a sudden, in November of 1984, my brother beat the living tar out of me and I said that was going to be the last. Either my parents got rid of him or I was leaving. I said, "I don't have to put up with this shit anymore," and moved out. I spent everything I had saved for school on my own place.

The times weren't much better away from home, so I decided to join the Marines. It was the hardest of all the branches, but I knew I worked best under pressure. The more that's demanded of me, the more I'll give. If I choose something less stringent, I'm more likely to kick back and not give it my all. I knew this would be the best for me.

Here I was, twenty years old and hitting it hard in my basic training program. At first I was ready to quit. I wanted to get the heck out, but then I thought about it. About that same time, my grandmother sent me a letter saying how proud they were of me, and that they knew I could do it. Since I always came through no matter what, it made me put my whole heart into it. From then on, it was smooth sailing. I graduated second in my platoon and was meritoriously promoted to lance corporal.

Lance Corporal Baum,
U.S. Marine Corps, 1986

In advanced training, I had the highest score. There were other honor grads, but I got 97 percent. I was actually considered "distinguished" honor grad out of the Corrections School, because they gave a special award for such an achievement. I knew I was learning what I was supposed to do. I realized that in a couple months I'd be out on the road doing my job and getting paid, so motivation was high for learning. I also knew I wasn't stupid—oh, maybe I acted dumb once in a while, but intellectually I wasn't stupid, and this certainly helped bring it home to me.

In these early days of my training, I was concerned about getting through school. I really didn't tune in to anything about homosexuality until someone in my basic training unit brought it to my attention. One day, we were sitting on our bunks and this gal started pointing out who was and who wasn't. I was shocked and said, "You're crazy. Did you read the enlistment? When you sign up, there's a question that specifically asks, 'Have you ever had any homosexual contact?' or something like that. You can't get in if you're gay." You know, the thought of lying on a piece of paper never occurred to me. That's how naive I was. I really was. I had no thought of that at all.

As I recall, it was my first roommate who made me aware of the fact that she was gay. Normally, I mind my own business. I don't worry about anybody else but me; regarding what's going on, I don't care as long as they're happy. When she admitted to me she was gay, it kind of scared me, especially having her as my roommate. So naive me became good friends with a young lance corporal named Diana who eventually put me in jail.

I can't say I wasn't warned, once it was obvious about Diana. The people I worked with did warn me about a few women, which were the same ones I was interested in hanging around. When they would say, "Hey, she's gay, or *she's* gay," I'm like, "You're crazy," because I refused to believe it. For the longest time I refused to believe it about one girl who was eventually discharged.

Granted, I was scared, but curious. I was looking for something that everybody else was doing. I was partying with everybody and became known as the group's little drunk. I'd go to all the parties and just pass out. I felt I was having fun, but some people got so irritated with my drinking that they didn't want to talk to me. Still, I'd show up, was always let in, but never got involved with anybody.

As I began to feel more comfortable, I finally gave in to my sexual urges, during one of my drunken escapades. Diana asked to spend the night in my room. Even as drunk as I was, I was still scared she wanted to go all the way, whatever that meant. She wanted to do all these things, and I'm like, "Look, this may sound stupid, but I don't do that the first time I'm with somebody, and besides, I've never even done this before." I wasn't going to jump in the first time the offer was made. The actual night we went all the way, both of us knew something was going to happen, something different, so we plunged in, so to speak. Afterward, I was so—how do I say it?—"let down," that I went for a drive in my car. I can't really remember, but it left me with a feeling that it wasn't really what I wanted or what I thought it might be. It didn't do anything for me. I mean, we made love several times, but basically, I did it because I didn't want to lose her. I wanted to say I was with somebody, like everybody else, that I was involved with somebody.

To be very honest, she always did everything to me. I never did anything, so I guess that made me the passive one. I'm sure all of my "positioning" related directly to my past and those horrible experiences with my dear brother. To this day, I've never done anything sexual to another woman. The military refuses to believe me, but I swear that's the honest-to-God truth. I was petrified. I didn't know what to do and I was afraid of looking like a fool, so she was the active partner in bed. To top it off, anytime anything happened between us, I was always drunk. And during that time, my drinking was totally out of control.

It was hard, because it seemed I was always being distracted, plus I was usually hung over. I'd get off work at eleven at night, come home with a six-pack and drink, just get drunk. I'd go to sleep, wake up at nine or ten in the morning, feeling like a vegetable, then go back to work at two o'clock. This occurred over and over again. Believe it or not, no one ever thought I had a drinking problem. But from my observations, it appeared the military tended to look the other way unless it got severely out of control. Even though there were drug and alcohol programs, people still operated on a level similar to my own.

My drinking really had no major impact on my job, because the military police position wasn't all that challenging. Ass-kissing was a standard mode of operation. If an officer was caught driving drunk or speeding, and you'd pull him over, he'd simply want to bitch at you instead of letting you tell him he'd done something wrong. And as an officer, he always got his way. He'd complain to the provost Marshal and they'd come back to you and say, "Hey, chill out a bit, okay? You're not in the real world, you're here, at Parris Island." To me, we weren't able to do our jobs the way we were supposed to do them. It was a real joke.

I continued with my drinking and my relationship. It wasn't the best situation, but it was better than what was about to happen to me. It was the day before Thanksgiving, in 1986, when we were called in for the first of several interrogations. Diana was called in one day, and I the next. They told us we were under investigation and that there were allegations, but since neither of us volunteered any information, they wouldn't give us many facts. When we requested a lawyer, they definitely didn't give us any further information regarding the allegations.

The next think I knew, I was being counseled by my commander on my "apparent drinking problem," for a short time; then, for what seemed like hours, he counseled me on my personal behavior. He talked about letting my hair grow longer, and wearing makeup. I said, "That's not me. I don't care what anybody thinks." He said, "Well, you'd better care about what other people think, because that can make or break you." I replied, "Fine, maybe the military's not for me." To this day, and all through my military experience, I never changed anything about my personal image or appearance. I am who I am.

He didn't stop with those two issues, because he also wanted me to start dating some of the local guys. "You don't seem to go out with the fellows." (All I could see were visions of my brother, and I hoped I could control that kind of situation.) I said, "If you knew about my past, you might understand." We ended our discussion at that point, but it didn't stop what the original investigators had in store for me.

After the counseling session, my life went from bad to worse. To make matters more involved, Diana had also been going with one of the guys on the base, and now she was trying to dump him. However, he was not convinced she really meant it, and started following us around. He followed us to a motel we had gotten one weekend. All of a sudden . . . I mean, nothing was going on, we were just lying there about to drift off to sleep. Granted, we weren't wearing any clothes, but we were not doing anything . . . and you hear this loud *boom*. What the hell's going on? you know. *"Oh shit!"* I'm trying to calm the situation down and Diana's picking up a chair, yelling "Rape!" and "Fire!" and I'm like, "Shut up! You're going to wake up the whole friggin' neighborhood here and everybody's going to be checking it out. I know we can talk this over, if we can get him to settle down." Finally, Diana gets down . . . he grabs both of us . . . she breaks away and takes off.

Of course, he reported us to the Naval Intelligence Service. I was sent into a rehabilitation program for my drinking problem, and reports were being assembled about our sexual activities. I decided to get away from Diana, so once out of the program, I began in earnest to become a good troop. I began by going back to my old cross-country training routine from high school.

During this time, I met my lieutenant friend, and we began running together. After we'd run, I'd talk about things in my past and realized she was someone I could trust. We formed a good friendship from this. Once she decided to run cross-country, we trained together every day. We didn't think this or anything else was wrong, but people began noticing my car at her place. Then, new allegations started coming forward. When the investigation started, these same individuals volunteered their observations, so my friend was under investigation as well.

It was one of the Marine Corps' biggest blowups and became a huge witch hunt. The Marine Corps was releasing information on everybody charged. Before it was all over, they disciplined, discharged, or jailed twelve to fifteen women. It was a scandal, to be sure.

At the time, nobody really trusted anybody. It was like somebody had to be talking and no one knew who it was, but they were getting all the right people. No one could figure out how they were doing it. It had to be somebody in the group. Everybody was kind of afraid. I didn't know what else to do, so I started drinking again.

The NIS called me into the prosecutor's office. I had the prosecutor right there. It was like a pre–court-martial hearing, but I didn't know it at the time. Before they began the interview, I said, "I'll answer your questions, but for my own personal protection, I'm going to record this interview." This bitch sitting next to me, the NIS lady, said, "I won't allow that." I said, "Fine," and we ended the session. They accused me of playing games, but I was the only one having enough nerve to tape my own interrogation. I just wanted it all on tape, so when they came up with my statements, I could say, "Hey, this is what I said right here. You

can hear every word of it, and I did not say this and I did not say that."
I had my lawyer after that.

I was put on legal hold, from January until March. At that time they started final separation proceedings on me, or so I thought. I was afforded the opportunity of appearing in front of an administrative hearing board. This is where the pretrial questioning was to take place. They were supposed to make a decision of either an honorable discharge or a dismissal [of charges] so that I could stay in.

I decided to waive my rights and didn't appear in front of the board. Since I was under the impression there would be no question about the type of discharge, if it were given, I felt fine about waiving my rights. However, I wasn't back in my office more than an hour when I got a call from my lawyer saying, "Get up here. NIS has been talking to Diana. She's spilled her guts, and you're going to jail!"

Diana gave them pages of information, which were converted into charges of obstruction of justice, indecent acts with women, and sodomy. They dragged out countless other charges. Under each one there were different charges for indecent acts; twenty in all. I felt so betrayed by her. It made me feel cheated and . . . I don't know. I should have expected it. At that point it was like, "Oh, let's just drink." And I did, for a week straight, every night. I went to work, but that's when they had transferred me down to a different office and my hours were nothing, so I hardly worked.

Under immunity, Diana sang like a songbird. Maybe she was frightened at the time, because she was pregnant and didn't want anything to happen to her baby. In fact, I think that's how they threatened her, by saying she would lose custody of her child if she didn't give them what they wanted. She had made a comment like that back in February, something like, "No matter what they say, I'm not going to lose this baby."

Yes, the big boys got what they wanted. They wanted me, and even told her *I* was the *head honcho* in this whole mess and that they felt it was like a Mafia operation. I was even charged with threatening to *kill* somebody. I mean, if you saw me, you'd know I'm not a threat to anybody. I couldn't hurt a fly. They were making an example of me in the most ridiculous manner possible.

The pressures of it all were beginning to take their toll. I would wake up in the middle of the night from a recurring dream about some evil, wickedly smiling person putting me in jail, and all I could hear, over and over, were the jail doors slamming behind me. I'd wake up in a cold sweat—it was so frightening yet seemed so real. I knew something was going to happen and it was not going to be good. Everybody kept telling me, "They can't put you in jail for being gay, they just can't, it's not right, they're just trying to scare you."

I tried to listen to everybody, but deep in my heart I knew something terrible was going to happen. However, I am still proud to say, the night before my court-martial, I had my last taste of alcohol. I realized all my mental sharpness would be needed for the trial that lay before me.

The court-martial was a horrid repeat of the other confrontations. I was totally degraded, made to look like some kind of sex maniac, and treated like I didn't have a single redeemable human characteristic. It was sickening, a truly dehumanizing experience. I had to sit in that courtroom while Diana verbally gave evidence that would figuratively become my "death sentence" in the Marine Corps. Love can be a costly and devastating endeavor. I think I would have been better off dead at that point. I was left without any sense of worth when the officers were through with the trial.

Once my court-martial was over, the presiding officer found me guilty of everything except the threats to kill. It took about an hour and a half, while they decided on an appropriate sentence. The courtroom was overflowing with news media covering the case, and other curious bystanders. I was aware that the news of this case hit all the major papers across the country. It was so terrible. It seemed like we were all under the circus bigtop and I was the circus freak.

In the end, when the sentencing was given, I didn't move, didn't cry, but just stood there, then went to my lawyer's office and mentally fell apart. I called my friend the lieutenant and called my folks. They were all quite supportive of my situation. The authorities were pressing to take me to jail, but I told them I'd come whēn I was damn good and ready.

It was so difficult to realize I had just been given a *dishonorable discharge and one year in a military prison, stripped of all rank, and required to forfeit all pay* for simply being gay. Actually, the court originally asked for *thirty-eight years* in prison but reduced it to the one year, which was later shortened to six months. The discharge was also changed to bad conduct discharge. This was a relief because the second type of discharge did not carry the stigma that would have made me a felon. However, I do understand I was being made an example and that this would send a message loud and clear to gays regarding toleration of such activities in the military, particularly in the U.S. Marine Corps.

It was like a nightmare. I was devastated. But you know, I made history, because no other female marine had ever been given such a sentence for being gay. On the other hand, I guess that's not the kind of thing I would like to be remembered for as I grow older!

Through it all my mental health, as well as my physical health, was deteriorating. I had gone down from 125 pounds to 100 pounds. They were checking me daily to make sure I didn't have any serious health problems. I was severely depressed from the courtroom ordeal, but particularly from the evidence about my past childhood abuse, both sexual and physical. My lawyer felt the information might help our case. It didn't help, and all it did do was make me recall some terrible wounds that have never healed. I was monitored and given antidepressants. And believe me, I can tell you, knitting baby clothes for the Navy relief was *not* a way of getting me out of my depressed condition [prison duty].

After I was in prison for a week or so, the authorities paid me a visit. They wanted me to make statements about other women I knew, so proceedings could begin against them. After much thought and soul-searching, I decided to cooperate. When I had finished, I read part of my statement, and I don't remember . . . I mean I was scared and so afraid that I wasn't going to be able to tell them anything. They wanted me to say I had a sexual relationship with the lieutenant, and with So-and-so and So-and-so, but I hadn't. I told them I had never been involved with anybody other than Diana. The investigator kept trying to put words in my mouth. He kept trying to twist what I was saying. "Oh, so you're with the lieutenant, and you're in a hotel room together one night, and nothing happens." I said, "That's right, nothing happened; we slept. Drop it, okay. Nothing." It really pissed me off.

When my friend, the one in question, did take the chance of visiting me, it seemed to turn everything around. She was someone I trusted with all of my feelings. She was pretty upset upon seeing my physical condition. I was nothing but skin and bones. My attitude had become that if I didn't wake up, it didn't matter. I wasn't going to do anything to hurt myself, but I didn't care if I ever woke up. Talking to her at least helped me realize that there was somebody out there who still cared. Even though I was jeopardizing her career, she was more concerned about my welfare, and gave me hope.

It gave me the boost I needed at that point, because after finishing the statement, I just lost it. I couldn't believe I had done it, and I wanted to take back every word but couldn't. To make matters worse, soon after her visit, *she* was put on legal hold. They put her up for an Article 32 hearing, which was similar to a civilian grand jury hearing, and wanted to court-martial her. However, she requested resignation of her commission and was allowed to resign. *My* situation was bad enough, but what a waste of a well-trained, well-educated U.S. Naval Academy graduate. She spent all those years preparing for a military career, and for what?

I couldn't have felt worse about what they did to her. Of course, she was upset but knew what I was going through and knew I didn't sell out a bunch of women for my own sake. Even so, I can't help but believe her forced resignation was directly related to our friendship. To this day, that weighs heavily on my mind. When all the evidence was assembled, we were only two of the final twelve to fifteen removed or punished.

Shortly after I was in the brig and had made that statement, Cheryl arrived to serve her sentence. We basically got each other through the worst of it. I know she had a tremendous impact on my survival. We weren't allowed much outside contact, so we gave each other support. Cheryl had an attitude like, sock 'em, so I took on her attitude. She had another three months to go once I left. It's pretty sad to think that Cheryl lost all of the benefits her nine years could have given her. She was a career soldier.

I survived my ordeal, and now that I'm out, I've had time to think about it. I don't feel it changed my values because those will never change, but it's made me appreciate things that I took for granted, like freedom. I was put in jail and treated like a criminal, lost all my rights and privileges as an American citizen, for something that's not criminally wrong. Gays make up about 10 to 15 percent of the Corps, whether they want to accept it or not. Since the military is unable to identify these members, where is the problem? If we are causing problems, why can't the *authorities* seek us out? Why must they use informers? Simple— because, except for our sexual orientation, we look and act like everyone else. Do they ever question the sodomy that takes place between men and women that are married? Oh no, that's different! And how so? Just *who* is causing the problem?

Tell me, how can the military powers that be justify those marines who left a comrade out in the desert to die? That wasn't a problem? They took a human life, and only *one guy* got three months in prison, and that was all. He took a life, he was responsible for a human life, and he got *three months*. Yet I went to jail for six months, Cheryl was there for nine, for being gay? And *who* were we hurting?

Needless to say, I have few regrets, and actually gained from the experience, particularly by taking control of my drinking. I haven't taken a drink since I was released, and that has had a tremendous impact. It's changed my life, because if I were to start drinking today, I'd probably end up killing myself or hurting somebody else. It's not worth it. I know what it's like to lose my freedom, and I don't plan on doing anything to jeopardize it again. I will not willingly or knowingly do something to break the law.

Believe it or not, this whole experience has allowed me to be freer. I don't practice any kind of sexuality—I'm too afraid of people. I must go through counseling to deal with the feelings from my past, as a child, and from what's happened now. When you look at it . . . the sexual experiences I've had have been traumatic—one landed me in jail and the others left me scarred as a child—so it makes me fearful of any kind of involvement. Actually, I don't mind being by myself. All I really want is to be free, live my life the way I want, and have others stay out of it. I'm trying to overcome everything that's happened, learn from it, and be happy. Right now I'm not sure how I'm going to solve my problems, but I survived before and I can do it again.

I know I need to get over my fears, my lack of trust, because I don't want to live my whole life alone. I'm really afraid to get involved with anybody, whether it be sexual or not. I'm just afraid to be close to anybody. I'm so afraid of being hurt and going through that loneliness and pain I felt when I was in the brig. I detach myself from things so I won't have the fear of losing whatever it may be.

AUTHOR'S NOTE: *On February 20, 1990, a Military Appeals court cited bias among members of a court-martial jury in overturning Ms. Baum's conviction for having sex with another woman.*

☆ ☆

"I've never lost faith in America . . . I never thought America would let me down . . . I am standing accused of being unfit, for doing one thing and one thing only—saying four words about myself: I am a lesbian."

MIRIAM BEN-SHALOM

Age 42, U.S. Army Reserve, 1974–76, 1987–88 (reinstated), enlisted. Present occupation: substitute teacher.

I lived in Israel for five years, when I was about nineteen years old. During part of that time, I fought in the Israeli Army for almost a year and a half. Women served as guards, transportation-type drivers, and the like, which many of the women resented. They had passed a civil rights laws for gays in Israel around 1969, prohibiting discrimination, which just took my breath away, but it didn't do much for women in general. I drove an armored personnel carrier around and also stood guard duty up on the heights of Golan. It was during one of these assignments that I saw two of my friends killed, one by a land mine and the other in a terrorist bombing. In fact, even I killed someone while I was there. I believe because of those two incidents I don't have the same problem with killing another person from a defensive position as some people might—not willy-nilly to kill somebody, but when pushed, in danger.

After my time in Israel I decided to return to the United States for my advanced education degree. Along the way, and quite possibly because of my experience in Israel, I felt a need for some mental counseling and went in for psychotherapy, but I was outraged at the *sexual* approach by this male therapist. However, through it all, I realized my lesbian identity without the benefit of a lover. I am a lesbian, have not regretted it, and the best thing about it all is that I finally discovered who I am.

In 1974, I joined the U.S. Army Reserve, initially because I thought it would be a good way to augment my income. I maxed all my military exams. . . . I was one of the first two female drill sergeants in the whole 84th Division.

About my second year, there were a whole spate of discharges, so I went to my commanding officer and said, "Gee, why is the Army removing all of these people and you're not kicking me out, too?" And he said, "Oh, there's this regulation, but it's up to the discretion of the commander. Besides, you're really good at what you do. We have no arguments with you, so don't worry about it." At that point it was certainly a mixed message.

Staff Sergeant Ben-Shalom,
U.S. Army Reserve, 1988

My sexuality wasn't any secret. I'd just been on TV. I've been an activist ever since I came out, so it was no state secret. It wasn't like nobody knew. But after about two years of my enlistment, pressure came down on me, and *I* was removed in 1976, with an honorable discharge. Yep, I was kicked out. It was honorable because they had no other choice; at no time did the Army ever accuse me of any misconduct or any inappropriate activities.

As it happened, my commander had to start the action. I think he did it just to see what would happen. He had some idea, I think, that he was honest with me. He didn't really start the discharge action; he actually put in for the commendation award that I was due, and it was up to the Army then to either discharge me or remove the flag. A flag is placed on anyone's personnel file when some action is pending. In my case it had to do with my verbal statements about being a lesbian. They chose to discharge me.

I remembered while I was training at Fort Leonard Wood, I had mentioned to somebody that I was a lesbian. It was "Just shut up, you don't say anything about it, be quiet." Now I know what they meant, because they were trying to tell me something could happen to me, but at that time it was "Just shut up about it, do your job." I don't know whether it was from all of that, but I do know they went around and asked people about me. I know that my phone was tapped for a while, because I could tell. I used to say, "Hello, CID and whoever else is there."

Once I was out, and took my case to the courts, I promised myself I would never, ever put anybody else at jeopardy. Have I met other gay people in the military? Yes. Where were they? I can't tell you. This fight is mine. I will not acknowledge if I see somebody that I know—I refuse to do that. I know there are gay generals and admirals. I know who they are, because I know other gays in the military, not that I served with but that I've come in contact with throughout the years. I have personal knowledge of several colonels, light colonels, and majors. I mean, does the American public and particularly the military, who would never admit to it, think we are only in the enlisted ranks? You would be amazed and shocked if tomorrow— Okay, postulate tomorrow a miracle happened and everybody who was gay turned lavender. This country would die!

My commander told me I did a real good job for them. I've done everything the Army has asked me to do and I've done it well. I guess that's why the removal was so hard to take. Of course, I didn't take it with a grain of salt, or turn the other cheek—no, no. I began what was to become this very long and emotional road to plateaus of success and letdown. I went through all the administrative appeals starting in '76. In 1978, all of those appeals had been exhausted, and we went into federal court. In May of 1980, we won a decision out of the district court, which ordered me immediately reinstated with all rank, honor, and privilege. But for the next seven years, the Army just had a damnably hard time understanding what the word *reinstatement* in English meant. At first they offered me $991.36—bullshit! That was supposedly the back pay that I would have been entitled to for the year that was still on my Reserve contract. Well, I didn't fight for money. That wasn't the point. Besides, that was a stupid thing to offer me anyhow.

When the Seventh Circuit U.S. Court of Appeals realized they weren't going to take me back in, and that circuit court ruled unanimously that the word *reinstatement* meant putting me back in, and the Army was threatened with a contempt ruling against them if they did not do it. Finally, they were forced to take me back in. This was after *seven years* of wrangling over it. It was real stupid. . . .

The money was not the point. Fuck the money. The issue was that I wanted my job back, and I didn't care about money. Besides, there's not enough money in the world that they could offer me. I mean, if they wanted a cheap lay, they can take the $991.36 and shove it. If they want to have a good lay, let them go someplace else. If they want to pimp me, forget it. I went back in on September 12, 1987, because they were forced to take me, and was allowed to finish the rest of my original contract. On August 11, 1988, I completed my contract and wanted to reenlist for another six years. Then the whole thing started all over again.

Now they're denying my reenlistment for exactly the same reason they kicked me out twelve years ago—new regulation. . . . If you say you are, you're automatically out, considered unfit, regardless of whether there is any misconduct or not. It's the assumption of the label that makes you unfit, which is one of the bases we're using.

I believe it violates my freedom of speech. A black can say, "I'm black and I'm proud." A woman can say, "I'm a feminist." A Jew can say, "I'm Jewish. I don't want to go to church services, I want to speak to a Jewish chaplain." I do not want to sashay down the main street on a military base wearing lavender fatigues. I don't want to carry any banners saying, "Ha, ha, I'm a lesbian, I'm gay, fuck you." I want to be seen as an individual. I want to be judged on my capabilities as an individual. If I'm a good soldier and I do the job, then what does it matter what my private life may or may not be, as long as I do not do any dishonor or any discredit to this country, the flag, or the uniform that I wear? Why does it matter? The military says I'm a detriment to morale and a threat to national security and I damage the esprit de corps. Why would I be an honor graduate if I'm so bad? Why would I receive compliments from the people I've served with if I affect morale so terribly? Okay, these are facts, not fantasy. So they say, "Well, there's a reg, and we say there's a reg, and since we say it, then therefore it has to be," which is circular reasoning. They are using the same type of argument toward gay people that they did toward blacks when the services were forced to integrate. There was that same argument that blacks were somehow unfit, a detriment to morale. And let's not leave out Asians and women, although in each of these situations, the military hasn't been as blatant as with the blacks, but more particularly with gays.

There's always this cadre of people that want to stand behind these poor shredding banners of personal bias, bigotry, and discriminatory attitudes. They want to stand fast, and just as these attitudes have been shown to be incorrect in the instance of people of color in the military and in the instance of women being integrated into the service . . . all fallacious . . . I have not done anything. I choose not to live with the label "unfit to serve my country" for the rest of my life. I've never lost faith in America. . . . I never thought America would let me down. . . . I am standing accused of being unfit, for doing one thing and one thing only—saying four words about myself: I am a lesbian. I felt when I walked into that courtroom I was judged guilty before I was innocent, and the Army has not offered any proof to back up their arguments. If only they were as rigorous about misconduct toward heterosexual members of the service as they want to be with us.

Their arguments just don't hold up. When I went back in after all those years of waiting, I had to catch up as a drill instructor. I caught up, to the point where I was told I did a superior job. Then my job classification was changed to a 71-Mike, which is chaplain's assistant. I'm now the drill sergeant for people who don't have a prayer! But don't ask me their reasoning, other than further harassment, which the court specifically said they couldn't do. I'm sure the Army still feels they run their own show, and they were going to teach me a lesson for being forced to take me back.

The discrimination in the military is ever present, no matter what they try to say. Yeah, it's there. Racism is there, like any other place in this society. I don't think they do anything about it. They aren't as rigorous in enforcing their own policies as they should be, and that's a damn shame. And they're worried about people like me? Give me a break! It's like the previously mentioned "security risk" of the homosexual. Heterosexual males are *known* security risks. When was the last time—say, for instance, in the last ten years—you heard of a gay person committing treason as a spy? Think about it, and you will be hard pressed for a name. And I'd be damned if I'd sell out my country for a little old roll in the hay. I know how to keep my zipper up. There might be a gay person who would, just like there might be a heterosexual who would, but they don't do it *because* they're gay; they do it because it's a flaw in their character. . . .

I'm a recalcitrant pup myself and a minority, so I know what it is to be harassed. I know what it is to be discriminated against. I've had "Nazis" threaten my life. . . . I've lost so much . . . lost my house, custody of my daughter for a while, employment. It's real hard to get a job when you're on the front page of the newspaper and people think that you're highly radical and highly adversarial. I was shot at in Indianapolis . . . somebody loosened the lug nuts on the drive wheel of my truck . . . I had my brake linings cut.

I get lots of phone calls from creeps threatening to kill me, and my response is "Well, at least I'm honest. You're using the anonymity of the telephone." I don't resent the threats—that's bullshit. What I resent is the cowardice . . . because the phone calls were obnoxious . . . just referring to me as a lesbo, a lezzy, or a dyke. Yeah, I've had stupid-assed phone calls from people. I told one guy who called, I said, "You know how boring and mundane this is? Don't you dare call me back until you can make it interesting for me as well." I said, "Are you so lacking in creativity that all you can do is say you want to suck my pussy?"

The whole thing hurts a lot, that's all, and the lack of support from the gay community doesn't help the pain. There was no support whatsoever. I've taken more harassment and more hurtful things from the gay community than I ever have from heterosexuals. It's phenomenal that in 1988 there's *no* national defense fund to help people challenge discrimination. It seems just awesome that while we're fighting for our very lives with AIDS, we cannot fight for our equality of life. I have no patience for it, and that's too bad. But I, single-handedly, challenged the largest white, male, heterosexual power institution in the world and won, so, yeah, it's hard to have any patience for all that crap. But not to have that support can really take its toll.

I was on welfare for a while, which was a very dehumanizing experience. . . . People didn't want to be seen with me in public. I don't understand why. If you're seen with a black person, nobody thinks you're black. If you're seen with a Jewish person, nobody thinks you're Jewish. But if you're seen with a queer, walking down the street, well, my God, you must be a queer too. And I've never quite understood that. It's been very solitary.

I will not hide what I am. I speak three languages, have a master's degree, and I'm a trained teacher. It would appear that the military has missed out on a lot by not having my services available to them all those thirteen years. In fact, the military shortchanges many women, not just gay women. I think women can handle it just as well as men can. I think many women go in because there is so much offered in terms of MOSs [jobs/positions], and many times the gay woman, in particular, is an independent individual who would be interested in pursuing such avenues of endeavor. Every lesbian that I have ever met or spoken to in the military has, for the most part, been a very superior soldier. I sense that many lesbians are chronic overachievers but also figure, "Well, if I'm found out, I can point to my impeccable work record." I think they do it because they're doubly women and lesbians, and women still have to work three, four times as hard as any man to get where they want, but fortunately, that's easy enough to do!

I wish that America had a system wherein it would be mandatory to give at least two years' service to your country, not necessarily in the military. I'm not a pacifist. It is a given that we need a military—we cannot just destroy it all—but I would hope for a day when we do not need an army, though it is still necessary today. I'm just saying that there might be some other alternatives.

There are days where I wish I'd never opened my mouth, because of the price I've had to pay. . . . I'm forty-two years old and I don't have money in the bank. When I get old and I want to retire, I don't know what will happen. Maybe I'll end up out on the streets. . . . I've put everything into challenging discrimination . . . thirteen years is a long time to fight. Every day, every moment, every second, it's there with me every moment. I have not lived without it for thirteen years.

I still feel anger. I still feel a lot of rage. My sense of injustice in the world around me is heightened more than ever. . . . The general public needs to know about the pain, anger, hurt and all the *loss* that has gone on. This is a *very* important thing. That any of us could survive as whole human beings is a miracle. It's a testament to the strength of the human spirit and the human soul. . . . I get tired. I feel terribly alone right now, terribly filled with pain, all the memories. . . . I feel desperately close to tears, desperately close to pain that I haven't thought about in a long time.

☆ ☆ ☆

A call recorded on August 4, 1988, in the author's presence, to Ms. Shalom's Sergeant at her Reserve unit:

This is Miriam Ben-Shalom calling. Five minutes ago my attorney called me, and we got a decision. We won. The Army has a preliminary injunction prohibiting them for considering my sexual orientation in any discharge proceeding or any reenlistment proceeding. It appears that the request for considering my orientation was upheld, and all of the First Amendment, all of the constitutional issues were definitely upheld. We won on every point. I can't tell you any more because I haven't seen the brief myself, but I did want you to know we won on every count. I can't believe it!

> AUTHOR'S NOTE: *On August 8, 1989, the Seventh U.S. Circuit Court of Appeals reversed a lower court decision allowing Miriam Ben-Shalom to rejoin the Army Reserve. In October 1989, Ms. Ben-Shalom was informed of a stay of the lower court's decision, and filed a writ of certiorari with the Supreme Court. On February 26, 1990, the Supreme Court refused to consider Ms. Ben-Shalom's constitutional challenge to the military's policy against homosexuals.*

☆ ☆

"People respect me as a physician and they think I'm a good doctor. I know that I'm a good doctor, and whether I'm gay or straight should make absolutely no difference at all."

"EMILY BLACK"
Age 29, U.S. Army, 1984–present, officer. Present occupation: physician in military medical hospital.

When I finally came out, it occurred during a real difficult point in medical school, which happened to be my second year. I just said, "The hell with it, I'm going to be who I am, who I've known I've been for years, and I don't give a damn about anything else." I stopped fooling myself and hiding. I weathered my sexual storm, and graduated in the top 10 percent of my medical school class.

It was the Army medical program that made it all possible for me. So here I was, gay, a lieutenant in the Army, and cruising through medical school. They paid all tuition, reimbursed me for all my books, and I received about $600 a month for living expenses. And for that, and a bill of about $100,000 to get me through, I owed the Army four years of being a physician for them. It really was a good deal, but the drawbacks were that you weren't going to be in a location of the country that you might have chosen, and you had all of the problems related to the paranoia of being gay while in the military.

I was leery when I went in for my initial interview for the Army physical. I don't think there was a question about homosexuality, but then, I wasn't out at that time either. However, they did ask me if I knew any communists—it was actually written down whether I knew or ever had anything to do with any communists! Once I passed all of the testing, a group of us went to our basic training. Trust me, that was a big joke. We got to shoot M-16s, which was actually kind of fun, they tried to teach us how to march, and we had to run PT every morning at six o'clock. The nuclear/biological chemical training we had was watching someone else dress up in all this gear. We never had to wear the gear. You know, it was just a joke. The group had many more men than women. It was really hilarious, so yeah, we had three weeks of officers' basic.

I met my current partner during my third year of medical school. Then that next summer, I went off to Germany for six and a half weeks. We had barely been lovers for more than three months at that point, and it was really difficult being split up so soon into our relationship. I was the only woman in the group and was missing her terribly. From an emotional standpoint, it was a terrible summer. We wrote letters every day, and boy, was I happy to get home! She still won't tell me how much she spent on telephone bills for that period.

After I finished all the medical school training and the summers of "Army training," I was recommissioned as a captain and sent to my first permanent medical station. When I arrived at my hospital, of course, people want to know about you, about your life and what's going on. So now I'm dealing with a certain bit of secrecy about myself, and the growing anxiety in the guise of paranoia. It's very difficult to decide who is safe to come out to, and who you can't come out to, for fear of exposure. You have to ask questions in certain ways so you're not suspect . . . you don't want to be too obvious and make people raise their eyebrows, and there's always a little bit of paranoia that you'll do something to make them angry and they'll turn around and report you or make accusations.

So far, I've had good excuses, like being on call in the hospital, being on duty in the hospital when there's a social thing that people are supposed to attend. I've been able to skirt the issue so far. Many times I've planned on being out of town the weekend something social was going to occur. . . . It makes you feel terrible. You think, I'm a person too, and I'm working just as hard as the other people, so why shouldn't I be able to live like I want? And yeah, it's a terrible thing that you can't be open and out. (I really hope that Perry Watkins's [see pages 248–57] case turns out good for us.) I am also sure there may come a time when I will feel the need to ask a male gay friend to be my date for a Christmas ball or a dance, just to act as cover, you know, if there's any indication that people suspect me. Yes, I'd probably do that. I am aware of probably one senior staff person in my department that is probably gay, but I don't feel comfortable with even attempting to come out to him, because what if he isn't? Or what if he is and feels threatened because I am? It just presents all kinds of ramifications. And because of this stupid regulation, I realize that I will never be able to take my own partner to any military functions, period.

The thing is, there are so many of us who are gay, what's the big threat with us against them? I know a full colonel who is gay. There are a handful of physicians that either I know for sure or I suspect are gay. It seems like there's even more gays in the Nurse Corps. We are in all the medical fields, just as we are in all occupations in life. That is not going to change. Yes, there are a lot of gay nurses, and it's probably good because of their innate sensitivity to the human pain that seems so much a part of what each gay person must deal with anyway, throughout his/her life. Like we know pain, because of what the straight society does to us every day to tell us we shouldn't have rights, feelings, or even an existence.

This paranoia affects everything I do. You practically can't say a thing in the hospital about being gay. You have to be careful when talking about things you're going to see. I couldn't just openly say, "Are you going to the gay pride parade next weekend?" You know, that just wouldn't go over in a military hospital. You have to be careful talking on the telephone. There are even signs posted on the telephones everywhere, THIS CONVERSATION MAY BE BUGGED, so you have to be careful. At nighttime, just so I get a chance to talk with my lover before she turns in for the evening, I will call when I'm on duty in the hospital. We have to be careful and contour our conversation, because we don't know if we're being listened to or not. The gay nurses that I've talked with are the same way. We all feel a grave need to be very careful about what is said, what you can let out, and not looking overly gay (whatever that means) for fear of raising eyebrows. It's like the system makes you feel there's something wrong with you when you know there isn't, and I resent that. I resent having to be closeted so much on the job. Yet I chose the military because of the scholarship, but *only* because it was a means to an end. Did I sell out? No, I don't think so.

I've made some lesbian friends in the hospital, but generally, I socialize with nonmilitary friends and I'm only out to a handful of other physicians in the hospital, both straight and gay. It causes quite a bit of inner turmoil when I feel I am a normal person, professionally and privately, and they continually have the feeling I am suspect. It's tough always being confronted by straights that make digs about gay people, about gay people in general. And people (medical types) in the hospital will—

and I really resent this—will make digs about people with AIDS. At some point you *must* stand up, without making yourself too obvious, and say, "Come on, we're supposed to be health care professionals and we're not supposed to be . . . and it's a terrible disease and we shouldn't be making digs about gays and AIDS. You know as well as I do that AIDS is a disease of the immune system and has nothing to do with a particular sexual orientation." You may feel quite strongly about certain ideas, but you just can't be real open or else it will cause people to suspect those very feelings. It's a pretty sad situation, especially for someone in the medical profession, in the Army. I took the oath, the Hippocratic oath, and yet I am limited in what I can do. And on top of that, the confidentiality for the victims of this terrible disease is a joke. Once someone has a positive test result, everyone knows about it. In one case, this sergeant's whole group knew it, and that's totally unacceptable.

I do go to gay bars and I hope I'm not wrong about this, but I would hope that the places I go to are safe for me. You know, I'd hope that the military wouldn't be so underhanded as to plant people in gay establishments and try to seek, find, and destroy us. I guess I haven't let that affect me too much, but that paranoia is still ever present. I just don't think they would ever send people [CID] in to try and identify gays at the places where I socialize. [The military does set up decoys for that very purpose; it has long been a common practice.]

Well, the military has their claws into me for a few years, because I have an obligation to pay them back—so I don't think they're going to kick me or other gay physicians out too soon. After all, they have us as guaranteed, indentured servants for a few years. And because of that, they might look the other way just a little bit, knowing that you're going to be a doctor in the military for a selected period of time. So perhaps, just perhaps, my own personal fear is not as valid as, say, a regular foot soldier that hasn't the same amount of responsibility as I might have to the service, in the form of my medical training. They are much more expendable than I. Of course, dismissal is an absurd joke anyway, but that's probably how the powers that be think. Getting rid of someone with my training would not be a good business move. So I don't think I'd ever be at risk of being arrested and being sent to Leavenworth. Come to think of it, I only know of one physician that was nearly removed for being gay. The pressure was so great on this individual that she even seriously pondered leaving the medical field all together once her obligation was completed. Fortunately, she finished without being dishonorably discharged.

I don't think I would deny it. I think I'd say, "Yeah, I am," and see what happened. I feel strongly enough about my own personal credentials that even if I were kicked out, I'd be able to go to any number of civilian programs and be successful. People respect me as a physician and they think I'm a good doctor. I know that I'm a good doctor, and whether I'm gay or straight should make absolutely no difference at all. Sometimes I get very frustrated with the whole situation. I've done very well. I've gotten excellent OERs, just really tops. I'm getting very good specialty training and I know I'll be a good professional when I'm done. My last OER said that out of all my cohorts I was the best. It was a recognition by my staff, as a group, with all the senior members in the department. They decided that of my group, my year, I was the best. That's the most important thing.

Now that I'm fully active and considered a real Army doctor, there are other little things about the military that irk me, like if you're married you make more money than if you're single, and I resent that. Why should they make more money than somebody who's single? I resent that, and if I could fight it I would, but again, I'm trapped by the regulation. I mean, if it's either go on one salary versus being separated for two years, I think we'd try to go on one salary and make ends meet.

Evaluations and small problems aside, the regulation is not necessary. I think it's actually directed more at the enlisted people living in the barracks. They don't want rampant sexual behavior in the barracks, as if it would occur if the regulation were not there, but that is probably an illogical statement anyway. Those are the same comments and the same arguments that were made when we had a nonintegrated Army. Before blacks and whites were in the same barracks, they made the same comments: "There's going to be too much fighting, there are going to be riots, and we won't be able to handle things. We can't have blacks and minorities living with whites in the same barracks." Well, it took fifty years before the Army became integrated, and as far as I know, that seems to be working out pretty well. So I'm hopeful that the same situation would occur if they ended the restrictions on gay people.

It's pretty sad that the Army, in a sense, can take away many of your civil liberties with the Code of Military Justice, because it seems to supersede the laws of the land. By being in the military, you're risking giving up civil rights that you should have as an American citizen. There has always been that military attitude that you are guilty until proven innocent. And gays are guilty, no matter what!

There's really no difference between gay and straight people. If you're talking about professional ideas, we have the same rights, same ideas, and same aspirations as anyone. I mean, we're just people. There's no reason why we should be treated any differently. I didn't have a choice about being gay. I think I had a choice in *acting* upon my gayness, but ultimately, whether it takes a person five years, ten years, or whether their denial is so great that they *never* overtly express their gayness, they are still gay in their orientation, in their chemistry. I believe that. I feel that I was gay to begin with, grew up as a tomboy, and had feelings about my girlfriends from the fifth grade on. No, I don't think that I had a choice about whether or not I was going to be gay. Some people decide never to express those feelings, and they try to fool themselves into leading a straight life. Those are the same ones that come out at thirty or forty, after having tried to deny it through marriage in the legal sense. They didn't just "turn gay"; it was always in place.

As a qualified and well-trained physician who happens to be gay, I will do my utmost to uphold that Hippocratic oath and care for you and my fellow soldiers, even though the Army feels I am unworthy of the uniform and the respect due my position.

☆ ☆

"I had done something that had never happened to me before: I fell in love with a man."

DAVID KRAFT ECKERT
Age 44, U.S. Air Force, 1969–89, officer. Honorable Discharge. Present occupation: seminary student.

I had a stirring within myself before I went into college. I felt there wasn't much time to consider that, because I had a call to the Presbyterian ministry, and that was my priority at the time. My college years were pretty much straight. There were just a couple of incidents that happened, and both of them made me real uncomfortable. I had two very strong romances during college. One ended up being the girl that I married. Aside from the fact that I still had these little urges, I really felt those inner feelings were never going to be a problem.

I had begun to fly in 1965. By the time 1967, 1968 came along, I was really bitten with the flying bug. So flying, the love of flying led me to thinking about things other than seminary. The Air Force became my choice of career at that time. I marched down to the seminary, and said, "Guys, I'm going to do the best that I can. I'm going to fly hospital airplanes." That's what I told them. I didn't know what a hospital airplane was. I didn't know if they had any. I said that to them because it made me feel better about leaving that atmosphere, going off in a new direction which they considered to be totally alien.

In 1969, I went in as an officer trainee. It was horrendous. It was absolutely gut-wrenching for the first two weeks. Here I came out of this religious, pacifistic—militantly pacifistic—atmosphere into something that was exactly 180 degrees opposite. I'll never forget the second day we were there. We were all herded into this room right after we all got our little haircuts, and listened to good old Colonel Somebody. I still remember him. He was the most decorated colonel in the United States Air Force. His wings would not fit on his suit because of the ribbons. He had so many ribbons, it was just too much. He got them all in Vietnam. He stood there, ramrod straight, in front of this bunch of shaven recruits and told us that if we didn't want to go to Vietnam, we were cowards. He said, "You're cowards if you don't want to go to Vietnam, if you don't want to serve your country in Vietnam." I thought to myself, "God,"—I talked to Him a lot—"what have you gotten me into? How am I ever going to be able to do this?" For about a week and a half to two weeks, I thought—the fence was there every minute—for sure I was going to jump that fence. There was no way I was going to deal with this. However, as faith would have it, I just put my head down and got through it as a "distinguished graduate."

I went on to pilot training for a year and came out of there as number two in the class. . . . Once again, I finished as the distinguished graduate, and also won the academic training trophy . . . and sure enough, the day came, about two weeks before we graduated, that I got my C-9 (which is a converted DC-9). When I saw that, I went to my knees and said, "Thank you, Lord." He had led me to something that I didn't even know was there. . . . I stayed in that airplane for the next eight years.

Colonel Eckert on flight duty, 1989, San Francisco

As luck would have it, I did go to Vietnam. I flew over Vietnam a lot. . . . In April 1975, when Saigon fell to the Viet Cong, the C-5 carrying the babies (the baby lift) crashed. In a desperate effort to get as many people out of the country as possible, we had taken all these children and stuck them into this C-5 for a flight to Clark Air Force Base in the Philippines. The airplane, at 23,000 feet, blew out the back pressure bulkhead and scattered people all over the landscape. It turned around and tried to make it back to Saigon, but crashed in a rice paddy going about 300 knots. One hundred and sixty-five people, mostly babies, were killed.

We were asked to volunteer so we could get those folks out. I said, "I'm going to do that." My wife almost killed me. She said, "We have come this far. Now you've raised your hand to go back in there, fly over enemy territory, land your airplane in blackout, at night, to get those people out? I can't believe it." I said, "I'm sorry. I've got to do it, because I've got more experience than most of the other guys." We flew them out of there approximately fifteen days before Saigon fell. During that time frame, I got a Meritorious Service Medal, two Commendation Medals, and a couple of outstanding unit awards. The first half of my career was medical evacuation.

In 1978, I applied for the 89th, which is the presidential hauling wing. I was assigned to the detachment out of Hickam Field, Hawaii, and stayed there four years giving lifts to the ranking admiral in charge of the Pacific fleet. We also flew the overall Commander for the Pacific Air Forces and the Commander-in-Chief United Nations Command. I was a captain half the time and a major the other half. I made major in 1980 . . . and during this tour in Hawaii, I finally came out.

I think what really accelerated the process a little bit was that my brother had come out in 1977, and I had begun to realize that my own feelings were getting stronger. I think I just kept feeling an attraction. I kept going to the Officers' Club or other bars, and would watch the wrong things. I'd watch the men and not the women. There was a restlessness within me, that same feeling I had before going into the seminary. There was an incompleteness that I could not for the life of me understand. My brother, his lover, and I hit some bars and a bath or two. For me, it was fun and games, new toys, and a totally enlightening experience. It was really wonderful. My wife didn't have any trouble with it, because in her mind the physical part of the whole business didn't bother her so much, as long as she knew where my heart was. As long as she knew where my affections and emotions were, she didn't give a darn.

All of a sudden, here comes this little commander's job, a detachment commander out of Clark in the Philippines. This was 1982, and a career decision was now due. It had a lot of things going for it. It was a real small detachment for two people, so I would be the commander. However, the primary thing about the assignment was that it would be a comfortable place for me to pursue my new lifestyle. Of course, the military really gets uptight and tense when they find out that a senior officer is involved with enlisted people in a homosexual manner. Boy, it just sends them up the wall. In fact, that is the very reason they sent Paul Starr [see pages 227–35] to Leavenworth. But I guess love has no rank, because my first real involvement was also with an enlisted man.

I had come to Clark a couple of weeks before my family. I met this man shortly thereafter. We went down to the bay and stayed for about a week. When I came back from there, I had done something that had never happened to me before: I fell in love with a man. Oh, I loved my wife. Dearly. I'll tell you, there are so many of us (I think men and women both, but I can certainly speak for the men) whose watershed time in their walk as a gay person comes with that first love. Because men are different from women sexually, in the sense that men can go out and just diddle and have a wonderful time and leave all that mushy stuff, romance and commitment, somewhere else. In the gay culture particularly you do that. We do that. We get physical, we get real promiscuous, and there are outlets and places where you can go and you don't even have to know your partner's name. You can do that, and a lot of us do that more or less for a period of time, but then all of a sudden, something happens and we meet that individual, something turns the lights on, and we say, "Whoops, I'm in love." And you know it; there's no doubt about it, and in my case, it was literally like a floodlight coming on, because I looked at myself and said, "When have I felt like this before?" I looked back in my eyes and said, "I felt like this in high school!" That was my most overwhelming sensation. "My God, I feel like I'm in high school. It feels absolutely right and it feels absolutely wonderful."

This involved my heart, my emotions, and to use a slightly clinical term, an affectional preference. I looked at this individual and we were beginning to share, but we were sharing something else as well. All of a sudden, I just fell in love (and fortunately, he did too). He was an airman first class. I was a major and a commander. I was totally blind. I couldn't turn my back on this person. It was just wonderful. Absolutely wonderful. It was the most life-turning-over experience I'd ever had.

This all occurred about two weeks before my family arrived at Clark from Hawaii. After my wife came to the island, I "tap-danced" for about two weeks. I had a desire to be with him and a desire to be with her, too, in a way that we had been, but I was just terribly confused. Finally she said, "Okay, when are you going to tell me what's going on?" I went, "Huh? Who, who me?" She said, "Look, I know there's something about that kid. Now, what is it about that kid? Is that kid your lover?" She said, "Good grief, the minute he walked in the house, I could tell something was going on." Well, I should have known better. The woman knew me too well. She had figured it out from the beginning. She had simply waited a respectful amount of time before she brought it up, hoping to catch me off guard.

Fortunately, he left for Crete shortly after that, but we carried on a torrid romance for months, over the telephone and through the mail. It continued throughout my entire tour of the Philippines. But I had a real hard time making a commitment to him at that time because I was just coming out. I was real new and fresh. There was a little community out there, I had to be there, so why should I have denied myself?

Somehow, my wife and I decided we were going to stay together, no matter what, and get through this Philippines assignment. We'd gone over there to get promoted, to get that little thing out of the way, and we were not going to screw it up. I continued "seeking the other lifestyle" and hoped I wouldn't get caught. Oh, there were a few tiny inquiries into what I was doing, but they were so innocuous that the OSI didn't even bother with them. I felt I was invincible . . . you get complacent, emboldened, or whatever you want to call it, and you do a little more and a little more. We were living this "military family" existence . . . but my sexual activities were starting to add up.

At one time, we had a going-away party for one of my new friends, who was being sent to Hawaii. I also agreed to meet him there and help him get settled. I met him in Hawaii as planned. Somehow, he seemed so distant. He hadn't told me that the day before he left Clark, the OSI had jerked him into a dismal room with a light bulb and had grilled him for four hours, all because of what had gone on at that party. He made up the damnedest story about how I was a lecherous old major who preyed upon these young airmen and made them do things they didn't want to do, and that I'd been chasing him but nothing had ever happened. He made it up because his butt was on the line. As long as he said that nothing ever happened between us and that I was just doing all these things, they were going to let him go, because they now had the *big fish*. Also at that time several others were investigated after the party, but no one said a thing. The reason, of course, was not so much a loyalty to me but that these people were all military and couldn't afford to say they saw or did anything. They all kept their mouths shut out of self-preservation.

I was put under investigation, so I got the air defense counsel to represent me. I put him between me and them, and they never talked to me. In my entire military career I've never talked to OSI about anything regarding an investigation. We gave out neither statement nor interview. We simply refused. It's absolutely the smartest thing you can do, not to talk to these people. I can't get that over to enough people. You just don't talk to them. They have no jurisdiction over you. They have no power over you. When they come in wearing those little suits, looking through those little teardrop glasses, flashing those badges and representing themselves as something else, people fall apart. They wind those people up like dolls and just let them chatter. It's real depressing. And for me it lasted for five and a half months. At the end of it all, there was not enough evidence to pursue it.

I came out of there pretty shaken but still basically intact. And I got my promotion. I got promoted just before all this stuff really hit the fan— too bad for them. The only major fallout was that the wing commander at Clark said that he would drop dead before he saw me pin on lieutenant colonel oak leaves. He said, "I'm not going to have that son-of-a-bitch walking around here a lieutenant colonel after all the shit that's been going on." He had all the credentials. He was thoroughly homogenized. When he was told that I wasn't going to pin them on until after I left Clark, he was happy.

When we came back in August 1985 to McClelland, my wife and I separated. I needed to step out on my own and see if this was really what I wanted to do. It was a terribly hard decision. It involved telling the kids, and at first I didn't tell them why. As I look back, I should have, right off the bat. It was hard for them to understand. We never yelled. We never had fights. There was nothing outwardly that would tell others our marriage was in trouble. It hit the kids like a bombshell; they were asking why. I made it sound like a midlife crisis. How clichéd. That wasn't me. I wasn't any different. I hadn't changed. There was nothing in the house that had particularly changed. They couldn't understand it; it was not until I shared who I was that it all made sense.

Finally, I met someone—someone who was not in the military. This was what I wanted. This was everything I wanted. I wanted a relationship, and I had a relationship. I had somebody to come home to, somebody who knew how to cook, and somebody warm and fuzzy to curl up to at night. It was what I had sacrificed my family, my life, and everything for, and now I had it. I was a happy clam. Then the first cloud appeared over the horizon. On September 17, 1986, I found out that I was HIV positive. (I had gone to a private physician, and had managed to miss all of the mandatory testing in the military at that point.)

In any event, I went home to my lover; there were tears and crying. I said, "This is the way it is. You need to leave, you need to get out of here. You don't need to be a part of this." He said, "Oh no, I can't do that. I love you. You're just too wonderful. I can't do that, I can't leave you." So he stayed, and because we were never particularly active with each other, it fit very well. It worked out very well. So overall, from August of '86 until July of '87, things were pretty cool. We enjoyed one another, we went places together, we did things together, we loved one another.

In July of '87, I found out that he had made unauthorized use of my credit cards to the tune of $3,400. I was not a happy puppy. I found out what *we* bought. We bought limousines, hotel rooms, restaurants, drinks, and boy, we just had a fine old time. When I'd go on trips, temporary duty with the airplane, he was having a good time. There were tears, apologies, and "Gee whiz, I'll pay this back" and a lot of "You bet you will." I decided to give him a second chance. The next time it was a Discover card at 19.8 percent. I said, "That's it. We're done, we're finished." He wept and wailed, and I said, "I'm sorry. This is it. Once was enough, but twice—no way."

Two months later I found out all of his story, like he was on parole for credit card fraud. I got a mistaken call from his parole officer. I almost died. He left on the twentieth and on the twenty-first of April, 1988, the first of the anonymous phone calls came in to the Air Force. The investigation started. They called me in and said, "Yes, sir. There's an investigation, and now let us march down to the clinic, because we're going to draw blood." And we marched right down to the medical lab. My commander was right behind me, and they drew blood. No questions.

There were absolutely no questions on my part. It was done—it was going to be done. I sighed and accepted, and, of course, two weeks later it came out positive. They sent me to Wilford Hall at Lackland.

The medical center personnel went over me with a fine-tooth comb and did all the tests. I was a guinea pig for some of the experiments they were doing. They asked, "How do you think you got this?" Of course you say, "I don't know. I just don't know." That was all they could put down: "I don't know." There was an assumption that there were probably some people that were gay in there. We had doctors who came in and talked about how interesting it was to have all these HIV-positive people to study, because the Department of Defense was the largest organization that had mandatory testing. The thing they touted the loudest was that this pool of HIV people come from a cross section of America, that all the medical people on the outside only have to work with IV drug abusers and queers. And we're all sitting there going, "Hmmm, uh-huh. Right, Yeah, darling." Tell me another story I don't know. What did those people think was going on there?

The Army went in with their report to the big boys and said 38 percent of their people getting the disease were heterosexual. These were unbelievable, exotic figures. They were laughed out of the room. They actually *damaged* AIDS research because they skewed the numbers in a direction they don't go. They skew groups, protecting their image. Actually, they're not so much protecting their image as taking at face value what these people are telling them, which is worse than that.

Through all of this the stress was the most horrible thing. The flight surgeon prescribed a little green pill, a mood relaxant/depressant–type thing. When I took it, I went comatose until nine-thirty the next morning. The rest of the day I walked around in a fog. I said, "This is ridiculous. I can't possibly function with these stupid things. I'm going to throw these things down the toilet." And I did. I was classified a Walter Reed 2-A, 6 being the worst and 1-A being the best. The physical evaluation board elected to retire me. That paperwork went out to Randolph, to the Secretary of the Air Force, and came back approved. I had nineteen years in at that point. On the twelfth of August, 1988, they preferred charges. When they did that, the whole retirement process stopped.

Presently, I am formally charged: two counts of sodomy and about four counts of conduct unbecoming an officer. If this results in dismissal, it probably will be dishonorable. The best is that they simply acquit and/ or drop charges and give me my medical retirement. An intermediate process can happen. They can bring some charges forward, find me guilty, and decide on some kind of punishment. Whether it includes dismissal or not I don't know. The worst thing that can happen, of course, is dismissal and jail. I really am not anticipating that one.

If they quietly said, "Why don't you just take this retirement and go away?" I'd grab it and run. If they want to get out from under these headlines and all the crap that's going to come down the road if it's continued, then just give me the retirement and let me get the hell out of here. And the headlines keep coming. I had the editor of the local monthly gay newspaper call me. "I heard that you were married." I said, "Yeah." She said, "Is it a marriage of convenience?" I said, "Yes. I've been conveniently married for twenty years." She said, "Do you love one another?" I said, "Honey, you don't go through this and not love one another." She was flabbergasted.

The Air Force contends: "We're not trying Colonel Eckert on the fact that he's gay, we're trying him on specific charges." Homosexuality per se, they contend, is not a crime, but the acts are. If you look in the supplemental books to the Uniform Code of Military Justice there are definitions for a class 1, 2, or 3 homosexual. A class 3 just feels like it but doesn't do anything. A class 2 has consensual sex with an adult. A class 1 either forces, rapes, or gets involved with a man. Right now they're saying I'm a 1. Why? Because one of the charges involves a minor.

I realize that I'm not going to make chief of staff! I have one year left until regular retirement. Looking back over my life of forty-three years, I have asked myself, "Where does all this fit in with the big picture? Who am I and why did God . . . ?" I've come to the understanding and belief that we are unique creatures and that God has created us just the way we are. I really believe that we're not an accident, that we're not a mistake. There are too many people who have this orientation for it to be a mistake. We're not a screwed-up gene. I'm sorry. I do believe that there is a very definite genetic predisposition to homosexuality . . . which may cause you to go in this direction. Whether you choose to act on it or not is another question, but I do believe the primary thrust is genetic. If I do believe that, then I must also contend, for my own religious feelings, my own Christian belief, that God, in creating the different types of human beings that there are . . . that this is one variety He has certainly created. He has done this for a purpose.

If there are differences, then there should be acceptance. I really believe with all my heart that if God made me the way I am and has brought me to this place, as rough as it is right now, it's a journey; it's for a purpose. I believe that the call I had to the ministry twenty years ago has been reaffirmed in my experience over the last three years. I'm ready to take up the call and go with it as long as I'm alive, as long as my health allows me to do that. I feel that very strongly. I believe there is a gospel that has to be preached—preached loud and clear, both to the gay community and to the others: You are committing a terrible mistake. The military is committing a terrible mistake. People make a terrible mistake when they choose to persecute and discriminate against gay people. We have as much right as blacks or any other racial group to the civil rights of this country for one very simple reason—that we have no more choice over our sexual preference than the black man has over his skin or the Oriental person his eye slant, except that ours is not visible.

That's the key. That's the real key. Because we *can* get by, because we are the invisible minority. You may look at us and think you can tell whether we are gay, but that's bullshit. You can't look at any of us and know that we're gay for real. I think everybody accepts that the number is almost as big as blacks, twenty million. Twenty million gay people, if you go by the straight statistics. But we're invisible. And we're invisible not only to them, but we are invisible to ourselves. Because we are invisible to ourselves, we do not hold the kind of power that the other obvious minorities have.

AIDS has been the most devastating blow to our political strength, not because of the fact that people are afraid of it but because we have used all of our political energy to fight AIDS instead of fighting discrimination. And we're losing our leaders. In every facet, whether it's religious, political, or social, we're losing them. It's tragic, absolutely tragic, and nobody's paying attention. My destiny is to be right where I am.

I'm not doing this because I'm brave, believe me. I'm being forced to do it. It's a decision that I made on whether to simply knuckle under or stand up and take these people on. If I wanted to be remembered for anything, it's for this situation, here and now. If what happens here causes increased pressure to be put on the military to change its policy, then I would like to be remembered for that. When I say the military, I'm really talking about the President of the United States, I'm talking about the Commander-in-Chief, because he's the only one who can do it. He doesn't have to have Congress, all he has to do is issue an executive order and the military regulation against homosexuality is gone. Now, Congress, if they wanted to be real nice, could put us under the 1964 Civil Rights Act, which would also do away with it. But I put my money on the President of the United States, who actually has the power to eliminate this brazen discrimination in one fell swoop.

If what I do and how I conduct myself in this case can bring us any closer to that, or if I go down in horrendous flames but it brings us one step closer, for that I want to be remembered. Do I want to be another Leonard Matlovich? Heaven help us—see what Leonard went through. But if that is what it takes, then I'm ready to do that. Somebody's got to stand up. Somebody's got to do something. I just love to see them get nervous over this issue. They just can't stand it. They just don't want to talk about it.

AUTHOR'S NOTE: *On September 1, 1989, Colonel Eckert received full military medical retirement and benefits. He will also be returning to seminary so that he can continue his work in the ministry.*

☆ ☆

*". . . that's when I found out he had been seeing this rear admiral . . .
you may as well have lit bullets under me. I was like well, that bigoted
son of a bitch (the admiral) . . . wanted him to have a little party, an
orgy of sorts . . ."*

J. W. "SKIP" GODSEY

Age 38, U.S. Army, 1967–70; U.S. Navy, 1970–86,
enlisted/officer. Honorable Discharge. Present
occupation: military counselor.

I liked it fine. I didn't like the fact that we were in
Vietnam, but yeah, I was taught . . . where I came from in Kentucky . . .
my family came from a very long line of military people. My grandfather
was a rear admiral, and from World War I, clear back to the Revolution-
ary War, we had pictures. I got the nice lecture about being patriotic and
serving my country, and so off I went to Vietnam, as a corpsman, which
was a lot like being a preacher.

When you talk to the preacher, you kind of let your guard down and
say a lot of things that you wouldn't say to anybody else. And the thing
about being a combat medic was that everybody just dumped on you . . .
many times it was about a homosexual affair. I can't refer to people in
particular because of confidentiality, even twenty years later, because of
the oath that I was sworn to at that time, but there were lots of activities
going on. Of course, it was very, very, extremely closeted . . . but it definitely existed. And there were bigots. There were people who absolutely
hated it. There were fag-bashers, and many a time I sewed up a few heads
and straightened a few broken arms because somebody was queer. I can
remember one guy in particular, they almost killed, and he was one of
the best radiomen I've ever known in all my years of service—he was
probably right up there in the top 3 percent.

I got out of the Army in 1970 and was out for a year. Actually, I was
discharged four times in my career. I'd get out and then I'd go back two
or three months later or a year later. I stayed in the Navy as enlisted for
ten years. So I had lots of friends. Most of them were not military. I did
have many gay friends in the military. I'd be the first to say, "Take all
the queens and all the lesbians out of the Navy and it'll sink." I'm convinced of that. There's no doubt in my mind. And the Marine Corps—
now that's another story. They always had some excuse about not being
gay: "It was the heat of the night, I guess," or some lame excuse to that

effect. Most of the gays I knew were like that. Not all, because there's always one or two screaming queens running around, but most of them . . . as the MC per se, and the Navy. It's all just, you know, it's playing Navy. But the stories I could tell . . .

J. W. "Skip" Godsey, 1988, San Diego

Now, I had a real problem when people came to me, especially after I became an officer, and they came to me—"Well, I'm gay and I want to get out of the service." So fucking what! There was nothing that I absolutely hated more, and still probably do, than people using the gay issue as an excuse to get out of the service. I think it's a crock of shit. I was gay. It never came up, I was never on the carpet, I was never asked—except for one time. I was asked by a commander, so I asked him what difference did it make? I later found out he was an old queen himself. So I never admitted it nor denied it, but it never came up. In this particular case, he wasn't just somebody trying to nail me for being a faggot. He was a friend, who in passing conversation . . . just asked me, "Are you one of those funny boys?" "What difference does it make if I am or if I'm not? *I* think I'm pretty funny." And he came to my house many times after that with his boyfriend. They were together for thirty-four years.

So I played Navy well. I was a 4.0 sailor—on a scale of 1 to 4, just like a grade point scale. I was never written up, never turned down for advancement, and never turned back for any duty that I ever asked for. I always got it. I have a full stack of ribbons. I've got every one you can think of practically. I have a total of eighteen or so. And oh yeah, and I have a Purple Heart.

While I was in Vietnam, this one fella, I carried him for about seven or eight miles on my back. He was already dead, but I didn't know it because I was so spazzed out from my own injuries by that time. We'd just been under attack and I was determined he was going to hang on because he was my buddy. He was the one who was getting me through, and he'd tell me I was the one getting him through. But of course, by the time I got him back he was dead already. There wasn't anything I could do about it. That was one of the major reasons I decided I wanted to leave the medical profession, because I felt totally helpless in this situation. And you know, I didn't like watching people fall dead, that same feeling of helplessness . . . I couldn't do anything about it.

During that same time, reality faced me even more directly when I was forced to kill another human being in order to save my own life. The first one I shot was probably about fourteen years old. I woke up with him standing straight over my face, and it was either blow or get blowed. We'd just bedded down and had probably been under attack for a couple of days. Everybody was totally worn out. I'd lain down, was just dozing off, when I heard something. When I opened my eyes, he was right there. And to this day, I can see the look in his. Well, it literally blew his face off. Literally.

I began to have problems, because his face wouldn't go away. It was constantly in my mind's eye. Today I could probably sit down and draw it, just because of the expression that was on his face. I'm sure I won't ever forget that face—never. You just can't . . . you know, but it's not like I wake up fifty times a night like I used to. There are times that I just weird out. I mean, boom, there it is. But it's not anything, not even a grain of salt, compared to what it was before, absolutely nothing. On the other hand, it was one of those things you had to do or had to get done. Some of us are still paying for it emotionally, mentally. . . .

It was the last thing they told us when they kicked us out of those choppers, like, look out for your own ass because nobody else was going to do it for you. It doesn't make any difference where you're from or what country you're fighting for, it's each man for himself. The reason I went in as a medic was that they told me my job would be saving lives, not *taking* lives. What they didn't tell me was that when somebody fell over there, I might have to kill five to get to him. They didn't tell us that part, you see. That part they left out. Otherwise, I wouldn't even have been a medic, if I'd known.

I found out damn early that, as a medic, you do not wear a cross on your hat, not on your lunch pail! You don't carry a medic box with a cross on it either, because the first person they're going to take out is the corpsman, the second is the radioman—guaranteed, guaranteed. They told me to wear it. I said, "Fuck you" . . . and didn't wear it. That's definite, that's also good advice.

People always ask if there were drugs and alcohol abuse in active combat. If there wasn't, we wouldn't have any sanity left. None of us would have come back that did. We'd have all been dead. That's my personal opinion. When you have people shooting at you from every direction, sometimes for as long as three days at a time, nonstop, if you don't find some sort of ventilation or an escape, you just lose it, and I've seen that happen. I've seen a lot of people go off, just completely go off the deep end. Some of those were classified as suicides and some of those were missing in action.

It was a difficult theater of battle, to say the least. You could be a little more open with emotions and feelings, not sexual but nonsexual. It's like you have this old cliché that men don't cry and men don't do this and they don't do that. Well, in combat you didn't really give a fuck what men did and what men didn't do. All you cared about was that you looked over and the guy you were talking to last night was still there the next day. It didn't make a rat's ass of difference whether he was black, white, queer, or straight, nobody gave a fiddle-dee-fuck. It was simply the fact that he was there, breathing, because most of them weren't; they were dropping like flies at one point. I remember writing in my journal they were "going like flies." So, sure, you were able to show a little more affection, I suppose, in that aspect. But as far as the homosexual part of it, it was still very, very much under wraps, even in combat. You didn't actually . . . as a matter of fact, I never saw actual sex acts going on at the time in the heat of battle. Now, I've seen it at the end of the day, or early in the morning, little interim periods.

We were the peace generation, so if I were going to call myself a peace-maker, then that meant I couldn't have prejudices. Those things could not exist. I was in the gay march in Chicago when they cut queens apart. One in particular, they found in five dresser drawers. Just because he said he was gay. They totally decapitated him! But in the war situation . . . they weren't labeling people and saying get the fuck out of here be-cause you're queer. Not during war. In fact, there was this one instance where I'm sure the commander knew this guy was gay and was trying to get out because of it. But the commander's overall concern was that he would lose men, and he wasn't going to give up any of them without a fight, and he didn't, so he told the gay fellow to prove it. That's exactly what he said—prove it. "So you're a gay boy, prove it." Consequently, the guy didn't get to go home.

After Vietnam I was still in the Navy, and had completed my education in order that I could be commissioned. That occurred in 1979. I had a lover for eleven of my military years; he died in September of 1987, with AIDS. I was an officer and he was an enlisted man, but we lived together for all of that time. When I was at work, I was strictly service. I strictly did my job, didn't talk about being queer, didn't talk about queer things. I talked about Navy and my job. When I went home, it was a totally different ball game. When I was home, it was *my* time, even though you're government property twenty-four hours a day. We never had any prob-lems on a personal level. However, I did run head on into a gay-related problem with a rear admiral I personally knew was gay. Not that there aren't many more in the general/admiral ranks.

I worked for him at one time, and if there was ever a hypocrite that I've known in thirty-eight years of living, he was class A. No doubt about it. Even though he was gay, he really shit on other lower-ranking military gay people. He loved to bust somebody for being gay. It so happened my corpsman was having an affair with another man who was also in the Navy. At the time, I did not know it was this admiral. This corpsman had been doing fine on his job, then things just started falling apart. It caused me some concern as his supervising officer.

I asked him what the hell was going on. And he goes, "Well, nothing. I'm doing my job." I said, "Listen, don't get defensive with me. I'm just asking you as a friend, not as your commanding officer." I said, "I just don't know what's happened. You know, you can talk to me, see if there's something I can do." He told me he had been seeing this rear admiral . . . you may as well have lit bullets under me. I was like, well, that bigoted son-of-a-bitch, I know him! I let him tell me all about what was bothering him. Apparently, the admiral had wanted him to have a little party, an orgy of sorts, and he wouldn't do it. He was very, very possessive, and so naturally he didn't want anybody else around, not in a compromising position. When he refused, the admiral got pissed off and, since he had friends all the way down the line, got a little shit stirred up, and the next thing you know, my man was on the carpet because he was a homosexual, unfit for active duty!

I decided to step in at that point. That's when the admiral and I butted heads . . . I told him, with all due respect to his rank, "Sir (then he couldn't get me for insubordination), I know that you're a goddamn closet queen, and if you want to know how much I know, I can name the last twelve boys you've had! You happen to have one of my corpsmen on the carpet, and I can tell you he is not going out of the service." I started naming names, and his eyes got right big and he kind of sat back. It was like, "Oh, the queen knows what he's talking about, yeah." So he said, "Well, who is this person, who is this corpsman?" and I told him. I said, "You don't need to tell me any explanations, I don't want to hear them. I don't care. In fact, I could care less." Now, you have to take into consideration, I had my job on the line, because it was as much my responsibility to turn him in (for being gay) as it was the admiral's, but I knew, or at least I hoped, I had enough "tearoom" stories on him to call his bluff, and I did. The corpsman just retired last year. And the admiral has since retired as well.

If they called for us to go to war tomorrow, as long as I was convinced that we were fighting for us, for our rights, for our country, for our mothers, for our fathers, for our kids, then I'd be the first in line. I'd have no problems. I'd go right back. They wouldn't take me now because I have AIDS, but I'd be the first in line, absolutely. No doubt about it, no qualms. Anybody that won't fight for their country has got no goddamn business here—that's the way I see it, period. Personally, I think the peacetime service is full of shit. Because it's like, is your gig line straight, or is your hair combed the right way? Who cares? If they're pointing a gun down your face, they're not going to look at your shoes!

I would have retired at twenty years, but I got out at eighteen because I was diagnosed. And I was amazed that I had gone through eighteen years of bullshit and survived. So when I was diagnosed, I just went to my commanding officer, who was a female captain in charge of the operating room, and told her exactly like it was. But I was pissed, very pissed. But there wasn't much I could do with it. I had just finished my Ph.D., in hospital administration, thirteen months before I was diagnosed. But just the fact that they're dealing with the AIDS issue could help. By them investigating and getting involved in the AIDS crisis, in the process they're going to learn and are already learning that, hey, these guys are just normal sailors, squids, jarheads, or GIs. They're just like everybody else. I think that it made them stop and think about what they were doing, instead of just doing it.

I live a day at a time. Oh, I have short-range goals . . . I just try to keep up my quality of life, I'm not concerned with the quantity. Mind you, you don't have to live on death row or let your life be a shambles. I'm learning to take control of my own life, but it comes in stages. I thought mine would go on as planned, but I found out differently. And if anything is taken from this, let it be that just because you're gay doesn't mean you should be removed or forced to get out of the service—nor should you be afraid of the service. You may not beat the system, but you can massage it, make it work for you, that's all.

☆☆☆☆☆☆☆☆☆☆☆☆☆☆☆☆☆☆☆☆☆☆☆☆☆☆☆

". . . doing things that . . . weren't really wise. Like getting dropped off to drill and kissing my girlfriend good-bye . . . all these people in my company were in the first sergeant's office getting a bird's eye view . . ."

"LESLIE GRAHAM"
Age 30, National Guard, 1981–present, enlisted.
Present occupation: leather apparel craftsman.

I was a tomboy. I played with GI Joes. In fact, my parents, knowing how much I loved my toy soldiers, GI Joes, and playing war, bought me a little OD green sergeant's uniform when I was about six years old. I wore that thing until it was threadbare—I've still got the stripes that went with it. So I had plenty of illusions of being the typical soldier. I had friends along the way; not all of them wanted to play war. Most of those I became close to were female. There was never any overt sexual activity, though. I mean, not in the physical sense, like making love.

Actually, my sexual experiences began with a man. He was bisexual and liked his girlfriends to be bisexual as well, so that we could do three ways. In that, having introduced me to women, I found out, oh, that's the missing piece. The proverbial light dawned, and I suddenly realized this was why I hadn't been getting crushes on boys like all of my friends had, and had this inordinate attraction to my female friends. Suddenly everything fell in place, and I said, oh, that's why I always felt a little bit different, and realized that's where my attractions led, that's where my orientation was. Several months later, I thanked him and warned him that, unfortunately, he'd been too successful!

I went through the normal college life, activist kinds of things, but I realized there was still this pull toward the military. A lot of my attraction to the military wasn't just—I joke about having a uniform fetish, which I probably do, but it wasn't just playing soldier but also some very strong convictions in terms of old-fashioned patriotism. And I decided that that was something I wanted to do. So I joined the National Guard. I enjoyed the concept of the military but just didn't want to do it full-time. I remember that stupid question about my sexuality, and I lied through my teeth. I mean, "Have you ever had any homosexual contacts or experience?" is a horribly open question, and if people answer truthfully, at least according to Kinsey, a lot of heterosexuals wouldn't be in the military. I didn't feel it was a question that should be included anyway. But I got in.

When I went to basic, I felt really angry, because in my company I could look at the first three platoons and see dykes all over the place. And somehow I ended up being the only dyke in my entire platoon. I was a little upset at the fact that there was no person in my group I could turn to for moral support. I didn't go in purposely with a lavender triangle on my forehead, but I might as well have. Because from day one, everyone knew I was a dyke, and I got a lot of resentment and problems from the other women in the platoon.

One sergeant in the company . . . now, I shouldn't put a label on her, but it was pretty obvious she was a dyke. I felt good about that, but that didn't stop the catcalls and snide comments. It was like she didn't care what was coming down on me. I didn't truly mind, but I guess it was the fact the other women found me somewhat different. The word *dyke* was thrown out while passing in the hall, you know, and *pervert*, or just plain avoidance, especially in the showers. That seemed to be the biggest place where they harassed me the most, real hate, real petty bullshit. There was no way I would ever do anything in any of those situations, but somehow the straight person believes otherwise. I meet and get involved with an individual using the same techniques as any other person. What is the big concern that so many straights seem to have about us?

My platoon sergeants' attitude was to purposely goad me into performing at a high level of excellence, so I'm not sure whether they honestly thought I was incompetent or not, or that they didn't want one of "their own" to let them down. I proved myself by being one of the first ten people from my company to graduate, and it was a self-paced course. I came out of basic training as an expert grenadier and sharpshooter. At AIT there were only nine women. And once again, I was the only dyke there. I was beginning to question all the stereotypes I had heard about lesbians in the military, that was for sure!

I came back home and entered my unit, performing my monthly week-end drills. I was ecstatic to find there were some other lesbians . . . but for the first couple years in the unit, I was extremely naive . . . naive just doing things that probably weren't really wise. Like getting dropped off to drill and kissing my girlfriend good-bye in the car, then walking into the unit to find that my first sergeant, my company commander, and all these people in my company were in the first sergeant's office getting a bird's-eye view of the *kiss.* One of the other lesbians in the unit was also in the same room at the time. She came up to me later and said, "Leslie, what were you doing?" I said, "What are you talking about?" "Do you know who was in that room when you kissed your girlfriend?" She named them off, and it's like, oh, geez. I can tell you, I only made that mistake once.

I'm the only woman in my section. And that has been a real problem regarding a lot of women in the military, in terms of men not following orders or wanting to be supervised by a woman. It's a basic issue of respect, not wishing to treat a female section sergeant the same way, with the same respect or obedience that you would give normally to a male. And I'm not sure if that's because I'm a woman or I'm a lesbian. Actually, men tend to get along with me and the other lesbians much better, and I simply think it's because they see us as more assertive. Once again using labels and major stereotypes here, but by and large, it seems lesbians are more likely to be assertive or aggressive, willing to take authority, to take responsibility, to operate in leadership capacity. A lot of the straight women I see in the military don't seem as comfortable with it or willing to accept those situations as well. Not to say there aren't straight women who do excellent work, but . . . It's more of a re-flection of our society as opposed to the women themselves or their role in the military, but I'd have to say a lesbian makes a hell of a lot better soldier than a heterosexual soldier does. It sounds cliquish, but we aren't worried about breaking our damned fingernails!

When all the other women are in their skirts or class A's, I'm in my pants. I don't have long hair, don't wear makeup. They don't need to worry about telling me to take off a pair of earrings, so perhaps I don't fit the appearance of a "standard" (whatever that means) female soldier. My appearance is closer to a male soldier, within the regulations, of course. Be that as it may, I have gotten lower ratings on appearance because of this very issue. I don't think it is at all fair, particularly when I am within the regulation and am getting my job done.

I have never been approached while on the job for any kind of sexual favor—most people know where I am coming from on the issue. Besides, I made it a point a long time ago to never fool around while on duty. My sexual life doesn't mix; however, my civilian job has in fact mixed over. I'm sure everyone in my unit knows not only that I'm a lesbian but that I work in a leather shop. The important point here is that no one has chosen to do anything about it. They're looking the other way—about knowing and choosing to ignore it—probably because I'm a good troop and haven't caused any problems. Now, I feel if I were a problem, they would damn well do something about using the regulation to get rid of me, but so far . . .

People in my unit have learned over the course of the years not to make fag jokes. And I don't care to hear any AIDS jokes . . . I jumped all over this one guy who I felt went too far on the subject, because I had heard just one too many cracks about it. And so people know. At the moment, there are only a couple of us in the unit right now, and she is pretty open about it. I don't know how she handles the crude, cruel jokes that are made about gays in general and AIDS. But I just won't stand for it. I think even if I were straight I wouldn't. Where is the humor in joking about a terminal disease? People don't make jokes about cancer.

I'm inclined to believe that the gay men in the military are harder to pick out than we are. That's probably why more of us are harassed and even kicked out, percentagewise, compared to how many of us are actually in, than the men. I think the men feel a need to be more in the closet, where the lesbian in society in general and certainly in the military is maybe tolerated more but, again, at the same time more obvious. In the military you can expect it, because she's a strong woman and she's willing to pull her share of the work. A gay man would be such a threat. It is certainly a fucked-up kind of rationalization, to say the least. Unfortunately, many women who are drawn to the military may have all those tomboyish characteristics and *not* be gay, yet they are still harassed because they fit the gay stereotype.

The Guard has now become a smaller part of my life. I entered a relationship, and my lover has a hard time with the identity, my being there. So I'm finding that I may need to reevaluate my dedication to the Guard. Before, I was always single and did not have to make these choices. Since the military is opposed to such relationships, it makes it even more difficult. Recently, I went inactive, to give myself some time to think about my options. I had begun to feel some resentment toward my unit, you know, the regulation and all.

I have been able to gather some support for my situation from another woman in the unit, a straight woman who knows of myself and several of the other lesbians, and she's always been there, in terms of moral support and encouragement. It's good to have her support, because if nothing else, the people that have made various comments or inquiries have always assumed that I had a lover, and she can help act as a sounding board for me and some of the others. It's funny how people draw their conclusions, because at various times they have just assumed the other women in the unit and myself are lovers.

Even with the negative aspects, the Guardship always enabled me to keep some semblance of financial security. I always knew I was going to be getting at least a hundred dollars every month plus, and of course my two weeks' annual training has certainly been a holiday! When you are a reservist, your regular job, as previously mentioned, can sometimes be a problem, especially in my position as a leathercrafter. I will probably never get rich, and it's a blue-collar dirty job, but I love working in it, and I'm also very out and actively involved in the scene around here, as a civilian.

I've received a lot of flak and problems for the fact that I'm a lesbian. They assume the worst because the leather shop is primarily an "adult" store, so a lot of the leather equipment is related to bondage and different things. I get plenty of "Hey, Leslie, did you bring your whips and chains to drill this weekend?" It's basically good-natured, but many times it is a bit uncomfortable. Even if I were straight, I would tend to keep my personal life my own private business, in terms of these people that I see once a month. I mean, hey, they don't tell me about their sex life, and I don't expect them to wonder about mine.

☆ ☆

"Well, being MI, I don't want to put myself in a blackmail situation, so I've always been up front about it. I don't want to put myself in a compromising position."

"KEN HANSON"

Age 35, U.S. Army, 1971–1977, enlisted; U.S. Army Reserve, 1978–present. Honorable Discharge (from active). Present occupation: printing field.

I recall, before I had my first experience, I was stationed at Heidelberg and there were two gay men on the floor of their barracks . . . they were caught in a sexual act, and I thought it was totally disgusting. I thought it was horrible. And I said, "Well, why doesn't someone tell the commander?" Older people in the military said, "Just leave them alone, it's none of your business . . ."

In my twenty-first year, I basically came out. We were good friends, and I went over to his house because I'd gotten dumped on; I had a date for New Year's Eve and she dumped me. I was feeling badly about it, so I went over to his house and we got shit-faced drunk together. Then he started playing around with me, and I didn't resist it that much. It was a real strange feeling. But I decided it felt right. There was something missing when I was involved with women, and I felt this was what was missing. I was in military intelligence then, and so was he. I personally think you tend to have more gays in MI than you do in other fields. There was also more compassion back then. . . . In fact, in most environments where I worked, it was not an issue. Everybody had to work so damn hard, no one cared who you were or what you were, just as long as you were a good worker.

Once I really came out, I was a screamer. When I was stationed in San Francisco, I was loud, and fairly obvious, so there was never a question of whether I was gay or not. A major went into my commander one day and blew up, screamed, ranted and raved: "I want you to process that man out of the Army right now. He's gay, he's a homosexual. Get him out." And my commander said, "I don't give a damn what he is, he's the best troop I've got. What I do with him is my business, not yours." Even while that guy wanted me out by stepping over commands, he seemed to miss all the other officers that were gay. Hell, while I was at the Presidio, I hung out with several majors and knew a couple full colonels.

I'd say the Presidio's high in the number of gays assigned there, period. Many people who get stationed there are obviously gay. It was real funny, I had a lover at the time who was an E-8, stationed at Presidio. I knew within two weeks of my arrival probably thirty people, and he'd been there for two years and had never met anyone. They were working in his office and everything. I think I was, I know I was, a little bit more open, more friendly too. I got to know people. Most of the people he knew had been removed. So I think he was working under a great amount of fear and paranoia—rightly so, of course.

It seems most people I've encountered that were prosecuted out had other reasons included as well [minor problems, i.e., being late, average EERs]. It was like an excuse to get rid of them in a lot of areas. They were mad for some other reason, and homosexuality became an issue. In fact, in my last duty assignment, it wasn't an issue of my homosexuality so much that made me leave the Army but an issue of compromise. I was being blackmailed into doing things because of it. And that's when I refused to be blackmailed. I said, "Fine, I quit." When I first arrived at this duty station, after two weeks the personnel guy goes, "You're queer, aren't you?" And I went, "Yeah." I've never lied if asked about it. Well, being MI, I don't want to put myself in a blackmail situation, so I've always been up front about it. I don't want to put myself in a compromising position. And that guy had known for six years, so when we got a new commander in, he said, "Now, this man is a vicious antihomosexual and is going out there looking for them, so you'd better lay low, and quit *acting* like a homosexual!" His comment blew me away, particularly since I had previously had straight commanders come so far around as to say, "I would like to recruit gays into the unit, because they work harder than the straight troops do."

My previous commander was *very* progay. He thought people were people. So I go from a commander like that to one who's trying to prosecute us out of the Army. I went, "No, I can't deal with this. You know, after six years of active duty, I am me and I get things done and I'm damn good." It was a question of judgment, and since I'd had six years' experience with my position, I also thought I was being told I didn't know what the hell I was doing. I wasn't going to put up with someone that was still operating under the witch hunt system.

I mean, in my career I've run into the Navy "plants" that go to the gay bars and take down the names of their service people. I am familiar with that whole process. I've sat and talked with them. I'm real up front about stuff like that. I usually walk over and face them off right away. I have talked to them for hours and found that they were gay as well, but their job in the military was to identify others, gather evidence, and file the paperwork to aid in final expulsion. I found them to be sleazy and disgusting. They were active duty, and I'd ask them how they could live with themselves; I personally couldn't. Somehow, they could justify it to themselves, but I felt they were a very low form of life. Usually they had been caught themselves for one reason or another, and had made a deal with the military in order to stay in.

In most cases, they'd been in eight or ten years and agreed that they would turn in . . . would go around to all the bars and other gay establishments, and write down all the names of the servicemen. You'd have to be very stupid to be caught by one of these people. You'd have to be totally drunk, out of your mind, and rattling off about something. Normally, they would sit in a bar and cruise like everyone else, you know, like they were looking for somebody, and then they'd eavesdrop on different conversations. I saw this one prick seduce this one fellow so he would talk. As soon as he started talking about his position in the Navy, he was gone. This spy was quite efficient, and got their name, unit address . . . whatever was needed. Personally, I guess I have tempted fate, because I would usually give them my name, rank, and social security number, what unit I was currently assigned to, and phone numbers to call. I'm not afraid of Virginia Woolf!

I learned from my assignment at the Presidio that if you're good, people are not going to fuck with you, especially if you're in a power position. I felt I was in such a position with this new commander. But it didn't happen that way. It was, basically, "Keep your mouth shut and gracefully get out or we're going to burn you." This commander was like a little old lady. It's a horribly sexist term, but he was vicious, bitchy, self-centered . . . I talked to him all of twenty minutes in the total six months that I was under his command. I was totally shut out as soon as he became commander.

The old commander said he *wanted* gay people in his command because it was a psychological operations unit. He wanted gays because they were already living a dual life—gays have to do that constantly with the straight world—they were already playing games, were aware, more acutely aware, of propaganda and smear campaigns and the vicious whole aspect of the redneck propaganda machine. But not the new one, oh no: "Let's tar and feather 'em!" Consequently, I got out of the active Army but went into the Reserves, in a new unit, in a new state. I got a slot in another MI unit, and they were thrilled to have a man with my background and expertise.

I feel there was a lot more support during my active-duty time, and that was because of a large networking system. When people transferred, they could link you up with other people, so you would immediately walk into a friendly situation. It was like a club, and if you left, you informed anyone that came in of the status of different people. . . . It's protective to an extent. There are very strict rules that are unwritten. It's always been there, like a fraternity, an unspoken knowing. . . .

In order to make it work, you've got to be a total workaholic. You've got to be good. If you get out of line the network will be the first people to slit your throat. But mentally, I don't think being gay in the military should be an issue. I don't think it should be there, and I go through life saying that it's not. I'm me, goddamn it, so get used to it. I didn't ask to be who I am. I am who I am. I like who I am. I'm a good person, and I have no problems with it. If it comes down to a pissing contest, it's *going* to be a contest—I'm not going to run away and hide. However, when it's a no-win situation, I will just walk away. I don't have a scary area that I'm going to fall into or need to avoid. I know how I am, 360 degrees around me. I can't get backed into a corner because I can see behind me, and if you can get yourself into that position, it's a good way to go through life in the military.

You know, it's like that question when one first goes in about one's sexuality. Well, for one thing, it's really not a problem, and "tendency" is probably an incorrect statement regarding the information they wish to gather. I have a real hard time dealing with it. I think people are people. I don't think of a person as sexual; I think of the person as a human being. I could and have fallen in love with a woman before. It's the person that I fall in love with; sex comes into it after that. No, I don't think the question has any merit or basis for being there. And besides, the last Army physical I had, the *doctor* was gay! So what's the big deal?

I feel I did well in my six years in the service. I received two Army Achievement Medals and two Air Force Commendation Medals. I was on a joint Army–Air Force base statistics program when I received the medals. They expected me to shut up and be quiet, and I wasn't. They said, this particular problem needed to be addressed. I was given the task of solving the problem and I did an outstanding job. I did out-briefings for two Air Force generals and one Army general, and obviously did a super troop job there as well, so I think I received the medals for several reasons.

I've encouraged several friends who were gay to go into the military just to get their heads screwed on, give them time away from a situation. It *can* be good. I think it might be easier for a woman to be gay and remain in the military. Soldiers are expected to be tough. Your typical stereotype gay woman fits into the military mold—I mean, your stereotypical woman—more than your stereotypical male does. And I think women running around with each other is a little bit more common, so people don't raise their eyebrows.

I've thoroughly enjoyed the military and the people I've encountered. I mean, even the bad times were growing experiences. Sometimes it's hard dealing with other gays in the military. The people that stay have been protected or they know how to protect themselves. I wish there was some way of teaching people that talent. The most dangerous time you have is when you first join a unit. You haven't proved your value to them; they will do whatever is necessary to make points. It's a very *dangerous* thing to switch units or switch chains of command. You don't always have protection, that networking. You have to very well watch yourself. But as a whole, if you lay low and see where the cards fall, you can make it. It's real hard, because you have to make a very strong decision on who your friends are, and you need to make a decision as to when you will let them into that personal aspect of your life, because at that point you become very vulnerable. But it also opens a lot of doors, because they come to you with very personal, private things. It opens as many doors as it closes. And I think the people that truly accept you are the people worth having as friends. And the people that don't, it's better to know right away.

You can't live in fear. You've got to keep on going, keep on trucking. I've gotten totally drunk and made an ass out of myself a few times and let too much information out, but luckily, I usually tend to drink with friends. They watch out for you, and there's usually somebody there that can deal with the situation, talk to the person that you've made an ass out of yourself with or whatever. I remember one time when a friend covered my butt by talking to this officer that I had "shocked." He told him, "He's an ass tonight, he's said too much and revealed too much, but he's very important to me, so will you please disallow what you heard?" I was terrified of what I'd done, but later, I got a call from that officer. He said, "You know, you were a real jerk the other night, but you've got very good friends and they said that was you that night and that was not you the rest of the time." So I think it's quite important when friends are selected that know and care. Yes, that network of friends. I have an incredible safety net . . . I would do the same for any of them. A lot of people don't have that safety net. I've got too many friends that are interrogators, and we know how to deal with the situation. I can step back real quick!

I have found that the more redneck people are or the more hostile toward you, the lower they think you are on the chain of life, and they will tend to do things around you that they wouldn't be caught dead doing with their own friends. And if you have to, there's a lot of parties that you can remember. The only tricky thing is that that information is good only if you *don't* use it. Once you use it, it's gone. You don't have to mention the party or anything else; all you have to do is be aware of what takes place. In other words, turn the tables and have something on them, if they hassle you too much. You need to remember, they will do these things simply because they think you are a lower form of life than they. That makes it all okay.

My doors have always been wide open, and people knew where I was and tended to walk in and treat my house the same way. And it never became an issue because I never used it. Like I said, I never, ever used it, but it's there. If you're honest and open, people will be honest and open around you. And their behavior may be as low as what they think your behavior is, but by being open and honest you're not going to run into a situation. You're not going to have problems. You've got as much shit on them as they have on you.

I had incredible rapport with my troops. I mean, I couldn't ask for— They got together and bought me dress blues, because we had a military function and they wanted me in dress blues. They didn't wear dress blues, but they went together and bought me dress blues and brought them in to me one day. That was like a hundred and fifty bucks. I was shocked. I didn't realize that they thought that highly of me.

I've had people act like a mother to me, a father, an uncle. There's always been someone there, and what still shocks me is, your friends aren't the people you might think they are in the military. It is only under direct fire, when things are really rotten and nobody wants to talk to you, that you'll have some unfamiliar PFC walk up to you and say, "I've always respected you." You'll have some high-ranking officer, from God knows where, come down and say, "God, it's good to hear your voice again." And that has *nothing* to do with my sexuality, that's merely one human being relating to another, as it should be.

☆ ☆

"They had to revive him from the time he was born . . . I can't help but believe my baby died because of that incompetence. Underscoring it all, is the feeling that they weren't overly concerned because I was a lesbian."

"JANET K."

Age 24, U.S. Army, 1983–87, enlisted. Honorable Discharge. Present occupation: data controller.

I believed in God. I believed in doing what's right and all that. I felt that way and I still do, and I struggled with my orientation, and I'm just now beginning to accept things. I was still struggling in my mind, with what was right, what was wrong. I was really giving myself a hard time, and finally I just couldn't . . . you know it just overwhelmed me so much, I just couldn't stand still anymore and finally allowed my gayness to be.

When I was being recruited to go into the service, they asked me if I was gay or not. I remember now, the recruiter said that they don't allow homosexuals in and he needed to find out that information. I thought, "Wow, I can't believe you're asking me this." That's the way I felt at the time. That's none of his business to start with and I don't understand why it would matter anyway.

When I entered AIT [advanced individual training], it was like a whole different world. I was in the barracks, open bay, nothing but women, and it was open . . . I mean, there were lesbians everywhere, it was over-whelming. I just couldn't believe it. All of a sudden, I found myself. . . . All these women were attractive and they'd ask me out to drink with them and then finally, after they'd get me drunk, you know, we'd start talking about things, and so I knew . . . I was in all kinds of situations with all these different women. I finally realized my feelings.

This drill sergeant was really strict on gay women. He'd always say he was going to get all these gay women out, counsel them, read them their rights, and so forth. I didn't know what to believe after I heard all that. I thought, "Wow, I can't believe he'd do that." These corporals would always walk by and make all kinds of comments that were, to me, really insulting. They'd just . . . I don't know, rub it into the ground. They found great glee in making obscene comments about lesbians. They would tell me I'd better not take a shower when the lesbians were in there and all that. . . . Sometimes I would even be in the shower when they'd make these comments. I couldn't believe it. . . .

I met this one woman who lived in Philadelphia. So we would drive up there over the weekend. And that was kind of tense because her lover . . . I didn't know about at the time was an E-6 in the Army. When we were careful, it was really a good situation. We would go when her lover wasn't there, but when she did find out, she came back and threatened to kill me. But I felt so strongly about the one I was seeing, that wow, this was it, this was love, it didn't matter. We kept seeing each other, even though this other lover was going to kill me. She didn't. I found out that she had a broken leg at the time—probably from killing the last one!

I realized rather quickly that the straight people in the barracks who were homophobic treated lesbians like they were lepers. I had to develop a protection against that sort of treatment. If the women would not go out with the guys, they would definitely be called gay. Most of the men had that attitude, but especially the black guys seemed to think that way. If you didn't give them sex, that was it, there was something wrong with you. That was the label, all the way through my military career, yet almost every straight woman I knew in the Army was pregnant—was pregnant at one time or another. They slept around plenty—I was horrified by that—one guy one night and another guy the next night. They just kept repeating the pattern.

The investigation aspect of my career became more obvious as I added more years to my enlistment. I had one friend who was investigated while she was in Georgia. They had people staked outside of her house every day, day in and day out, for a couple of months, had a telephone tap, and she was continually being harassed. They'd call her in two times a week to ask her questions, the same questions over and over. She sent me a letter and she told me about it, and I immediately thought, "Oh no, this is it, oh God." The CID was scary to me. I didn't even know what they could do. I didn't even want to know what they were capable of doing to gays or lesbians.

I just tried to decide, okay, if I'm in my own home, if I'm not doing anything, bothering anybody, what was the problem? I was a damned good soldier, one of the best from basic training on. I had several letters of recommendation to prove it. But I started seeing it for myself, and I was getting scared, I was getting cold feet big time because . . . I didn't want any part of that. I didn't want—I had made a commitment to the Army, and I wanted to stay in because I had several goals I wanted to reach. So I thought I'd start dating guys, to either cover myself or just try to get away from my gayness. So I did that for a period of time, a few months, but when I was with a man, I'd continue to think about women.

I was just dating them, yeah. They'd get upset with me. Every time it came to sex, there was no way I'd do it and they couldn't understand why. This one guy got so upset, that we finally stopped seeing each other and he started spreading rumors that something was wrong with me.

That bothered me because, first of all, I was somewhat old-fashioned. I come from Kentucky, from the hills, and I was raised with the idea that you found one guy and got married. I didn't even date any guys until I went in the Army. I was beginning to understand what guys were all about and that all they wanted was sex. I felt like they were just using me, but besides that, I didn't feel anything with them, while with a woman it was a totally different feeling.

I went from stateside to Mannheim, Germany. I found that there was plenty of gay activity going on over there. I went to a private bar that was strictly gay. There were hundreds of people that patronized the bars, military and civilian. For some reason, I wasn't that concerned about the CID, but frightened enough to really watch myself, no matter what, about ever talking to anybody about my private life. I always thought deep down that I don't want the CID to find out, and I thought you never know if one of your friends could be CID. I really made a point to watch what I'd say around anybody, unless I knew for sure. I still felt harassed and couldn't be myself; I always had to live a lie. I've never done anything to hurt anybody, so why would they want to harass me? It really tripped my mind out—I couldn't believe all the harassment. If I'd known that when I went in the Army, I don't believe I'd ever have gone in the military, because I was put through so much.

I tried to be careful, which added a good deal of stress to my life. Finally, I started coming on to this lieutenant. She was flirting, very nice-looking, but there for a while she gave me the runaround, saying she was not gay and all of this, and then she was. We started seeing each other, but it was rather hard because she was a new lieutenant in the Army and had to really be careful. She always kept isolated from everybody because she was afraid. She talked to me about all the different things she knew. Remember, I was just a bit of a hillbilly.

But she couldn't understand, nor I, why they're so prejudiced to start with and why they would kick out homosexuals. It's not like we had some kind of disease or something, and I agreed with her. She was in the Army against her beliefs and was hiding what she was because of what the Army told her she'd better not be—she had a lot of energy about that. It was either be straight or you were out.

I also realized that being with her was another violation of the regulations—fraternization. I always thought it was exciting to ... I don't know ... exciting and daring to see someone with that much rank. To me, I thought the lieutenant was something else. And I loved it, personally ... the excitement ... but still I had to be cautious. Although I didn't like sneaking around, that was the fun of it.

Well, after Germany I got emotionally drained, totally zapped. And I thought, okay, three gay relationships were enough. I didn't want to be gay any longer, so I tried to play it straight again. I met this guy that I really thought I liked. If there was going to be any guy I loved, it would have been him, and I guess I did love him in some ways. But then I met

Ruth . . . I was fighting these feelings for her, because I fell for her from the very beginning. Even though we were totally opposite, I cared deeply for her.

When I first met Chris, we talked about everything. I told him I was gay and he thought that was neat, because he thought gay women were sensitive, special women. I think I loved him deep down. As luck would have it, I got pregnant. . . . At that point I felt really close to Ruth. I'd always wanted a child, and I wanted one with her, period. I don't know, maybe it was a miracle, meant to be, but it happened. I was totally loving the fact that I was pregnant. And Chris, he quietly stepped aside.

My military problems didn't become overwhelming until about my sixth or seventh month of pregnancy. The first instance occurred when Ruth and I were in the barracks (she still had a room on base), and I asked her if she would like to feel the baby kicking. Her roommate, just burst into the room, saw what she thought we were doing, and turned around and quickly walked out. But this woman and some of her friends had already been spreading rumors about us, and she slipped a note under the commander's door saying that we were kissing. We got called in by the commander.

He told me he was aware I was a good soldier but said he would not stand for any more business about lesbian activity. I was seven months pregnant, had high blood pressure, and he wasn't even concerned about that. I questioned him about why he would believe an unsigned note, whether it was true or not, and he just kept saying he had reason to believe that it *was* true. I was so upset, and had to be aware of my own health. I was starting to develop some severe physical problems.

While I maintained my relationship with Ruth, I was also living in an apartment with this colored girl and her boyfriend. That was another one of their regulations—about moving out of the barracks once you were pregnant. I think I lived there a couple of months, and my blood pressure started getting super high. There were just so many things coming down on me. Ruth and I decided that we had to get me out of that apartment situation, because it was causing so many unnecessary problems. The day that we were supposed to move, I was put in the hospital. I was about eight months pregnant. I was checked by an Army doctor, who didn't do much at all, even though my pressure was about 160 over 120, I mean, like sky high. This doctor sent me home with very few restrictions—duty was fine. Oh sure! Shortly thereafter, I was back in the hospital, for an emergency C-section.

My baby only lived twelve days—that was emotionally heart-wrenching. While I was in the hospital, not once did my commander come to see me, to see if I needed anything, not one time. My platoon sergeant only came in one time. I was in the hospital for nearly a month.

After the baby died, I had to set up the funeral arrangements and everything. The day . . . I didn't go to my baby's funeral . . . I couldn't. And that same day my dad had a slight heart attack. I called up my NCO that was in charge of me and told him I needed help, I needed to help my mom back in Kentucky. As I was leaving, who shows up but that damn bigoted commander! He came rushing in and asked if he could be of any help. And all that time I was in the hospital and needed somebody, he never even thought of asking . . . the bastard.

There wasn't any reason for them to treat me that way, because I always did a good job for them. I was one of the best soldiers they had. I was also the only female in their platoon. In fact, it used to gripe me when they'd address the whole platoon as men—"Men this" and "Men that"—and I started getting pissed off about it because I'm not no man! So finally I told my platoon sergeant, "I'm in your platoon too, and I don't want to be called a man, period." Then he'd address the platoon . . . call them men and look directly at me and say, "Excuse me, and one lady."

When everything was all over—the hospital, the funeral, and so forth—I wanted my furniture back from my other apartment (there was a problem with the roommate), and I brought it up to my platoon sergeant, who told me, "I can't help you. I can't go to the commander because he knows you're gay, and he won't do anything about it." I didn't know what to say. . . . They gave me the impression I was a burden to them, even though I was always there and did a top-notch job. Yeah, I think they were just trying to ride me out, so I'd just get out, be out of their hair. That's the way I felt about it. At the end of five years, and a great amount of emotional stress and pain, I decided to get out. The only time I could breathe a sigh of relief was when I was on the outside, when they cut up my ID card. . . . Before that we, Ruth and I, thought for sure we were going to get busted.

I was feeling victimized, I guess. I don't know. I was feeling like they're telling me being gay was wrong, that there was no place for homosexuals in the Army *or* anywhere else. So I felt like, wow, maybe I'm not right, because they all felt so strongly about it in the Army. I did not deserve what I was put through. If I was late for formations, came out half dressed, or was catching up on somebody every day, that would have been different. But now I feel very angry. I resent what was put on me. And I'm getting an attorney . . . matter of fact, regarding the death of my baby. It's still painful to talk about it, because it's only been about a year since he died.

I even had a stroke that had closed the vessels to the placenta, so he wasn't getting the blood supply he needed. They hadn't noticed! And all the amniotic fluid was gone. There was nothing in there. They hadn't checked. When the emergency C-section was performed, he was born almost dead. They had to revive him from the time he was born . . . then twelve days later . . . I don't like to think about it, holding him for such a short time, so helpless. I can't help but believe my baby died because of that incompetence. Underscoring it all is the feeling that they weren't overly concerned because I was a lesbian. And what appears to be a glaring answer is, everything that happened can be tied directly to the regulation, as to how I was treated—the fact that I am gay, and the reality of my baby dying. All so unnecessary. . . .

I take one day at a time. Granted, I'm a strong person, but I'm still trying to recover from my emotional devastation. I must have time to mourn, and need time to heal. I must move forward in my life, but it will take time. I do have a good job right now, and oh yes, Ruth and I are still together. But even that does not give me all I need. It's conceivable that I could sit here and feel sorry for myself, but that's not going to bring my baby back.

☆ ☆

"Your right to free speech, free assembly, and freedom from illegal search and seizure does not exist in the military."

PAUL STARR

Age 28, U.S. Air Force, 1982–88, officer. Dismissal under less than honorable conditions, one-year prison term. Present occupation: sales representative.

Long ago, I had decided to go into the Air Force and pursue a career as an officer. Since I'd been in Civil Air Patrol since I was thirteen, it seemed like such a natural. I went to the college of my choice. I didn't like what went on at the Academy, and couldn't honestly believe in their training philosophy for officers. Besides, once I got commissioned, my bars were the same color as theirs, so it really didn't make any difference to me.

After graduation from my ROTC program in 1982, my first duty was at Malmstrom Air Force Base in Great Falls, Montana—you know, "where the men are men and the sheep run scared." Yeah, and the good old boys would go fag-bashing on Friday nights, or Indian-bashing—whichever they found first. It's not a real good place to be out. Consequently, I played it very low key. But the Air Force took up a majority of my time anyway, so it wasn't a big problem. I was very, very dedicated to my work. While I was there, I was named SAC Outstanding Administrative Officer of the Year, Junior Officer of the Year, and Officer of the Year. I was pretty dedicated to the job of being the best there was at that base.

From this grand beginning, I was chosen for a position in Germany as a squadron commander. This particular position made me the youngest commander in Europe, which was kind of neat. So I left the big sky country and headed for Europe.

The base was in a rural area in the Eifel Mountains, about two hours from everywhere. I laid real low for a while, and then started seeking out the "tearoom" scene. The train stations were real good sources for that kind of stuff. I'd always known it was against the rules. I'd always known that if I got caught I could get kicked out. I really didn't want that to happen, so I thought I played it rather cool. After all, it was my private time while I was off duty. I was under the impression that if someone was caught and exposed as a homosexual, they would simply be removed. Prison was never in my thoughts, that's for sure.

I was able to move rather freely because of my command of the German language. I met a German national, and we were having a relationship. One night I tried to find him in this gay bar. I thought, "Well, he's probably in the bar," so I went to look for him and found him. As I was sitting there talking to him, about five GIs that knew me walked by, and I almost fell over and went, "Oh my God!" and they said, "Oh, hello, sir," real loud! So then at that point the word started spreading around the gay community in the Eifel that Lieutenant Starr was gay. I was the talk of the town. Suddenly, people that had never talked to me before started becoming real friendly. It was a pretty interesting situation.

Captain Starr, U.S. Air Force, 1985

Come October, we had a birthday party with a bunch of people, non-military gays and the gays we knew from the military. One of the guys was later court-martialed. He was very helpful to the OSI and gave them plenty on me. He told them all the details he remembered from the birthday party. That was the mainstay that made their case for my court-martial. Leo, the guy I was dating, was sitting on my lap. We were stroking, caressing, and kissing in front of the other party guests—the same thing any two people in love might do. One of the other guys at the party was in my squadron. Later, when the investigation was going on, they contacted him, and he gave a full confession of his sexuality as well as what he saw at the birthday party in return for an honorable discharge. Our actions at the party, which were not really out of line, became a favorite graphic description for many brought in for the investigation. It seemed that everyone who testified against me confessed their homosexuality and got honorable discharges in return for their testimony. Which bothers me just a little bit. Actually, my judgment must have been impaired during that time, because the *next* guy I dated sang like a canary as well when he was brought in. Once again, when he was finally discharged, it was for homosexuality in return for his testimony.

I was in Germany two and a half years. Almost three years, I guess, if you include the three months I was in Mannheim prison. I had routine contact with the OSI as part of my job, and suddenly that stopped and I thought, "That's odd. Why aren't they coming around to talk to me? Why aren't they coming to do their routine investigations? Why the sudden change of contact?" I found out that my records were getting checked out by bizarre people for no obvious reason. The wing commander and the chief of security police seemed to have an interest in me. So I thought something was up. I got real careful. The OSI called me in and said, "We've gotten this letter and wondered why your name would be on this list." I went, "I don't know." It was a very descriptive list—all the names were gay people, most of whom I knew. This OSI investigator, a woman, said, "Would you like to make a statement?" And I said, "Well, yeah." I wrote, "I am not now nor have I ever been homosexual, nor have I committed any homosexual acts," signed Paul Starr. *That* came back to haunt me later on in the court-martial for making a false official statement. That was one of my charges, but at that time I did not know that they were putting my case together from many sources.

I lived at the very edge of the town, and beyond me were fields. Many times, there would be a car parked out in front of my house with a Frankfurt license plate, and I lived two and a half hours away from Frankfurt. I thought, "Well, that's kind of odd." It didn't seem to make any sense, but it was there for long periods of time. Occasionally there'd be somebody sitting in the car. I thought, "OSI guys aren't real bright. I think I know what's going on." One guy tried to follow me on foot, but I always lost him—he wasn't real good at surveillance work. I needed to be real clean and real careful. I *wasn't* careful enough. My secretary apparently had planted a bug in my office, for the OSI. I thought she was a friend of mine. I was trying to help her out—little did I know!

The OSI called me in for questioning, and it was just like playing back a tape, with the OSI agent seeming to have all the answers, and, of course, that confirmed my thoughts about the source of their information: I'd mistakenly confessed a lot to this secretary, mostly locker room–type talk. So when the OSI confronted me, I confessed to what they had that I had *actually* done. I confessed to three charges of sodomy, two counts of fraternization, and one count of official false statements, which was that "I'm not a homosexual" statement. There was plenty that they *didn't* know. I really wanted to protect a lot of people, people that are still very special to me who are still in the military. They probably could have brought those people in as well and ruined their careers. I rationalized, "Well, either way, my career's over, so why drag them down with me?" So I said, "Take me, I'm yours. I confess to what you've got that I've done." They hemmed and hawed and finally said, "Yeah, okay."

I gave them a statement, a stipulation of fact, basically telling them that I had done these six things, with enough detail to convince the judge that in fact I had done them. We had prepared a pretrial agreement which would have given me no more than two years' confinement, no more than a dismissal and forfeiture of all pay allowances. A dismissal is not called a dishonorable. The discharge papers say that the type is "uncharacterized." But even so, it was still under less than honorable conditions.

It took two days for the trial results to hit the papers. It was a pretty big article, and the funny thing was I couldn't get that much for one of my troops who won Air Force Airman of the Year. But me being a homosexual captain seemed to get a whole lot of attention. It was in the *Stars and Stripes*, which covers all of Europe. It was in the German regional paper, which covers all of central Europe, as well as being broadcast on the local and regional radio news repeatedly during the day.

A lot of people attending the trial were my troops, people who wanted to see me get what they felt was my just deserts. You see, I was a hardcore squadron commander. I believed everyone was there to work and we all had the same mission to accomplish, and if you didn't play by the rules . . . I told them what the rules were. If you get a DWI, you lose your license for a year, and you're going to lose a stripe, no questions. If you do it again, you are discharged. I had very simple rules—tough but simple. I was known as a kick-ass commander, and so the troops that I had given reprimands to were there to watch me suffer. There wasn't a lot of seating in the courtroom. People were standing outside, listening through open windows. It was a lot of fun. The trial took three hours.

The prosecutor kept discussing anal intercourse, which was not part of the evidence. The judge kept saying, "Stop, wait a minute, unless you can bring in some new evidence . . . " Four or five times the prosecutor brought that up, and the judge was just getting real pissed at him. I think that it was to my advantage. He was calling for *twenty-one years' confinement* in prison. For my heinous crimes.

He made me out to be a walking sex maniac, looking for my next conquests, and if I couldn't find some young, single GI, maybe I'd look for children. He kept calling me "despicable" and it ruined the presentation. "What? I'm not a recruiter." My petition throughout was grown adults, fully consenting, age appropriate. Unfortunately, the military's a little different. They don't see it that way. Then it came to the sentencing part, and since we had established guilt, it was the next step. My lawyer presented my outstanding military record and all the medals I'd won, as well as my career in Civil Air Patrol and career in college and high school, the politics and everything else I was involved in, March of Dimes, rape crisis centers, and all the rest of that stuff. The prosecutor said, "We don't care. The guy is still despicable. I still want twenty-one years."

I thought everything seemed to be stacked well in my favor. Then it finally came down to the sentence of dismissal and eighteen months' confinement. No reduction of grade. Total forfeiture of pay allowances. Up until the day I went to court, I still didn't believe they'd actually court-martial me. I'd never heard of anybody being court-martialed. I thought, "They can't send me to jail for this. This is stupid." I went back to my little holding room, and twenty minutes later they came with the handcuffs and took me off to confinement. It was a holding cell there on base until they transferred me to Mannheim prison. And Mannheim was the last stop before Leavenworth prison in Kansas!

My holding cell on base was about four feet by ten feet by ten-foot ceiling. I had a wall locker, a bed, and a toilet. There was a shower outside in a little hallway and a sink for the morning shower and shave. That was it. I was there for four days. I was very cooperative—didn't make any waves. They were likewise. While I was in prison, I was still a captain. That was to my advantage, because officers got treated far better than the enlisted personnel. Especially at Leavenworth. We were segregated, we had an officers' tier—there were about thirteen of us—we had two color TVs for thirteen people. In the enlisted section there were two color TVs for two hundred people. It was a lot more relaxed for lockdowns and they treated us far, far better than the enlisted people.

The base judge and the OSI wanted to make a deal with me to cut down my prison time, by giving names and information, but I said, "I don't think that's my right. I think it's crazy for you to ask me that question. Sure, I could have given them all kinds of information—all the way up to full colonels and all the way down to basics—but I didn't think that was my right or my place and I wasn't going to do it, and as it turned out, I didn't serve the total time anyway.

While I was in the confinement cell, the guy who did the most damage against me came over to my cell about an hour after I had been there and said, "I'm really sorry. I had no idea it was going to turn out this way." I just looked at him. I'd been real remorseful at that point of the game. My whole career was just flushed down the toilet. I wasn't feeling really up. He came up with that and I said, "You didn't think what? You've got to be kidding!" He looked kind of shocked and I said, "Get the fuck out of my sight." His wife was the kingpin in making the OSI investigation stick. She felt a lot of guilt. Prior to the trial she came over to my house and brought me a bottle of wine. She said, "I know this is nowhere near enough to make up for what I did. I really feel sorry for what I've done. I was really stupid." I said, "I feel what you feel. You did this for your husband." She had no idea what her husband had been up to as far as his role in the gay community. I told her, "I thought of all the people it might have been except you. I'd saved your butt so many times. I'd saved his butt when his commander wanted to do something to him for beating you up. You're the last person I thought would betray me, but I'm not going to forgive you, I can't forgive you."

After those four days I was moved to Mannheim, and spent three months there while they were pissing around, getting my case finalized. For a prison, the facility was real nice. It was kind of like being in Army basic training. We had to get up early in the morning, scrub down the whole place. Buff, buff, buff, sweep, sweep, scour, scour. I had never done this before in the military. This was all new to me. The Army guy said, "No problem. We'll show you how to do it. We did our own time." I went, "Okay." They had one- and two-stripers as our guards. It was a perfect time for those low-ranking guards to "get even" with officer types. It was their chance to play drill instructor and pick on the captains! They took full advantage of that, and they treated us worse than what I'd seen Army basic trainees being treated, let alone Air Force basic trainees. They were allowed to haze us and harass us. We were being harassed and watched all the time, all our waking hours.

One day, while I was taking a shower, they ran a tour through. That bothered me. I'm still a human being. I still had some rights to privacy. So I kind of turned around and was oblivious to it. What else could I do? In fact, that kind of treatment goes on all the time in the enlisted section. They—the enlisted—don't have the knowledge or background to know that it's wrong. That they don't have to put up with that kind of harassment, of being treated like lowlifes.

From day one I said, "I'm going to cooperate and follow the rules." That was the way I was in the Air Force, except for the homosexuality issue—if I followed the rules, then I could enforce the rules. If I followed the rules in prison, I could complain when I was not being treated fairly. If I was not following the rules, and was getting special privileges, then I couldn't turn around and complain. I had exactly thirty letters, I had exactly fifteen magazines, I had exactly two sticks of deodorant, all the maximums I could have; I didn't have anything over. They tried to catch me, but apparently they were really disappointed. They came back and searched me two days later while I was at work, and two days after that, but still couldn't find anything.

Finally, I was evaluated and removed from Mannheim, and sent on my way to Leavenworth. This prison held about fifteen hundred inmates, and about thirty were officers. I had never been handcuffed until I left Mannheim. We were all handcuffed and shackled. Here I was in my service dress uniform and shiny captain's bars, handcuffed and shackled. It was very humiliating, especially walking through Kansas City International Airport with shackles and handcuffs. They let me put my overcoat over my handcuffs, but my shackles were still visible. I guess the fact that people couldn't see the handcuffs was supposed to make it better. I remember one woman was walking with her two children, and as we walked past, she pulled her children away. I thought, "What am I going to do?"

The cell that I finally made my home, sweet home, was four feet by ten feet by ten feet. I very carefully measured it with my little eight and a half by eleven piece of paper. In that cell, I had a single-sized bed, toilet, sink, chair, garbage bag, and a four-by-four locker that was four and a half feet high, cram-packed full of my military and prison uniforms. There wasn't a whole lot of space.

Word flew before I even got there that a homosexual was coming. That caused some friction with some of the officer inmates because it was very cramped quarters, communal showers and that kind of stuff. I said, "You don't mess with me, I won't mess with you. I'm not going to do anything while I'm in prison that might jeopardize my chances of parole. The last thing I'm going to do is get caught fucking around. You can rest assured." One guy really didn't like me being there. I said, "By the way, you're not even my type. I wouldn't mess with you if you were the last man on earth." That pissed him off more than anything else. "What do you want me to say—that I think you're attractive, so please sleep on your stomach instead of your back?"

There were a lot of gay people in there, a lot of people who were in there for drugs or whatever else, who just happened to be gay. There was no one else there for consensual sex, although there was one person, an Army captain, who'd left about six months before I arrived, who had a one-year sentence. That's the only one I could find any record of, who had been given a prison sentence for it. Actually confined for consensual, homosexual, age-appropriate sex. Prisoners were there for rape, murder, grand larceny, robbing banks—in anybody's book, these guys were criminals. I was there for loving a specific group of people: men. The child molesters got a whole lot of abuse; they called them Chesters. And that seemed to be what half the officers were there for, and, of course, these fellows were all straight, as are most child molesters. But they were at one end of the spectrum, the murderers were at the other.

Our uniforms were basic brown. Women had a blue uniform that was equivalent. They wanted to spot blue from a distance in case there was a woman who might have gotten in around the men. God forbid we'd have fraternization of prisoners. It was interesting, some of the men who'd been there many, many years and who had a chance to see a woman, would get all worked up, start panting, and foaming at the mouth. I thought, "I'm glad I'm gay. I don't have to go through all this or even pretend to go through all this."

There was a lot of homosexual sex going on in the enlisted wings. A whole lot of it. I was approached, but I told them that I wasn't going to do anything to jeopardize my parole. Besides, I could just as easily go back to my cell and beat off for my sexual release. There was one inmate who was HIV positive, and who was so prolific that he had people waiting at his cell to fuck him or get fucked. I confronted him on it, and he didn't seem to give a shit. "I'm going to die, I'm in prison, so who cares what happens, I'll get it when I can." He had a twenty-year sentence, and I honestly do believe he didn't care. And we're not talking high-risk groups, but high-risk behavior. The total situation was not a good experience, and fortunately, I was able to leave after six months.

Looking back on it, I think I must have been very naive, thinking I could have pulled it off for twenty years. I was very relieved when the OSI confronted me. I thought, "Okay, I'll be discharged and all this will be over and I can come out and be human about it." Not thinking they were going to court-martial me. I never thought that would be the worst-case scenario. I felt almost schizophrenic: two very different people. When I was playing Captain Starr, that was my entire life, my entire mental thought pattern. When I would take off my uniform and leave the military environment, I could be the Paul Starr that really exists.

I was really very military all along and very patriotic. The Air Force was a natural step for me. Academically, taking an officer with my credentials and my résumé from the Air Force and kicking him out because of consensual sexual behavior, nonprejudicial behavior against the Air Force, is in a business sense, stupid. After all, I received a Special Achievement Medal for working on and developing a prototype defense suppression system. If the enemy bombed an Air Force base, they wanted to see if it could survive. I came up with this prototype—a sewer pipe underground system for living quarters. It was a prototype for which I developed all the operating procedures and training manuals. I engineered the whole program, which is now being implemented worldwide.

It's routinely upheld in court that when you join the military, you give up your civil rights. I don't think that's appropriate either. Your right to free speech, free assembly, and freedom from illegal search and seizure does not exist in the military. Several of the officers I was very close friends with were also very good friends with enlisted people. I said, "Hey, you could be next." They heard it loud and clear. But of course, *that's* never prosecuted—being friends, yet fraternization just the same.

Getting out was the ultimate high point. There's really nothing else you can compare it to. It's like when you go Christmas shopping, you've bought that last present and you don't have to go out into the stores anymore. The hassle's over. That's what walking out the gate was like. It wasn't like, "Yay, I'm free!" The hassle was over, but I *wasn't* free, because I still had to set up a schedule with my parole officer, find a place to live, find a job, and so on. I thought, "When's my shit finally going to get together?" But I never lost my own self-value. I know what my value is in this world.

Now, I finally feel free. On a personal note, I had found a terrific lover shortly after leaving prison. We fell madly in love. From the first day I met him, we were together every single day. The second day he told me he was HIV positive. I didn't practice unsafe sex, so sexually that wasn't a problem. Since he was just HIV positive, I assumed we'd have several years together. I figured that would be no problem. In a period of six months, he went from HIV positive to full-blown AIDS, very, very quickly.

The last few weeks were very painful for him. Things were going on in the outside world over those last eight weeks that I was oblivious to. I spent every spare moment in the hospital. I'm now, only two weeks after his death, finally getting a grip on things again.

I have had a hard time understanding why the gods sent me the best person I ever loved in my life, and now, in the blinking of an eye, he's gone. It's like, "When will this ever end?" The heart-wrenching part of it is that somebody I might fall in love with again will be in the same situation and I'll have to watch him die. That part is very difficult for me right now. There's not an hour that goes by that somebody doesn't remind me of Mark. My whole enthusiasm grinds down. Where is the justice?

Superficially, I have never accepted the fact that I was a convict. I don't feel like an ex-con. I don't feel like I'm a felon even though legally I am. I don't think those are labels I use to describe myself. The only time it bothered me was when I came out here to do job hunting. . . . Being on parole . . . anywhere outside the parole district, I had to have written permission. I will have to wait about seven years before any federal court will even consider dropping the felony charges. I mean, I can't even vote because I'm a felon! For being gay! I spent nine months total confinement to the day, with six of those being in Leavenworth. I was on parole from March until September of 1988, for a total sentence of eighteen months. *For being gay!*

☆ ☆

"I was the only midshipman ever in the history of the Academy to do that, to sing . . . I was the only person ever to sing the national anthem at the Army-Navy games, twice. People recognized me."

JOSEPH STEFFAN

Age 25, U.S. Naval Academy, 1983–87, discharged six weeks before graduation. Present occupation: computer sales.

I was involved in things like student council. I was president of the student council my senior year, president of my senior class, voted most likely to succeed, and all the standard kinds of things the Naval Academy looked for in a midshipman. I pretty much fit all the criteria that they were certainly looking for as far as success in high school was concerned. I was also co-salutatorian of my graduating class with something like a 98.8 average throughout my high school career. So in 1983, after I received my appointment from my congressman, I entered the Naval Academy.

I wanted to do something meaningful and felt the military service would serve that purpose. The Academy itself provided a very elite, exciting chance to compete with the finest people in my generation, both academically and physically. I also entertained the thought that with an Academy education and naval military background, I would be fairly free to do whatever I wanted to in life.

Midshipman Second Class Steffan, U.S. Naval Academy, 1987, singing the national anthem at Army-Navy Game

I was always on the go. I got involved in three choirs and eventually took on leadership positions. I felt my time was really very constrained. I learned early on that the Academy was a very homophobic institution, and just about any naval officer, except for a few thoughtful individuals, would speak of gays for use in target practice. They *expect* fairly high-ranking officers to make sexual orientation jokes, because they know that the military supports that kind of thing. It's basically discrimination, and it's something that no one would ever dare talk about supportively, because it was so well ingrained that the military was against it, that even coming out in favor of some type of openness, being open about it, about discussing the issue, was considered grounds for suspicion.

Freshman are called plebes, derived from the word *plebeian*, and they are basically considered scum individuals. The core of the first-year experience is to place the maximum amount of stress on an individual to see whether or not he can make it. Once you make it through your first year, it's perceived that you have the ability to make it through the remaining three years. And so the plebes lead a very regimented life. It's immediately understood that academic requirements like chemistry and some very difficult courses confront a freshman. He must deal with that as well as this very, very strict, regimented lifestyle and the extra memorization that is forced upon him. This is intended to maximize the mental and emotional stress of the individual. That's the whole philosophy, to essentially see who breaks under pressure the first year, so that the remaining years can be a time of investing in the individual.

I recall, as a plebe, we were forced to jog in 120-degree temperatures, wearing plastic rain gear, while holding our M-1 rifles out horizontally away from our bodies. We continued to jog, brought our rifles down, and then held the rifles out again for forty-five seconds at a time. This ridiculous activity actually didn't stop until the individual directly behind me passed out and went into convulsions. I was involved in specific efforts that changed the indoctrination system. I was instrumental in rewriting, as a junior, the plebe indoctrination manual. Along with the basic hazing, there was also a great deal of negative attitude toward women, even when I started in 1983. The Academy changed a lot over the space of my four years. . . . By the time I was to graduate, there was enough ingrained support from the brigade that the women's issue was not really one that was particularly foremost in people's minds. I think that it sort of died away to some extent.

My feelings of homosexuality resurfaced during my sophomore year, but it was not something that I felt I could actively pursue without putting myself at great risk. I decided I couldn't afford to be involved with my sexual feelings, whatever they might be, because it was too risky, and I'd invested so much in the Academy, that I didn't want to get kicked out for something that stupid. So I basically wasn't involved much during my Academy years, mainly by my own choosing. I did have a few experiences, but they were few and far between and very, very secretive, conservative. Certainly none of the horror stories I've heard about football players with their girlfriends in their room and things like that.

On occasion, they would have a female midshipman girlfriend and have frequent sexual encounters in the hall or whatever, which was extremely taboo. So there was plenty of sex going on in the halls. Probably not much of it was homosexual because of the double risk involved. I mean, if you were caught having sex in the hall, you were certainly in big trouble, and you may have had to take a year off and serve in the fleet for a year, but it you were gay and caught, you were out. I mean, there are no questions asked. In my case, the situations I did encounter tended to be with other midshipmen in non-Academy surroundings.

We went on many trips over the years, with all the involvement in choir and performance. It was usually on those occasions that I had my secret contacts—something you'd never do on the Academy grounds. It was just too risky. You could sort of tell by how someone looked at you or how long they made eye contact. I think men are very sensitive to that, especially if you don't know them. You start to pick up little truths like that. It was something that just happened, nonverbally, and in most cases, it never happened again with that individual, because of the risk factor involved.

I finally accepted the fact that I was gay and was not going to change, which probably occurred during my junior year. I had made the acceptance after a lot of conflict as a sophomore, and by the time I was a junior, I realized I was gay. There were even certain groups who tried to find out, just to get you kicked out. Yeah, there was a lot of that there, probably because they were trying to cover up their own sexual uncertainties. I think a lot of that is covered up by supermachoism. I'm sure that 10 percent of the midshipmen at the Academy were gay. I wouldn't doubt that at all.

Overall, people liked me as a person and my involvement in other activities as well. I had decent grades and had performed very well as a plebe, being consistently ranked among the highest people in my company and squad. When I was a second class or a junior midshipman, I was selected as the regimental commander, which was basically someone who commanded half of the entire junior class. I was one step below the highest-ranking midshipman in my class. Then I became a battalion commander and commanded one sixth of the entire brigade. There's a lot of power struggle involved, and certainly my involvement with the glee club and singing the national anthem didn't hurt my position.

I was nationally televised, during my sophomore and senior years, while singing the national anthem. I was the only midshipman ever in the history of the Academy to do that, to sing . . . I was the only person ever to sing the national anthem at the Army-Navy games, twice. People recognized me. In fact, when my story hit the Academy, it was hard for my friends to realize what was going on. Even my closest friends, even my roommates, were outright and honestly shocked. I guess I was so well known and well thought of that "I couldn't be gay," which was a normal statement for someone to have made coming from that environment. I spent three years with one roommate, who throughout that entire time never had even the slightest suspicion that I was gay—which was exactly my point. What difference did it make? I never caused any moral decline. He never knew!

It all came out during the last half of my senior year, and I realize now that I probably trusted more people than I should have. It was probably because I felt so confident in my position and it was nearing graduation that I actually even considered confiding in a few close friends about my feelings. I basically told three people, those that I considered my closest friends. My understanding is that one of those friends then confided in another friend and so on, until the administration found out. I mean it was a *big deal*. I was a battalion commander, one of the ten highest-ranking midshipmen at the Academy. I certainly felt those I had told could keep this secret, and they did except for one. I felt a need to share it with someone because it was something that just eats away at you. I guess I made the wrong decision at that time, but it seemed more than I could hold inside.

Graduation was only two months away when I found out I was being investigated by the naval equivalent of the FBI. At that point I realized I was in big trouble, so I went to the chief of chaplains at the Academy, to see what I could do. I was honest with him and told him that I was gay but hadn't done anything to bring dishonor to the Academy. He didn't really give me a lot of direction but did agree that if they were at the point of investigating me, they would find something to disallow me from graduating.

The commandant said, "Yes, it is true, I'm *not* going to let him graduate, and I won't allow him to continue until graduation. We're going to kick him out." If I had all of the knowledge I do today, I would have realized that they didn't have enough to kick me out. They could not have kicked me out based entirely on the very small rumor-type information that they had gathered. If I had just kept my mouth shut, denied it, I would in all certainty have graduated. But I was *so scared*. Definite panic. I felt like I was in control of my emotions and things like that, but I needed to plan, to figure out what they knew. Getting kicked out as a very high ranking midshipman was extremely upsetting, so I went about trying to figure out how the effects of this could be minimized.

I talked to the legal adviser at the Academy and tried to get a meeting with the superintendent, who was the highest-ranking officer of the entire Academy complex. I was going to appeal to his sense of humanity, saying, "My God, I'm only six weeks from graduation, I've done nothing wrong, I've been an exemplary midshipman. At least let me graduate and get my diploma." They didn't let me see him, but the commandant said, "Are you willing to state that you're a homosexual?" I said, "Yes, I am." Then he asked, "Well, what do you want to do now?" So I said, "I guess I'll just have to leave." From that point in time, everything was put in motion for my dismissal. With no chance to speak with the superintendent, it came down to a question of how *fast* they were going to get rid of me.

Once I realized I was going to be kicked out, I called my closest friends together and said, "This is the situation: I'm getting kicked out because I'm gay, and it doesn't look like there is anything I can do about it." They were all very supportive, even more so than I had imagined. They all considered it really a tragedy, which it was. I also realized that when the story broke, I was going to be in physical danger—at least I perceived that—so I wanted to be prepared for that as well. That's when I began remembering those rumors about the blanket parties and things like that. . . .

The day after I had told the commandant, that same evening, I planned a meeting of my staff—I had about five staff people working under me at the time. I told them what was going on. I said, "Hey, I'm going to be kicked out because I admitted that I'm gay. There were no other people involved, and there were no acts involved." My whole reason for doing this was basically simple. I wanted to have a group of people know the *complete* story so that when the actual rumors started breaking, there would be people there to tell, with authority, that they knew the truth. Fortunately, that actually turned out to be very, very effective, which allowed them to dispel and defuse the rumors. By noon, everyone at the Academy knew the entire story.

Thank God I had called those people together, because rumors started flying everywhere by early morning. But by noon all of the rumors pretty much had been completely quelled, and everyone knew the truth. Had I not done that, the rumors would have been explosive and the most popular rumor would have reigned, so I felt it was something that was very well handled. I felt proud that I had managed to be that organized about my own dismissal, but you know, it's rather ironic, but I guess I also demonstrated quite nicely how a well-prepared officer, which I had aspirations of being, responded under the most adverse of situations. After all, wasn't that what they were training me for in the first place? But wow, I did all that, and I was gay to boot! Strange twist . . .

I was moved to another room at the Academy, away from the hall, in an area where teams stayed when they came to visit. I had my own little steel cot, similar to the furnishings in a prison cell. I was basically allowed to come and go as I pleased until they could get the appropriate boards together. The total board action was a two-stage process, the performance board and the academic board. I had straight A's and B's on my military performance throughout my four years at the Academy, but it just so happens that homosexuality falls into the performance area. By the Academy's definition, anyone who is gay is incapable of performing in the military, so despite everything I had accomplished from a military performance standpoint, it was null and void. I was brought in front of this board and told, "You are incompetent for performance, and we are recommending that you be reviewed by the academic board." But really, it was like, "Hey, everything else is irrelevant, so we're going to recommend you for discharge anyway, no matter what is said."

During the board, I was allowed to make a statement. I made a brief statement saying, "I've been a good midshipman. I haven't done anything wrong. It's true that I'm gay, but I wasn't involved with anybody, nor has it affected my performance, as validated by the documentation you have before you. I think that I've given a tremendous amount of my dedication and hard work to the Academy, and I don't think it's too much to ask that I be allowed to graduate." I realized, as I was speaking those words, that there was no way they were going to let me graduate. My words fell on deaf ears. The superintendent, who was in charge of the academic board, was there, as well as the commandant. Their only goal was to kick me out, and they really had no thought whatsoever toward my own personal feelings or my future, for that matter. Of course, this action did not in any way justify the thousands of dollars spent on my education and training. The waste of tax dollars for this kind of craziness is unbelievable [approximately $100,000 for four years at the Academy]!

I was not allowed to have lawyers present for the final board hearing. I did have a lawyer at the academic board proceedings, but he was not allowed to speak; he was just allowed to act as an observer. Now that's a great help, don't you think? Sure, you can have an attorney, but unfortunately, he will not be able to make any comments. It was obvious that they had their minds made up before I walked in, because of their entire assumption that homosexuality was "completely incompatible" with the military, no matter what my records indicated. I had been railroaded into it, and I didn't even realize they really didn't have a case. But by the time my lawyer and I got to the academic board, I had signed papers that indicated I was gay. I had two choices: resign with a discharge certificate that said "voluntarily resigned," or they were going to throw me out with a discharge certificate that said "discharged." Of course, they made a point of telling me that the latter would mean I would have difficulty getting a job and things like that, equating it to a dishonorable discharge, even though that wasn't it at all. I found out later about that little game they had played with me.

I did get an honorable discharge, never any question about that, but I was forced to resign. I chose to resign because that's what everybody does. But truthfully, you have no choice. Emotionally, I was trying to keep my own head above water. I had heard stories about midshipmen spreading rumors in class and others would just stand up and say, "Shut up, you don't know what you're talking about. This is a good individual, and he didn't do anything wrong. He openly admitted it, and you have no right to pass such rumors." No one accosted or threatened me, but somehow, deep down, I did not feel that would happen anyway. Anyone who knew and recognized me told me how sorry they were that it had happened and how unjust they felt it was.

Other gays that I knew at the Academy were undoubtedly feeling an inner heat over the whole situation. They were extremely, extremely worried that I was going to squeal. Some of these people were high-ranking. But I never told the administration about them. It's almost a tradition that if someone got in big trouble, they tried to take as many with them as they could, to somehow minimize their own guilt in any particular situation.

At the time I felt my entire life was ruined in that I'd never be able to get a job. I just knew people would ask me about why I left the Academy six weeks before graduation. Somehow, I felt they would be suspicious of such an obvious oversight. I still deal with that today. I try to hide that experience just to avoid the questions. It's a source of personal failure, and I don't like to talk about the Academy anymore, even though some of the best times of my life occurred there. Those four years of my life that I considered my proudest life's achievement are now a source of shame.

It took about six months for me to break out of the mentality to which I'd been brainwashed, that homosexuality was wrong. After I came out of that mentality, I became more and more angry about what had been done. I addressed the issue that I was gay, did a great job, and that even if I was gay, that was a nonvalid reason for kicking me out, regardless of anything else. The truth is that I had the capability to do well, that I had done well, and that gay people should not be kicked out of the military simply because they're gay. It's just a state of mind.

I gave up fighting my case at the beginning because of my family, my mother and father. You know, bad print and all that. I was almost getting angry at them for forcing me to give up the case, and the more that time went on, the more I realized I *did* have a good case. I found myself really becoming angry at my parents for forcing me to give up the fight. I resented their manipulation of me at that time, and I still hold that against them, but I've basically forgiven them. I realize the pressure they were under, but had they been more supportive of me, I feel that I would be in a much better position than I am right now.

It certainly broadened my perspective on the level of fairness in the world. I had been very idealistic, and thought that other people were idealistic and that in the end truth and honor would win out, which is not what happened in my case. I had been completely truthful and honorable, and prejudice had won out in the end. Some people want to be in the military to the point where they would be willing to live a secretive life, but I feel my honor would have been compromised in the long run if I lived that way. I do think there are thousands of gay people in the military doing a very good job, and if all the gay people in the military were kicked out tomorrow, we would have a national security crisis.

My patriotism has . . . it's changed a little bit. When I think of my patriotism . . . what I thought of my patriotism before, I thought of people fighting and dying for their country in some devastating war on some foreign shore. But when I think of patriotism now, I think of things like the Statue of Liberty, the Bill of Rights, and of people willing to fight to keep it free for everybody, whether they're gay, straight, black, white, male, or female. I think the most important fight that we have ahead of us is not a war outside this country but in making sure that the ideals that formed this country are carried through and applied to everybody, regardless of sexual orientation, race, religion, or origin.

I'm happy with my life now. I don't think that being gay is the easiest way to live, certainly not with all of the things that go on in our society, with the prejudices that still exist. But you know, I wouldn't trade my sexuality for anybody else's, because I realize that my personality and the person that I am has been motivated in many ways *because* I'm gay. Yes, I'm happy with the person that I am, and I know I have the ability to do anything I want in this life.

AUTHOR'S NOTE: *On December 29, 1988, Joe Steffan filed suit in U.S. district court in Washington, D.C., seeking readmission to the Academy, his diploma, and an assignment with the Navy. In November 1989, the district court dismissed the claim for reinstatement because he refused to answer court questions about whether he had engaged in homosexual conduct. He is appealing that decision.*

☆ ☆

"As a recruiter who happens to be gay, it is always difficult to address the question asked about homosexuality."

"ELIZABETH STRONG"

Age 32, U.S. Air Force, 1980–present, enlisted.
Present occupation: military recruiter.

I didn't come out till I was probably about twenty-two, twenty-three. I was a late bloomer, so to speak. I had heard rumors about a good friend of mine, and it made me uncomfortable, so I thought, "Well, let me talk to her." You know, I don't believe in rumors. I talked to her and she admitted, "Yes, I am." At first I was a little like, hmmm, not uncomfortable but a little surprised. I thought, well, I did not like her because she was straight or gay, I liked her because of who she was.

I started going to the bars with her and her lover. I would say, in my case, I mentally came out to the bars before I ever physically came out. I knew I was gay. Then this other friend came on to me during that same time period. I wasn't offended at her come-on. I just told her I wasn't gay, and at that time I wasn't, or I wasn't ready for it. I finally accepted her invitation to her home, knowing full well what would happen when I got there, and it did . . . I thought it was great. And we spent the whole weekend basically together . . . like a duck to water, as they say. I wasn't uncomfortable with anything. Boy, what a weekend!

Finally, as a young person wanting more out of life than just parties and running around, I became bored. My boredom was the impetus needed for me to join the Air Force. I knew I'd be qualified. And believe me, I certainly sidestepped that god-awful question about homosexuality.

I said, "no." I lied. I knew that I was telling an untruth, but who was to know?

The flight was all girls. I had one friend who I thought was cute, but I didn't want to jump on her in the middle of the night or anything. Like I don't even want to say sexual attraction, but God, I certainly met a lot of gay people there, lots and lots. I worked extra and helped in-process new recruits, so I saw everybody who came in my squadron, the new trainees . . . a perfect chance to check them all out—and I did! I recruited them to see if they wanted to stay in our dorm. There was one point in time when the whole bay, the whole dormitory bay, was almost all gay— probably twenty people.

It was a perfect place to meet, greet, wed, and bed the gay gals. It *was* a good opportunity for some, but I didn't have a lot of lovers. No, I never took advantage of the kids that were coming through. The sexual relations I had were with women that had been there for a while, more like friends. I never grabbed a kid off the bus, nothing like that.

My life in the Air Force has not been without the seemingly proverbial investigation. I didn't really come under investigation until I went to Georgia. I hadn't been in all that long. My supervisor called me into his office and said that the commander needed to see me. He gave me his car keys (he was a good guy). So I went in, scared as hell. The minute you're told the commander wants to talk to you, or your supervisor wants to talk to you, the first thing you think is "Shit, it's because I'm gay." It could be they need your signature on something, something totally different, but your immediate thought is "Oh shit, they found out!" And if anyone's stupid enough *not* to have those feelings about their supervisors, and so on, it should especially be felt when one is told to see the OSI—now, that's a dead giveaway. The good old Office of Special Investigation. They're all a little different for each one of the services, but they mean the same thing.

Anyway, he read me my rights and said that I was being investigated for homosexuality. Well, of course, I laughed and I became indignant, because I figured if I were a heterosexual and somebody accused me of being a queer, I'd be real pissed (unfortunately, I've seen that kind of heterosexual reaction), but that's how I played it.

I guess the commander needed reinforcements, so the boys from OSI were then called in. They started saying, "Do you know these people, do you know these people?" and these are all names of friends from my old base. Now it's like, "Well, yes, I do. I played softball with this person," and "Yes, I went to school with that person." Then they popped up with the name of a captain I knew from softball, and that's when I knew they were lying, because they said, "Well, we have a report that you had sexual relations with Captain So-and-so. (That was crap; she was with a lover for seven years. Yes, I knew her, but not on the level they were suggesting.) When they said that about her, I knew that they were trying to scare me into confessing. They were also trying to trip me up. "Well, do you know if these women are lesbians?" And I said, "I know them, but I wouldn't know who they slept with." But as the interview came to an end, there was one thing that stood out in my mind as an obvious threat. One of the agents told me, "We've been easy on you this time, but the next time we call you in, it's not going to be so easy." I left, and since I construed that as a threat, I went immediately to the judge advocate's office—the air defense counsel. He told me that I didn't have to go back and, the next time they called, to say that I had been advised by my lawyer not to talk to them. Case closed—never heard from them again, at least at that base.

About three years later, my new commander told me my security clearance had been pulled, canceled. Of course, let me guess why! He said, "You've got to do all this, this, and this." So, I had to see the physician at the hospital, a shrink basically, but by now I had gotten married, so I became real indignant. We had just gotten married about six months before I was called in. He was a good friend and knew I was gay. We were really best friends, and we had gotten married as a cover for me. He really didn't need it and shortly afterward, left for a different base. Nevertheless, we were still legally married. It was just a convenience, and when he got back from Korea, he went to California and ran into a woman that he'd known eight years before. Later, we got a divorce so that they could be married. But anyway, at this time, I said. "What the hell are you talking about? I'm married, for Christ's sake." At least I had that cover to throw in. No matter—I still had to see the shrink.

Of course, they never talked to my husband, but they did talk to my ex-lover (we had just broken up). . . . It was so bizarre. I mean, I couldn't believe all that was happening at one time. Let me see . . . my mother died, I broke my leg, my lover kicked me out, and then I was under investigation—all within a one-week period. But for some reason, nothing came of their investigation, and I was "let go."

Finally, I moved on and got into the recruiting end of the service, where I am now. It's very high-power stuff. I just love it. I had problems with this other recruiter, who was married but wanted to take me out. He was a real dick. I turned him down, which, as I found out, was not a good idea. He's the kind of guy who goes out of his way to screw someone if he doesn't get what he wants. So here we go with the OSI again!

I called my commander, who explained what happened, in that the OSI was doing spot inspections on certain offices and they went into my office and had gotten into my briefcase I had left there—government issue, of course, but still private property. I was stupid. I knew better than that, but I had a couple letters in it. I had been writing letters and needed the letters for their addresses. Nothing they could throw me out for but definite homosexual references. The commander told me that the OSI had confiscated my personal property and that he had informed the

OSI that he did not approve of their "Gestapo tactics," and then he told me he would get my letters and some pictures of my softball team . . . and give them to me the next time he saw me.

I don't think he really did approve of their Gestapo tactics. He probably authorized them to go into the office but not into my personal property. I soon found out why the whole incident occurred. It was the prick that had asked me out. A good friend asked me, "What the hell have you done to this guy? Why has he got a hard-on for you so bad as to get you kicked out?" I couldn't give the whole truth, so I just said that I didn't know. About two weeks later, the next time my commander saw me, he returned the things taken from the briefcase. Not a word was said.

I've tried to overlook the military's shortsightedness about the gay issue. You see, I really love this position, so my concentration on doing an outstanding job tends to keep most of their bigotry in its proper place. It's a fun job because you can see the turnaround with the ones recruited. You see the fruits of your labor, okay, because you put a kid in one month and he seems to change overnight. They will write you from basic training, and always, always, when they come home on leave, they will walk into my office in their uniform—now that's a real good feeling. You see the difference between those little punks of a couple months ago and these sharp young men and women standing in front of you.

As a recruiter who happens to be gay, it is always difficult to address the question asked about homosexuality. It's on one of the forms under "sexual history," so I've never asked the kids if they were gay or straight. None of the recruiters really do. We give them the form and have them answer the questions. Now, if a kid answered it "Yes," I would disqualify him and would feel no compunction in doing that. If he is stupid, stupid enough to admit it when everybody knows you can't do it and be in the military, then he's not smart enough to come into my Air Force, and that's how I feel. But I've never had anybody admit to it yet. In fact, I love this one: In the application for commissioning it states: "Are you a homosexual or have you ever engaged in a homosexual act?"— homosexual defined as sexual relations with the same sex. Then the question under that is: "Do you intend to engage in . . . ?" It's like, "I'm not now, but I think maybe in a month I might try it."

One thing I definitely feel is that 99 percent of your gays in the Air Force are your top-flight achievers, fast burners for promotion, top Airmen Award winners, top NCOs, officers of the quarter, and things like that. They're always outstanding. They're the cream of the crop because they have incentive. It's like that saying about women having to work twice as hard to prove they're half as good as a man. In the Air Force, if you're gay you've got to work twice as hard just to prove you're as good as the next guy. However, there is one twist to all of this, in that in the enlisted corps it's not who you know, it's what you know that gets you promoted, while the Air Force officer has to be more political.

I'm constantly aware of being paranoid, constantly aware. If I go out on a weekend or go to a gay bar, I'm aware of it. Being out in public with my girlfriend just buzzing around, I'm aware of it. It's like having the feeling that someone is always watching you. All the time. Always looking over your shoulder–type deal. I might be driving down the street with my lover and want to give her a kiss. Well, I'm always looking around to make sure there's no one I might recognize. It's a little bit easier in recruiting, because you are not normally assigned to a base. On the other hand, I am in a fishbowl, because I go out into the community and I'm seen in my uniform. It definitely increases my paranoia, so I'm just very cautious at all times with what I do and when I do it.

It definitely affects my personal life, because I'm constantly paranoid. My lover and I have had fights about it. She gets real fed up with the Air Force, very fed up, especially the crap that's going on because I am pregnant. We decided we wanted to have a family. So I was artificially inseminated. I felt it was none of their damn business how I got pregnant. Of course, it's also a good cover.

An interesting side point involves another recruiter. At the same time that I was pregnant, he found out his girlfriend was also pregnant. Now, they've been together several years, but they're not married. Okay, he informed his boss, and nobody's giving him crap. Nobody. Nothing was being said about relieving him of duty, but me—now that's another story. The point is that there is no regulation about being single, being in, and then having a baby. They were discriminating against me but not him. He was a good old boy that had knocked up his girlfriend, and that was perfectly all right! After basically threatening the higher echelon, I am now being told if I do my job, I'll be okay, which is the way it should be. If you screw your job up, you're out of there.

My security with this baby has me worried. I started questioning this pregnancy, and I resent the fact that I've had to do that. So now I'm considering finding a nice gay boy. Yeah, I need to meet a nice gay boy. I'd marry him and hopefully, that would take some of the heat off. But it's all so phony. I hate telling a lie. Yes, I do, I hate it, because I've had many very close friends in the military, heterosexual friends, who I would like to have told I was gay but couldn't.

I hope things change. I hope one day I will be able to take my lover to the dining out. That's one thing I really would like to do, because I'm proud of her and I would love for her to see me in my capacity as an Air Force staff sergeant. She's never really seen me working—she can't. There's no way she can see that without causing great suspicion. She can't see me when we have our annual awards banquet; she can't sit there and show her pride when I get all kinds of plaques, awards, and nifty things. I can't share my professional life with her and all that goes along with it. I resent the hell out of that, and hopefully, one day it *will* change.

☆☆☆☆☆☆☆☆☆☆☆☆☆☆☆☆☆☆☆☆☆☆☆☆☆

"I . . . checked the 'Yes' box for 'homosexual tendencies' [and they took me anyway]."

PERRY WATKINS

Age 42, U.S. Army, 1968–83, enlisted. Honorable Discharge. Present occupation: government civil servant, Social Security Department.

I was raised by my mother, my grandmother, two aunts, and a sister. Because of that, I never had a problem with the pressures of a male role model, of having to do the male-type things like football, basketball, and all that. So if I wanted to play jacks, play with dolls and things, nobody ever complained. And I was great! I mean, I used to give those girls hell in my neighborhood. They'd hate to see me coming with the jump rope, because they *knew* they were going to catch hell. I played with the girls, but my sexual feelings were for boys.

Junior high and high school was great, especially after I learned that you don't have to tell anyone you're gay in order to have sex. Let someone else do it for you, and you'll have all you can handle for the rest of your life. I guess I believed that after I met this kid one night who was about sixteen or seventeen. I had a weakness for blond hair and blue eyes. And I was quite bold in those days. The kid was close to five nine or ten, and I was maybe five two, if five feet. It was really funny. I walked by him on the street, turned around, and said, "Would you like a blow job?" The guy looked at me and said, "What did you say?" I said, "Are you hard of hearing, or what? You know, do you want a blow job?" He said, "Yeah, well . . . okay. Sure." So we went into this alley, and I did my thing with him.

This fellow happened to be a very good friend of a guy that was in my class. And he told him about this. He immediately spread it all around the school the next day. From that point, I never had to ask anyone else anything. They would all come to me. There was never any violence. Which was really interesting to me. It spread around school, and everybody started asking me, "Are you really a cocksucker?" "Yes." I thought, "Why the hell should I lie about it?" They wouldn't have much to do with me in school, but they were wonderful after school. Which was just fine with me. They'd do the most wonderful things to make sure I didn't get into trouble, get hit or beat up. All the boys wanted blow jobs and that was all. Quite honestly, it was purely a sexual thing—they knew it and I knew it, no problem. It was just wham, bam, thank you, ma'am. That was it. Ah, how I remember those days!

Perry Watkins at Gay Pride Day Parade, 1988, Portland, Oregon

The Army hired Perry Watkins, aka "Simone," to entertain the troops in Europe, 1971.

After high school I had planned, initially, to remain in Europe for three years and go to school. My father was a career military man, and he had been assigned to a base in Germany. I was studying and teaching dance. My plans were to enter the theater for professional training. I was going to remain in Europe after my father came back, because I would have been twenty-one, so it would have been fine. Well, the best laid plans of mice and men ... I got drafted the next year. However, the bottom line was that I knew I was gay, and knew the Army had a policy against gays being in the military, so I wasn't very concerned about them taking me. I wasn't aware of what the regulation actually said. I had never read the regulation. I just knew, that's all. Even though my father was a career military man, he never used the word *homosexual*—please! My father has never even discussed my case with me. No. No, no. If knowledge about homosexuality came from conversations with anyone, it would probably have been from other dependent kids that may have mentioned it to me.

I received my little draft notice, went down to the induction center, and checked the "Yes" box for "homosexual tendencies." Which I find amusing now. One of the arguments the Army made in court was that I didn't *say* I was homosexual. But of course, when they sent me to the psychiatrist immediately afterward—after checking the box—I specifically stated that I was gay. I specifically said to them, "No, I don't mind going into the military. If you want to take me like I am, that's fine with me." The Army's big argument was "Well, you're going to be taking showers with all these young men." Shit, I've been taking showers with naked men since I was twelve years old. Was there something new that I wasn't aware of, maybe a new military weapon or the like? *Please!*

Once at the center, we were all sitting in the room in our underwear, and this doctor looked at my form, looked at me, and said, "Well, what is this?" I thought, "Okay." I said, "What is what?" He said, "Well, what is this? You've checked this box." I said, "What does the box say?" He said, "Homosexual tendencies." I thought, "Isn't *this* cute? Are we embarrassed, or what?" But he continued, "Well, what does this mean?" I said, "Don't you *know*? I mean, you're the doctor, aren't you?"

He left the room for a while, came back in, and told me to get dressed. They put me in an ambulance and set me to the hospital for a psychiatric evaluation with a lieutenant colonel. I went in and filled out my little forms once again, and on the back it stated: "Why are you here?" I didn't write anything on the back, which was my first mistake. So this colonel brought it out, threw it in my face, and told me I didn't fill the form out right. So I put down that I'd expressed homosexual tendencies on my form 88. *Then* he yelled my name exceptionally loud. And I politely informed him, you know, "You don't yell at me like that because I'm not in your goddamn Army." I knew this man had no right to yell at me. Trust me, he did not scare me in the least, and I was not happy after being embarrassed, anyway.

You know, it's interesting when you're born black and you've been discriminated against all your life, or you've had to deal with it all your life. You can look at people and know this is not going to be easy. I looked at this man and I knew—"You're going into the Army. You're *going* into the Army! This man was pinched. You have upset him." And, sure as shit, I had. Now it was his turn to ask the same questions as before. He sat down and said, "Why did you check this box 'Yes'? Don't you want to go in the Army? Do you have a problem with going to Vietnam?" "No. I don't mind going to Vietnam." "Well then, why did you check the box 'Yes'?" It's getting pretty stale for me about this time. I'm also getting slightly irritated because I'm thinking, "Are you deaf? Or what is your problem?" I thought, "No, no, no, no. Let's not be rude." I said, "No, I don't have any objections about going into the Army." Then he said, "What do you do?" Now that one blew me away. I said, *"Excuse me?"* "What do you do?" I looked at him and said, "Do you mean to tell me you are the psychiatrist here and you don't know what a little homosexual does?"

He didn't find it amusing at all. *I* thought it was rather clever. He said, "I want to know." So I told him that I liked to suck dick, I liked to get fucked. You know, common, everyday things. Then he said, "Are you active or passive?" I had never heard those terms before. Everyone I was sexually active with, basically, were people of my own age who probably also knew nothing about gay communities as such. And you're talking 1968, so I said, "What does that mean?" He explained to me what it meant, and I said, "Well, I guess I'm both." I mean, I hadn't really decided whether I was—and still haven't. "Oh well, okay, tonight I get to be on top? Oh well, fine. How nice! No problem. You want to change places in the middle? No problem. No problem. We can do that, too."

After that line of questioning he made me talk about things that *I* liked to do. He made me state what I liked to do. I thought, "This is kind of strange." Then out of left field he looked at me and said, "Do you ever date women?" Now, this is the man who just asked me if I liked to suck dick. Or made me say I liked to suck dick. But yet, he's not going to ask me if I've ever *fucked* a woman. He's going to ask me, "Do you ever *date* women?" Obviously, this is a loaded question. Everybody dates women. I mean, I had to obviously take *something* to my senior prom!

The final upshot was that he made the determination that I *was* suitable for military service. Even though he had also made the determination that I *was* homosexual. Which is in contradiction to the regulation, because the regulation requires that the determination be that the person is *not* gay. That's the only way a person can then be inducted with this on their record. Confused, no matter, I was inducted anyway. It was at that point I realized being in the military was going to be real fun. *Real* fun. I thought, "Oh, this could be very amusing."

I'm surprised how well I performed through basic. After all, I wasn't the most macho guy there—quite the contrary. But I even got an accelerated promotion out of basic training, and only got attacked once by some guy in my barracks along the way. This man was determined he was going to fuck me, and I was determined he wasn't. I could kick myself today for being so determined—damn it! I decided I needed to develop a kind of attitude. I was determined that if I was going to be in this man's Army, then they were either going to treat me with the proper respect that I felt I deserved, or they could let me go home.

I never approached anybody for sex. It just simply wasn't necessary. I'd walk in and say, "I'm gay. Leave me the hell alone." All these people would just start traipsing to my door. You know, knocking at my door at all hours of the night. I also figured, basically, if I never asked anyone, they couldn't say I asked them. They were certainly not going to tell my commanding officer *they* asked *me*. When I was at Fort Dix, I actually got very fed up with all of it and said, "The hell with this. I want out." So I went to my commanding officer and said, "I want out of the Army. I'm gay and I want out. I had told that original dip-shit doctor I was gay and I didn't want to come in this son-of-a-bitch to begin with, so let me out of here." Would you believe I went to my commander and actually requested a discharge because I was gay and he said no? There was another person who went to his commander and told him the same damn thing and they let him go home. Of course, he was white. Which I think also had something to do with it—he was white and I was black. It was really funny, because they sent me to CID to fill out this paperwork. I refused to give them names of anyone I'd ever had sex with, because I didn't think that was their business. A month later they came back and said, "Well, we can't let you go because we can't prove you have ever done anything."

Then I went from there to Fort Hamilton, New York. I was going to be a chaplain's assistant. I got a phone call from the chaplain. He called me into his office. He was commandant of the school, a lieutenant colonel. "I've got a statement here from your records saying you're gay. I can't allow you to finish this course." I said, "Excuse me? Then you can allow me to go home, right? I mean, if you're going to put me out of the school because I'm gay, you obviously can put me out of the Army *because* I'm gay."

He sent me to more psychiatrists and psychologists for more evaluation. It was beginning to sound very familiar at this point. One man was such a nelly twit. I mean, I took one look at him and thought, "My God, and I thought *I* was a dizzy queen!" "Are you Private Watkins?" I don't know if he was trying to be funny or just trying to get me to jump up and grab him, but I thought, "Oh, this is rich, it's the blind leading the blind. Yes, girlfriend, I'm Perry Watkins." Well, I was evaluated, and one month later, I got told, "Sorry Charlie, you're not going anyplace. We *still* can't prove you're gay." So in my next bout with CID, they wanted names, and I decided to go for their request in earnest. "Okay, fine. You want names, I'll give you names!" I gave the name of one person I'd had sex with who was in the military and one who was not. I couldn't believe it—both people denied it! Three months later, they called me back in and said, "Since we can't prove any of this happened, you still have to stay in the Army."

Now, pay attention! This is the *third* time I've tried to prove what I had originally stated on my medical form the day I came into the Army. It has all become so ludicrous by now that I didn't really give a shit anymore. I was tired of playing games and I wasn't going to sit around and be abused. So I thought, "Fuck you and the horse you rode in on, Junior!" Since I was being forced to stay in, even though I was obviously and openly gay, I decided to join the gay bar scene. I liked going to the back room bars. They had back rooms where there was actually sexual activity taking place. Orgy rooms. Like, the Mine Shaft in New York, for example, was probably the most notorious sleaze bar. I mean, they had slings, and chains, and everything. It's definitely an S&M bar. That's basically what I really enjoyed. Still do.

When I started going out to the bars, I began having a bit more personal problems, but many of my problems due to my orientation weren't always from whites. I also ran into a lot of conflict from other blacks who wanted to set a double standard by publicly saying that I was an embarrassment because I was black and gay. That I was embarrassing to the race. When they'd get me alone, they'd want to hop in the sack and let me suck their dicks. I thought, "Well now, this isn't going to work at all."

I can remember situations that were truly ironic. There was this one guy, an ex-marine, who was now in the Army. Every day at lunch, he would come over to my office, take me down to his room, and want me to give him a blow job. Everybody in the whole company knew about it. But on the other hand, he was considered straight. He used to go downtown every night and fuck anything that walked. One day I walked into the mess hall, and he asked me to sit near him. This other guy sitting there was a typical asshole. He looked at the ex-marine and said, "I want to know something. I know you let him suck your dick every day, but why?" And without even looking up from his plate, he said, "Well, I like a good blow job, and the women downtown don't know how to suck dick worth a damn. But this man happens to suck mine better than anyone I have ever found in the world. I've been around the world several times and I ain't found nobody yet that can hold a candle to Perry's technique." I didn't hear much from that asshole again. And he was right, I did give good head!

Over the years, I traveled to many places. I did two tours in Korea. During my first tour, I was in the combat zone and pulled duty at the DMZ with live ammunition. People were being shot at, wounded, and killed. Believe me, when I heard shots, I ducked. People ask me, you know, "Were you getting shot at?" I don't know if they were shooting at me. I didn't ask, I didn't look, I didn't see anything. Here I was, you know, I ducked when I heard shots. Part of that assignment involved foxhole duty. It was fun in an adventurous sort of way. We didn't do much of anything in the foxhole. Normally, we just talked. I can't say I *didn't* have sex, but geez, I mean, you know, come on, you have to talk beforehand! If they asked nicely, I would submit to their advances.

In fact, once we did call in for a communication check. This poor man was breathing so hard, they said, "What are you guys doing?" Then the first sergeant decided that I could not be out there pulling duty anymore. You know, while I was there, I realized that the Soviet AK-47 had the strangest sound. You will never forget it if you hear one. And another thing, people don't seem to think of this area as a combat zone, but it is. In a lot of ways it's even more dangerous than Vietnam was, because you never knew what was going to happen. It was easier to be lulled into a false sense of security because there wasn't an actual conflict going on, as it was in Nam.

I came back from there, and got out of the service for a year with an honorable discharge, and performed drag for a year. Then I went back in the service and started *performing drag in the service*. That's when I was sent to Korea for my second time. And at my new unit they were getting ready for Organization Day. We had three guys in our unit—I'll never forget them—Tickle, Pickle, and Keyhole. The one setting it up asked Pickle if he'd play the banjo and he said yes. I volunteered that I had worked as a female impersonator for a year. So they asked me if I would do the show in drag. I did. After the show, there was an article written about me in the *Army Times*, which was carried at all the posts and installations worldwide. I got a call from a fellow who became my agent and booked me into recreation centers, Officers' Clubs, and NCO Clubs all over Germany. I even entered a beauty pageant as a joke, during Oktoberfest, with eleven other real girls—and *won*. Yes, girlfriend, this queen had the balls to take the top award, and did so. Nobody knew until

I took off my costume. "Simone" was a very popular entertainer! So I was doing it all at that time, and doing it quite well, if I do say so. When I returned to the States, I was stationed at Fort Hood, and was asked to do my act there as well. In fact, I even performed drag at our formal NCO ball. All this time, *I was being paid to do it*. It was authorized, if you will.

You know, I've had a strange military career throughout. I've seen combat, been candid about my gayness and even in the public view in drag. I also requested not once but three times that I wanted out of the Army—the first time at Fort Dix, the second time at Fort Hamilton, and the third time at Fort Belvoir. Now, the fourth time, the Army *itself* finally decided to remove me. They had actually given me a chapter 13 proceeding in 1975, during my second tour of duty in Korea. They ran a background check for my position of mail clerk. When they ran through the computer, they found all three of these statements that I had made requesting discharge. The statement that I had made naming people was also found. The information was given to my CO who said, "Now I have to process you for discharge." "Fuck it. That's okay, fine. Do that, you son-of-a-bitch" was my response. This was also the year after Leonard Matlovich's case.

They had a board of four officers. But would you believe they decided there was *no reason* for me to be discharged? My actions were not detrimental to the military, unit morale, or to mission accomplishment. Once again, they decided I should remain! However, interestingly enough, the board didn't find me guilty of two things I was accused of previously, and only recommended that I be discharged because I still stated that I was gay. The court said this decision was totally stupid and definitely in contradiction to their regulation and definitely double jeopardy. The Army did not appeal that decision. Then they turned around in October of '82 and said, "Now we're going to deny you *reenlistment* because you say you're gay."

The reenlistment regulation specifically states you cannot deny someone reenlistment for something they cannot be administratively discharged for. The Army blatantly violated their own regulation. So I went through a lot of harrassment during my last enlistment before being put out. For example, these same people went into court and said, "We can't promote this man because we have to consider his sexual orientation. You know how people are going to look at that." I wasn't given awards and decorations, because I was gay and they had to consider their "image" when they did things like that. It's absolutely stupid. But I went through it for several years. They were not going to do this to me. I was going out proud.

The whole thing was affecting me a lot. It really did. However, it didn't affect me that much while I was in. I think I was so egotistical and vain that it gave me a great deal of pleasure to be able to deal with the situation as well as I did. When it really, really began to affect me was after

I got out. Trying to find a job. I got to the point that I began to feel like maybe I didn't deserve a decent job. Maybe I really *was* worthless. That attitude seemed to prevail for a long while. They took away my pride, my self-esteem, all of it. . . . But I could still laugh. Even now, when I realize what I've been through, some of it is very humorous. Yet some of it is very sad.

You know, after you've put in fifteen years, an honorable discharge doesn't mean a damn thing. The first thing outsiders do is look at it and say, "Well, why didn't you stay in for twenty?" But . . . I'm not ashamed of the fact that I'm gay. You know, what the hell. If I were a personnel officer hiring someone for a company, I would be leery of a person who refused to answer that kind of a question. It made me mad, so I took the Army to court.

I'm not an activist. I'm not a militant person. Even though I'm obviously very stubborn and obviously very determined that I'm going to take this thing as far as it has to go to win, and do my best to do get it done, I'm not an activist, as such. I would have gone out at twenty years ever so quietly, but when someone lies to me, falsifies documents in my records file, and lies about my capabilities as a soldier, it just didn't set well with me. I decided, "This is stupid. Now you're attacking me directly and personally. I didn't lie to you when I came into this damn Army." That's what really pissed me off.

There were times when I felt a tremendous sense of anger, but I don't feel that anger as much anymore. Now I try not to think about negative things. I was taking a lot out on myself. I didn't realize how self-destructive I had become. Emotionally, I wasn't there. You know, the self-pity and the feeling sorry for yourself can really get to you. It's a lot like the feelings you go through when someone dies. You know, the depression. I didn't realize I was doing all of that until after I honestly started coming back from it. When you finally understand what's happening, it's like, "Whoa! I need to stop this bullshit. I need to turn this around." I'll never let that happen again. If anything, I've improved a lot. I know that I'm something, whether I am black or gay, and will always be something and will always be worth something. If I can be objective about all this, it would appear that it is based on both black and gay issues . . . both are ongoing and continuous.

It doesn't matter what kind of laws we have. People have asked me, "How have you managed to tolerate all that discrimination you had to deal with in the military?" My immediate answer to them was "Hell, I grew up black. Give me a break. I mean, to be discriminated against because I was gay was a joke." I mean, "Oh, you don't like me because I'm gay? Excuse me. I'm sorry, but *you've* got a problem." And discrimination is a very individual thing. If people are going to discriminate, they're going to find a way—regardless of what laws are in place. I do believe, however, specifically concerning the military, that if I had not been black, my situation would not have happened as it did. A couple of examples jump quickly to mind. I knew one E-7 who was boarded for incest with his twelve-year-old son. Do you know what the Army told him? "Oh. If you have that kind of problem, you need to take care of it at home. We don't need to get involved in your *private life.*" I'm still trying to figure out why my private life was not okay, but his was, or at least it didn't affect his job in the military. Like what he did to his own child was not a crime, and what I did with consenting adults was. Incest—no problem! And another example: Every *white* person I knew from Tacoma who was gay and had checked that box "Yes" did not have to go into the service. They were called in and asked, "What does this mean?" They said, "It means I'm gay. I like to suck dick." "Fine. You can go." Very interesting, don't you think?

Through it all, there were some things that I do hold near and dear. I still feel the military benefited me with an education, travel, and allowed me to learn a great deal about people. I had wonderful experiences meeting people, making friends, and growing up in general. I feel, quite personally, that they should reinstitute the draft. I think a two-year commitment to your country is very little to ask for what America gives. Everybody should go. You don't necessarily have to go into the military; you can teach, work in a hospital, do construction work—something. Learning to live and survive by yourself is one of the most beneficial things that could ever happen to a young adult.

I have few regrets about my overall fifteen years of experience. You can always learn from bad experiences as well as good ones. Everything can't be good in your life. You've got to learn to survive and exist and coexist in the world with other people, like them or not. And I'm a survivor, if nothing else. That I found out on my own. The message seems to be that as long as we continue to hide in the closet, we'll have to put up with this shit. Those high-ranking military members, ones that I met personally, need to stand up and be counted. As I see it, it must start at the top.

It's sad that we need to demand that. Unfortunately, if we don't, because of the way the laws are written, we're shooting ourselves in the foot. So let me reiterate that *as long as we continue to stay in the closet,* we give them credibility. Eliminate the regulation requiring people to admit whether they're gay or not, and then there will be no need to ask anymore. There are enough regulations dealing with moral conduct and professionalism already in place; we don't need any more. Unless it's a problem, then there isn't anything that should be done about it. The Army can always go to court, just like in my case, and say, "He's only one person. Why do we have to change all of our regulations to suit just one person?" It will only change when the courts have to stop and take a serious look and say, "What are you doing? Why are you doing this, and why do we have these *thousands* and *thousands* of cases?" So, if suddenly the Army or any of the armed forces were talking about fifty thousand people, instead of just one or two, if there were suddenly fifty thousand cases in the courts, people might say, "You know, maybe we *ought* to change that regulation." At this point, we seem to be spending millions of the taxpayers' money to carry out the requirements of this needless regulation.

I contend that if that gay *general* I met in Korea can succeed, it is obvious that he has not been limited by his gayness. However, in order to survive, he has had to maintain a very secretive and highly protected private lifestyle, but my point here is, why the hell should he or anyone else who is gay have to go to such extensive measures? Straight soldiers get a chance to prove whether they're good or not, and they're judged on their performance. Gay soldiers aren't. Whether you're good or not, if you're gay you're gone. No other reason necessary. And there is absolutely no basis in fact for any of the military's opposition to gays in the armed forces. When is this ruse going to be exposed as pure bullshit? I hope in my lifetime!

AUTHOR'S NOTE: *In an opinion handed down on May 3, 1989, the Ninth Circuit U.S. Court of Appeals ruled 7–4 that the Army must allow Mr. Watkins to reenlist, because Army officials had known throughout his fifteen years of service that he was gay and had continually praised his performance nonetheless.*

APPENDICES

U.S. Army Regulation
Defining Homosexuality/Sodomy

The definition of sodomy from the 1940s consisted of the following:

Article 125 of the Uniform Code of Military Justice: Sodomy

Discussion. Sodomy is the engaging in unnatural carnal copulation, either with another person of the same sex, or opposite sex, or with an animal. Any penetration, however slight, is sufficient to complete the offense, and emission is not necessary.

It is unnatural carnal copulation for a person to take into his or her mouth or anus the sexual organ of another person or of an animal; or to place his or her sexual organ in the mouth or anus of another person or of an animal; or to have carnal copulation in any opening of the body, except the sexual parts, with another person; or to have carnal copulation in any opening of the body of an animal.

Proof. (a) That the accused engaged in unnatural copulation with a certain other person or with an animal, as alleged; and if alleged, (b) that the act was done by force and without the consent of the other person or was done with a child under the age of sixteen years.

Definition of homosexuality from current U.S. Army Regulations:

AR 135–175, Separation of Officers, and AR 135–178, Separation of Enlisted

a. Homosexual means a person, regardless of sex, who engages in, desires to engage in, or intends to engage in homosexual acts.

b. Bisexual means a person who engages in, desires to engage in, or intends to engage in homosexual and heterosexual acts.

c. A homosexual act means bodily contact, actively undertaken or passively permitted, between members of the same sex for the purpose of satisfying sexual desires.

☆ ☆

APPENDIX B

*"Nonconforming Sexual Orientations and Military Suitability"**

JUDICIAL TRENDS AND SHIFTING FOLKWAYS

A case that drew national media attention in 1975 is that of Sergeant Leonard P. Matlovich ("Homosexual Sergeant," 1975). The bases for his separation from military service were the codified Department of Defense and Air Force regulations that persons who admitted to homosexual orientation or conduct could not serve in the Air Force. In 1978, the United States Court of Appeals in Washington, D.C., ruled that the Air Force had acted improperly in discharging Sergeant Matlovich without specifying appropriate reasons other than being homosexual. In 1981, the same court awarded him back pay and a retroactive promotion (Guevarra, 1988).

The more recent case of Sergeant Perry Watkins (Henry, 1988) may have profound implications for future legal challenges. Watkins entered the service in 1967 at age 19, admitting on a preinduction medical form that he had homosexual tendencies. At that time, the Army discharged soldiers for engaging in homosexual acts, but not for "homosexuality." The distinction between homosexual acts and homosexuality is difficult to draw. The authors of the regulation probably employed a notion that was influenced by the dichotomy: acts and dispositions. The abstract term, "homosexuality," could be employed to denote that a person might be disposed to act in certain ways, but would not necessarily engage in such overt actions.

In February, 1988, a three-judge panel of the United States Court of Appeals for the Ninth Circuit ruled two to one that the Army's discrimination against homosexuals was unconstitutional. The Court held that

*Government Document PERS–TR–89–002 (December 1988; excerpted)

the regulation violated the constitutional guarantee of equal rights under the law. The language of the court compared discrimination against homosexuals with racial discrimination. Writing the majority opinion, Judge William Norris included the following analogy:

> For much of our history, the military's fear of racial tension kept black soldiers separated from whites. Today it is unthinkable that the judiciary would defer to the Army's prior "professional" judgment that black and white soldiers had to be segregated to avoid interracial tensions.

To be sure, traditional attitudes are resistant to change. Not all legal rulings and social practices are favorable to policies supporting nondiscrimination on the basis of sexual orientation. Nonetheless, the instances cited above are more than straws in the wind. One interpretation to place on these judicial decisions is that folkways are shifting from intolerance to indifference, if not to open-hearted tolerance. This shift in folkways is reflected, in part, in the repeal of vaguely written and differentially enforced sodomy statutes in nearly half the States, thus decriminalizing homosexual conduct (not to mention decriminalizing unconventional but widely practiced forms of heterosexual conduct).

The world-wide prevalence of *exclusive* same-gender orientation is estimated as three to five percent in the male population, regardless of social tolerance, as in the Phillippines, Polynesia and Brazil, intolerance as in the United States, or repression as in the Soviet Union (Mihalek, 1988). This constancy in the face of cultural diversity suggests that biological factors may be the fundamental source of homosexual orientation.

Adult sexual orientation, then, has its origins, if not its expression, in embryonic development. Ellis and Ames conclude that:

> complex combinations of genetic, hormonal, neurological, and environmental factors operating prior to birth largely determine what an individual's sexual orientation will be, although the orientation itself awaits the onset of puberty to be activated, and may not entirely stabilize until early adulthood (p. 251).

The conclusions are consistent with those of John Money (1988), a leading researcher on the psychobiology of sex. According to Money, in his recent review and summary of current knowledge of homosexuality, data from clinical and laboratory sources indicate that:

> in all species, the differentiation of sexual orientation or status as either bisexual or monosexual (i.e., exclusively heterosexual or homosexual) is a sequential process. The prenatal state of this process, with a possible brief neonatal extension, takes place under the aegis of brain hormonalization. It continues postnatally under the aegis of the senses and social communication of learning (p. 49).

THE LEGAL CONSTRUCTION—
SEXUAL DEVIANCE AS CRIMINAL BEHAVIOR

To make rational use of the crime concept in the context of sexual behavior, it had to be consonant with accepted legal usage, as in crimes against the person, crimes against property, crimes against the Crown, etc. The linguistic formula "crimes against . . ." presupposes a victim. In following this logic, early practitioners of jurisprudence created "crimes against nature" as the label for unwanted sexual conduct. In so doing, they implied that "nature" was the victim.

In most of the criminal codes, and in the Uniform Code of Military Justice, the concept of "crimes against nature" appears frequently when sexual behavior is proscribed. The concept is sometimes rendered by the employment of language which includes the adjective "unnatural." Clearly, the authors of statutes that proscribe "crimes against nature" were not using "nature" as a descriptor for flora and fauna, mountains and valleys, oceans and deserts. When "nature" is the victim, something else is intended.

THE SICKNESS CONSTRUCTION—
THE MEDICALIZATION OF DEVIANCE

Although the mental health professions do not speak with one voice, the currently prevailing view was advanced by Marmor (Freedman, Kaplan & Sadock, 1975), at that time president of the American Psychiatric Association: ". . . there is no reason to assume that there is a specific psychodynamic structure to homosexuality anymore than there is to heterosexuality."

REGULATORY POLICIES IN THE MILITARY

The Office of the Secretary of Defense formulated a concise summary of official policy (Department of Defense, 1982) as follows:

> Homosexuality is incompatible with military service. The presence of such members adversely affects the ability of the Armed Forces to maintain discipline, good order, and morale; to foster mutual trust and confidence among the members; to ensure the integrity of the system of rank and command; to facilitate assignment and worldwide deployment of members who frequently must live and work under close conditions affording minimal privacy; to recruit and retain members of the military services; to maintain the public acceptability of military services; and, in certain circumstances, to prevent breaches of security.

Another article (Article 134) addresses "indecency" defined as:

> that form of immorality relating to sexual impurity which is not only grossly vulgar, obscene, and repugnant to common propriety, but tends

to excite lust and deprave the morals with respect to sexual relations (MCM, p. IV–131).

Although the intention of the articles is to provide clear definitions for criminal acts, some of the terms are ambiguous, for example, "unnatural," "sexual impurity," and "deprave the morals." These terms are drawn from remote sources that supplied the authors and translators of the Bible with guides to rule-making. Contemporary legal and linquistic analysis of these articles would lead to the deletion of rhetorical terms that could not be supported by empirical observation. The indecency article might be applied, for example, to the viewing of X-rated movies and other milder sexually stimulating materials on the grounds that they "excite lust."

A review of contemporary authorities of sexology, marriage, and family relations would raise questions about the UCMJ's criminalization of oral-genital sex play, especially since this is practiced by a large percentage of the general population (Katchadourian & Lunde, 1975). Since military personnel are drawn from the general population, it is reasonable to assume that large numbers of military men and women, married and unmarried, are in violation of the sodomy statute. If enforced, Article 125 would lead to punitive actions, including court-martials, for an untold number of military personnel.

If we look at separated homosexuals in terms of their security clearance, it becomes apparent that such homosexual service members are very likely to hold a security clearance. During the period 1981–1987, 4,914 men were separated from the Army and Air Force sample held Secret or Top Secret security clearances. It is reasonable to suppose that background investigations had yielded no information that would indicate that the subjects were security risks. It is interesting to note that only 28 percent of the homosexual servicemen were discharged in their first year; 72 percent continued to serve at least two years before their employment was terminated.

To account for the large discrepancy between the actual number of separations and the expected number of men and women who have same-gender orientation, several hypotheses may be entertained.

(1) Men and women who identify themselves as homosexual do not enter military service. This hypothesis is difficult to sustain. Harry (1984) found that homosexual and heterosexual men were equally likely to have served in the military. Homosexual women were *more likely* than heterosexual women to have had military service. Weinberg and Williams in a sworn affidavit state: "the vast majority of homosexuals in the Armed Forces remain undiscovered by military authorities, and complete their service with honor" (see Gibson, 1978). Ruse (1988) wrote:

Many soldiers, sailors and airmen are homosexual—and actively so. They do not get caught or prosecuted because they are discreet or lucky, or because authorities turn a blind eye. But the rules do exist, and every now and then some unfortunate gets enmeshed in the net (p. 240).

The fact that only an infinitesimal percentage of men and women are identified as homosexuals leads to an inescapable inference. Many undetected homosexuals serve in the military, enlisted and officers, men and women.

On the reasonable assumption that the number of military personnel who are homosexual may be as high as 10 percent, only a minute percentage are separated from the service. This discrepancy calls into question the usefulness of Article 125. It may be that the article is simply unenforceable.

Although not well-publicized, the available data all point to the conclusion that preservice background characterization and subsequent job performance of homosexuals in the military is satisfactory (Williams & Weinberg, 1971; McDaniel, 1989; Zuliani, 1986; Crittenden Report, 1957). The intensity of prejudice against homosexuals may be of the same order as the prejudice against blacks in 1948, when the military was ordered to integrate.

Social science specialists helped develop programs for combating racial discrimination so that now the military services are leaders in providing equal opportunity for black men and women. It would be wise to consider applying the experience of the past 40 years to the integration of homosexuals.

RESISTANCE TO CHANGE

In the belief system of current traditional military authorities, homosexual men cannot be rugged, tough, and macho.* The stereotype of homosexual men, as we mentioned earlier, centers on the feminized male who is unable to perform masculine tasks.

A recent exchange in the *Navy Times* reflects a criticism of current policy and a vehement defense of traditional military attitudes. Under the heading, *Man the barricades: The federal court is letting "them" in*, Michelle McCormick wrote a column poking fun at the arguments offered by supporters of discriminatory policies. Representative of her facetious bits of advice to future judges is the following:

Homosexuals are likely to bother people who don't want to be bothered. The bothering that goes on now is between men and women. It is the right and natural way of things that men should bother women who would rather be left alone. But men are not accustomed to being both-

*In Classical Greece homosexuality and homosexual bonds between soldiers were considered an asset to the performance of the fighting men in terms of patriotism and military courage.

ered; and they shouldn't have to put up with it (Navy Times, 29 February 1988, p. 62).

Ms. McCormick's column brought forth a letter to the editor from Major Randel Webb, USMC, who strongly defended the traditional point of view. Major Webb wrote (in part):

> . . . Clearly she accepts a main plank of the homosexual community agenda that denies their own profoundly aberrant behavior. It promotes the idea they are just like everyone else except for sexual preference. There are valid reasons homosexuals should not be accepted into the military.
>
> Homosexuals are a politically active special interest group. The services have adopted policies opposing homosexuals primarily because they are a threat to good order and discipline.
>
> Most people, though Ms. McCormick would probably consider them unenlightened, loath homosexuals. Their contempt is easily recognizable in the form of derision and jokes. Homosexuals would be harrassed, and discriminated against. What the armed services do not need is another political body within itself to create dissension.
>
> There are also real problems like homosexuals demanding recognition of their marriages and thus base housing and BAQ (Basic allowance for quarters) at the married rate, fraternization and all of its implications, morale and retention problems that would be caused by people who leave in disgust, and reduced effectiveness of homosexual officers and NCO's handling contemptuous subordinates. . . . The pointed end of the armed forces have a critical mission to prepare for and conduct war. It requires teamwork, camaraderie, and a sense of pride in being associated with other members of the unit.
>
> These elements are achieved by several factors, among them are discipline and good order. Tolerating homosexuals in the armed forces is contrary to good order and discipline.

Most of the issues raised by Major Webb, which reflect traditional anti-homosexual arguments are reminiscent of the issues raised when black athletes (then called Negro athletes) were first allowed to participate in professional baseball. Despite its early resistance to change, it is important to repeat that the military establishment is now looked upon as a model for racial and gender integration.

In his list of problems that would be created if homosexuals were freely admitted into the services, Major Webb failed to mention potential security risks. This has been one of the main reasons given for screening out homosexual men and women from the military, and from jobs requiring a security clearance.

Since the policy changes introduced in 1981, almost 100 percent of homosexual separations have been administrative, and 55 percent of these separations have been characterized as honorable. This indicates a softening of attitudes.

The unreasoned resistance to learning about or interacting with homosexuals has led to the formulation of the concept of *homophobia*. Some men experience uneasy feelings when in close proximity to other men who are identified as homosexuals. It is as if such nearness could pollute one's identity.

Homosexuals are like heterosexuals in being selective in their choice of partners, in observing rules of privacy, in considering appropriateness of time and place, in connecting sexuality with tender sentiments, and so on.

SUMMARY AND IMPLICATIONS

An examination of recent social and political history points to the fact that the courts are slowly moving toward eliminating discrimination on the basis of nonconforming sexual orientation. Under prevailing social conditions, a public admission of homosexuality carries less stigma than in earlier times, and is no legal bar to most employment. Thus, unless the military is willing to adopt nondiscriminatory policies, a mere claim of homosexuality, whether true or false, would excuse any person who wants to avoid military service.

Our analysis directs us to regard people with nonconforming sexual orientation as a minority group. Does atypical sexual orientation influence job performance? Studies of homosexual veterans make clear that having a same-gender or an opposite-gender orientation is unrelated to job performance in the same way as is being left- or right-handed (Williams & Weinberg, 1971).

For the purpose of military organization, however, quality of job performance may be less important than the effects of homosexuals (minority group members) on that important but ephemeral quality: group cohesion. The important question to be raised in future research must center on the claims that persons with nonconforming sexual attitudes create insurmountable problems in the maintenance of discipline, group cohesion, morale, organizational pride, and integrity.

In our study of suitability for military service, we have been governed by a silent assumption: that social attitudes are historically conditioned. In our own time, we have witnessed far-reaching changes in attitudes toward the physically disabled, people of color, disease, prevention, birth control, cohabitation of unmarried couples, and so on. We have witnessed a noticeable shift in tolerance for women and homosexual men and women in the civilian workplace.

Custom and law change with the times, sometimes with amazing rapidity. The military cannot indefinitely isolate itself from the changes occurring in the wider society, of which it is an integral part.

AUTHOR'S NOTE: *A complete copy of this document may be obtained by contacting the office of Congressman Gerry Studds, in the House of Representatives, Washington, D.C., or your state congressman.*

☆ ☆

APPENDIX C

Gay and Lesbian Support Organizations and Other Miscellaneous Services

I. VETERANS GROUPS

Alexander Hamilton American
Legion
    Post 448
    401 Van Ness Avenue, Room 128
    San Francisco, CA 94102
Gay Veterans Association
    263A West 19th Street
    New York, NY 10011
Gay Veterans Association, Inc.
    346 Broadway, Suite 814
    New York, NY 10013
Lavender Veterans
    650 Shrader Street
    San Francisco, CA 94117
New England Gay and Lesbian
Veterans
    P.O. Box 1392
    Back Bay Annex
    Boston, MA 02117

San Diego Veterans Association
    P.O. Box 89196
    San Diego, CA 92138
Swords of Plowshare
    400 Valencia Street
    San Francisco, CA 94103
Veterans C.A.R.E.
    P.O. Box 69961
    West Hollywood, CA 90069
Veterans C.A.R.E.
Chuck Schoen
    8031 Mill Station Road
    Sebastopol, CA 95472

II. VETERANS/MILITARY LEGAL GROUPS

American Civil Liberties Union
    132 West 43rd Street
    New York, NY 10036
    (Local affiliates in every state)

Citizen Soldier
Tod Ensign
    175 Fifth Avenue, Suite 808
    New York, NY 10010

Gay and Lesbian Advocates and
Defenders
100 Boylston Street
Boston, MA 02116
GI Assistance Project
P.O. Box 6586
T Street Station NW
Washington, DC 20009
Lambda Legal Defense and
Education Fund
132 West 43rd Street
New York, NY 10036
Midwest Committee for Military
Counseling
343 South Dearborn Street, Suite
1113
Chicago, IL 60604
Militarism Resource Project
P.O. Box 13416
Philadelphia, PA 19101

Military Law Task Force
1168 Union Street, Suite 201
San Diego, CA 92101
National Gay and Lesbian Task
Force
1517 U Street NW
Washington, DC 20009
National Gay Rights Advocates
540 Castro Street
San Francisco, CA 94114
(Local affiliates in most states)
National Lawyers Guild
2208 South Street
Philadelphia, PA 19146
Veterans Education Project
P.O. Box 42130
Washington, DC 20015
Vietnam Veterans of America
Claims Service
2001 South Street NW, 7th Floor
Washington, DC 20015

III. COMMUNITY SUPPORT GROUPS

East End Gay Organization for
Human Rights
Marie Manion
P.O. Box 708
Bridgehampton, NY 11932
Gay Historical Archives
P.O. Box 38100
3340 Country Club Road
Los Angeles, CA 90038-0100
GLOE—Operation Concern
1853 Market Street
San Francisco, CA 94103
The Information and Referral
Program
P.O. Box 38777
Los Angeles, CA 90038-1292
The International Gay and Lesbian
Archives
1654 North Hudson Avenue
Los Angeles, CA 90028
Lesbian and Gay Pride, Inc.
c/o Multnomah County Library
801 SW 10th
Portland, OR 97205

Lesbian Community Project
P.O. Box 5931
Portland, OR 97228
Lesbian Herstory Educational
Foundation, Inc.
Deborah Edel, Archives
P.O. Box 1258
New York, NY 10116
Metropolitan Community Church
(MCC)
1644 NE 24th
Portland, OR 97212
(Local affiliates in most states)
National Organization for Women
(NOW)
425 13th Street, NW, Suite 723
Washington, DC 20004
Olympia/Black Hills Chapter of the
Dorian Group
P.O. Box 5022
Lacey, WA 98503

ONE, Inc.
(Gay Archives)
   3340 Country Club Road
   Los Angeles, CA 90019

Outlook on Justice Newsletter
American Friends Service
   Committee
   2161 Massachusetts Avenue
   Cambridge, MA 02140

IV. MISCELLANEOUS SERVICES/POINTS OF CONTACT

The Advocate
   6922 Hollywood Blvd., 10th floor
   Los Angeles, CA 90028
Among Friends
   P.O. Box 426
   Madison, WI 53701
Different Drummer Bookshoppe
   1027 North Coast Highway
   Laguna Beach, CA 92651
A Different Light Bookstore
   548 Hudson Street
   New York, NY 10014
   or
   489 Castro Street
   San Francisco, CA 94114
   or
   4014 Santa Monica Blvd.
   Los Angeles (Silverlake), CA 90029
Giovanni's Room
   1145 Pine Street
   Philadelphia, PA 19107
Guardian
   33 West 17th Street
   New York, NY 10011
Just Out
   P.O. Box 15117
   Portland, OR 97215
Kentucky Gay and Lesbian
   Educational Center
   David Williams, Director
   1464 South Second Street
   Louisville, KY 40208
Lesbian and Gay Heritage Alliance
   of the Pacific Northwest
   1425 Prospect Street, #E5
   Seattle, WA 98112

Minerva: Quarterly Report on
   Women and the Military
   Dr. Linda Grant DePauw, Director
   1101 South Arlington Ridge Road,
   #210
   Arlington, VA 22202
New Directions for Women
   108 West Palisade Avenue
   Englewood, NJ 07631
New York Native
   P.O. Box 1475
   New York, NY 10008
Representative Cal Anderson (D)
   House of Representatives
   Olympia, WA 98501
Representative Barney Frank (D—
   Mass.)
   U.S. House of Representatives
   Washington, DC 20515
Representative Gerry Studds (D—
   Mass.)
   U.S. House of Representatives
   Washington, DC 20515
S.A.G.E. (Senior Action in A Gay
   Environment)
   208 West 13th Street
   New York, NY 10011
So Proudly We Wave
   Lily Adams, Editor
   P.O. Box 1703
   Mill Valley, CA 94941
Washington Blade
   724 Ninth Street NW
   Washington, DC 20004
World War II Project
   Allan Bérubé, Director
   P.O. Box 42332
   San Francisco, CA 94101

REFERENCES

GENERAL BOOKS

Adair, Nancy, and Adair, Casey. *Word Is Out: Stories of Some of Our Lives.* New York and San Francisco: Dell Publishing and New Glide Publications, 1978.

Adelman, Marcy, et al. *Long Time Passing: Lives of Older Lesbians.* Boston: Alyson Publications, 1986.

Aldridge, Sarah. *All True Lovers.* Tallahassee: Naiad Press, 1985.

Altman, Dennis. *Coming Out in the Seventies.* Boston: Alyson Publications, 1979.

Arnold, June. *The Cook and the Carpenter.* New York: Daughters, 1973.

Austen, Roger. *Playing the Game: The Homosexual Novel in America.* New York: Bobbs-Merrill, 1977.

Baldwin, James. *Tell Me How Long the Train's Been Gone.* New York: Dial, 1968.

Bannon, Ann. *I Am a Woman.* New York: Arno Press, 1975.

——. *Odd Girl Out.* New York: Arno Press, 1975.

Baker, Mark. *NAM.* New York: Berkley, 1981.

Barnard, Mary. *Sappho: A New Translation.* Los Angeles: University of California Press, 1958.

Barrus, Tim. *Anywhere, Anywhere.* New York: Knights Press, 1987.

Bérubé, Allan. *Coming Out Under Fire: Gay Men and Women in World War II.* New York: Free Press, 1990.

Blumenfeld, Warren J., and Raymond, Diane. *Looking at Gay and Lesbian Life.* New York: Philosophical Library, 1988.

Boggan, E. Carrington, et al. *The Rights of Gay People (An American Civil Liberties Union Handbook).* New York: Avon Books, 1975.

Boswell, John. *Christianity, Social Tolerance and Homosexuality: Gay People in Western Europe from the Beginning of the Christian Era to the Fourteenth Century.* Chicago: University of Chicago Press, 1980.

Brown, Rita Mae. *Rubyfruit Jungle.* New York: Bantam, 1977.

Bryant, Clifton D. *Khaki Collar Crime: Deviant Behavior in the Military Context.* New York: Free Press, 1979.

Costello, John. *Virtue Under Fire.* New York: Little, Brown, 1986.

Curb, Rosemary, and Manahan, Nancy, eds. *Lesbian Nuns: Breaking Silence.* Tallahassee: Naiad Press, 1985.

Damon, Gene, et al., eds. *The Lesbian Literature*. Bates City, Mo.: Naiad Press, 1975.

Day, Donald. *The Evolution of Love*. New York: Dial Press, 1980.

D'Emilio, John. *Sexual Politics, Sexual Communities: The Making of a Homosexual Minority in the United States, 1940–1970*. Chicago: University of Chicago Press, 1983.

Elbert, Alan. *The Homosexuals*. New York: Macmillan, 1977.

Enloe. *Does Khaki Become You?: The Militarization of Women's Lives*. Boston: South End Press, 1983.

Falk, Richard Q.; Kolco, Gabriel; and Lifton, Robert Jay, eds. *Crimes of War*. New York: Random House, 1971.

Fisher, Peter. *The Gay Mystique: The Myth and Reality of Male Homosexuality*. New York: Stein and Day, 1972.

Gibson, Lawrence E. *Get Off My Ship: Ensign Berg vs. the U.S. Navy*. New York: Avon Books, 1978.

Grief, Martin. *The Gay Book of Days*. Pittstown and Secaucus, N.J.: The Main Street Press and Lyle Stuart, Inc., 1982.

Hall, Radclyffe. *The Well of Loneliness*. New York: Simon and Schuster, 1975.

Hellman, Lillian. *The Children's Hour*. New York: New American Library, 1962.

Hudson, Rock, and Davidson, Sara. *Rock Hudson: His Story*. New York: William Morrow, 1986.

Humphries, Laud. *Out of the Closets: The Sociology of Homosexual Liberation*. Englewood Cliffs, N.J.: Prentice-Hall, 1972.

Janovitz, Morris. *The Professional Soldier*. New York: Free Press, 1960.

Jordan, Robin. *Speak Out, My Heart*. Bates City, Mo.: Naiad Press, 1976.

Katz, Jonathan. *Government vs. Homosexuals*. New York: Arno Press, 1975.

Kramer, Larry. *Faggots*. New York: Random House, 1978.

Lahr, John. *Prick Up Your Ears: The Biography of Joe Orton*. New York: Alfred A. Knopf, 1978.

Loulon, Jo Ann. *Lesbian Sex*. San Francisco: Sprinsters Ink, 1984.

Lusk, Susan, et al. *Sappho: The Art of Loving Women*. New York: Chelsea House, 1980.

Lynn, Elizabeth. *A Different Light*. New York: Berkley, 1978.

Marmor, Judd, ed. *Homosexual Behavior: A Modern Reappraisal*. New York: Basic Books, 1980.

McCarthy, Mary. *The Group*. New York: New American Library, 1964.

McIntosh, Harlon. *This Finer Shadow*. New York: Dial Press, 1941.

Melville, Herman. *Billy Budd, Sailor: An Insider Narrative*. Chicago: University of Chicago Press, 1964.

Meyer, Carol. *The Writer's Survival Manual*. New York: Bantam Books, 1982.

Miller, Isabel. *Patience and Sarah*. New York: Fawcett, 1973.

Miller, Neil. *In Search of Gay America: Women and Men in a Time of Change*. New York: Atlantic Monthly Press, 1989.

Mollo, Andrew. *The Armed Forces of World War II: Uniforms, Insignia and Organization*. New York: Crown Publishers, 1981.

Morgan, Claire. *The Price of Salt*. New York: Arno Press, 1975.

Murphy, Lawrence R. *Perverts by Official Order*. New York: Harrington Park Press, 1988.

National Gay and Lesbian Task Force. *National Anti-Gay/Lesbian Victimization Report.* New York: 1984.

Nelson, Charles. *The Boy Who Picked the Bullets Up.* New York: Avon Books, 1981.

Rader, Dotson. *Gov't. Inspected Meat.* New York: Paperback Library, 1972.

Rechy, John. *The Persian Boy.* New York: Pantheon, 1972.

Richmond, Len, and Noquera, Gary, eds. *The Gay Liberation Book.* New York: Ramparts, 1973.

Ries, Al, and Trout, Jack. *Positioning: The Battle for Your Mind.* Warner Books, 1981.

Rutledge, Leigh W. *The Gay Book of Lists.* Boston: Alyson Publications, 1987.

Samois, et al. *Coming to Power.* Boston: Alyson Publications, 1982.

Sanders, Dennis. *Gay Source: A Catalog for Men.* New York: Coward, McCann, 1977.

Schneider, Carl J., and Schneider, Dorothy. *Sound Off: American Military Women Speak Out.* New York: E. P. Dutton, 1988.

Schur, Edwin M. *Crimes Without Victims.* Englewood Cliffs, N.J.: Prentice-Hall, 1965.

Selby, Hubert, Jr. *Last Exit to Brooklyn.* New York: Grove Press, 1974.

Shilts, Randy. *And the Band Played On: Politics, People, and the AIDS Epidemic.* New York: St. Martin's Press, 1987.

——. *The Mayor of Castro Street: The Life and Times of Harvey Milk.* New York: St. Martin's Press, 1982.

Stanton, Shelby L. *Vietnam: Order of Battle.* New York: Galahad Books, 1987.

Terkel, Studs. *The Good War: An Oral History of World War Two.* New York: Ballantine Books, 1984.

Tiger, Lionel. *Men in Groups.* New York: Random House, 1969.

Torres, Tereska. *Women's Barracks.* Greenwich, Ct.: Fawcett, 1950.

Truscott, Lucian K., IV. *Dress Grey.* New York: Doubleday, 1979.

Vida, Ginny, et al. *Our Right to Love: A Lesbian Resource Book.* Englewood Cliffs, N.J.: Prentice-Hall, 1978.

Walker, Keith. *A Piece of My Heart.* New York: Ballantine Books, 1987.

Warren, Patricia Nell. *The Front Runner.* New York: William Morrow, 1974.

Weinberg, George. *Society and the Healthy Homosexual.* New York: St. Martin's Press, 1973.

Williams, C. I., and Weinberg, M. S. *Homosexuals and the Military.* New York: Harper & Row, 1971.

Young, Ian. *The Male Homosexual in Literature: A Bibliography.* Metuchen, N.J.: Scarecrow Press, 1975.

LEGAL BOOKS

National Organization for Women. *Lesbian Rights: Military Policy.* Lesbian Rights Resource Kit, 1981.

Rivkin, Robert S., and Stichman, Barton F. *The Rights of Military Personnel* (An American Civil Liberties Union Handbook). New York: Avon Books, 1977.

Woodward, James M., ed. *The Gay Military Counselor's Manual.* San Diego Center for Social Services, 1976.

LEGAL BRIEFS

Allen, Katherine M. *"Dronenburg vs. Zech:* The Wrong Case for Asserting a Right of Privacy for Homosexuals." *North Carolina Law Review,* vol. 63, pp. 749–66.

"Armed Forces: Discharges." *United States Law Weekly,* 45 LW (August 17, 1976), pp. 2074–75.

Ben-Shalom v. Secretary of the Army, No. 78-C-431, U.S. Seventh Circuit Court of Appeals for the Eastern District (Berigan). September 9, 1985.

Ben-Shalom v. Secretary of the Army, No. 87-1217, U.S. Court of Appeals for the Seventh Circuit (Berigan). May 22, 1987.

Ben-Shalom v. Secretary of the Army, No. 88-C-468, U.S. District Court, Eastern District of Wisconsin (Berigan). May 3, 1988.

Bourdonnoy, Katherine; Johnson, R. Charles; Schuman, Joseph; and Wilson, Bridget. "Fighting Back: Lesbian and Gay Draft, Military and Veterans Issues." Chicago: Advocate Enterprises, 1985.

Diamond, David Harley. "Homosexuals in the Military: They Would Rather Fight Than Switch." *John Marshall Law Review,* vol. 18, no. 4 (Summer 1985), pp. 437–968.

Hunter, Nan, and Spears, James M. "Gays and the Military." American Bar Association, April 11, 1988, pp. 36–37.

Hunter, Nan D. "Appeals Court Rejects Army Rule Against Gays." American Civil Liberties Union, Winter 1988, pp. 10–14.

Loda, Gifford. "Homosexual Conduct in the Military: No Faggots in Military Woodpiles." *Arizona State Law Journal,* 1983:79, pp. 79–112.

Lynch, N. B. "The Administrative Discharge: Changes Needed." *Marine Law Review,* 22, 1970, pp. 141–69.

Matlovich v. Secretary of the Air Force, No. 75-1750, U.S. District Court for District of Columbia (Gesell). July 16, 1976.

McGrevy, Susan. "Norton Sound Case Shows Investigations Rely on Intimidation and False Evidence." American Civil Liberties Union, June 1981, p. 6.

Rivers, Rhonda. "Our Straight-Laced Judges: The Legal Position of Homosexual Persons in the United States." *Hastings Law Journal,* vol. 30 (March 1979), no. 4, pp. 837–55.

——— . "Queer Law: Sexual Orientation Law in the Mid-Eighties, Part II." *University of Dayton Law Review,* vol. 11:2, 1986, pp. 287–324.

——— . "Recent Developments in Sexual Preference Law." *Drake Law Review,* 311, 1980–81, pp. 319–24.

Scandy-Carbetta, Kelly. "The Armed Services Continued Degradation and Expulsion of Their Homosexual Members: Dronenburg v. Zech, 741 F. 2d 1288 (D.C. Cir. 1984)," *Cincinnati Law Review,* vol. 54, pp. 1054–67.

Suskind, Jerome A. "Military Administration Discharge Boards: The Right to Confrontation and Cross Examination." *Michigan State Bar Journal,* 44 (January 1965), pp. 25–32.

Woodward v. United States and United States Navy, No. 86-1283, U.S. Court of Appeals for the Federal Circuit, District of Columbia (Groat). March 29, 1989.

NEWSPAPERS

Army Times:
December 1, 1971. "Geraldine, Meet Simone!" John B. Ward. P. 58.
February 29, 1988. "On Issue for Congress."

The Blade:
August 7, 1980. "U.S. Navy vs. the Lesbian Eight." Jeff Britton. Pp. 1, 21.

The Body Politic:
November 1980. "Dyke Challenges U.S. Army Sex Rules." P. 17.
October 1980. "Navy Drops 'Lesbian' Charges After Sailors Win in Two Cases." P. 22.

Boston Gay Community News:
January 8, 1977. "Widened Vietnam Pardon Could Aid Gay Veterans" (Community News Syndicate), Neil Miller.

Boston Globe:
October 23, 1989. "Pentagon Is Said to Bar Gays Anew."
October 30, 1989. "New England in Washington: Studds Speaking Out for Gays in Uniform." Michael K. Frisby. P. 3.
November 2, 1989. "Military Seeks Third Study of Policy on Gays." Michael K. Frisby. P. 1.

Boston Herald:
November 6, 1989. "Congress Unlikely to Fight Military Gay Ban" (AP). P. 21.

The Bridge:
February 18, 1988. Letter to the editor: "Armed Forces Not for Homosexuals." Bill E. Volz. P. 2.
February 25, 1988. Letter to the editor: "Sound Off." Pp. 3–4.
January 11, 1990. "'Crusader' Aims to Educate Society." Serena Lesley. Pp. 1, 4.
January 11, 1990. "'Vendetta' Charge Untrue: VonTagen." Serena Lesley. P. 4.

The Bugle-American:
October 8, 1976. "Ben-Shalom Discharged: Army Marches Against Lesbianism." R. Reuel Karp. Pp. 20–21.

The Bulletin:
August 1, 1980. "Drugs, Bisexuals Are Common at Base, Woman Sailor Claims." P. B-3.

Cape Cod Times:
October 29, 1989. "Studds Reveals Pentagon Report Supporting Gays" (AP). John Diamond. Pp. 1, 10.

Cincinnati Post:
February 11, 1988. "Activists Praise Ruling Against Army's Gay Ban" (AP). P. 2A.

Daily Californian:
May 21, 1976. "Lesbian Seeks Support." P. 25.
May 21, 1976. "Lesbian Sergeant Challenges Military." Larry Sterne. P. 1.

Daily Cardinal:
  October 1, 1987. "Lesbian Discusses Her Battle with Army." Elleen Zaffiro.
  P. 1.

Daily News:
  July 10, 1986. "Lesbian at War: Lt. Ellen Nesbitt Fights Discharge from Air
  Guard." Michele Willens.
  May 21, 1987. "Lesbian to Sue National Guard." Robert Carroll.

Downtowner:
  February 27, 1989. "Doctor to Discuss 'Gays in the Military.' "

Gay Community News:
  November 6, 1982. "Lesbian in Air Force Appeals Conviction." Jil Clark.
  P. 3.
  March 26, 1983. "Newak Loses Appeal, Press Rule Relaxed." David Morris.
  P. 3.
  October 29, 1989. "Military Shocked by Pro-Gay Report." Jennie McKnight.
  Pp. 1, 14–15.

Gay Scene:
  August 1988. "Leonard P. Matlovich." P. 20.

Greensboro News & Record:
  October 24, 1989. "Operation Ostrich: The Pentagon on Gays." P. A14.

Guardian:
  April 6, 1983. "Women Loving Women: A Crime in the Air Force." Tod Ensign.

Just Out:
  July 1988. "Leonard Matlovich." Mike Hippler. P.8.
  August 1988. "Life On a Seesaw: Dr. Mary Ann Humphrey Tells All." Kamila
  Al-Nijjar. P. 11.
  March 1989. "TV Show Features Gays in the Military." Jay Brown. P. 4.
  June 1989. "Military Expertise?" Jay Brown. P. 5.
  June 1989. "Documenting the Gay Americas." Ed Schiffer. P. 26.
  October 1989. "Navy Scapegoats a Dead Sailor." Jack Riley. P. 5.
  February, 1990. "Marine Corps Admits Error in Sodomy Prosecution." Jay
  Brown, P. 10.

Los Angeles Herald Examiner:
  October 24, 1989. "Gays and the Military."

Los Angeles Times:
  October 23, 1989. "Challenge to Military's Anti-Gay Stance Found in Report
  Dismissed by Pentagon."

Louisville Courier Journal:
  July 25, 1982. "Army Warns Six Law Schools to Lift Their Bans on Recruit-
  ing" (*New York Times* News Service). Warren Weaver, Jr. P. A11.
  October 30, 1983. "Navy Charges Officer With Homosexual Affair."
  January 22, 1984. "Discharge Recommended for Accused Homosexual."
  October 9, 1985. "Marines Want Proof Before Discharging Gay" (AP). P. A8.
  January 15, 1987. "Soldier Gets More Advice on Cross-Dressing Habits."
  Abigail Van Buren.

February 11, 1988. "Court Overturns Army Ban on Gays." *(Washington Post)*, Ruth Marcus.

February 17, 1988. "Justice on the March."

April 8, 1988. "Marine Officers Probe Charges of Lesbianism Within Corps' Ranks" (AP). P. A10.

June 10, 1988. "Army Gay Rights Reviewed."

Milwaukee Sentinel:
February 12, 1988. "Military Exclusion of Lesbians/Gays Overturned." Pp. 11–12.

January 11, 1989. "Man, 49, Has Friends, Humor, Courage, and AIDS." William Janz.

Navy Times:
February 29, 1988. "Man the Barricades: The Federal Court Is Letting 'Them' In."

February 29, 1988. "More Women Than Men Discharged as Homosexuals." Grant Willis.

March 21, 1988. "Homosexual Women in Uniform Describe Pride and Daily Fears." Grant Willis. P. 34.

March 21, 1988. "Two Marine Cases Up This Month at Parris Island." Mel Jones.

March 21, 1988. "Witch Hunt Decried as Extreme." Grant Willis. P. 34.

New York Native:
March 1986. "Lesbian Scores Landmark Victory over Army." Sarah Schulman.

March 1989. "Gays in the Military on TV." Mary Ann Humphrey.

New York Newsday:
June 25, 1986. "Lesbian: Uncle Sam Wants Me Out." Janine Coughlin.

New York Times:
July 6, 1975. "Self-styled Bisexual Sues to Stay in Naval Reserves" (AP).

June 29, 1980. "Navy Sends More Women to Sea, Despite Problems." Robert Lindsey.

September 14, 1980. "Navy Shifts Two Women Found Guilty of Lesbianism."

October 25, 1980. "Court Upholds Navy on Homosexuality Issue."

November 16, 1980. "Army Allows Clearances to Gays."

August 9, 1989. "West Point Picks Woman to Lead Cadet Corps." Lisa Foderaro. Pp. A1, B8.

August 10, 1989. "Bush Plans to Name Colin Powell to Head Joint Chiefs, Aides Say." Richard Halloran. Pp. A1, A12.

August 10, 1989. "Top Military Man: A Model General." Andrew Rosenthal. P. A12.

August 10, 1989. "Lesbian Struggles to Serve in Army." Sharmen Stein. P. A10.

February 27, 1990. "Justices Refuse to Hear Challenge to Military Ban on Homosexuality." Linda Greenhouse, Pp. A1, A12.

On Guard:
Issue no. 2, 1986. "Citizen Soldier to Fight Discharge of Homosexual Officer." Tricia Critchfield. P. 9.

Issue no. 3, 1986. "Sailor Jailed and Discharged for Refusing to Take AIDS Test." Adam Wood. P. 2.

Issue no. 4, 1987. "Lesbian to Be Promoted While Facing Discharge?" Tricia Critchfield.

Issue no. 6, 1987. "Air Force Officer Resists Ouster." Tricia Critchfield. P. 8.

Issue no. 3, 1988. "Military Represses Gays Despite Court Ruling." Stuart Sender. Pp. 9–10.

Issue no. 3, 1988. "Navy Recruit Harassed After Testing HIV Positive." Tod Ensign. P. 6.

Issue no. 4, 1988. "Witch-hunts Continue for 'The Few and the Proud.' "

Oregonian:
February 11, 1988. "Army's Gay Ban Illegal" (AP). Bob Egelko. P. 1.

February 12, 1988. "Ruling on Gay Rights to Have Wide Effects" (AP). Richard Carelli.

February 18, 1988. "Court Ruling on Army Sergeant a Victory for Individual over State." James J. Kilpatrick.

June 24, 1988. "Discharged Hero Dies." Pp. A14, 3M.

July 3, 1988. "Man Who Fought Gay Ban Buried" (AP). Pp. A12, 3M.

July 13, 1988. "Gay Issues: Societal Sanctions, Origins of Sex Orientation." Mary M. Chandler and Donald L. Weston. Pp. 3M, B9.

October 13, 1988. "Military AIDS Tests Make Case for High Accuracy of Screening" (AP). Daniel Q. Haney. Pp. 3M, E3.

December 30, 1988. "Homosexual Ex-Midshipman Files Suit" (AP). Matt Yancy. Pp. A12, 3M.

April 20, 1989. "Lesbian Label Described as Sexual Harassment" (Knight-Rider News Service). Bill Arthur. Pp. D10, 3M.

May 4, 1989. "Appeals Court Rules Army Must Allow Homosexual Ex-Sergeant to Re-Enlist" *(New York Times* News Service). Katherine Bishop. Pp. 3M, F3.

June 8, 1989. "Homosexuals Face Surge in Violence, Study Finds" *(Los Angeles Times–Washington Post* Service). Lee May. Pp. A14, 3M.

July 10, 1989. "Persecution Act Makes North Rich" (Chicago Tribune). Mike Royko. P. B7.

August 10, 1989. "West Point First." News in Brief, P. A3.

August 10, 1989. "Ex-Aide Powell in Line to Head Joint Chiefs." Suzanne M. Schafer. P. A9.

August 10, 1989. "Appeals Court Rejects Lesbian's Bid for Re-enlistment in Army Reserve." David Rocks. P. A17.

September 7, 1989. "Sodomy Law Struck Down" (AP) P. A15.

September 7, 1989. "Navy Blames Sailor for April Explosion Aboard USS *Iowa.*" Donna Cassata. P. A12.

September 8, 1989. "Navy Ties Sailor to Blast on *Iowa.*" (AP). Suzanne M. Schafer. P. A12.

September 17, 1989. "Rep. Frank's Public, Private Lives Clash in Controversy" *(New York Times* News Service). Michael Oreskes. Pp. A2, 3M.

September 23, 1989. " 'Coming Out' Will Help End Gay Discrimination" *(Los Angeles Times–Washington Post* Service). Andrew G. Webb. P. A2.

September 23, 1989. "Documents Detail FBI Spying on Gay-Rights Movement" *(San Francisco Chronicle)*. Randy Shilts. P. A2.

September 25, 1989. "Spectre of Sailor Haunts Questionable *Iowa* Investigation" *(Newport News Daily Press)*. Robert Becker and A. J. Plunkett. Pp. A2, 3M.

October 22, 1989. "Study Asks Military to End Bias Against Homosexuals" *(New York Times* News Service). Elaine Sciolino. Pp. A1, A25.

October 29, 1989. "Contradictions on Role Frustrate Military Women" *(Los Angeles Times, A3–*Washington Post Service). Molly Moore. Pp. A2, 3M.

October 30, 1989. "Pregnancy, Birth, Child Care Become Military Concerns" *(Los Angeles Times–Washington Post* Service). Molly Moore. Pp. A2, 3M.

October 31, 1989. "Canadian Women Find Infantry Training Hinders Equality" *(Los Angeles Times–Washington Post* Service). Molly Moore. Pp. A2, 3M.

November 7, 1989. "Bias Alleged in Denying Medal to Jew" *(New York Times* News Service). William E. Schmidt. Pp. A1, A11.

November 7, 1989. "Insurer Agrees to Pay USS *Iowa* Crewman" (Knight-Ridder News Service). Donna Gehrke. P. A11.

November 9, 1989. "SF Voters Reject Domestic Partners Law" *(New York Times* News Service). Pp. A15, 3M.

November 18, 1989. "House Plans to Look into *Iowa* Inquiry" (AP). Donna Cassata. Pp. 4M, A15.

December 5, 1989. "Faculty Wants ROTC Off Campus if Gay Ban Isn't Lifted" (AP). Julie Aicher. Pp. A12, 3M.

January 4, 1990. "Woman Leads Attack in Panama" *(New York Times* News Service). Michael Gordon. Pp. A8, 4M.

February 20, 1990. "Marine Lesbian Case Overturned" (AP). Pp. 3M, A9.

February 27, 1990. "Armed Forces Sex Policy Stands" (Knight-Rider News Service). Arron Epstein.

February 28, 1990. "Man Attempts to Change Gay's TV Image" (AP). Richard De Atley. Pp. 3M, D3.

March 3, 1990. "House Panel Raps *Iowa* Inquiry" *(Los Angeles Times–Washington Post* Service). Melissa Healy. Pp. 3M, A11.

March 6, 1990. "Is a Gay Publication Always Suspect?" *(Washington Post)*. Niles Merton. Pp. 3M, B7.

Out!:

March 1984. "Ruling Due Soon in Case Against Army." Sue Burke. P. 3.

April 1984. "Battles Won, But the War Goes On: Ben-Shalom Holds Out for Victory." Sue Burke. P. 1.

October 1984. "Commentary: Lesbian and Gay Soldiers Get the Cold Shoulder." Miriam Ben-Shalom.

March 1986. "Fight with Army Wins Rights for All." Sue Burke.

Patriot Ledger:

October 30, 1989. "Gays Are Well Qualified for Military, Report Says."

Philadelphia Inquirer:

February 9, 1976. "Ensign Vows to Fight Discharge over Sexuality." Robert Fensterer. P. B-2.

May 28, 1977. "Navy Ban on Homosexuals Upheld." Aaron Epstein. P. 5-A.

January 4, 1988. "The Marines: A Few Good Men Doesn't Include Gays."
David Ross.

Post Intelligencer:
July 1988. "Matlovich Dies." P. 2.
July 1988. "V.A. Extends Benefits to Gay Veterans." P. 1.

Roanoke Times:
June 4, 1976. "Gay Ensign Checks Out of Navy" (AP).
June 28, 1976. "Homosexual Tries to Rejoin Navy: Claims Case Mishandled" (AP).
June 25, 1977. "Army Woman Near Explosion" (World News, AP).

Sacramento Bee:
September 1, 1989. "Gay Officer Given Full Retirement." Steve Gibson. P. B1.

San Francisco Chronicle:
August 6, 1980. "Navy Lesbian Hearing Opens: None of Your Business, Uncle Sam" *(Los Angeles Times).* Beth Ann Krier. P. 2.
August 7, 1980. "Navy Threat in Lesbian Case Criminal" (AP). P. 25.

San Francisco Examiner:
June 4, 1990. "Gay in America—An Examiner Special Report." This was a 16-part special report subjects and dates as follows:

June 4, "The Gay Movement"	June 14, "Impact of AIDS"
June 5, "National Poll"	June 18, "A Change of Heart"
June 6, "Gay Poll"	June 19, "Gay Teenagers"
June 7, "Violence"	June 20, "Joe Comes Out"
June 8, "Religion"	June 21, "Gay Culture"
June 11, "Going Home Again"	June 22, "Gays in the Arts"
June 12, "Gay Families"	June 24, "Parade Review"
June 13, "Politics"	June 25, "Gay Freedom Day"

San Francisco Sunday Examiner:
May 9, 1976. "Gay Sergeant vs. the Army." Lon Daniels. Section A, p. 4.

Seaside Tribune:
May 10, 1979. "Monterey Man Challenges Sodomy Conviction: Case Could Affect All Homosexuals in Army." Bonnie Lemons.

Seattle Weekly:
March 8, 1989. "Gay Soldier—'I'm Not Trying to Be a Hero.' " Gary Atkins. Pp. 24–31.

Sentinel:
November 9, 1989. " 'Gay's Okay!'—Uncle Sam." Michael Colbruno.

Stars and Stripes:
June 27, 1986. "Lesbian Lieutenant Won't Resign."

Statesman Journal:
July 3, 1988. "Military Funeral Honors Homosexual War Hero."
February 27, 1989. "Book Looks at Military and Gays." Ron Cowan. Pp. 1B, 2B.
April 18, 1989. "Gay Literature Moves into Sales Mainstream" (Gannett News Service). Dave Berns. P. 5B.
April 20, 1989. "Women Charge Sexual Harassment by Military" (AP).

Times (San Diego Gay Times):
  February 22, 1990. "Let Us Learn . . ." Bill Mondigo. Issue 113, Pp. 8–10.
TWN:
  November 1, 1989. "Pentagon Squashes Own Pro-Gay Report." Cliff O'Neill. P. 3.
U.S.A. Today:
  August 10, 1989. "Top Cadet Rejects Limits." P. 2A.
  February 27, 1990. "Justices Reject Challenge to Pentagon Ban on Gays" P. 6A.
Village Voice:
  April 12, 1983. "The Court-Martial of Lieutenant Joann Newak." Nat Hentoff. P. 8.
  March 13, 1990. "The Gay Cadet." Francis Wilkinson. Pp. 23–31.
Washington Blade:
  December 17, 1982. "A Happier Time." Lisa M. Keen.
  September 11, 1987. "Milwaukee Lesbian Sets a Military Precedent." Lou Chibbaro, Jr. P. 1.
  October 27, 1989. "Controversial Report: Gay Recruits Are 'As Good or Better.' " Lou Chibbaro, Jr. Pp. 1, 11.
Washington Post:
  May 28, 1975. "Homosexual G.I. Fights Release from Service." Jay Mathews.
  June 14, 1980. "Female Sailors Asked to 'Red Pencil' Names of Lesbians, ACLU Says." Margot Hornblower. P. A7.
  October 23, 1982. "Her Sentence: Six Years' Hard Labor" Colman McCarthy. P. A23.
  January 9, 1983. "The Two Faces of Military Justice." Colman McCarthy.
  November 6, 1989. "Rethinking DOD Policy on Gays." Howard Schneider.
Washington Times:
  October 23, 1989. "DOD Nixes Report on Homosexuals."
Willamette Week:
  March 2–8, 1989. "Public Interest: Portland Lesbian Mary Ann Humphrey Guest on Sally Jessy Raphael Show." P. 7.
Windy City Times:
  February 13, 1986. "Lesbian Wins 10-Year Battle over U.S. Army." Sue Burke. Pp. 1, 12.
  August 27, 1987. "Activist Wins Major Legal Battle Against U.S. Army." Sarah Craig. P. 1.
  November 9, 1989. "Pentagon Officials Blast Report on Homosexuality." Cliff O'Neill. P. 9.
Wisconsin State Journal:
  January 4, 1987. "These 10 Made a Difference." Frank Renton. Pp. 6, 8.
Woman News:
  May 1983. "Join the Air Force . . . and see Ft. Leavenworth." Catherine Dillon. P. 3.
  July–August 1983. "Uncle Sam Wants a Few Good Men." Paula Martinac. Pp. 1, 19.

PERIODICALS / MAGAZINES

The Advocate:

August 13, 1975. "Second Sergeant Comes Out," and " 'Unfit' WACS Going to Court."

February 25, 1976. "Annapolis Graduate Decides to Fight." Pp. 11–12.

June 15, 1977. "The Watergay Scandal: A Personal View." Vernon E. Berg. Pp. 6–7, 43.

June 23, 1987. "Monumental Dreams: Remembering Our Lesbian and Gay Heroes." Leonard Matlovich. P. 9.

July 7, 1987. "Soldier Court-Martialed for Unsafe Sex." Mark Vandervelden. Pp. 26–27.

September 29, 1987. "After 11-year Battle, Ben-Shalom Set to Return to Army." Dave Walter.

December 22, 1987. "Northwest Airlines Turns Away Leonard Matlovich." Mark Vandervelden. P. 13.

January 5, 1988. "Obscene: Overseas Witch-Hunts." Peter Cummings. Pp. 10–11, 20.

February 16, 1988. "Newsfront: U.S. Army Private Adrian Morris." P. 25.

March 15, 1988. "Court Strikes Army's Ban on Gays." Peter Freiberg. Pp. 10–13.

March 29, 1988. "So They Say." P. 25.

April 26, 1988. "Gay Veterans Unite." Mike Varady. Pp. 12–13.

July 19, 1988. "Gay Air Force Hero Matlovich Dies: Well-Known AIDS Activist Was 44." Rick Harding. P. 16.

July 19, 1988. "A Mixed Bag in the Courts: Army Case Sent Back to Appeals Court." Peter Freiberg. Pp. 14, 16.

August 30, 1988. "News in Brief: South Carolina." P. 30.

September 13, 1988. "A Controversial Hero." Mike Hippler. Pp. 42–45.

February 14, 1989. "Suit Charges Navy with Bias: Case Focuses on Gay Midshipman." Rick Harding. P. 9.

April 11, 1989. "A Midshipman vs. the Military. Joseph Steffan Fights Navy Dismissal with Quiet Valor." Mark Chekola. Issue 522, pp. 38–39.

May 23, 1989. "Military Bias Charged. Women Say Antigay Harassment Is Extreme." Rick Harding. Issue 525, p. 10.

June 6, 1989. "Court: Reenlist Gay Soldier, Judges Duck the Big Question, Though." Rick Harding. Issue 526, p. 18.

June 6, 1989. "War and Remembrance—Gay and Lesbian Veterans Tell Their Tales." David Perry. Issue 526, pp. 38–42.

July 4, 1989. "In Love and War." Mary Ann Humphrey. Issue 528, p. 4.

July 4, 1989. "Blast Bombshell Torpedoes Activists." Rick Harding. Issue 528, pp. 6–7.

August 1, 1989. "The Tyranny of 10%." Gregory Herek. Issue 530, pp. 46–48.

August 29, 1989. "Ship Blast: Navy Still Looks Hard at Gay Man." Rick Harding. Issue 532, p. 16.

September 12, 1989. "Gay Officer Loses Fight to Overturn Military Ban." Robert W. Peterson. Issue 533, p. 10.

September 12, 1989. "A Reluctant Hero." John Preston. Issue 533, p. 65.

September 26, 1989. "Lesbian Soldier's Long Fight Against Policy Is Nearly Over." Peter Freiberg. P. 19.

December 5, 1989. "Report: Gays Make Good Soldiers." Rick Harding. Issue 539, p. 14.

December 5, 1989. "Of Vice and Men." Jonathan Ned Katz. Issue 539, p. 35.

December 19, 1989. "Steffan Lawsuit Dismissed. Former Midshipman Wouldn't Talk About Sex." Rick Harding. Issue 540, p. 24.

January 16, 1990. "ROTC Flunks Out with Wisconsin Profs." Chris Bull. Issue 542, p. 13.

February 13, 1990. "Lawyers Admit Lesbian Marine Was Bamboozled in Military Trial." Rick Harding. Issue 544, p. 26.

February 13, 1990. "News In Brief: Texas." Issue 544, p. 28.

Baim, Tracy. "Ben-Shalom Back in U.S. Army." *Chicago Outlines*, September 19, 1987, pp. 1, 12.

Bérubé, Allan. "Coming Out Under Fire." *Mother Jones*, February/March 1983, pp. 23–29.

———. "Rediscovering Our Forgotten Past." *The Front Page*, vol. 5, no. 11, (June 26–July 9, 1984), pp. 8–11.

Bjorklund, David, and Bjorklund, Barbara. "Straight or Gay." *Parents Magazine*, October 1988, pp. 93–98.

Chiles, John A. "Homosexuality in the United States Air Force." *Comprehensive Psychiatry*, vol. 13, no. 6. (November/December 1972), pp. 529–32.

Clausen, Jan. "Is Militarism a Feminist Issue? (and Other Pertinent Questions)." *WIN*, vol. 17:4, (March 1, 1981), pp. 9–11.

D'Emilio, John. "The Military and Lesbians During the McCarthy Years." *Signs*, Summer 1984, pp. 759–75.

Doidge, William T., and Holtzman, Wayne H. "Implications of Homosexuality Among Air Force Trainees." *Journal of Consulting Psychology*, 1960, pp. 9–13.

Druss, R. G. "Cases of Suspected Homosexuality Seen at an Army Mental Hygiene Consultation Service." *Psychiatric Quarterly*, 41 (January 1967), pp. 62–70.

Duberman, Martin. "The Case of the Gay Sergeant." *New York Times Magazine*, November 9, 1975, pp. 16–17, 58–71.

Frontlines. "Military Gays Fight Back." *Mother Jones*, June 1976.

Gibson, Lawrence E. "Homosexuality in the Navy: The Suppressed Findings of the Crittenden Board." *Gai Saber*, vol. 1, no. 2 (Summer 1977), pp. 132–35.

Gilbert, Arthur. "Buggery and the British Navy, 1700–1861." *Journal of Social History*, 1976, 10: pp. 72–98.

Hooker, Evelyn. "Facts that Liberated the Gay Community." *Psychology Today*, December 1975, pp. 52, 54–55, 101.

Humphrey, Mary Ann. "The Lavender Corps: Gays in the Military." *Guide*, March 1989.

Irwin, P., and Thompson, N. L. "Acceptance of the Rights of Homosexuals. A Social Profile." *Journal of Homosexuality* 3 (2) 1977, pp. 107–21.

Katz, Susan. "Hanky-Panky Is Strictly Off Limits." *Insight*, vol. 4, no. 7, pp. 22–23.

Kopkind, Andrew. "The Boys in the Barracks." *New Times*, August 8, 1975, pp. 19–27.

Kroll, Jerome. "Racial Patterns of Military Crimes in Vietnam." *Psychiatry*, 39, (February 1976), pp. 51–64.

Lester, Marianne. "Homosexuals in Uniform." *Family: The Magazine of Army/Navy/Air Force/Times*, March 27, 1974, pp. 4–9, 12–13.

Levy, Charles. "ARVN as Faggots. Inverted Warfare in Vietnam." *Transaction*, 18 (October 1971), pp. 18–27.

Little, Roger W. "The Sick Soldier and the Medical Ward Officer." *Human Organization*, 15 (Spring 1956), pp. 22–24.

McDonald, Boyd. "Great Moments in Journalism." *Christopher Street*, issue 119, 1988, pp. 8–14.

Morrison, David C. "Gays in Uniform." *National Journal*, November 11, 1989, p. 2785.

Morrow, Mark W. "DOD Stance on Gays Headed for Change? Allies' Policies Vary Widely." *Armed Forces Journal International*. December 1989, p. 15.

National Geographic. "A Newcomer to Australia." February 1988, p. 259.

Newsweek:
February 22, 1988. "A Milestone for Gay Rights?" P. 8.

March 21, 1988. "Out of the Closet onto the Shelves." Walter Clemons. Pp. 72–74.

June 5, 1989. "Foul Play on the *Iowa*?" Eloise Salholz and Richard Sandza. P. 22.

September 25, 1989. "Barney Frank's Story." Tom Morganthau. Pp. 14–18.

September 15, 1989. "Gays in Washington." Jonathan Alter. Pp. 19–20.

March 12, 1990. "The Future of Gay America." Eloise Salholz and others. Pp. 20–25.

March 12, 1990. "The Younger Generation Says Yes to Sex." James N. Baker and others. Pp. 23–24.

March 12, 1990. "Lesbians: Portrait of a Community." James N. Baker and Shawn D. Lewis. P. 24.

March 12, 1990. "Degrees of Discomfort." Jonathan Alter. P. 27.

Parade's Intelligence Report/Parade Magazine:
November 9, 1980. "Ship of Shame." Lloyd Shearer, Intelligence Report. Pp. 16–17.

August 13, 1989. "It Can Be Done." David Wallechinsky, Profile. Pp. 4–6.

Thomas, Charles, J. "Of Dirt Roads and Dragons." *Northwest Magazine*, April 3, 1988. P. 5.

Time:
September 8, 1975. "Gays on the March." John Leo. Pp. 32–43.

February 15, 1988. "Redefining a Woman's Place." Jacob Larmar, Jr. P. 27.

February 22, 1988. "Uniform Treatment for Gays." William A. Henry, III. P. 55.

Unger, Craig. "William Calley." *People Weekly*, November 20, 1989, pp. 153–58.

U.S. News & World Report:
February 15, 1988. "The Sexes: Wider Field of Fire." Ted Gest. P. 13.

November 20, 1989, "The Pentagon's Fight to Keep Gays Away." Peter Cary. Pp. 57, 61.

Wallinga, J. B. "Severe Alcoholism in Career Military Personnel." *U.S. Armed Forces Medical Journal*, April 7, 1956, pp. 551–61.

West, Jolyon Louis, Doidge, William T., and Williams, Robert L. "An Approach to the Problem of Homosexuality in the Military Service." *American Journal of Psychiatry*, 115 (November 1958).

Williams, Colins J., and Weinberg, Martin S. "Being Discovered: A Study of Homosexuals in the Military." *Social Problems*, 18 (2) (Fall 1970), pp. 217–27.

——— . "The Military: Its Processing of Accused Homosexuals." *American Behavioral Scientist*, 14 (November/December 1970), pp. 203–17.

MISCELLANEOUS

Schreiber, E. M., and Woelfel, John C. "Women in Men's Boots: Performance and Adjustment of Women in the Coed American Army of the 1970's." Paper presented at the 72nd annual meeting of the American Sociological Association in Chicago, Illinois, September 9, 1977.

FILMS, DOCUMENTARIES, AND VIDEO PROGRAMMING

Battered Lesbians, Battered Lovers. Geraldo. Paramount Television Domestic Distribution. November 21, 1989.

Before Stonewall. Jezebel Productions/Cinema Guild Productions, Division of Documents Associates, New York. 1984.

Controversy Over Granting Custody to Homosexuals. Sally Jessy Raphael Show. Multimedia Entertainment, New York. November 27, 1989.

Dear America: Letters Home from Vietnam. Bill Couturie and Thomas Bird Productions. 1987.

Gays Come Out. The Oprah Winfrey Show. King World Distribution, Harpo Production, Inc., New York. October, 11, 1989.

Gays in the Military. Phil Donahue. Multimedia Entertainment, New York. March 12, 1990.

Homosexuals Discuss Love. Phil Donahue. Multimedia Entertainment, New York. August 21, 1989.

Homosexuals in the Military. Sally Jessy Raphael Show, Multimedia Entertainment, New Haven. March 3, 1989.

Homosexual Soldiers and Police Officers. Geraldo, Paramount Television Domestic Distribution, May 4, 1988.

Lesbian Custody. Geraldo. Paramount Television Domestic Distribution. May 19, 1989.

Lesbian Parents. Phil Donahue. Multimedia Entertainment, New York. September 20, 1989.

Marching to a Different Drummer: Lesbian and Gay Americans During World War II. Allan Bérubé. Documentary slide presentation. San Francisco Lesbian and Gay History Project. 1987.

Ruined by Rumors. Phil Donahue. Transcript #120487. Multimedia Entertainment, Inc., Cincinnati. 1987.

Senior Gays. Phil Donahue. Multimedia Entertainment, New York. September 29, 1989.

Should Gay People Be Allowed to Be Legally Married? The Oprah Winfrey Show. King World Distribution, Harpo Production, Inc., New York. December 19, 1989.

Should Homosexuals Be Given Special Rights? Ken Schram. Town Meeting, KOMO TV, Channel 4, Tacoma, Washington. Barbara Groce, producer. November 5, 1989.

Silent Pioneers. Produced by Patricia Ginger Snyder. Pioneer Film Production, in conjunction with New York Center for the Humanities, Film Makers Library. 1985.

Sonia Live From L.A. "Interview with Joseph Steffan." CNN/Cable News Network, Inc., Hollywood. February 7, 1989.

Teenage Lesbians and Their Mothers. Geraldo. Paramount Television Domestic Distribution. March 3, 1989.

The Times of Harvey Milk. Produced by Robert Epstein and Richard Schmiechon. Television Laboratory—WNET Thirteen. Black Sand Production. 1984.

To Serve with Honor: Midshipman 1/C Joseph Steffan, Warren, Minnesota. Over the Edge. Woody Fraser Productions in Association with Reeves Entertainment Group, Reeves Communication Company. March 19, 1989.

Torch Song Trilogy. RCA/Columbia Pictures Home Video. New Line Cinema. #L11918. 1989.

Who Becomes Homosexual and Why? Phil Donahue. Multimedia Entertainment, Cincinnati. April 14, 1989.

Women in the Military. Phil Donahue. Transcript #09030. Multimedia Entertainment, Inc., Cincinnati. 1980.

Word Is Out. Produced by Nancy Adair and Casey Adair. Mariposa Film Group and Adair Films. 1978.

ABOUT THE AUTHOR

Mary Ann Humphrey received a direct commission in 1979 as a captain in the United States Army Reserve. During her nine years of service, she was awarded the Army Reserve Component Achievement Medal (First and Second Oak Leaf Cluster) and the Army Commendation Medal. She served in the Administrative branch (AG) as an Affirmative Action–Equal Opportunity Officer and also completed qualification in the quartermaster and military intelligence branches, QM and MI, respectively. Because of her sexual orientation, she was denied promotion to major and forced to resign her commission in November 1987. She is currently a member of the Alexander Hamilton American Legion, Post 448.

Her other works include the historical background contribution to *Gays in Uniform: The Pentagon's Secret Reports* (Alyso Publications, 1990), a book containing the Defense Department's recent research documents on the subject, and *Waterplay* (Wm. C. Brown, 1990), a book of water games and other activities based on her many years of swimming experience and teaching physical education at Portland Community College, in Portland, Oregon. She holds both a B.S. and an M.A. in physical education, an M.Ed. in educational counseling, and an Ed.D. in teacher evaluation and training. She serves as the coordinator of physical education and health at the Rock Creek campus of the college.

The author's time is divided between administrative duties, lecturing, writing, restoring antiques, and collecting Mickey Mouse memorabilia. She shares her home with her seven-year-old son, Parke, and her long-time partner, Debra Sue Keever. A feisty cocker spaniel named Addie Rae, two Manx cats, and a mini-lop-eared rabbit named Jessica complete the household.